Enterprise JavaBeans For Dummies®

D0901478

Summary of Frequently Used EJB Interfaces

The following table identifies the interfaces you need to implement for each type of Enterprise JavaBean (EJB) that you create:

Interface/Class	Message-Driven Bean	Session Bean	Entity Bean
Remote interface	None	`javax.ejb.EJBObject`	`javax.ejb.EJBObject`
Local interface	None	`javax.ejb.EJBLocalObject`	`javax.ejb.EJBLocalObject`
Remote Home interface	None	`javax.ejb.EJBHome`	`javax.ejb.EJBHome`
Local Home interface	None	`javax.ejb.EJBLocalHome`	`javax.ejb.EJBLocalHome`
Bean class	`javax.ejb.MessageDrivenBean`	`javax.ejb.SessionBean`	`javax.ejb.EntityBean`

Basic Description of a Message-Driven Bean

The following block of XML illustrates a typical description of a message-driven bean in the deployment descriptor:

```xml
<message-driven>
  <ejb-name></ejb-name>
  <ejb-class>fully.qualified.BeanClassName</ejb-class>
  <transaction-type>Container | Bean</transaction-type>
  <acknowledge-mode>
    Auto-acknowledge | Dups-ok-acknowledge
  </acknowledge-mode>
  <message-driven-destination>
    <destination-type>javax.jms.Queue | javax.jms.Topic
    </destination-type>
<!- use the following only if destination type is Topic.->
    <subscription-durability>
      Durable | NonDurable
    </subscription-durability>
  </message-driven-destination>
</message-driven>
```

For the `<transaction-type>` attribute, the value can be either `Container` or `Bean`. For the `<destination-type>` attribute, the value can be either `javax.jms.Queue` or `javax.jms.Topic`. For the `<subscription-durability>` attribute, the value can be either `Durable` or `NonDurable`. More information on Java Messaging Service (JMS) and message-driven beans is available in Chapters 9 and 10. Chapters 11, 12, 14, and 15 supply additional information on deployment descriptors.

Basic Description of an Entity Bean

The following block of XML code is a typical description for an entity bean class in the EJB application's deployment descriptor:

```xml
<entity>
  <ejb-name>EJBComponentName</ejb-name>
  <home>fully.qualified.RemoteHomeInterfaceName</home>
  <remote>fully.qualified.RemoteInterfaceName</remote>
  <local-home>fully.qualified.LocalHomeInterfaceName</local-home>
  <local>fully.qualified.LocalInterfaceName</local>
  <ejb-class>fully.qualified.BeanClassName</ejb-class>
  <prim-key-class>fully.qualified.PrimaryKeyName</prim-key-class>
  <persistence-type>Container | Bean</persistence-type>
  <reentrant>False</reentrant>
  <persistence-type>2.x<persistence-type>
  <cmp-field><field-name>fieldName</field-name></cmp-field>
  <primkey-field>primaryKeyFieldName</primkey-field>
</entity>
```

For the `<persistence-type>` attribute, the value can be either `Container` or `Bean`. Chapters 6, 7, and 8 focus on topics specific to the creation of entity bean components. Chapters 11, 12, 14, and 15 supply additional information on deployment descriptors.

Basic Description of a Session Bean

The following block of XML contains a typical entry for describing a session bean in the EJB application's deployment descriptor:

```xml
<session>
  <ejb-name>MyEJBName</ejb-name>
  <home>fully.qualified.RemoteHomeInterfaceName</home>
  <remote>fully.qualified.RemoteInterfaceName</remote>
  <local-home>fully.qualified.LocalHomeInterfaceName</local-home>
  <local>fully.qualified.LocalInterfaceName</local>
  <ejb-class>fully.qualified.BeanClassName</ejb-class>
  <session-type>Stateless | Stateful</session-type>
  <transaction-type>Container | Bean</transaction-type>
</session>
```

For the `<session-type>` attribute, the value can be either `Stateless` or `Stateful`. For the `<transaction-type>` attribute, the value can be either `Container` or `Bean`. Chapters 4 and 5 contain more information on session beans. Chapters 11, 12, 14, and 15 supply additional information on deployment descriptors.

For Dummies: Bestselling Book Series for Beginners

™

BESTSELLING BOOK SERIES

References for the Rest of Us!®

Are you intimidated and confused by computers? Do you find that traditional manuals are overloaded with technical details you'll never use? Do your friends and family always call you to fix simple problems on their PCs? Then the For Dummies® computer book series from Hungry Minds, Inc. is for you.

For Dummies books are written for those frustrated computer users who know they aren't really dumb but find that PC hardware, software, and indeed the unique vocabulary of computing make them feel helpless. For Dummies books use a lighthearted approach, a down-to-earth style, and even cartoons and humorous icons to dispel computer novices' fears and build their confidence. Lighthearted but not lightweight, these books are a perfect survival guide for anyone forced to use a computer.

> *"I like my copy so much I told friends; now they bought copies."*
> — **Irene C., Orwell, Ohio**

> *"Quick, concise, nontechnical, and humorous."*
> — **Jay A., Elburn, Illinois**

> *"Thanks, I needed this book. Now I can sleep at night."*
> — **Robin F., British Columbia, Canada**

Already, millions of satisfied readers agree. They have made For Dummies books the #1 introductory level computer book series and have written asking for more. So, if you're looking for the most fun and easy way to learn about computers, look to For Dummies books to give you a helping hand.

Hungry Minds™

1/01

Enterprise JavaBeans™

FOR

DUMMIES®

Enterprise JavaBeans™ FOR DUMMIES®

by Mac Rinehart

Hungry Minds™

Best-Selling Books • Digital Downloads • e-Books • Answer Networks • e-Newsletters • Branded Web Sites • e-Learning

New York, NY ◆ Cleveland, OH ◆ Indianapolis, IN

Enterprise JavaBeans™ For Dummies®

Published by
Hungry Minds, Inc.
909 Third Avenue
New York, NY 10022
www.hungryminds.com
www.dummies.com

Library of Congress Control Number: 2002100257

ISBN: 0-7645-1646-9

Printed in the United States of America

10 9 8 7 6 5 4 3 2 1

1B/SU/QU/QS/IN

Distributed in the United States by Hungry Minds, Inc.

Distributed by CDG Books Canada Inc. for Canada; by Transworld Publishers Limited in the United Kingdom; by IDG Norge Books for Norway; by IDG Sweden Books for Sweden; by IDG Books Australia Publishing Corporation Pty. Ltd. for Australia and New Zealand; by TransQuest Publishers Pte Ltd. for Singapore, Malaysia, Thailand, Indonesia, and Hong Kong; by Gotop Information Inc. for Taiwan; by ICG Muse, Inc. for Japan; by Intersoft for South Africa; by Eyrolles for France; by International Thomson Publishing for Germany, Austria and Switzerland; by Distribuidora Cuspide for Argentina; by LR International for Brazil; by Galileo Libros for Chile; by Ediciones ZETA S.C.R. Ltda. for Peru; by WS Computer Publishing Corporation, Inc., for the Philippines; by Contemporanea de Ediciones for Venezuela; by Express Computer Distributors for the Caribbean and West Indies; by Micronesia Media Distributor, Inc. for Micronesia; by Chips Computadoras S.A. de C.V. for Mexico; by Editorial Norma de Panama S.A. for Panama; by American Bookshops for Finland.

For general information on Hungry Minds' products and services please contact our Customer Care Department within the U.S. at 800-762-2974, outside the U.S. at 317-572-3993 or fax 317-572-4002.

For sales inquiries and reseller information, including discounts, premium and bulk quantity sales, and foreign-language translations, please contact our Customer Care Department at 800-434-3422, fax 317-572-4002, or write to Hungry Minds, Inc., Attn: Customer Care Department, 10475 Crosspoint Boulevard, Indianapolis, IN 46256.

For information on licensing foreign or domestic rights, please contact our Sub-Rights Customer Care Department at 212-884-5000.

For information on using Hungry Minds' products and services in the classroom or for ordering examination copies, please contact our Educational Sales Department at 800-434-2086 or fax 317-572-4005.

For press review copies, author interviews, or other publicity information, please contact our Public Relations Department at 317-572-3168 or fax 317-572-4168.

For authorization to photocopy items for corporate, personal, or educational use, please contact Copyright Clearance Center, 222 Rosewood Drive, Danvers, MA 01923, or fax 978-750-4470.

Hungry Minds™ is a trademark of Hungry Minds, Inc.

About the Author

Mac Rinehart is President of Sextant Technology Consulting, Inc., a business dedicated to providing high-quality consulting services for the planning of Web-based, transactional applications development. For more information on the author and Sextant Technology Consulting, visit www.sextanttech.com.

Dedication

This book is dedicated to my good friends Brian Tawney and David Jacob.
A person couldn't ask for better friendship than these two have shown me.

Author's Acknowledgments

While my name may be the only one on the cover, there are many people who deserve credit for making this book a reality. Without the support of my acquisitions editor, Steven Hayes, this book wouldn't have been possible. The project editor, Paul Levesque, deserves special credit for helping to shape my first draft into a superior book. Copy editor Nicole Laux deserves both my thanks and yours. Finally, I'd like to thank my technical editor Al Williams, whose contributions have helped to strengthen this book significantly.

On this book I had the honor of working with a fine group of peer reviewers, whose contributions and insights have been above and beyond the call of duty. The peer review team was composed of individuals who were either familiar with EJB technology or just wanted to get exposed to it for the first time. Their insights helped iron out wrinkles in difficult passages, and they've helped to shape the overall content of the book. Although several people were involved, I want to single out Fred Loney of Spirited Software, Fred Obermann of Sundancer Systems, and Andrew Steckley of @Once Software Consulting. In addition, I'd like to thank the many members of the Portland Java User's Group, who have freely shared their collective experience to help make this a better book.

Finally, I'd like to thank my wife, Kristin Schuchman, and my family and friends for their continued support. They are my anchors in the world of reality as I dive into the obscure and often murky waters of computer technology.

While I share the credit for the making of this book with many people, only one person is ultimately responsible for its content: me. While we all strove to make this the best book it could be, I take the blame for any errors or omissions. If you find fault with something in these pages, please contact me at feedback@sextanttech.com. I encourage feedback, and I'm happy to respond to questions and inquiries, as well as provide support on any of the software examples available with this book

Publisher's Acknowledgments

We're proud of this book; please send us your comments through our Hungry Minds Online Registration Form located at www.dummies.com.

Some of the people who helped bring this book to market include the following:

Acquisitions, Editorial, and Media Development

Project Editor: Paul Levesque

Acquisitions Editor: Steven Hayes

Copy Editor: Nicole Laux

Technical Editor: Al Williams

Editorial Manager: Constance Carlisle

Permissions Editor: Laura Moss

Media Development Manager: Laura VanWinkle

Media Development Supervisor: Richard Graves

Editorial Assistant: Amanda Foxworth

Production

Project Coordinator: Erin Smith

Layout and Graphics: LeAndra Johnson, Stephanie D. Jumper, Jackie Nicholas, Shelley Norris, Jacque Schneider, Ron Terry, Julie Trippetti, Jeremey Unger, Mary J. Virgin

Proofreaders: Andy Hollandbeck, Carl Pierce, Linda Quigley, TECHBOOKS Production Services

Indexer: TECHBOOKS Production Services

General and Administrative

Hungry Minds Technology Publishing Group: Richard Swadley, Vice President and Executive Group Publisher; Bob Ipsen, Vice President and Group Publisher; Joseph Wikert, Vice President and Publisher; Barry Pruett, Vice President and Publisher; Mary Bednarek, Editorial Director; Mary C. Corder, Editorial Director; Andy Cummings, Editorial Director

Hungry Minds Manufacturing: Ivor Parker, Vice President, Manufacturing

Hungry Minds Marketing: John Helmus, Assistant Vice President, Director of Marketing

Hungry Minds Production for Branded Press: Debbie Stailey, Production Director

Hungry Minds Sales: Michael Violano, Vice President, International Sales and Sub Rights

Contents at a Glance

Cartoons at a Glance

By Rich Tennant

page 11

page 51

page 105

page 237

page 265

page 361

Cartoon Information:
Fax: 978-546-7747
E-Mail: richtennant@the5thwave.com
World Wide Web: www.the5thwave.com

Table of Contents

· ·

Part III: Entity Beans: The Way Things Are *105*

Introduction

Welcome to the wonderful world of Enterprise JavaBeans! Whether you're a student fresh out of the programming academy or an experienced programmer looking for a straightforward reference to Enterprise JavaBean technology, this book is for you. To get you off on the right foot, I'd like to dispel a couple of myths right off the bat:

- ✔ **Reading a Dummies book doesn't make you a dummy.** This book isn't a "dumbed down" reference. Rather, it's a book that doesn't make assumptions about what you know about Enterprise JavaBean technology. While other references may leave you wondering about the definition of some insurmountable term, this book presents every topic in a clear, straightforward, practical style.

- ✔ **Writing Enterprise JavaBean programs isn't beyond your reach.** Let's be clear: Enterprise JavaBeans (EJBs for short) aren't simple. But they're not obscure either. Instead, they're programs that must be constructed according to specific guidelines. After you understand the formula for creating EJBs — and get a couple under your belt — you'll be ready to rumble.

My goal in writing this book is to dispel the mysticism of EJBs and to provide a practical reference for discovering the nuts and bolts under the hood of EJB technology. If that's the kind of reference you're looking for, this book is for you.

What's in the Book

Enterprise JavaBean technology is based on a specification developed by Sun Microsystems. A *specification* is a document that provides a detailed description of the nuts and bolts that hold a technology together. The latest EJB specification is *Enterprise JavaBean Specification, Version 2.0*. There have been a lot of changes in the EJB specification since the Version 1.1 release. This book presents Enterprise JavaBeans from the Version 2.0 perspective.

You don't have to read this book from cover to cover to get the most out of it. Instead, go directly to the section that has the information you need. The index is your topical guide to subjects in the book and where to find them — use it to your advantage.

Part 1: Enterprise JavaBeans: Taste 'em Again for the First Time

If EJB technology were a house, Part I would be the lumberyard. This part drills down on all of the technology underpinnings and assumptions that contribute to great EJB applications:

✔ Chapter 1 examines the technical "materials" of EJB applications, such as home interfaces, remote interfaces, and EJB classes to name just a few. In this chapter, you discover what the heck I'm talking about and get a bird's eye view on major EJB features.

✔ Chapter 2 shows you the ropes by examining the process of developing, deploying, and administering EJB applications.

✔ Chapter 3 illustrates a simple yet practical EJB scenario, examining the role of EJBs in a banking application.

If you're looking for background in EJB technology, Part I is the place to go.

Part II: On the Couch with Session Beans

Your therapist is no match for a good session bean. *Session beans* are one of three types of Enterprise JavaBeans — the others are entity beans and message-driven beans — and are used to perform tasks in an EJB application. If you're looking for information about implementing business processes or writing programs that perform tasks, this is the part for you. And you don't pay by the hour to partake in Part II.

✔ Chapter 4 introduces you to stateless session beans — EJBs used to perform tasks that can be completed in a single step. Stateless session beans are the simplest of the EJB components, and they're a good choice for beginners looking to get their feet wet.

✔ Chapter 5 turns up the volume a notch, introducing stateful session beans. Stateful session beans are used to coordinate tasks that require multiple interactions between a client program (the user of the EJB application) and the session bean.

Part III: Entity Beans: The Way Things Are

Entity beans are EJB components used to represent business data. If you're familiar with database programming, you'll have a leg up when it comes to working with entity beans. But be prepared for some differences. Entity beans aren't the same as rows in a database. Even if you're not familiar with database programming, you'll get off on the right foot in Part III.

 ✔ Chapter 6 addresses the creation of entity beans with container-managed persistence. *Persistence* refers to the process of storing data in a physical location, such as a disk drive or a database. With container-managed persistent, the EJB application manages its own persistence, so you don't have to worry about it.

 ✔ Chapter 7 introduces the EJB Query Language (EJB QL), which is a new addition to the Enterprise JavaBean Specification, Version 2.0. This language is used by entity beans in conjunction with container-managed persistence to get access to business data.

 ✔ Chapter 8 covers the construction of entity beans with bean-managed persistence. This is the counterpart to container-managed persistence (covered in Chapter 6) and allows you to take control of the persistence process. In Chapter 8, you can read about the differences between the two approaches and the steps to implementing entity beans with bean-managed persistence.

Part IV: Expressing Yourself with Message-Driven Beans

Message-driven beans are EJBs used to receive messages from remote programs through the Java Messaging Service (JMS). Message-driven beans are a new addition to the Java enterprise architecture. Part IV explores the JMS framework, allowing you to discover the role of message-driven beans in an EJB application.

 ✔ JMS applications are applications that allow a client program and the server program to perform tasks in parallel to each other. Chapter 9 investigates the new JMS framework, giving you the background you need to maximize your use of JMS and message-driven beans.

 ✔ Chapter 10 blows the cover off message-driven beans themselves, exploring the components of message-driven beans and giving you the knowledge you need to take advantage of this great new feature.

Part V: Putting It All Together

Every technology book has to draw a line on coverage, and this book is no exception. But I don't want to leave you hanging when it comes to developing EJB applications. Part V is devoted to covering special topics inside the EJB framework as well as in related technologies. The goal is to provide you with a complete starter toolkit in principles of EJB programming so that you can be productive right away.

✔ Chapter 11 takes a close look at what every EJB component developer needs to know about the *deployment descriptor*, a special XML file that every EJB component must use to describe itself. At the end of this chapter, you get a close look at packaging EJB applications in a deployment file called an `ejb-jar` file, which holds all the contents of the EJB application and is used to distribute the application.

✔ Chapter 12 examines the use of the Java Naming and Directory Interface (JNDI) API. JNDI is used by Java programs to look up and get references to objects that may be located on remote computers. JNDI is essential for EJB applications as well as for the client applications that use them.

✔ Chapter 13 examines a process called application assembly and deployment. In this phase of EJB application development, various EJB components are put together to form an application. Application assemblers provide additional information in the application's deployment descriptor while deployers map EJB applications to services provided by a host environment (called the EJB container).

✔ Chapter 14 enhances your toolkit of skills with coverage of transaction support and management in EJB applications. *Transactions* are groups of actions that must all succeed as a set. If one piece of a transaction does not succeed, the entire transaction must revert to its original state.

✔ Chapter 15 investigates the EJB security features that protect your EJB applications from attacks by malicious users. Implementing EJB application security is completed almost entirely in the application's deployment descriptor, and it's very easy.

✔ Chapter 16 takes a closer look at integrating EJB applications with *client applications* (programs that users interact with). For example, your users can interact with an EJB application through a JavaServer Pages application located on the Internet, or they can interact with the EJB application through a program that resides on their local computers.

Part VI: The Part of Tens

Every *For Dummies* book contains a Part of Tens — full of useful and cool little tidbits that don't quite fit anywhere else in the book — and this title is no exception!

✔ Chapter 17 is your reference to great Internet resources for more information and for support as you develop EJB applications. I identify the Web sites that you should turn to first for questions and answers.

✔ Chapter 18 gives you some great strategies for optimizing the performance of EJB applications that you create.

Glossary

With this book you also get a glossary — your one-stop resource for the definitions of key terms that appear in the book.

System Requirements

It's time to underline the Enterprise in Enterprise JavaBeans. While you don't need a super computer to develop EJB applications, you'll certainly find a powerful server is necessary if you plan to use EJBs in an enterprise scale application. In this book, I focus on your needs as a developer.

If you'll be using Enterprise JavaBeans in a large-scale application, you should get some professional advice on hardware from vendors such as Sun Microsystems, IBM, or Intel.

System requirements for EJB development

You can program EJBs on a single computer, using any of the following operating systems:

- ✔ Microsoft Windows NT, 2000, or XP
- ✔ Linux or Unix
- ✔ Mac OS X

For the examples in this book, I use a Microsoft Windows 2000 computer with an Intel PIII processor and 512MB of RAM. I confess; I'm a bit of a hardware fanatic. In the following list, I identify some minimum requirements that you can get by with.

The hardware requirements for EJB applications are largely dependent on the specifications of the EJB containers that host them. Be sure to check out the requirements for each container because they may be different from the figures I identify here.

- ✔ **150 MHz processor minimum** (Intel PII or equivalent).
- ✔ **128 Megabytes of RAM.**

✔ **The Java 2 Standard Edition, Version 1.3.x developer's kit (JDK).**

You can get the JDK from Sun Microsystems at `http://java.sun.com/ j2se/1.3/`. The JDK Version 1.4 was released shortly before the completion of this book. Be sure to check with the application server vendor that you choose to determine whether or not they support the new JDK before you start using it.

✔ **Windows 2000, NT, XP, Linux, Unix, or Mac OS X operating system.**

✔ **Your favorite Java development tools.**

I recommend using Together Control Center from TogetherSoft, Inc. This Integrated Development Environment (IDE) includes a complete Unified Modeling Language (UML) modeling solution that allows you to design your software using diagrams and to automatically generate source code.

✔ **An Enterprise JavaBean container (a fancy way of saying "a program that can run Enterprise JavaBeans").**

Several different EJB containers satisfy this need; consider one of the following:

- **JBoss Application Server:** This EJB container is an open source project run by JBossGroup, LLC. The product is very impressive, and you're sure to be happy with it. Be sure to download version 3.0 or later, as earlier versions don't provide complete support for version 2.0 of the EJB Specification. You can get JBoss at `www.jbossgroup.com/binary.jsp`.

- **WebSphere Application Server:** This EJB container is produced by IBM, and it's the Mercedes-Benz of application servers. Be sure to pick up version 4.0 or later. A trial version of WebSphere is available from IBM at `www4.ibm.com/software/webservers/ appserv/`.

- **WebLogic Application Server:** This EJB container is produced by BEA, and it's a strong competitor in the market of EJB container vendors. WebLogic 6.1 and later provide full support for EJB 2.0 applications. Download a copy of WebLogic from `www.bea.com/ products/weblogic/server/index.shtml`.

System requirements for EJB testing

Enterprise JavaBeans are intended for developing *distributed applications*, applications that run on more than one computer. Thus, if you're developing components of an EJB application that should run on different computers, testing them using more than one computer is a good idea. For most testing purposes, you can use computers that conform to the same configuration as your development computer. The only major difference is that your testing computers must be able to communicate with each other across a network or the Internet.

If you're doing a performance test, you'll want to use a computer that's configured identically to the computer that you used for your production system. A *production system* is the computer environment you use to run applications after the development and testing is complete. To get a good idea of the performance characteristics of your application, you need to use the same configuration as the production system when conducting a performance test.

Conventions Used in This Book

Before you dive into the book, take a moment to review the conventions regarding fonts and symbols. The book is the road, and these are the road signs. If you can't read the signs, your progress down the road is going to be slower. So, if you get this bit of driver's education under your belt first, you'll be able to put the pedal to the metal with confidence.

Fonts and symbols For Dummies

The various fonts and symbols in this book are used to illustrate code and special instructions. Here's a simple guide to help you interpret these symbols:

- ✔ All code samples are presented in the `code monofont` style.

- ✔ *Syntax keys* are code samples used to illustrate the syntax of a statement.

  - In a syntax key, square brackets ([ ]) are used to delimit optional syntax elements.

  - Angle brackets (<>) are used to enclose variable syntax elements that you should replace with your own variables.

  - Repeatable elements of a syntax key are followed by an ellipsis (. . .).

  - If you need to choose one of several options in a syntax key, I surround the options with curly brackets ({ }). Each option inside the curly brackets is separated with a single pipe character (|).

- ✔ From place to place, I may provide you with explicit instructions on things you should type into your computer. In these instructions, the portion you should type will be indicated in **reverse bold**. If the surrounding text is a normal font, the portion you type will be in a **bold font**. But if the surrounding text is in a **bold font, the portion you should type will be indicated in a** normal font.

✔ You'll occasionally come across step lists that guide you through performing a particular task; these lists usually describe interactions with your computer's desktop and menus. So, for example, if you need to open a file in a program, I tell you to "Choose File➪Open." That means that you need to click the File menu in your program, and then choose the Open option from that menu.

These are the Icons of our time

One of the greatest features of Dummies books is the margin icons. These icons help you identify the key points in the book, particularly if you're in a hurry. Here's a guide to the margin icons and their meanings.

I'm full of advice on developing Enterprise JavaBean applications. And when I have a particularly useful piece of information that will help you create faster, smarter, or better EJB applications, I use this Tip icon to draw attention to it.

If your eyes are about to glaze over, you're reading the content delimited by a Technical Stuff icon. While you can skip the Technical Stuff icons, the material they denote may be useful if you're seeking a deeper understanding of a particular topic.

Some information is consequential over the long run, and some is not. I use this icon for two related purposes. First, I may be refreshing your memory on a topic covered elsewhere in the book or the chapter that applies to the current topic. The second reason is simply to tell you to remember this information because it's important.

This icon identifies information that you can find on the Internet. The companion Web site (`www.dummies.com/extras/ejbfd`) for this book contains the source code for many of the examples in this book.

Beware of the warning icon. In every programming solution, there's a few right ways to do something — and a lot of wrong ways to do it. I indicate the things to avoid doing by putting a Warning icon in the margin.

Throughout the book, I identify other books and articles that you can refer to for information on related topics and deeper information about EJB technology. The Cross-Reference icon identifies text that tells you about resources beyond this book for developing EJB applications.

Foolish Assumptions

This book isn't a hitchhikers guide to everything. It's a book on Enterprise JavaBean development. So I had to make a few assumptions about what you know before I started writing. I want to get these assumptions out in the open in advance, so you'll have a better experience with this book in the end. To that end, I describe what this book is not:

- ✔ **This book is not a reference on the Java language.** If you don't already have some background with Java or an object-oriented programming language (such as C++ or Smalltalk), you'll find that the material in this book is a little difficult to navigate.

- ✔ **This book is not a reference on the Structured Query Language (SQL).** Some portions of this book will address interacting with a database and using Java Database Connectivity (JDBC) to query, insert, update, and delete data in a database. I provide the necessary background on JDBC, but if you aren't familiar with SQL, you'll need an additional reference on that topic.

- ✔ **This book is not a reference on developing client programs that interact with EJB applications.** This book presents information on using EJB applications in *client programs* (programs that users interact with). Two typical types of client programs are JavaServer Pages applications and SWING applications. If you plan to develop client programs, you need additional references for the type of program you intend to develop.

I know you're thinking, "Throw me a bone here, Mac!" So following are some resources that you can refer to for more information about the topics that are outside the scope of this book.

The *Java 2 Bible*, by Aaron Walsh, Justin Couch, and Daniel Steinberg (published by Hungry Minds, Inc.), is a great resource for those who are just getting their feet wet in the Java programming language. You'll find complete coverage of all the fundamentals of the Java programming language, and you'll be programming like a pro when you get finished with that book.

For excellent coverage of the Structured Query Language, check out *SQL: the Complete Reference*, by James R. Groff and Paul N. Weinberg (published by Osborne). It's a huge book, but it provides the background you need to develop simple and sophisticated SQL programs, and it covers SQL from the Microsoft and Oracle perspectives.

JavaServer Pages For Dummies, by Mac Rinehart (published by Hungry Minds, Inc.), is my favorite reference on developing JavaServer Pages applications. I've met the author and had numerous conversations with him. He and I agree on almost everything, including the fact that *JavaServer Pages For Dummies* is a pretty good read as far as technical references go.

Where To Go

It's time to get the show on the road. Remember, you don't have to read the book from cover to cover to get everything you need. Instead, focus on the points that you need to explore and skip around as you need. Be my guest and dive into this book whither you will.

If you're not sure where to start, Chapter 1 is a good choice. Have fun!

Part I

Enterprise JavaBeans: Taste 'em Again for the First Time

The 5th Wave   By Rich Tennant

And finally, do you feel your client/server environment keeps you well connected to your department?

In this part . . .

In Part I, I review fundamental concepts of Enterprise JavaBeans (EJB). In this section, you'll discover the structure of EJB applications, explore the various roles of EJB application developers, and investigate the technological foundations of EJB applications. I also introduce you to the running example EJB application I refer to throughout the book.

Chapter 1

Enterprise JavaBean Ground Rules

In This Chapter

▶ Looking at the component view of Enterprise JavaBeans (EJBs)

▶ Discovering the types of EJBs

▶ Making the case for EJBs

▶ Deciding whether EJBs are right for you

*E*veryone is talking about Enterprise JavaBeans (EJBs). Because you've purchased this book, you've probably heard the buzz. Perhaps your business is planning to implement an EJB application, or perhaps you want to discover more about this technology for personal enrichment. Whatever your reason, you're about to discover that there's a lot more to EJB programming than writing code.

To be a successful EJB programmer, you must first understand the conceptual model of the Enterprise JavaBean architecture. The *architecture* is the conceptual model that structures EJB applications and ensures that different parts of the application can work together. Understanding the EJB architecture is important because, as an EJB developer, you must adhere to certain development practices in order to ensure that the EJB application works properly. Your responsibilities are referred to as the *EJB developer contract*.

In this chapter, I introduce you to the general terms of the contract. As you proceed through this chapter, you discover the fundamental characteristics of EJB applications, investigate the types of Enterprise JavaBeans, and gain an understanding of some of the general characteristics of each type of bean. You also see the benefits that EJBs bring to a software project. Finally, you examine some criteria for determining whether using Enterprise JavaBeans is the right choice for you.

Introducing Component Model of EJBs

EJBs are software components. A *software component* is a program that runs inside a container. (What's a container? Read on!) The component provides some unique functionality that is specific to the application you develop, whether it's a shopping cart for an online retailer or an account management service for a bank. The *container* (see?) provides your software components with *system services*. System services are generic services that any type of application can benefit from, such as security and transaction services. Basically, that means you can benefit from many very powerful system features in your software components without writing any code to create those features.

The EJBs you develop in your EJB application should provide services that are unique and special to the business problems your software needs to address. If your EJB components don't address a unique problem, then you don't necessarily need to develop them yourself; you can probably buy existing components that do the job.

Now for the catch. (You never get somethin' for nothin'.) In the case of EJBs, in order to benefit from any container's services, you — as the EJB developer — must adhere to a *contract* with the container. The container agrees to provide certain features to your EJBs according to a specified set of rules. In exchange, you must develop your EJBs to conform to a specified structure that the EJB container can understand.

Think of this component concept in the same way that you might think of your stereo system. If you're an audiophile, you have the ability to choose between a variety of brands for the different components for your stereo system. You may get one brand of receiver, another brand of amplifier, and yet another brand of speakers. You can plug them all together because each component adheres to a convention that requires consistent interfaces for plugging into a stereo system. Likewise, Enterprise JavaBeans can be added and removed from any EJB container because the EJB specification requires consistent interfaces between the container and the EJB component.

Figure 1-1 illustrates a simple view of the component model for Enterprise JavaBeans.

The figure shows the following three key players in an EJB application:

> ✔ **The *client* is a software application that makes use of EJB components.** The client can reside on the same computer as the EJB component, or it can reside on a remote computer. The client can also be virtually any type of application. You may have a JavaServer Pages (JSP) application as a client, or a desktop application residing on a user's computer. The client may also be another Enterprise JavaBean.

✔ **The container is the host for EJB components.** It provides a variety of system services to the EJB component so you don't have to develop them yourself. When a client application — such as a JSP application — invokes a method on an EJB component, the call is passed through the EJB container first. The container performs these extra services and then passes the client's call to the EJB component. Ultimately, the EJB component performs the operations requested by the client. This entire process is completely transparent to the client application; as far as the client is concerned, it thinks it's talking directly to an EJB component.

✔ **The EJB component is a provider of business services or business data.** *Business services* and *business data* are processes and information that *you* define and which are specific to the needs of your business. As an EJB component developer, your development responsibilities are two fold:

  • **Your EJB components must implement the methods required by the EJB component architecture.** These methods are collectively referred to as the *application programming interface* (API). The methods defined in the API allow the EJB container to provide system services to your EJB components. They also allow you to make requests to the container to perform certain actions, such as getting the identity of a user.

  • **You must implement the business methods required for the application you're developing.** That allows the client to receive business services and business data from your EJB component. For example, if you're developing a shopping cart application for your business, you'll need to define methods to add items to the cart and remove items from the cart.

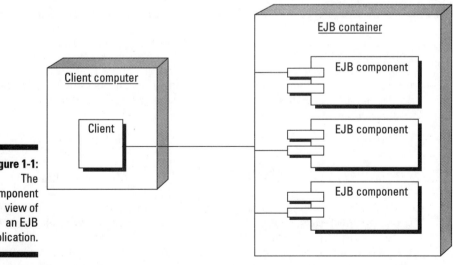

Figure 1-1:
The component view of an EJB application.

EJBs: For distributed applications only?

A *distributed application* is a program that runs on many computers at once. Each computer in a distributed application provides a subset of the total application's behavior. Enterprise JavaBeans are designed for building distributed applications and are ideally suited to perform the task. Some argue that Enterprise JavaBeans are only for distributed applications. I've heard opposing points of view on this issue. I'm casting my vote against it; EJBs are *not* only for distributed applications.

While enabling distributed computing is certainly a key feature of the EJB approach, distributed computing is not the only thing to be accomplished with EJB applications. EJB applications also provide a variety of services to business application developers that are completely independent of the distributed computing question. These features include transaction and security services, which should be considerations in all business applications regardless of whether they're distributed or not. You should not feel that you can't take advantage of these features just because you don't intend to create a distributed application.

In addition, you shouldn't make your EJB application a distributed application just because you can. Distributed computing with Java is enabled with a technology called *Remote Method Invocation.* Anytime an EJB application talks with a client that is located in a different Java Virtual Machine (JVM) — even if the JVM is located on the same computer — the application uses RMI. RMI is orders of magnitude more expensive to perform — in terms of system resources — than communicating with Java programs locally. RMI is expensive because when you pass an object from one JVM to another using RMI, the computer must make a copy of the entire object and send it to the remote computer, which then reconstructs the object before it can do anything. In Java, local communication allows you to pass an object by reference, which means that only a reference to the object is passed across the method invocation, not the object itself.

The good news is that EJB applications don't have to use RMI. As you make your way through this book I'll show you techniques you can use to ensure that your EJB components use local communication to improve their performance.

Implementing business services in an EJB application is little different from implementing them in any other Java application. There's no mystery or magic to it. As I review each type of EJB component in this book, I'll provide additional information about defining business methods in that type of component.

Responsibilities of the EJB Container

The EJB container is responsible for providing a number of services to your EJB programs. The services the EJB container must provide are enumerated by the Enterprise JavaBean Specification. That means that you can deploy your EJB to any specification-compliant container and receive the benefit of all the mandated services. Those services include the following key features:

- ✔ **EJB containers provide support for remote and local communication between your EJB components and client applications.** This is accomplished in a manner that's virtually transparent to you, so you don't have to worry about how it's implemented when you're developing EJB components.

- ✔ **EJB containers provide *pool* and *cache* services to EJB components.** A *pool* is a repository of unused EJB components that are supplied to a client on demand. A *cache* is a storage area for EJB components that are assigned to a client program, but not currently in use. These services minimize the memory requirements for the EJB container while providing high performance service to the client program.

- ✔ **EJB containers must provide security services for EJB programs.** When you deploy an application you can configure these services according to guidelines laid out in the specification, but you don't have to perform any special programming to utilize them.

- ✔ **EJB containers must provide transactional services for EJB programs.** *Transactions* define units of work that must all succeed or all fail as a set. Transactions can contain many EJB programs, including EJB programs residing on remote computers. The transactional characteristics of an EJB container can be configured when your EJB application is deployed, but require little to no special programming from you as the EJB developer.

- ✔ **EJB containers provide transparent integration between your EJB components and external data sources such as databases.** As a developer, you don't have to manage storage and retrieval of data from a database, although you may choose to do so if it fits your needs.

The EJB container provides these and other features according to the rules that you define. This is referred to as *declarative programming*. Declarative programming is a mechanism that allows you to declare the services you want in an XML formatted document. This XML document is called the *deployment descriptor,* which is deployed with your EJB application. The server reads the deployment descriptor and automatically implements the services you request according to the rules that you declare. Thus, the complexity of implementing these services is completely hidden while you retain the ability to configure the EJB application to suit your needs.

While the EJB specification defines many of the options that you can modify in the deployment descriptor, it doesn't prohibit EJB container vendors from creating their own custom deployment descriptors to extend existing configuration options or to add new options. All container vendors provide extensions to the deployment descriptor; they use these extensions to connect the generic EJB deployment descriptor to container-specific services. While these extensions are often essential, they're not standard and not portable. EJB component developers are not responsible for working with container-specific extensions to the deployment descriptor. The service is generally reserved for someone who has specialized knowledge of administering the EJB container.

Psychoanalyzing EJB Components

Enterprise JavaBeans may have a simple API, but because each Enterprise JavaBean is actually made up of three separate classes, they present a multifaceted personality to the EJB component programmer. As the EJB component programmer, you have the responsibility of creating these three classes for each EJB that you develop. Think of these three parts as the split personality of EJB components, which you must integrate into a cohesive whole.

Now, it's time for a reality check. If you're not sure about the definition of a class, then you're not yet ready for developing EJB applications. To be an effective EJB application developer, you should have a pretty good understanding of the fundamental concepts and syntax for the Java language. You can pick some of that up from *Java 2 For Dummies,* by Barry Burd.

Figure 1-2 provides a more detailed view of the component model illustrated initially in Figure 1-1.

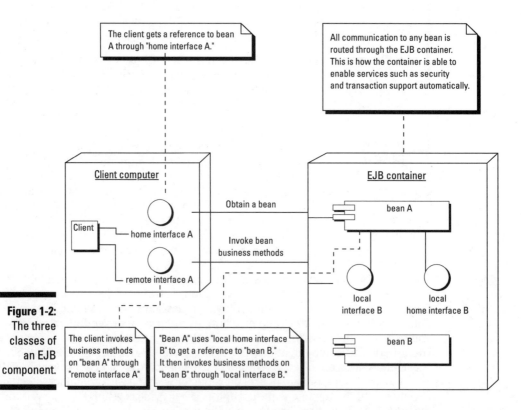

The client gets a reference to bean A through "home interface A."

All communication to any bean is routed through the EJB container. This is how the container is able to enable services such as security and transaction support automatically.

Client computer

Client

home interface A

Obtain a bean

Invoke bean business methods

remote interface A

EJB container

bean A

local interface B

local home interface B

bean B

Figure 1-2: The three classes of an EJB component.

The client invokes business methods on "bean A" through "remote interface A"

"Bean A" uses "local home interface B" to get a reference to "bean B." It then invokes business methods on "bean B" through "local interface B."

With this detail, you can see the physical layout of the different classes that make up an EJB component, as follows:

- ✔ **The *bean* is the actual provider of services to the client.** This class supplies all the business service methods, and also implements the API methods necessary to interact with the EJB container. Depending on the type of bean you're working with, the EJB container may store this component in a pool or in a cache.

- ✔ **The *home interface* is a Java interface that coordinates client access to beans.** The home interface is the second class required by EJB components. The client gains access to a bean by requesting a bean through the home interface. This in turn sends a message to the EJB container to create or retrieve a bean and make it available for use by the client. The two types of home interfaces for EJB applications are remote home interfaces (often referred to simply as home interfaces) and local home interfaces. Remote home interfaces are used by client applications that reside in a different Java Virtual Machine (JVM) — possibly in a different computer. Local home interfaces are used by client applications that reside in the same JVM.

- ✔ **The *remote interface* is the Java interface a client talks through to invoke business methods on the bean.** The client never actually has a copy of the bean because the bean always lives in the EJB container. The client does have a copy of the interface, and through the interface can make use of methods supplied by the bean. The remote interface provides the client with access to business methods of the EJB while hiding all the details of the system services that the EJB container provides.

  The local interface in Figure 1-2 is a cousin to the remote interface. It provides access to business methods for clients that reside inside the same Java Virtual Machine (JVM) as the EJB component, which is useful when other EJBs need to interact with a local EJB component. The local interface and remote interface are generically referred to as *component interfaces*. The component interface of the EJB component is the third required class.

Reviewing the Types of EJBs

Currently, there are four types of Enterprise JavaBeans. Each type plays a unique role in a complete EJB application. When you create an EJB component, you need to implement a component that is appropriate for the type of task you need to perform. The purposes envisioned for each type of EJB component are outlined here:

✔ *Stateless session beans* are EJBs that are used to implement processes that can be accomplished in a single step. They're referred to as stateless because they cannot remember information about a client program from one method invocation to the next. A good example of a stateless session bean is a bean that deposits money into a bank account. This bean provides a service that a) can be completed in a single step and b) doesn't need to remember anything from one invocation to the next. Stateless session beans exhibit the following characteristics:

- There is a one-to-one correspondence between stateless session beans and the client that uses them. Thus, each client gets its own stateless session bean.

- Stateless session beans are pooled when not in use. After each client invocation, the stateless session bean is cleaned up and returned to a pool of beans available for the next client invocation.

- Stateless session beans don't preserve any state between invocations. State is the data stored inside the bean. After each client finishes using the bean, the state is discarded.

✔ *Stateful session beans* are EJBs that are used to implement processes that require a multiple step dialog between the client and the EJB. They're called stateful because they can remember information supplied by a client application across multiple method invocations. A good example of a stateful session bean is a shopping cart; a client should be able to add any number of different books to a shopping cart and each client should have its own shopping cart. Stateful session beans exhibit the following characteristics:

- There is a one-to-one correspondence between clients and stateful session beans, meaning that each client gets its own stateful session bean.

- Stateful session beans are used to handle multiple step interactions with a given client. To accomplish this, the state of the session bean is preserved across multiple invocations from a client.

- A stateful session bean may be cached by the client in between client invocations. This takes the session bean out of the server's memory to make room for other session beans that are actively being used.

✔ *Entity beans* are EJBs that are used to represent business data in an application, such as a bank account. Entity beans share the following characteristics:

- Entity beans correspond with information stored in a database or other persistent storage. *Persistent storage* is any location where data can be stored and survive a shutdown of the computer. (For example, a disk file or a database.)

- Entity beans have a primary key that a client can use to find them. A primary key is a value that uniquely identifies an entity bean. When a client needs to interact with a specific entity bean, it can look up that entity bean by using a primary key. For example, if you want to deposit money into your bank account, you need some means to find *your* account, instead of deposing the money into any old account. A primary key allows you to find your account.

- Multiple clients can access and work with the same entity bean.

- When an entity bean isn't in use, its state is preserved in a persistent location and the bean is returned to a pool. When an entity bean is in use, it can be cached between invocations. When an entity bean is cached, it is stored in a temporary location.

✔ *Message-driven beans* (MDBs) are the newest addition to the EJB architecture. These beans are fundamentally different from other EJBs because they don't have a home interface or a remote interface. MDBs are used to integrate with the Java Messaging Service (JMS), a service that allows clients to give orders to your EJB components without hanging around waiting for a response. For example, you may need to tell your EJB application to generate bank statements for all the customers of a bank, but you wouldn't want to sit there waiting for the job to get done (boring), so you just send a message through JMS. MDBs are called JMS message consumers, which means they listen for messages from a JMS server. When a message is sent, the MDB "consumes" the message and performs a set of actions you define.

As you design EJB applications, be sure to tailor the design to conform to the roles of the four different EJBs.

Defining Roles for EJB Developers

The EJB architecture is designed to be a highly flexible, robust, and modular system for creating business applications. Speaking of modular, the creators of the EJB specification envisioned that the creation of EJB applications would involve a number of different developers, with each developer tailoring his or her specialized skills to a narrowly defined set of roles. The roles are

✔ **EJB bean provider:** The bean provider is responsible for creating EJB components and defining some of the characteristics for these components in a deployment descriptor. For more about the deployment descriptor, check out the earlier section "Responsibilities of the EJB Container."

✔ **EJB application assembler:** The application assembler is responsible for taking EJB components from various sources and putting them together in a complete package. This task primarily involves defining many of the attributes of the deployment descriptor XML file.

✔ **The EJB deployer:** The deployer is the administrator of an EJB container. The deployer's domain is to deploy applications (assembled by the application assembler) to a particular server and then to administer that server.

✔ **The EJB container provider:** The container provider is an organization that develops an EJB container. There are several vendors that supply EJB containers.

✔ **The EJB server provider:** Typically the same entity as the EJB container provider, the server provider is a specialist in the system services — such as transaction management, security, and other services — provided by the EJB container.

Because I've focused the content of this book to fit the needs primarily of EJB component developers and application assemblers, you'll find no information in this book on creating EJB containers or EJB servers. In addition, the responsibilities of the deployer are specialized to a particular EJB container and are thus outside the scope of this book. To get additional information on deploying EJB applications, you'll have to refer to the documentation supplied with the EJB container you use.

Deciding Whether EJBs Are Right for You

Enterprise JavaBeans are not the end-all and be-all of application programming. That doesn't mean that you won't find them extremely useful; if you need them, they are wonderful. What I mean is that EJBs aren't the right choice for every application. When you're deciding whether EJBs are right for you, consider the following:

✔ **Does your application need to be distributed?** Distributed applications are applications that reside on multiple computers at once. Because EJBs hide the complexity of communicating between different computers, they're ideally suited for this type of application.

✔ **Do you need to develop applications that are completely independent of a database or other persistent storage?** This is a typical scenario for third-party application vendors that provide applications for back office systems — including financial applications, supply chain management, and point-of-sale systems. EJBs are ideal for this scenario because they can be developed to be completely database independent, allowing you to swap databases depending upon your client's needs.

✔ **Do you need to develop applications that can be easily integrated with business partners?** Examples of these types of applications are business-to-business (B2B) applications and supply chain integration applications.

✔ **Do you need to take advantage of the services provided by the EJB container to maximize the performance and flexibility of your business application?** EJB containers provide a lot of benefits for your business applications, and hide a lot of complexity in developing solid, effective business applications. If you're looking for the benefits of security, transaction management, object pooling and caching, and ease of integrating with a database, then the EJB model is a good approach.

If you answered yes to any of the preceding questions, then EJB applications are probably a good choice for your needs. If you didn't answer yes to any of the questions, then you should think carefully before pursuing the development of an EJB application. If you don't need the services of an EJB application, you're adding a lot of complexity to your application with little benefit in return.

Although EJB applications are typically integrated with Servlet or JSP applications, it's possible to run a Servlet or JSP application without EJB application services. Consider this strategy as an alternative to using EJBs in your application if you think that EJBs aren't a good choice for you.

EJB applications provide business services and business data. They provide an interface through which client programs can interact and benefit from the services provided by the EJB container. However, end users cannot interact directly with an EJB application. So if you use EJB components in your business applications, you must also take advantage of other application solutions. Your options include Servlet or JSP programs — if your application is Web-based — or you can develop client-side applications that use EJBs to interact with a central server.

Chapter 2

A Practical EJB Scenario

In This Chapter

▶ Development lifecycle recommendations

▶ Discovering the running example for this book

*T*hey say a picture is worth a thousand words. This chapter provides a picture of the running example used throughout the book to illustrate every aspect of EJB development. I'm devoting an entire chapter to introducing this example for a couple of reasons:

✔ The most important goal is to deal with introducing the example up front, so I don't have to cloud the EJB presentation with a lot of extraneous explanation of the example.

✔ This chapter gives me the opportunity to address some software development methodologies that will help you create better Enterprise JavaBeans faster.

As you proceed through this chapter, you'll get a sense of how EJB components fit together to form a cohesive application. If you're seeking information on a particular topic, you'll also find lots of internal cross-references in this chapter.

If you're a non-linear reader, this chapter is a great place to start. Just find the topic you're interested in and follow the cross-reference to the chapters that address your topic.

The ATM Scenario

The ATM scenario is a favorite among EJB sample solutions. Automatic teller machines lend themselves to EJB development for many reasons:

✔ Pretty much every Tom, Dick, or Harriet has used an ATM machine. It's woven into the fabric of our lives, which makes it accessible to the average Joe. That means I can spend my time talking about Enterprise JavaBeans instead of example applications. (If you haven't used an ATM, seek professional help.)

✔ ATM operations are transactional, which means that each ATM transaction you perform should complete successfully before the changes are saved. Thus, they're great for illustrating the transactional features of EJB applications.

✔ ATM operations require security, so there's a natural opportunity to take advantage of security services supplied by the EJB container.

✔ A standard ATM software solution exercises all API features of Enterprise JavaBeans, so you don't have to fumble through contrived scenarios as you're discovering the EJB API.

The running example in this book is by no means production quality. It's a hypothetical ATM scenario used to illustrate EJB development — not to illustrate my prowess in the field of banking applications. In fact, the solutions are pretty simplistic. So if you're a banker, I don't want to hear about it.

Application view

The ATM application used in this book implements a limited number of use cases. A *use case* describes a process through which a user and a computer system interact with each other. In some contexts, a use case is referred to as a *user-system dialog* because it involves a logically related group of interactions between a user and a software system. Figure 2-1 shows a component diagram that illustrates the structure of the ATM application. The use cases of the ATM application in this book include

✔ **Selecting from a list of available accounts:** Let's face it — as a banking customer, you won't get far in this world unless you know what your accounts are.

✔ **Depositing funds into an account:** In the real world, this step involves inserting an envelope of money into the ATM machine. As an alternative, I'm requesting that you send the envelop directly to me — cash only please. I'll make sure it's properly spent.

✔ **Withdrawing funds from an account:** Again, you're welcome to send this request to me. I'll look into it and get back to you.

✔ **Transferring funds between two different accounts:** This operation is an ideal solution to illustrate the transactional features of EJB applications. After all, a transfer is nothing more than a withdrawal from one account and a deposit into another. You're reusing the EJB components from the preceding two bullets to implement this solution while discovering the transactional semantics of EJB applications.

✔ **Requesting an account statement:** In this EJB component, you exercise the features of the message-driven bean to request and receive a statement of your bank account delivered to your e-mail address.

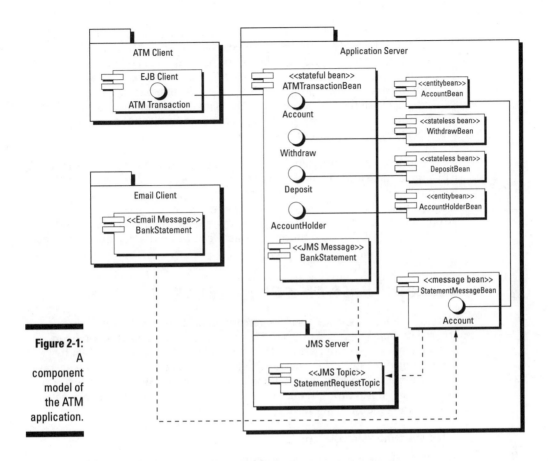

Figure 2-1:
A component model of the ATM application.

As with any real world application, you have a variety of ways to achieve the ends that I describe in these use cases. The book covers a variety of alternative approaches in this running example. Here are a couple of the alternatives you'll get to see:

✔ While the "pure EJB approach" for the ATM scenario contains several entity beans, many companies avoid the use of entity beans in their applications. Entity beans are generally less efficient than other types of EJB components. Throughout this book, I show you EJB solutions that implement all the previous features without using entity beans.

✔ EJB containers have the ability — known as *container-managed persistence* (CMP) — to implement all the interaction between an EJB application and a database without any explicit coding. The alternative to CMP is *bean-managed persistence* (BMP), which requires you to code all the interaction between the bean and a database explicitly. You'll get to review both approaches in the context of the ATM application.

> ✔ EJB applications are pure *server-side* application solutions. That means that they reside entirely on an application server and have no direct interaction with an end user. It also means that you can implement different kinds of client applications. *Client applications* provide an interface (typically a graphical user interface) that allows a user to interact with the EJB application. You'll investigate some good strategies for preserving flexibility in the types of client applications you implement, using the EJB application as a model.

As you look at the component diagram in Figure 2-1, you may recall that each EJB should have a home interface that's used to look up a reference to the EJB on the server. I didn't display the home interface in the component diagram to avoid stretching your brain too much in one spot. (Those brain stretch marks are so out of vogue.) Just remember that except for message-driven beans (MDBs) each Enterprise JavaBean has to have a home interface.

Stateful session components

Stateful session beans are used to perform tasks that require multiple steps. The *state* is equivalent to the information the stateful session bean accumulates in order to perform the desired task. To bring that down to earth, consider the ATM scenario: When you transfer funds from one account to another using an ATM, you have to traverse several screens. Each screen may record information pertaining to one step in the transfer process with the following required steps:

1. **Select the source account.**

   The state is the account number for the source account.

2. **Select the target account.**

   The state is the account number for the target account.

3. **Specify the amount to transfer.**

   The state is the amount of money to be transferred from the source account to the target account.

For the transfer process to work, the states captured in each of the three steps must be preserved until all the information is captured. Only then can the transfer process be completed. That makes this solution ideally suited for a stateful session bean.

In the ATM application that I've developed for this book, there's one stateful session bean — a generic ATMTransaction bean that represents the process of completing a transaction using an ATM. I've devoted Chapter 5 exclusively to developing stateful session beans.

Stateless session components

Stateless session beans are software components that don't have to preserve state in between client interactions. As an example, consider an activity such as withdrawing funds. Withdrawing funds can be accomplished in a single step. Just tell the bean to withdraw a specific amount from a specific account and you're done. Because the bean doesn't have to preserve any information about the action for the client to refer to later, it can be easily modeled with a stateless session bean.

The running ATM example in this book has two stateless session beans: a `WithdrawBean` and a `DepositBean`. You find more information on stateless session beans in Chapter 4.

Business entity components

Entity beans are software components used to represent business data. Entities are different from session beans because entity beans describe *things* while session beans represent *processes*. The sample ATM application has three entity beans: an `AccountHolderBean` that describes a person holding an account, an `AddressBean` that describes an account holder's address, and an `AccountBean` that contains information about an account holder's bank account.

Working with entity beans is a pretty broad subject. I've devoted several chapters in this book to entity beans:

- Chapter 6 covers the basics for developing entity beans with *container-managed persistence (CMP)*, meaning that the EJB container coordinates storage and retrieval of the data in an entity bean.

- Chapter 7 covers the newly defined EJB Query Language (EJB QL), which is used in conjunction with CMP to support looking up entity beans.

- Chapter 8 covers all the basics of working with entity beans that use *bean-managed persistence (BMP)*, meaning that the entity bean coordinates its own storage and retrieval of data.

Message-driven bean components

Message-driven beans (MDBs) are a new addition to the EJB 2.0 specification, intended to perform tasks where the EJB client doesn't need to wait for the result of the task. Such tasks are referred to as *asynchronous* because the activity between the EJB client and the EJB doesn't happen simultaneously.

Instead the client says, "Go take care of this while I do something else." MDBs are very useful in cases where a request can take a long time to process, and the client doesn't care what the result of the task is.

The sample ATM application has just one MDB: the `StatementMessageBean`. The `StatementMessageBean` creates a bank statement and e-mails it to the `AccountHolder`. Because the ATM client shouldn't wait for this process to complete, the MDB is an ideal solution to generate and send bank statements.

You'll find complete coverage of message-driven beans in Chapters 9 and 10. Chapter 9 provides the background you'll need in Java Messaging Service (JMS), which is a necessary prerequisite to working with MDBs. Chapter 10 delves into the topic of creating MDBs. These beans are remarkably easy to work with if you have the appropriate background information under your belt (which I supply in Chapter 10).

Here's a security tip: Before providing access to MDBs, require your EJB client to authenticate itself with the EJB container. That ensures the client cannot generate tons of MDB tasks without identifying itself. If you don't require authentication, a malicious user may be able to launch a denial of service attack on your EJB container by rapidly generating thousands or tens of thousands of messages for the server to process. If you require a user to authenticate, and you monitor usage of the EJB application, you can block such attacks by disabling the user's account.

Putting it all together

EJB applications involve more than just writing EJB components. You'll also need to define the *deployment descriptor* (which describes the EJB component to the container) for each EJB component and package your EJB components in an *EJB-JAR file* (the file that holds all your EJB components and the deployment descriptor). The ATM application needs to have a deployment descriptor that describes its various components and declares the use of EJB container services (such as security and transaction services). It also needs to be put into an EJB-JAR file so that it can be deployed to an EJB container.

The good news is that I address all of these topics in this book. Here's a guide to finding the chapters you need to address these concerns:

✔ Chapter 11 covers the packaging of EJB components and the definition of the EJB deployment descriptor from a bean provider's perspective. If one of your responsibilities is creating Enterprise JavaBeans, you'll want to take a look at this chapter.

✔ Chapter 12 picks up where Chapter 11 leaves off by examining a service called Java Naming and Directory Interface (JNDI) that EJB components need to talk to each other.

✔ Chapter 13 covers the assembly of EJB applications and investigates the elements of the EJB deployment descriptor that are defined when an EJB application is deployed. If you're responsible for assembling various EJB components into a complete application, this chapter is for you.

✔ You'll find substantial coverage of transactional management with EJBs in Chapter 14. *Transactional management* is implemented in XML for EJBs and, while it's pretty simple from a syntax perspective, the implications of various transactional decisions can rapidly become complex. Chapter 14 takes a closer look at a variety of transaction scenarios and illustrates the implications of different transactional choices you can make in an EJB application.

✔ Chapter 15 is devoted to the coverage of oft-neglected security issues. This chapter presents the subject of security in the context of creating EJB applications.

✔ Chapter 16 investigates strategies for creating EJB clients. While this book doesn't endeavor to be your definitive reference for creating EJB client applications, I've included some examples in this chapter to serve as pointers in the development process.

Advice on EJB Development Strategies

This book doesn't aspire to be your definitive reference for software development practices nor can I promise that reading this book will keep your projects out of trouble. Nevertheless, I'd like to pass on a few tips that will help keep you on the right track. These aren't original ideas, but I've used them and they've proven effective for me.

Define the proper scope

Each Enterprise JavaBean you create should represent one *atomic unit* of work — either a complete business process or a complete entity. An atomic unit is an entity or process that represents a single unit of work. Apply the principle of *atomicity* when you design your Enterprise JavaBean components.

Deciding how to apply the principle of atomicity can be difficult. To help you decide whether a unit of work is truly atomic, ask yourself these questions:

✔ **Are parts of the EJB I'm creating reusable in different contexts?** If the EJB can be subdivided so that parts are reusable in other contexts, then you've probably defined it too broadly.

✔ **If I had to undo some of the work in this EJB, would I also have to undo work in another EJB to restore a consistent state to my application?** If you have explicit dependencies between two or more EJBs, then you may have defined the EJBs too narrowly. And you may consider combining the two to make a single entity.

In some cases you, may find that the atomic metaphor doesn't work well with a given task. If you have a business process that requires a multiple step conversation between an EJB client and the EJB server, and in which the server must remember data between each step in the conversation, then it may be more convenient to think of this process by using a *molecular* metaphor. Such conversational tasks are ideally suited for stateful session beans. Just remember that while a multi-step process is okay, if an EJB component serves more than one purpose, it should be subdivided into more EJB components.

Seek opportunities to reuse EJBs

Enterprise JavaBeans are part of a component-based architecture, meaning that each EJB component should be reusable in a variety of contexts. One of the first steps in making reusable EJBs is to apply the principle of atomicity that I explain in the preceding section. But after you've done that, be sure to maximize the benefit of all your little atomic EJB components by reusing them in different contexts.

You can often find opportunities for reuse when you have to compose several beans to complete a larger unit of work. As an example, consider the sample ATM application in this book, which has two tasks (deposit and withdraw) that can be combined to implement a transfer (which requires a deposit from one account and a withdrawal from another).

Pick your EJB tools carefully

For each task you must perform with Enterprise JavaBeans, you have four types of EJBs to choose from. I go into more detail about deciding which components are appropriate for which uses throughout the book, but following are some basic guidelines you can apply to making the decision:

✔ **Use stateless session beans to implement the solution whenever you have a task that can be accomplished in a single step — and which doesn't require a multiple step interaction between an EJB client and the EJB server.** Stateless session beans are truly atomic units of work in the purest sense.

- ✔ **Use stateful session beans only when you have a task that requires a multiple step conversation between an EJB client and the EJB container.** Remember that the conversation should also require the preservation of state across each part of the process. If you can accomplish the same task with several stateless session beans, then do so. Stateless session beans are more efficient than stateful session beans.

- ✔ **Use entity beans to represent data in your application.** Don't use entity beans to represent a business process; you should use entity beans to represent data only.

- ✔ **Use message-driven beans to perform asynchronous tasks.** An *asynchronous task* is one that a client can start but doesn't need to wait for a response before it continues to the next step. For example, if you have a sales application that triggers a reorder process when quantity falls below a given level, the client triggering the reorder doesn't need to wait until the reorder process is complete in order to complete an order. The alternative is a *synchronous task*, in which the client must wait for the task to be completed before it proceeds to the next task.

To entity bean or not

Entity beans have come under criticism from a lot of different camps, particularly during the EJB 1.1 specification. The original vision for these beans was to serve as the platform independent view of data, meaning that you could technically use any kind of database that you want to store your EJB components, and you could change the database without changing any of the code in your EJB application. Unfortunately, that model doesn't work well for all applications, and it sometimes comes at a high cost to performance. Don't feel that you have to use EJBs just because they're there. Consider these options when deciding if entity beans are right for you:

- ✔ If you're developing an application for resale, entity beans are a great choice. You can develop entity beans without knowing what type of database your customers use, maximizing the flexibility of your application.

- ✔ If you expect to have multiple EJB clients that make use of the same data at once, entity beans may benefit your application because a single entity bean can be shared between many EJB clients.

Sharing a single entity bean across multiple clients is beneficial because it limits the number of connections between your application and a database. In terms of application performance, interacting with a database is a very expensive process. Limiting the amount of interaction required between your EJB application and the database may substantially improve performance.

✔ If you have an existing database that you're building an EJB application on top of, entity beans may not be a good choice. Your existing database probably represents a significant investment that you'll want to leverage into your EJB application. Reverse engineering your database into entity beans will probably be very difficult — and not very beneficial.

One of the most important optimization considerations with entity beans is to ensure that your application server has enough memory to hold all the entity beans in use at any given time in memory. When an application server runs out of memory, it starts to cache entity beans to disk. Doing so means they have to be retrieved from the cache the next time they're requested, which is much slower than accessing them from memory.

Chapter 3

EJB Technology under the Hood

In This Chapter

▶ A simple EJB example

▶ Investigating the building blocks of EJB technology

▶ Discovering the patterns behind EJB components

*1*f you're like me, you have two important steps to conquering a new technology: Discover what you need to do; then discover why you need to do it. In the case of Enterprise JavaBeans, the *what* is the EJB API; the *why* is the principles of Java technology that make EJB technology work. This chapter is intended to impart meaning to why EJBs are the way they are. To accomplish that end, I take a look at the technological underpinnings of the Java language that make EJBs possible, and I also illustrate some of the design patterns that are used in the EJB components.

The best way to get started with a new technology is to start with the simple stuff. And there's nothing simpler than the ubiquitous Hello World application, in which you create an EJB that says, "Hello World!" Using the Hello World application, you get the chance to see what makes Enterprise JavaBeans tick. I've devoted this chapter to general principles that can be applied to virtually all Enterprise JavaBeans. This is boot camp for all new EJB developers, and you'll find that the principles in this chapter really lay the foundation for the rest of the book.

Note that I said these principles apply to *virtually all* Enterprise JavaBeans. The exception to the rule is the message-driven bean, which is a special case. To discover why, check out the section "Messaging systems and message-driven beans."

EJB Technological Underpinnings

EJB technology was originally developed to accomplish two basic goals:

- **To provide a simple way to create distributed applications in Java.** *Distributed applications* are programs that can run on many different computers at the same time, and which can communicate across a network. That means you have a single application running on many different computers at the same time.

- **To simplify the writing of application components that take advantage of a variety of services (such as security and transaction support) that are implemented in a container.** Because these services are provided by the container, the EJB programmer doesn't have to be a jack-of-all-trades. Instead, programmers can specialize in addressing the needs of their customers and leave all the complexity of application services to the developer of the EJB container.

With the introduction of the EJB 2.0 specification, a third important goal was identified — performance. While EJB applications are designed to be distributed, in practice, many EJB components tend to reside on the same computer. In the EJB 2.0 specification, new features were introduced to optimize communication between EJBs that reside on the same computer.

It's easier to see why Enterprise JavaBeans work through an illustrative example. Without going into the details of how to create EJBs, the example I use is the Hello World EJB, shown in Figure 3-1. The source code for the Hello World application is available at the Enterprise JavaBeans For Dummies Web page (www.dummies.com/extras/ejbfd).

Figure 3-1: Deployment diagram for the Hello World EJB.

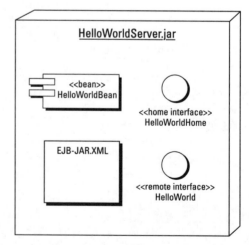

Before proceeding, take note of the following points illustrated in Figure 3-1:

✔ Enterprise JavaBeans are deployed in two files. Both files are called JAR files, and I'm not talking about your mother's cookie jar. A *JAR file* is just a collection of other files that are all packaged together so that you can move them around easily.

  • The client JAR file (HelloWorldClient.jar in Figure 3-1) contains interfaces that the client needs to make references to EJB components.

  • The server JAR file (HelloWorldServer.jar in Figure 3-1) contains the client interfaces, the bean component, and also an ejb-jar.xml file, which is the deployment descriptor. The EJB container needs all the server files to run the EJB application.

✔ While EJBs are referred to as components, each EJB — with the exception of the message-driven bean — is composed of three separate classes:

  • The *bean* is the part that resides inside the EJB container and implements all the business methods.

  • The *home interface* is used by an EJB client to create or to find a bean component in the EJB container. The home interface is deployed both to the EJB server and to the EJB client.

  • The *remote interface* is used by the EJB client to execute business methods of the bean located in the EJB container.

✔ The ejb-jar.xml file and vendor-specific XML files provide information that the EJB container needs to name beans. The filename ejb-jar.xml is the official filename given to the deployment descriptor, which is a required feature of every EJB application. The EJB container may require an additional XML file to initialize container-specific services.

Introducing Java Naming and Directory Interface

As you can see in Figure 3-1, EJB components are deployed in their entirety to the EJB server, but only the interfaces of the EJB component are deployed to an EJB client application. In order for a client application to make use of these interfaces, it must have access to the objects in the EJB container that implement the interfaces. Thus, the first task of the EJB client is to locate and obtain a reference to an EJB component. More properly, the client needs a reference to the home interface for an EJB component.

Java Naming and Directory Interface (JNDI) is a Java service that provides the EJB client with the ability to find an object located in a different computer. EJB applications and their clients use JNDI in the following way:

✔ The EJB container registers a reference to an EJB component's home interface in JNDI. This reference has a name that's assigned by the deployer of the EJB application. When a client requests the EJB component's name, the JNDI server returns a reference to the component.

✔ When a client application needs to use an EJB component, it requests a copy of the component from JNDI. The client application provides the JNDI name for the component.

✔ When the JNDI server receives a request for a component, it looks up the component requested using the name supplied by the client application. When it finds that component name, it gets a reference to the object the name refers to, and then returns that reference to the client application.

Figure 3-2 shows JNDI in action. In Figure 3-2, notice that a client has requested the home object through the JNDI Directory Service. JNDI finds the object and returns it to the client.

Don't worry about understanding all the mechanics behind JNDI. Most of the work in interacting with JNDI is performed for you by the EJB container. Looking up and obtaining a reference to the EJB home object is accomplished with a few simple lines of code, shown here:

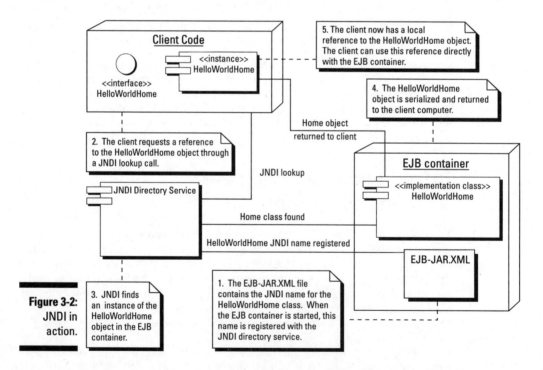

Figure 3-2:
JNDI in
action.

```
// This method uses JNDI to find a home interface
public HelloWorld() throws NamingException, RemoteException,
    ClassNotFoundException {

  /* First I get a reference to the JNDI context, which
   * contains the names for all the components registered in
   * JNDI.
   */
  context = new InitialContext();

  /* Next I request the HelloWorldRemoteHome from JNDI. The
   * "ejb/helloWorldEJB" is the name that this EJB component
   * was registered under in JNDI.
   */
  Object obj = context.lookup("ejb/helloWorldEJB");

  /* Finally, I am casting obj to HelloWorldRemoteHome
   * interface. I have to use the
   * PortableRemoteObject.narrow method because reference is
   * to an object that resides on a remote computer, in the
   * EJB container.
   */
  home = (HelloWorldRemoteHome)
    PortableRemoteObject.narrow( obj,
    HelloWorldRemoteHome.class);
}
```

 You can see the complete Hello World solution — including this JNDI example — in the Hello World application example, on the Web at www. dummies.com/extras/ejbfd.

Passing the buck with Java serialization

Java *serialization* is a process whereby a Java class is converted into data that can be stored on a disk or transported across a network. Serialization is one of the key features that makes EJB applications possible. One of the nice things about serialization is that, as a programmer, all you have to do is tell the Java Runtime — the program that runs Java programs — that you want a class to be serializable. To be serializable, a Java class has to implement the java.io.Serializable interface.

 The cool thing about the Serializable interface is that it has no methods. The entire effort is illustrated in the following code snippet:

```
Public Class SerializableClass implements Serializable{. . .}
```

You might assume that EJB components have to implement `Serializable` to participate in Java serialization. Instead, the architects of the EJB specification made EJB components serializable for you. So the magic of serialization is completely invisible to you as an EJB component developer.

Invoking methods remotely

Because EJB clients and EJB components often reside on different computers and because the method of the EJB component actually resides on the server (and isn't visible to the EJB client), it isn't possible for a client to execute a method directly on an EJB component. Instead, the client executes a method on the remote interface. Through a transparent service called Remote Method Invocation (RMI), the remote interface is able to deliver the method invocation to the server — where the work is performed — and the result is returned to the client. RMI is a service provided in the standard Java API and is another critical enabler of EJB technology. Figure 3-3 illustrates some of the magic that occurs behind the scenes with RMI technology.

Creating RMI applications without using an EJB container is possible. While RMI applications can be distributed across a network, they don't automatically offer the services available in an EJB container.

In Figure 3-3, you can see that RMI introduces some additional pieces to the EJB puzzle that I haven't yet addressed. You already know that the EJB components are composed of a remote interface, a home interface, and a bean. This view is augmented by what's shown in Figure 3-3:

✔ All RMI solutions are composed of a stub, and may also include a skeleton:

- The *stub* is an object that resides in the remote application and contains services that help it to invoke methods on the *skeleton* (see the next bullet). In the case of EJB applications, the EJB client is the remote application. Another term for stub is *proxy*, which is used because the stub accepts input and relays it to the skeleton.

- The *skeleton* is an object that resides in a local application and is responsible for forwarding method invocations to the local object. In the case of EJB applications, the EJB container is the local application. In pure Java 2 applications, a skeleton isn't required; instead, the stub forwards method invocations directly to the local object.

- When the client invokes a method in the stub, the stub forwards the invocation to the skeleton. The skeleton directs the method to the local object, which executes the method and returns the result back to the skeleton and ultimately to the stub.

✔ The home interface in an EJB component is required to extend the `javax.ejb.EJBHome` interface. In turn, `javax.ejb.EJBHome` extends `java.rmi.Remote`. The implementation of the `EJBHome` object is provided by the EJB container, and supports the underlying RMI communication protocol.

✔ The remote interface in an EJB component is required to extend the `javax.ejb.EJBObject` interface. As with the `EJBHome` interface, the `EJBObject` interface also extends `java.rmi.Remote`. Again, implementation of the `EJBObject` is provided by the EJB container and supports the RMI communication protocol.

Because an EJB client only interacts with the EJB through the remote interface, the RMI process is completely transparent, which means that the client programmer doesn't have to think about RMI at all. In fact, an EJB container can implement RMI in a variety of ways. Thus, while Figure 3-3 illustrates a possible implementation, the EJB container you use may work differently.

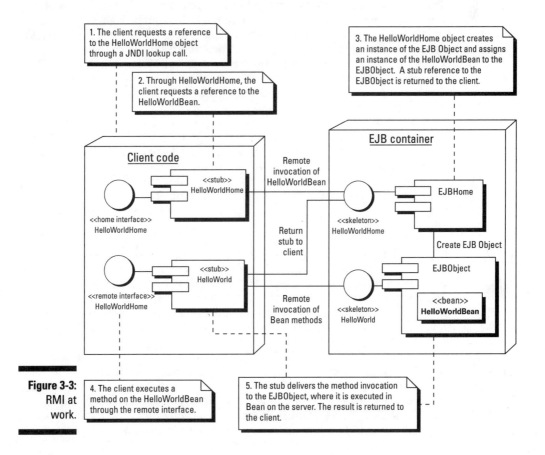

Figure 3-3: RMI at work.

1. The client requests a reference to the HelloWorldHome object through a JNDI lookup call.

2. Through HelloWorldHome, the client requests a reference to the HelloWorldBean.

3. The HelloWorldHome object creates an instance of the EJB Object and assigns an instance of the HelloWorldBean to the EJBObject. A stub reference to the EJBObject is returned to the client.

4. The client executes a method on the HelloWorldBean through the remote interface.

5. The stub delivers the method invocation to the EJBObject, where it is executed in Bean on the server. The result is returned to the client.

At this point you should be noticing a pattern evolving in EJB development; you don't have to do a lot to take advantage of some sophisticated services. The EJB container is a service provider — kind of like the local water company. You provide the plumbing for the EJB component by extending a couple of interfaces (EJBHome for your home interface and EJBObject for the remote interface), and the EJB container provides the water.

Improving performance with local calls

With the first major release of the EJB specification (Version 1.1) the innovators at Sun Microsystems were able to let the dust settle a little and see how EJB technology was used in the industry. The lessons learned have contributed to a lot of improvements in the EJB 2.0 specification. One of those improvements is the added support of local communication between EJB components.

This support was in high demand because, in practice, a lot of EJB applications aren't distributed, and yet they were required to depend on RMI for method invocation. A simple fact about RMI that's important to keep in mind is that it's a labor-intensive process. In fact, RMI is much more expensive than the local communication in terms of performance. And while RMI works between EJBs that reside in the same JVM (Java Virtual Machine), it involves a lot of extra work that local method invocations don't require.

Specifically, it used to be that in order to support RMI, the home interface had to extend the EJBHome interface and the remote interface had to extend the EJBObject interface. To provide a facility for local communication, the EJB 2.0 specification introduces two alternatives to EJBHome and EJBObject: EJBLocalHome and EJBLocalObject. If you want to create Enterprise JavaBeans that don't use RMI, you can do so by having the home interface extend the EJBLocalHome interface and a remote interface that extends the EJBLocalObject interface.

While local method invocation gives you a big boost in performance, it also reduces the flexibility of your EJB application. If you use local method invocation, your EJB component cannot be invoked from a remote location. Thus, before you decide which interfaces to implement, think about how you intend to use an EJB component. If you anticipate the need for remote communication, stick with implementing the EJBHome and EJBObject interfaces.

Many EJB containers allow you to take advantage of local communication even if you implement EJBHome and EJBObject. See, behind the scenes, EJB containers determine whether an EJB invocation is from a local resource. If the resource is local, the container automatically supports local communication. You get all this as a *transparent service* — you don't have to do any special work to get local communication whenever it's possible.

Managing lifecycles with callback methods

An EJB container provides your EJB components with a variety of services, which you can take advantage of without writing any special code. Many of those services have to do with managing the lifecycle events of your EJB component. For example, a stateful session bean can be stored in and retrieved from an EJB container's cache. Storing a stateful session bean to cache is called *passivation* while retrieving a stateful session bean from cache is called *activation*.

Activation and passivation are two of several tasks referred to as *lifecycle events* because they denote important actions in the lifecycle of an EJB component. While the server performs these actions automatically, you may want to perform some special actions during these and other lifecycle events for an EJB component. To illustrate, consider how an EJB component should handle a connection to a database in the following lifecycle events:

- **When the EJB component is activated, you may want to obtain a connection to a database.** The component needs this connection to interact with the database while it's active.

- **When the EJB component is passivated, you'll want to release the database connection so that other active EJB components can use it.** Because database connections are typically scarce resources, you don't want to lose access to one by passivating it with an EJB component.

- **When an EJB component is removed, you'll want to release the database reference so that it isn't destroyed with the EJB component.** Again, your database connection is a scarce resource, and in terms of performance, it's expensive to create new connections. So, when another component is about to be destroyed, making connections available to other EJB components is a good idea.

When using entity bean components, the EJB container can manage database connections for you. However, if you need to connect to a database from another type of bean, then you need to manage your database connections with methods in the EJB bean class called callback methods. *Callback methods* are methods that an EJB container executes when lifecycle events occur in an EJB component. Callback methods are defined in the interfaces you must implement with the bean element of your EJB component. To implement custom behaviors during a lifecycle event, all you have to do is provide the code in the appropriate callback method.

As I explain each type of EJB component available, I point out the callback methods. For now, it's just important to know that they're there for you to use if you need to provide support for some custom action that must occur during a lifecycle event.

Incidentally, while you're required to implement all callback methods defined for a particular kind of bean, you aren't required to do anything with those methods under normal circumstances. In many cases, the callback methods do nothing. Programmers in the know have a name for methods that don't do anything: *no-ops* — as in no operations performed.

Declaring your intentions with deployment descriptors

Taking advantage of the services provided by an EJB container means that you need to tell the EJB container what you want it to do. Telling the EJB container what to do is accomplished with an XML file called the *deployment descriptor*. For working with EJB applications, the EJB specification defines one deployment descriptor: the ejb-jar.xml file.

Deployment descriptors use a style of programming called *declarative programming* to tell the EJB container what services the EJB component needs. The EJB container then provides those services to the component. Declarative programming is simple because you don't need to know how to implement a particular service; all you have to do is declare that you want the service. The EJB container then handles all the implementation details.

Here's a short list of the types of services that you can declare with the ejb-jar.xml file:

- ✔ **The JNDI name for a component.** In order for a client to find an EJB component, it uses JNDI to look up the component based on a name; refer to Figure 3-2. A component's name is declared in the ejb-jar.xml file.

- ✔ **The transactional rules of a component.** Transaction support — which ensures that changes to data are properly executed — is a service provided by the EJB container to each EJB component. Each EJB component can elect the type of transaction support required by declaring its needs in the ejb-jar.xml file. Read more on this topic in Chapter 14.

- ✔ **The security roles and method permissions of a component.** EJB containers also provide security services to EJB components. The ejb-jar.xml file is used to declare various security roles and method permissions that the EJB container should implement.

In addition to the `ejb-jar.xml` file, each vendor's EJB container may have additional deployment descriptors to configure services for the container that exist outside the scope of the EJB specification. Note that, while I cover all the standard syntax and semantics of developing EJB applications in this book, you also need to know vendor-specific information for your EJB container to deploy and use EJB applications.

Messaging systems and message-driven beans

The EJB 2.0 specification introduces a new kind of Enterprise JavaBean called the message-driven bean (MDB). MDBs are different from all other EJB components because they don't have a remote or a home interface. MDBs are special because they're designed to interact with the Java Messaging Service (JMS) API. JMS is an enterprise Java service that allows applications to deliver messages and listen for messages on a message server.

JMS is similar to RMI in that it facilitates remote communication between a client and a server. The difference is that the client doesn't have to wait for a response to a message before it can continue about its business. In fact, JMS can even hold messages in a mailbox for an EJB container until the recipient is ready for them.

- In RMI method calls, the client invokes a method remotely, the method is executed on the server, and the return value of the method is returned to the client. The client can't execute the next line of code until the server has completed its task. Because the activities of the server and the client are happening serially, this type of operation is referred to as a *synchronous* operation.

- With JMS, the client delivers a message to a topic or a queue in the JMS server. The client can then continue about its business. Meanwhile, the EJB container has a MDB that subscribes to the JMS topic or queue as a listener. When the message is delivered, the JMS server forwards the message to the MDB, which can then perform some operation making use of the information in the message. Because the activities of the client and the server are happening simultaneously, this type of operation is called *asynchronous*.

Figure 3-4 illustrates JMS in action. Because of the fundamental differences between RMI and JMS that I identify in the preceding bullets, the MDB doesn't need a home interface or a remote interface.

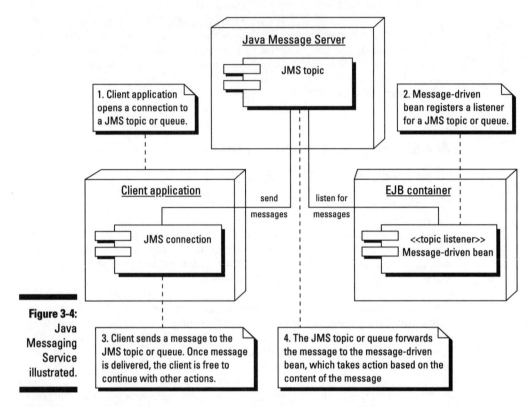

Figure 3-4:
Java
Messaging
Service
illustrated.

Java Message Server

JMS topic

1. Client application opens a connection to a JMS topic or queue.

2. Message-driven bean registers a listener for a JMS topic or queue.

Client application

JMS connection

send messages

listen for messages

EJB container

<<topic listener>>
Message-driven bean

3. Client sends a message to the JMS topic or queue. Once message is delivered, the client is free to continue with other actions.

4. The JMS topic or queue forwards the message to the message-driven bean, which takes action based on the content of the message

For client applications to use message-driven beans, they must implement interfaces and operations that are part of the JMS API. Read more about JMS in Chapter 9. I cover message-driven beans in Chapter 10.

EJB Design Patterns

Another way to think about Enterprise JavaBeans that lends to understanding why they're structured the way they are is to consider them in terms of software design patterns. *Software design patterns* are designs for software that address a particular design problem with a standard solution. Each software design pattern addresses a particular kind of design problem, and has both benefits and consequences. Ultimately, design patterns help software developers apply proven techniques to address common design issues that occur in the software development process.

Software design patterns are general rules in software design that apply to the problem being solved by software, and not necessarily to a particular language or technology. Design patterns can help define why EJB technology is structured in the way that it exists without getting into the technical details of the Java language.

Assembling EJBs with the Factory Pattern

Imagine the world without factories. If you wanted a car, you'd have to build it yourself. In fact, you'd have to start by machining all the parts. Well, that doesn't make much sense to car owners because cars are complicated machines. Likewise, some software products are so complex that they require a factory to create them. Instances of EJB components are a case in point — they are created for you by a factory because the details of implementing an EJB component are too complex for mere mortal programmers like you and me.

You can get a reference to the home interface of an EJB by performing a JNDI lookup on the home interface, as I discuss in the earlier section "Introducing Java Naming and Directory Interface." The next task to creating an EJB is invoking the constructor method on the home interface that most suits your need. When you do so, that invocation is forwarded to the server, where the EJB component is created and a reference is returned to the EJB client. The process for creating an EJB component can be described with a design pattern called the *Factory Method Pattern.*

The Factory Method Pattern provides a means for delegating the creation of a complex object to a special class referred to as a *factory.* The three basic roles in a Factory Method Pattern are

- **The consumer requests the creation of an object.** This object is typically referred to as the *product.*

- **The *factory* (a class) receives the consumer's request for an object.** The factory then performs some magic that isn't visible to the consumer, ultimately returning the object (see next bullet) requested by the consumer. The factory class can have one or more methods called *factory methods,* which are responsible for assembling the product.

- **The factory creates an object that's called the *product* and returns it to the consumer.** Typically, the consumer only has an abstract notion of what a product is. In implementation, that means the consumer is referring to the product through an interface or an abstract class. The factory is able to take that abstract request and apply concrete implementation details that result in returning a concrete product to the consumer. The bottom line here is that the factory can change the internal implementation of the product without having to change any code in the consumer.

These three points should resemble the process of getting a reference to an EJB component. In the case of Enterprise JavaBeans, the EJB client application is the consumer. The EJB client application obtains a reference to an object factory, which is the home interface. The client application then tells the home interface, "Create an EJB component for me." In EJB applications, the factory method is named `create` and exists in the home interface. The home interface can define one or more `create` methods. Each `create` method can take different arguments, but they all return an object implementing the remote interface to the client.

Just as most car owners are oblivious to (and don't need to know) the process of creating cars that occurs in a factory, EJB component developers don't need to know the details of how an EJB component is created to make use of it. All you need to know is that the EJB container is like a factory. As a consumer, the EJB client requests an EJB component from the factory, and the factory returns one to the client.

Enabling distribution with the Proxy Pattern

If you've ever cast a ballot in an election, you've participated in a proxy process. The ballot is a proxy that represents your desires, allowing you to influence decisions that are made too far away for you to participate in directly. If you think that the idea of voting is flawed, consider the alternative of all voters going to the seat of power to participate directly in an election. The result would be a mass confusion.

Just as our electoral process benefits from the use of proxies, EJB applications also benefit from a software design pattern called the *Remote Proxy Pattern*. Each EJB you use from a client application is referenced through a remote interface. Although you never implement the remote interface, you're able to invoke methods on the interface, and — as if by magic — the EJB component, which resides on a different computer, takes actions on your behalf. The Remote Proxy Pattern provides insight into how this magic works.

In the previous section, I explain how the Factory Method Pattern returns a product — a reference to the EJB component on the remote computer — to the EJB client. This returned product is effectively a Remote Proxy.

In the case of Enterprise JavaBeans, the Remote Proxy implements the remote interface, which defines all the business methods the client may need to invoke. Indirectly, the Remote Proxy also implements the `javax.ejb.EJBObject` interface and the `java.rmi.Remote` interface. Depending upon the EJB container you use, this Remote Proxy might also implement additional interfaces or define additional methods. Taken together, all of these methods are the object that I previously refer to — in the earlier section "Invoking methods remotely" — as the RMI stub.

Remote Method Invocation is basically an implementation of the Remote Proxy Pattern. The RMI stub is a Remote Proxy. While you may only invoke the methods of the remote interface on the Remote Proxy, all of the underlying methods are there to help the Remote Proxy object transport your method invocations to the EJB container and deliver the response from the container to the EJB client.

Enhancing productivity with the Object Pool Pattern

Imagine going to a dinner party where there are 100 guests but only 5 table settings. If you want to eat while the food is still warm, I'd recommend getting to that party early. While this scenario sounds absurd, it's not far from the mark in many software applications. Because of limitations in memory or processor power, you may be prevented from creating more than a few of each type of object that you need in your EJB container. Yet you may have hundreds or thousands of users interested in using those few objects. How do you handle the load? You use the *Object Pool Pattern*.

The EJB Server makes use of the Object Pool Pattern for managing stateless session beans and entity beans when they aren't in use. An *object pool* is nothing more than a collection of objects that are stored and made available for use by anyone who needs them. When requested, an object is removed from the pool and provided to the requestor. When the requestor is finished with the object, the object is cleaned and returned to the pool. This solution offers the following benefits:

✔ Creating new objects is a labor-intensive process in Java. When an object pool is employed, the creation of an object occurs before that object is needed. The object is then stored where it can be made available very quickly when demanded. The result is a substantial improvement in performance.

✔ Object pools are an effective tool for managing memory utilization in your EJB container because they prevent the creation of more objects than those you specify. They also reuse those objects over and over. Reduce-reuse-recycle and your application performance goes up while memory utilization goes down. That's a pretty good deal.

✔ Object pools are often used to manage scarce resources, such as database connections. Because database customers are often charged additional fees based on the number of concurrent connections to a database at any given time, the object pool allows the consumer to manage the total number of connections available and thus the total cost of an application.

 When demand of an object in a pool substantially exceeds the supply of objects in the pool, the pool forces those who haven't yet received an object from the pool to wait until one is available. Thus, your application performance can take a serious nose dive if you don't have enough objects in the pool to address your EJB clients' needs.

Protecting your investment with the Cache Pattern

Because EJB servers can service hundreds and perhaps thousands of clients at the same time, it's very important for the container to provide an environment that can easily scale while not over utilizing the RAM on your computer. To facilitate the goal of robust scalability, EJB applications implement a memory management pattern called the *Cache Pattern. Cache* is a storage place on your computer where an application can put things when they're not in use.

The Cache Pattern defines a mechanism that allows the EJB container to move EJB components that aren't actively being worked with by clients to a temporary storage system. Cache management allows the computer to free up memory by taking EJB components and storing them on a disk, typically in a file, where they can be accessed and then restored the next time they're needed.

By using the Cache Pattern, EJB containers can optimize their utilization of memory on a computer and prevent or minimize the risk that the EJB server will consume too much memory and cause the computer to crash. Stateful session beans and active entity beans can be stored in cache by the EJB container in the event that the container needs to make extra room for new clients.

While cache management is good for stability, it isn't good for performance. The process of storing an object in cache and retrieving it from cache is labor-intensive and can result in performance degradation of the EJB container. So I recommend minimizing the need for cache by making sure the computer that runs your EJB container has plenty of RAM.

Top EJB container vendors will have system administration tools that enable you to monitor your system's utilization of cache. Administration tools are a good investment in this respect because they allow you to monitor the performance of your EJB container and make decisions about the need for additional RAM.

Part II
On the Couch with Session Beans

The 5th Wave   By Rich Tennant

"We're here to clean the code."

In this part . . .

*H*ere you'll explore the creation of session bean
components. The workhorses of EJB applications,
session beans are used to implement business processes
and perform actions. In the following chapters, you'll see
how session beans work and what you need to do to
create them.

Chapter 4

Constructing Stateless Session Beans

● ●

In This Chapter

▶ Discovering the lifecycle of the stateless session bean

▶ Investigating the stateless session bean API

▶ Identifying the do's and don'ts of stateless session bean development

▶ Creating your first stateless session bean

● ●

Stateless session beans — EJBs that complete a task in a single step — are arguably the simplest of all EJB components. They make minimal demands on the EJB component developer and are used to implement very simple operations. Nevertheless, you have several important rules regarding stateless session beans that, as an EJB developer, you must remember.

Stateless session beans can be tricky because of the way the `EJBHome` and `EJBObject` interfaces are defined. All types of EJB components implement these two interfaces, which must be generic enough to support the methods needed by stateless session beans, stateful session beans, and entity beans. Because stateless session beans are so simple, they don't need all of the methods that the `EJBHome` and `EJBObject` interfaces define. Consequently, some of the methods in the stateless session bean always throw exceptions if they're invoked. As you proceed through this chapter, I'll point out the times when you have to be concerned about this issue.

Take a note — when defining your own classes, it's a good idea to define interfaces so that they hide methods that are irrelevant to a particular implementation. You accomplish this simply by defining the narrowest interface first, and then extending it to add additional methods for a broader interface, and so on until you have all the required methods defined. Doing so eliminates the messiness that results from having methods implemented in a class that doesn't need them and can't use them.

To clarify which methods of the home and remote interfaces are relevant to stateless session beans, this chapter begins with a brief overview of the life-cycle of stateless session beans. From there, you dive into developing stateless session beans with both remote and local interfaces. Finally, you move into defining a simple deployment descriptor and creating a basic EJB client.

Stateless Session Bean Lifecycle

Stateless session beans are EJB components designed with two simple objectives in mind:

- ✔ To perform simple tasks that can be accomplished in a single method invocation.
- ✔ To be shared by many clients at the same time. This is the root cause for the session bean being stateless.

The term *stateless* refers to the fact that the stateless session bean cannot hold any information for an EJB client between method invocations for that client. The reason stateless session beans are stateless is because the beans are held in a shared pool on the EJB container between each method invocation on the bean, a process shown in Figure 4-1.

When a client invokes a method on a stateless session bean, it is removed from the pool, the method is executed, and the bean is immediately returned to the pool. Consequently, if you executed two concurrent methods on a stateless session bean variable, they would probably be serviced by different beans in the EJB container.

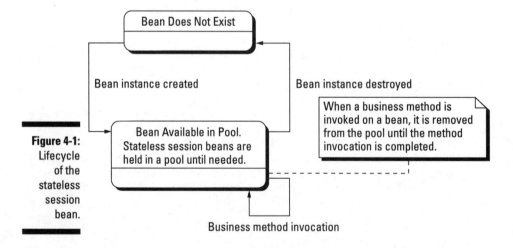

Figure 4-1: Lifecycle of the stateless session bean.

When to use stateless session beans

Given the abundance of EJB component choices available to you, it can sometimes be difficult to decide whether the stateless session bean is the right tool for your task. A couple of simple guidelines can assist you in making that decision.

✔ First, consider whether the task your application needs to perform can be accomplished in a single method invocation. Remember that a stateless session bean cannot remember state specific to a client between method invocations. Thus, if the task at hand involves more than a single step, the stateless session bean isn't the right choice. But if you can perform the task in a single step, then always use the stateless session bean.

✔ Second, determine whether the process your application is performing needs to be visible to multiple clients at the same time. If the application needs to share information and state between multiple clients, then you have only one choice — an entity bean.

Remember that a stateless session bean provides substantial performance benefits to your application. Generally, if you can design the application to maximize the use of stateless session beans, your application server will be able to respond to client invocations more quickly.

While stateless session beans offer a big performance benefit, they're not the right choice for all tasks. If you need your session bean to remember information supplied by a client across multiple method invocations, then you should use stateful session beans.

Ideal cases for the use of stateless session beans are for simple tasks, such as processing a payment, making a deposit, or making a withdrawal. These tasks all have two common features: They represent actions, and they can be performed in a single step.

API of the Stateless Session Bean

Depending on how you intend to use the stateless session bean, you have the option of creating local or remote interfaces for the bean. It is also within your discretion to create both remote and local interfaces. Remember that remote interfaces can be created for EJB 1.1- and EJB 2.0-compliant containers, but local interfaces are available only on EJB 2.0-compliant containers. As I illustrate creating a stateless session bean with the `DepositBean` from my handy sample ATM application in the upcoming sections, I investigate each of the interfaces and relevant objects in the stateless session bean.

Defining EJB remote interfaces

Remote interfaces are used by EJB client applications that need access to your EJB component from a remote computer. The remote interfaces are built over the Java Remote Method Invocation (RMI) API, which supports communication between applications across Java Virtual Machines (JVMs). Developing EJB components with remote interfaces was the de facto standard in EJB 1.1 applications.

The EJB 2.0 specification introduces a new set of client interfaces called *local interfaces,* which provide access to EJB components for clients in the same JVM. Because of the new option, you now have to decide whether to develop remote interfaces or local interfaces. When determining whether you should implement remote interfaces for your EJB component, consider the following points:

- ✔ Implementing remote interfaces promotes flexibility in EJB application design. EJB applications are traditionally meant for distributed computing systems, and the remote interfaces are essential to supporting distributed computing.

- ✔ Remote methods invocations are implemented in pass-by-value semantics. *Pass-by-value* means that instead of passing a *reference* to a Java object, a remote method passes the values that represent *the state of the object,* and the object is then reconstructed when arriving at its destination.

- ✔ Objects passed as parameters or returned through remote calls must implement the `java.io.Serializable` interface.

- ✔ Remote method invocations are typically less efficient than their counterparts in the local interfaces — because methods have to be serialized and transported across a network.

- ✔ Implementing remote interfaces may force EJB client applications to handle additional exceptions resulting from network communication issues and the state of resources on remote computers.

- ✔ Casting of objects by using RMI requires the use of the `javax.rmi.PortableRemoteObject.narrow` method. This step is necessary for the EJB container to ensure that the cast operation is allowed.

As you can see, remote communication has both benefits and some drawbacks. Ultimately, the decision is a design decision that falls on the shoulders of the EJB component developer. One important consideration is that nothing prevents you from implementing both remote and local interfaces. By providing both remote and local interfaces, you give developers that use your EJB component flexibility in deciding which interfaces they want to use.

The remote home interfaces

The remote home interface defines a means for accessing the EJB server to request a reference to an EJB component. The remote home interface must always extend the `javax.ejb.EJBHome` interface. Listing 4-1 illustrates the remote home interface for the `DepositBean`.

Listing 4-1   The DepositRemoteHome Interface

```
package com.sextanttech.transactions.interfaces;

import javax.ejb.EJBHome;
import javax.ejb.CreateException;
import java.rmi.RemoteException;

public interface DepositRemoteHome extends EJBHome{
    /* This create method defines the only way for the client
            to obtain
     * a reference to a DepositBean.
     */
    public Deposit create() throws CreateException,
            RemoteExeption;
}
```

As you can see in the preceding sample code, the `DepositRemoteHome` interface is pretty simple. Its single purpose is to return a reference to an EJB component in the EJB container. A few critical considerations to keep in mind are

- **The remote home interface for a stateless session bean must define one and only one** `create` **method that takes no arguments and returns a reference to the bean's remote interface.** Although other types of EJB components allow `create` methods that take arguments in the remote home — and overloading of the `create` method — that isn't allowed with stateless session beans.

- **The** `create` **method must throw a** `javax.ejb.CreateException` **and a** `java.rmi.RemoteException`. Both of these exceptions are used by the EJB container to notify a client in the event that a system-level error occurs when the client attempts to get a reference to an EJB component.

With the release of the EJB 2.0 specification, it is considered a good programming practice to use the suffix `RemoteHome` on all the names of all remote home interfaces.

Don't forget to throw the `java.rmi.RemoteException` and the `javax.ejb.CreateException` in the `create` method. Your code will still compile, even if you don't implement these exceptions. But you'll end up with really obscure errors when you try to run it.

Because the remote home interface extends `javax.ejb.EJBHome`, it is technically possible to override methods of the `javax.ejb.EJBHome` interface in your remote home interface. Don't do it, or you'll get a lump of coal for Christmas. The EJB container is responsible for implementing the `EJBHome` interface for you. Overriding methods of the `EJBHome` interface in your remote home interface may have unpredictable side effects.

The remote interface

The remote interface defines the *business methods* used by an EJB component. Business methods are methods in a class or interface that perform operations of a business-oriented nature. Contrast business methods with *system methods*, which perform operations related to the EJB system. The methods of the EJB API are system methods. Any special method you define for an EJB component to perform a task related to your business activity is a business method.

Regardless of the type of EJB component you create, the remote interfaces for each component are extended from the `javax.ejb.EJBObject` interface. The remote interface for the `DepositBean` is defined in Listing 4-2.

Listing 4-2   The DepositRemote Interface

```
package com.sextanttech.transactions.interfaces;

import javax.ejb.EJBObject;
import java.rmi.RemoteException;
import com.sextanttech.transactions.*;

public interface DepositRemote extends EJBObject {
    public void deposit( DepositEnvelope dep ) throws
            RemoteException, DepositException;
}
```

In Listing 4-2, the remote interface for the `DepositBean` implements a single method. While this stateless session bean has only a single method, it is reasonable to have stateless session beans with more than one method. Several important rules are illustrated in Listing 4-2, as follows:

- ✔ **All remote interfaces must extend** `javax.ejb.EJBObject`. This interface defines API system methods for the EJB container.

- ✔ **Each method of any remote interface you define must throw the** `java.rmi.RemoteException`. The EJB container and other APIs use the `RemoteException` to notify the remote interface in the event that some system level error has occurred.

- ✔ **Remote interface methods may also implement application exceptions.** An *application exception* is an exception that pertains to an application error, as opposed to a system error. While not mandatory, implementing application exceptions is a good practice. In the case of the

DepositRemote interface, I've defined a DepositException class, which can be used to tell the client why a deposit failed.

In the core Java API, all exceptions implement the java.lang.Throwable interface, which extends the java.io.Serializable interface. Thus, you don't need to implement java.io.Serializable in your application exceptions.

✔ **You can define custom support classes for use in the business methods of your EJB component — but those support classes must implement the java.io.Serializable interface.** In Listing 4-2, notice that the deposit() method has an argument of type DepositEnvelope. The class implementing this method is illustrated in Listing 4-3. Implementing java.io.Serializable is critical because the class will be passed to the EJB container using RMI.

Just because you can override methods of the javax.ejb.EJBObject in your remote interface doesn't mean you should. You don't really gain anything by overriding the EJBObject interface in your remote interface — and you could potentially cause problems.

Listing 4-3   The DepositEnvelope Defined

```
package com.sextanttech.transactions;

import java.io.Serializable;
import com.sextanttech.entities.interfaces.AccountKey;

public class DepositEnvelope implements Serializable {
    private double amount;
    private AccountKey account;

    public DepositEnvelope(double amount, AccountKey account){
        this.amount = amount;
        this.account = account;
    }

    public double getAmount() {
        return amount;
    }

    public AccountKey getAccount() {
        return account;
    }
}
```

Defining local interfaces

As with remote interfaces, local interfaces provide EJB clients with access to an EJB component. But unlike remote interfaces, local interfaces can be used only by EJB client programs that reside in the same Java Virtual Machine (JVM) as the EJB component. Local interfaces were first implemented in the EJB 2.0 specification. Here are some points to keep in mind when considering the use of local interfaces:

- ✔ Local interfaces cannot be used to access an EJB component that resides in a different JVM from the client. Thus, local interfaces are typically used for bean-to-bean communication, such as when one EJB component needs to communicate with another EJB component residing in the same EJB container.

- ✔ Local interfaces pass object parameters by reference. That means a *reference* to the object is passed, rather than the *actual value*. Pass-by-reference does not required serialization and is, consequently, more efficient than pass-by-value.

- ✔ Type casting in local interfaces does not require use of the `javax.rmi.PortableRemoteObject.narrow()` method.

- ✔ Objects passed as parameters in local interfaces do not have to implement `java.io.Serializable`.

While local interfaces will likely improve performance of your EJB components, they will also limit flexibility. This tradeoff must be carefully considered in the design of EJB components.

Naming conventions explored

Prior to the release of EJB 2.0, it was considered good practice to name remote interfaces according to their business name. According to that guideline, I should have named the `DepositRemote` interface `Deposit` instead. But because EJB 2.0 introduces local interfaces, following the business name convention could lead to confusion regarding whether the `Deposit` interface is a remote interface or a local interface. I'm recommending that you now attach the suffix **Remote** to the end of remote interfaces and **Local** to the end of local interfaces to indicate whether the interface is local or remote. If you've been following the EJB 1.1 naming convention for remote interfaces and need to preserve backward compatibility with your naming convention, then forget about the

Remote suffix, and just use the **Local** suffix on your local interfaces.

When it comes to naming home interfaces since EJB 2.0, you're also able to choose between a remote home and a local home interface. I've seen naming conventions where developers use the suffixes **HomeRemote** and **HomeLocal**. I personally feel that's a little hard to read, and opt for the suffixes **RemoteHome** and **LocalHome**. My rule is to name it how you say it.

The final convention pertains to the beans themselves. For clarity, it's again generally accepted that the bean should be named with a suffix of **Bean**, to indicate that it is the bean.

If you choose to implement local interfaces — but want to preserve the ability to implement remote interfaces at a later date — you need to consider the design very carefully. One simple task of preserving flexibility is ensuring that all your support classes implement the `java.io.Serializable` interface so that they can be used in a remote interface down the road.

The local home interface

The local home interface is virtually identical to the remote home interface from an EJB-competent developer's perspective. When it comes to developing stateless session beans, virtually all the same rules apply. Listing 4-4 illustrates the local home interface for the `DepositBean`.

Listing 4-4   The DepositLocalHome Interface

```
package com.sextanttech.transactions.interfaces;

import javax.ejb.EJBLocalHome;
import javax.ejb.CreateException;

public interface DepositLocalHome extends EJBLocalHome {
    public DepositLocal create() throws CreateException;
}
```

In Listing 4-4, take note of the following features of the local home interface:

✔ All local home interfaces must extend the `javax.ejb.EJBLocalHome` interface. The `EJBLocalHome` interface is used by the EJB container to implement the bean home API functionality.

✔ For stateless session beans, the local home interface must define one and only one `create()` method. The `create()` method returns a reference to the local interface for the bean component.

✔ The `create()` method must throw a `javax.ejb.CreateException`. Unlike the remote home interface, it doesn't throw a `java.rmi.RemoteException`.

As is the case with the remote home interface, the local home interface should not override any methods of the `javax.ejb.EJBLocalHome` interface. The `EJBLocalHome` interface is implemented by the EJB container, and overriding methods may have unpredictable side effects on the EJB container.

The local interface

The local interface for a stateless session bean provides access to the application methods for the EJB component to a local client. Once again, this interface is very similar to its remote interface counterpart. Listing 4-5 illustrates the local interface for the `DepositBean`.

Listing 4-5   The DepositLocal Interface

```
package com.sextanttech.transactions.interfaces;

import javax.ejb.EJBLocalObject;
import com.sextanttech.transactions.DepositEnvelope;
import com.sextanttech.transactions.DepositException;

public interface DepositLocal extends EJBLocalObject {
    public void deposit( DepositEnvelope dep ) throws
            DepositException;
}s
```

Listing 4-5 illustrates the following rules of local interfaces:

✔ All local interfaces must extend the `javax.ejb.EJBLocalObject` interface. The `EJBLocalObject` interface is implemented by the EJB container on your behalf.

✔ The local interface should define all of the application methods for the EJB component. In the case of the `DepositLocal` interface, there is only one application method.

✔ Unlike the remote interface, local interface methods do not have to throw the `java.rmi.RemoteException`. You may choose to create application-specific exceptions and throw those exceptions in the local interface.

✔ As with the remote interface, the local interface may make use of support classes as arguments or return values. In this case, I've used the same `DepositEnvelope` class I used in my remote interface. Refer to Listing 4-3 to see the code for the `DepositEnvelope`.

Don't override the methods of the `EJBLocalObject` in your local interfaces. The `EJBLocalObject` interface is intended for EJB container developers and not for EJB component developers.

Defining the session bean class

At the core of every EJB component is a class that implements all the business methods for the component. For stateless session beans, that class is the *session bean class*. As with the development of the home interface and remote interface, a lot of seemingly arbitrary rules dictate the development of the stateless session bean class. The simple explanation for these rules is that the stateless session bean must be developed according to relatively rigid guidelines so that the EJB container can interface with the class. The task of developing a session bean class can be broken into four steps:

✔ **Each stateless session bean must implement the** `javax.ejb.` `SessionBean` **interface.** The `SessionBean` interface defines several lifecycle methods that are called by the EJB container when various lifecycle events occur. To discover more about the `SessionBean` interface, see the later section, "Responding to lifecycle events."

✔ **Each stateless session bean must define one public constructor that takes no arguments and has a return type of** `void`. A *constructor* is a method used to create instances of a class. By making the constructor public, you allow other classes to invoke it. When a constructor has no arguments, that allows applications to create instances of an object using a Java technology called *reflection*. Reflection is a little too deep to get into in this context, but it's how an EJB container creates instances of your EJB components.

This rule is easy to meet — the default constructor of a class is a public no-argument constructor that returns `void`. So, by not defining a constructor, the Java compiler will address this requirement for you. However, if you define a constructor other than the default constructor, the Java compiler will not define the default constructor and you must supply it yourself.

To avoid any complexities associated with constructors, don't define any constructor on your stateless session bean class. There should be no reason to have a constructor other than the default constructor.

✔ **Each session bean class must define an** `ejbCreate` **method corresponding to each** `create` **method defined in the EJB component's home interface.** When developing stateless session beans, adhere to the following guidelines when defining the `create` method:

- In the case of stateless session beans, there can be only one `create` method and, by inference, there can be only one `ejbCreate` method.

- The stateless session bean's `ejbCreate` method must take no arguments and must have a return type of `void`.

- The method must be declared `public` and must not be `final` or `static`. The terms `public`, `final`, and `static` are modifiers of a method declaration that respectively mean that the method is accessible to all external callers, that the method cannot be overridden in a subclass, and that the method is associated with a class instead of an object. The `ejbCreate` method must be publicly accessible, and it cannot be `final` or `static`.

- The `ejbCreate` method can optionally throw application exceptions, and may also throw the `javax.ejb.CreateException` and the `javax.ejb.EJBException`. Determining which exceptions to throw is a design decision of the EJB component developer.

✔ **The session bean class can define any number of business methods.**
Each business method must adhere to the following principles:

- Business method names cannot begin with the prefix **ejb**. The EJB specification reserves the **ejb** prefix for use by API methods of the EJB component.

- Business methods must be declared `public` and cannot be `final` or `static`.

- The arguments and return types of each business method must be remotable — which means that they must implement the `java.io.Serializable` interface. Failure to do so will undermine the ability of the EJB component to talk to the remote interface in a client application.

- Each business method can throw any appropriate application exception, and may also throw the `javax.ejb.EJBException` in response to system exceptions.

Listing 4-6 illustrates the creation of a stateless session bean through the implementation of the `DepositBean`. Note that while this class implements the lifecycle operations of the `SessionBean` interface, those methods do not perform any operations. It isn't uncommon for EJB components to do nothing in their lifecycle operations.

Listing 4-6   The DepositBean Class

```
package com.sextanttech.transactions.implementations;

import javax.ejb.CreateException;
import javax.ejb.EJBException;
import javax.ejb.SessionBean;
import javax.ejb.SessionContext;
import javax.ejb.FinderException;

import com.sextanttech.transactions.DepositEnvelope;
import com.sextanttech.transactions.DepositException;

import com.sextanttech.entities.interfaces.AccountLocalHome;
import com.sextanttech.entities.interfaces.AccountLocal;
import com.sextanttech.entities.interfaces.AccountKey;

import javax.naming.Context;
import javax.naming.InitialContext;
import javax.naming.NamingException;

public class DepositBean implements SessionBean {

    private SessionContext context;
```

```
  /**
   * Default ejbCreate for a stateless session bean. This
   * method typically does nothing in a stateless session
   * bean.
   */
public void ejbCreate() throws CreateException,
        EJBException {
}


  /**
   * Container lifecycle method.
   */
public void setSessionContext( SessionContext context ) {
    this.context = context;
}


  /**
   * Container lifecycle method. Invoked by the EJB
   * container before a bean is destroyed. If you have
   * system resources that need to be released prior to a
   * bean component's destruction, release those resources
   * in this method. Examples of resources may include
   * logging utilities or database connection pools.
   */
public void ejbRemove() {
}


  /**
   * Container lifecycle method. Does nothing for
   * stateless session beans.
   */
public void ejbActivate() {
}


  /**
   * Container lifecycle method. Does nothing for
   * stateless session beans.
   */
public void ejbPassivate() {
}


  /**
   * The only business method of the stateless session
   * bean follows. Note it has the same return type as the
   * corresponding method in the remote interface and the
   * local interface. Also note it takes the same argument
   * as the local and remote interfaces. Finally, it
   * throws the same application exception. Since EJB 1.2
   * all business methods should throw an EJBException if
   * a system error occurs.
   */
```

(continued)

Listing 4-6 *(continued)*

```
public void deposit( DepositEnvelope dep ) throws
        EJBException, DepositException {

    /*
     * The bulk of this implementation interacts with
     * the Account remote interface of the Account
     * Entity Bean component. The code of this method
     * illustrates how an EJB client interacts
     * with an entity bean.
     */

    AccountLocalHome accountHome = null;
    AccountLocal account = null;

    try {

        Context naming = new InitialContext();
        accountHome = ( AccountLocalHome )naming.lookup(
            "java:comp/env/ejb/accountEJB" );

        account = accountHome.findByPrimaryKey(
            dep.getAccount() );

        account.debit( dep.getAmount() );
    }
    catch ( Exception e ) {

        /**
         * Throwing a system exception such as the
         * EJBException will automatically cause any
         * transaction the stateless session bean is
         * enrolled in to be marked for rollback. That
         * means that any changes made within the
         * transaction will be unmade.
         */
        throw new EJBException(e);
    }
    finally {

        account = null;
        accountHome = null;
    }
  }
}
```

Inside the `deposit` method illustrated in Listing 4-6, you can see the client code required to make use of the `Account` bean. The `Account` bean is an entity bean. You can discover more on the topic of invoking EJB components from client applications in Chapter 16. To investigate the creation of entity bean components, refer to Part III.

Casting a Vote for transactions

Transaction management is one of the most important features provided by the EJB architecture. *Transactions* define a set of operations that must all succeed or all fail. If you're familiar with database operations — and database transactions — you'll find significant differences between an EJB transaction and a database transaction. Database transactions are able to transact state, which means that they can remember the state of a database attribute before it was changed and restore that state if the transaction fails. EJB transactions, on the other hand, do not transact the state of a session bean. EJB transactions provide the following basic features:

- ✔ Identify all the EJB components that participate in a transaction, which is referred to as the *transactional context*.

- ✔ Delimit atomic units of activity within a transaction. EJB methods participating in a transaction represent an atomic unit of activity.

- ✔ Support API callbacks to each EJB component participating in a transaction, allowing that component to respond in the event that a transaction fails or succeeds. These callbacks are methods that you can use inside an EJB component to "cast your vote" on whether or not you want a transaction to fail.

- ✔ When a transaction fails, the container "rolls back" the transaction, which causes any changes made to "transacted data" to be restored to its state prior to the start of the transaction. An EJB application only transacts the data held in entity bean components.

The following highlights the basics of transactional participation for stateless session beans:

- ✔ Each stateless session bean must declare whether or not it participates in container-managed transactions through the `<transaction-type>` attribute in the `ejb-jar.xml` file. This task is illustrated in the upcoming section, "Defining the ejb-jar.xml File."

- ✔ If a stateless session bean participates in container-managed transactions, it must notify the EJB container if the business method fails by invoking the `SessionContext.setRollbackOnly()` method. To see this task implemented, refer to the bold code in Listing 4-6.

Because the transaction context of a stateless session bean is not set until a business method is invoked, you can use the `SessionContext.setRollbackOnly()` method only from within a business method. Invoking this method from any other type of method will result in a `java.lang.IllegalStateException`.

A single vote for a transaction rollback in any transaction context will cause the entire transaction context to be rolled back. Thus, while each EJB component gets to cast its own vote, all components must be against a rollback in order for a commit operation to be performed.

The `SessionSynchronization` interface is used in stateful session beans to add optional support for transacting the state of the stateful session beans. Because stateless session beans do not contain any client state by definition, and because a stateless session bean is always released between EJB client invocations, a stateless session bean should never implement the `SessionSynchronization` interface.

If you're performing an operation in a stateless session bean that may need to be rolled back in the event of transaction failure, then it is a good practice to invoke the stateless session bean from a stateful session bean. This is recommended because the stateful session bean is capable of responding to transaction events and can reverse the action taken in a stateless session bean under its scope if a transaction fails. Chapter 5 illustrates the process for accomplishing this task.

Responding to lifecycle events

The stateless session bean has a limited number of lifecycle events, as illustrated in Figure 4-1. Thus, while it implements the `SessionBean` interface, several methods of the `SessionBean` interface have no bearing on the stateless session bean. Table 4-1 identifies the methods of the `SessionBean` and their significance to the stateless session bean class.

Table 4-1	Lifecycle Methods of the Stateless Session Bean
Method	*Description*
`void ejbCreate()`	This method is executed after the stateless session bean's constructor is invoked and before the `setSessionContext()` method is invoked.
`void ejbActivate()`	This method has no bearing on a stateless session bean.
`void ejbPassivate()`	This method has no bearing on a stateless session bean.
`void ejbRemove()`	This method is executed by the EJB container immediately prior to destruction of the stateless session bean component. You can use this method to release system resources of a stateless session bean prior to its destruction.

Method	Description
void setSessionContext (SessionContext ctx)	This method is executed by the EJB container after the stateless session bean is created and before the bean is placed in the object pool. You can use this method to initialize access to system resources inside the stateless session bean.

One of the most important factors that an EJB component developer should keep in mind while developing the lifecycle methods of any EJB component is the management of system resources. Common system resources that may be made available to stateless session beans include

- Logging resources for recording activity that occurs in the stateless session beans.
- References to database connection pools for managing database access.

If access to these resources is accomplished through the JNDI ENC — a special naming context that's local to each EJB component you create — they can be initialized during the ejbCreate method. If access to these resources is defined in the SessionContext object, then the resources should be initialized in the setSessionContext method.

For more information about accessing JNDI ENC, refer to Chapter 14. For more information about initializing the session context, check out the upcoming section "Defining the ejb-jar.xml File."

Defining the ejb-jar.xml File

For each EJB component that you create, you must declare certain basic information about the bean in the ejb-jar.xml file. I've devoted Chapters 13 and 14 entirely to investigating all the possibilities of the ejb-jar.xml file. In the case of the DepositBean, the relevant portions of the ejb-jar.xml file are illustrated in Listing 4-7.

Listing 4-7   The ejb-jar.xml File

```
<!DOCTYPE ejb-jar PUBLIC "-//Sun Microsystems, Inc.//DTD
         Enterprise JavaBeans 2.0//EN"
         "http://java.sun.com/dtd/ejb-jar_2_0.dtd:>

<ejb-jar>
  <enterprise-beans>
    <session>
      <description>Used to deposit money.</description>
      <ejb-name>DepositEJB</ejb-name>
```

(continued)

Listing 4-7 *(continued)*

```
        <home>
    com.sextanttech.transactions.interfaces.DepositRemoteHome
        </home>
        <remote>
    com.sextanttech.transactions.interfaces.DepositRemote
        </remote>
        <local-home>

            com.sextanttech.transactions.interfaces.DepositLoc
            alHome
        </local-home>
        <local>
            com.sextanttech.transactions.interfaces.DepositLocal
        </local>
        <ejb-class>

            com.sextanttech.transactions.implementations.Depos
            itBean
        </ejb-class>
        <session-type>Stateless</session-type>
        <transaction-type>Container</transaction-type>
      </session>
    <enterprise-beans>
</ejb-jar>
```

The ejb-jar.xml file, as shown in Listing 4-7, defines a couple of important features of a stateless session bean. The following list summarizes some of those features:

✔ The classes for all the elements of the stateless session beans are identified in the ejb-jar.xml file.

✔ The only feature that identifies a stateless session bean as stateless is the <session-type> attribute of the ejb-jar.xml file, which must have the value Stateless.

✔ The stateless session bean must indicate the type of transaction management required for the bean component. The <transaction-type> element in the ejb-jar.xml file allows two values — Bean for bean-managed transactions, and Container for container-managed transactions.

Investigating Related Classes

In addition to the classes that I cover in the previous sections of this chapter, there are several related EJB API classes that are accessed through the component interfaces and the home interface for a stateless session bean. For entry-level EJB programmers, these classes probably aren't of much use, but I provide an introduction for the sake of completeness.

Using the SessionContext interface

Each stateless session bean is endowed with a `SessionContext` shortly after it is created. The `SessionContext` contains methods providing access to the following resources:

- ✔ References to the `EJBLocalObject` or `EJBObject`
- ✔ References to the `EJBLocalHome` or `EJBHome`
- ✔ Access to security resources implemented by the EJB container
- ✔ Access to transaction resources for container-managed transactions and bean-managed transactions

Of the three types of resources that the `SessionContext` object provides, most EJB components should only attempt to work with the transactional management resources.

Bean developers should avoid interaction with the security resources presented in the `SessionContext` interface. Interacting with those security resources may undermine the flexibility of container-implemented security services and can make the application assembler's job more difficult.

Not all the methods of the `SessionContext` can be accessed at all times. Table 4-2 identifies at what stages of a stateless session bean's lifecycle each method in the `SessionContext` can be invoked. Table 4-3 identifies the methods of the `SessionContext` and their definitions.

Okay, I confess. A lot of the methods in Tables 4-2 and 4-3 are actually defined in the superclass of `SessionContext` — the `EJBContext` interface. Basically, that means that you can invoke the methods through the `SessionContext`, but they aren't actually part of the `SessionContext` class — just like having some of my father's genes doesn't make me the same as my father to anyone other than my therapist. Let's just be thankful there's no such thing as software psychoanalysis.

Table 4-2	Lifecycle Considerations of the SessionContext	
Lifecycle Method	*Legal Methods of the SessionContext*	*Comments*
Constructor invoked	none	
`setSessionContext`	`getEJBHome`, `getEJBLocalHome`	

(continued)

Table 4-2 *(continued)*

Lifecycle Method	Legal Methods of the SessionContext	Comments
ejbCreate, ejbRemove	getEJBHome, getEJBLocalHome, getEJBObject, getEJBLocalObject	
Business method invocation	getEJBHome, getEJBLocalHome, getEJBObject, getEJBLocalObject, getCallerPrinciple, getRollbackOnly, isCallerInRole, setRollbackOnly, getEJBObject, getEJBLocalObject, getUserTransaction	getRollbackOnly and setRollbackOnly are available in container-managed transactions only. getUserTransaction is available in bean-managed transactions only.

Invoking a method of the SessionContext at an improper lifecycle state will cause the method to throw a java.lang.IllegalStateException.

Table 4-3   **Methods of the SessionContext Interface**

Method	Description
EJBLocalObject getEJBLocalObject()	Returns a reference to the EJBLocalObject, if one exists.
EJBObject getEJBObject()	Returns a reference to the EJBObject if one exists.
Principal getCallerPrinicipal()	Provides access to the Principal object, which is part of the security API. Not recommended for use by EJB bean developers.
EJBHome getEJBHome()	Returns a reference to the EJBHome object, if one exists.
EJBLocalHome getEJBLocalHome()	Returns a reference to the EJBLocalHome object if one exists.

Method	Description
`boolean getRollbackOnly()`	Indicates if a container-managed transaction is marked for rollback or not. A return value of `true` means that the transaction is marked for rollback.
`UserTransaction getUserTransaction()`	For use in implementing bean-managed transactions. Refer to Chapter 15 for more information on this topic.
`boolean isCallerInRole (String roleName)`	Indicates if a client invocation has a given security role. Not recommended for use by EJB bean developers.
`void setRollbackOnly()`	Marks the current container-managed transaction for rollback. For container-managed transactions only.

Investigating the EJBHome and EJBLocalHome interfaces

The `EJBHome` and `EJBLocalHome` interfaces present methods to EJB client application developers that may be tempting, but, for the most part, should be avoided. Table 4-4 takes a closer look at the `EJBHome` interface.

Table 4-4	The EJBHome Interface
Methods	**Description**
`EJBMetaData getEJBMetaData()`	This method returns a reference to the `EJBMetaData` object. `EJBMetaData` is intended for software development tools.
`HomeHandle getHomeHandle()`	This method returns a reference to the `HomeHandle`, which can be used to pass references to a home interface across JVMs. While this capability appears to be useful, the implementation details are left largely to each EJB container. Consequently, the results of working with a HomeHandle are unpredictable unless you have a fairly deep understanding of the implementation details in your EJB container.

(continued)

Table 4-4 (continued)

Methods	Description
`void remove (Handle handle)`	This method is used to remove an EJB component from the EJB container. The method has little practical value in the case of stateless session beans. That's because you cannot predict which stateless session bean will be removed — the client application never holds a reference to a specific stateless session bean.
`void remove (Object primaryKey)`	This method only applies to entity beans. Use of this method by a stateless session bean always throws a java.rmi.RemoteException.

The `EJBLocalHome` interface only defines a single `remove` method. The `remove` method has little practical value in the case of stateless session beans. Because the EJB container is responsible for pooling EJB components, stateless session bean removal is managed by the EJB container. Thus, it isn't advisable to use the `remove` method for stateless session beans.

Investigating the EJBObject and EJBLocalObject interfaces

The `EJBObject` interface and `EJBLocalObject` interfaces provide an EJB client application developer with access to EJB API methods through the remote and local interfaces respectively. In the case of stateless session beans, many of these methods are not that useful. Table 4-5 investigates the methods of the `EJBObject` interface. Table 4-6 investigates the methods of the `EJBLocalObject` interface.

Table 4-5	Methods of the EJBObject Interface
Methods	Definition
`EJBHome getEJBHome()`	Returns a reference to the `EJBHome` interface.
`Handle getHandle()`	Returns a handle to the `EJBObject` that can be used to pass the object to another JVM and reconstruct the reference to the `EJBObject`. This approach is not recommended because a client application never gets a specific reference to a particular stateless session bean, so there is little benefit to passing the session bean's handle to a different JVM.

Methods	Definition
`Object getPrimaryKey()`	This method returns a primary key to an entity bean. Invoking this method on a stateless session bean always throws a `java.rmi.RemoteException`.
`boolean isIdentical (EJBObject obj)`	This method compares two `EJBObjects` for equality. This method is not intended for use by stateless session beans. In a stateless session bean, the equality of two `EJBObject` references does not correspond to equality between the stateless session bean instances. That's because an `EJBObject` reference could refer to different stateless session bean instances on each method invocation. Thus, invoking the `isIdentical` method tells you nothing about the equality of two stateless session bean references.
`Public void remove()`	Invokes the `remove` operation of the `EJBObject`. This method is not recommended for stateless session beans because the EJB container is responsible for managing removal of stateless session beans from the pool.

Table 4-6	Methods of the EJBLocalObject Interface
Methods	Definition
`EJBLocalHome getEJBLocalHome()`	Returns a reference to the `EJBLocalHome` interface.
`Object getPrimaryKey()`	This method returns a primary key to an entity bean. Invoking this method on a stateless session bean always throws a `java.rmi.RemoteException`.
`boolean isIdentical (EJBLocalObject obj)`	This method compares two `EJBLocalObjects` for equality. This method is not intended for use by stateless session beans. In a stateless session bean, the equality of two `EJBLocalObject` references does not correspond to equality between the stateless session bean instances. That's because an `EJBLocalObject` reference could refer to different stateless session bean instances on each method invocation. Thus, invoking the `isIdentical` method tells you nothing about the equality of two stateless session bean references.

(continued)

Table 4-6 *(continued)*	
Methods	*Description*
`void remove()`	Invokes the `remove` operation of the `EJBLocalObject`. This method isn't recommended for stateless session beans because the EJB container is responsible for managing removal of stateless session beans from the pool.

Accessing the HomeHandle

The `ejbHome` interface provides EJB client application developers with access to an object called the `HomeHandle`. The `HomeHandle` is a serializable class that can be used to pass a reference to the home interface from one JVM to another. While this initially seems to be a nice feature, it requires a lot of sophisticated coding to be useful and is really an invitation for disaster when mismanaged.

EJB containers manage security on references to a `HomeHandle`. If you pass a `HomeHandle` to another JVM, the recipient of the `HomeHandle` may not have sufficient security permissions to use the handle. The security permissions of the new client may not be known until runtime. Consequently, this approach to managing references to the home interface isn't recommended.

Accessing the Handle

The `ejbObject` and `ejbLocalObject` define a method for getting a reference to a `Handle` object for an EJB object. This class has a similar function to the `HomeHandle`, but applies to the EJB object instead. You can use the `Handle` to pass a reference to an EJB object from one JVM to another and reconstruct the reference.

Using the `Handle` has the same risks associated with it as those found with the `HomeHandle`. If the recipient of the `Handle` reference doesn't have the appropriate security permissions, it won't be able to use the `Handle`, and security permissions of the new client may not be known at coding time. Thus, using the `Handle` to pass references to the EJB object across JVMs isn't recommended.

Another important consideration for the use of the `Handle` in the context of a stateless session bean is that a reference to the `Handle` isn't the same as a reference to the stateless session bean class. Stateless session beans are returned to a pool after each business method invocation. So a reference to a `Handle` doesn't guarantee access to any particular stateless session bean.

Using the EJBMetaData interface

Through an EJB component's home interface, it's possible to get a reference to the EJBMetaData object. The EJBMetaData object provides access to all the elements of an EJB component — the remote home interface, remote interface, local interface, bean class, and information about the type of bean (that is, whether or not the bean is a session bean and whether or not it's stateless).

The EJBMetaData interface is primarily intended for use by software development tools. This is one of those objects that may seem inviting and potentially useful to EJB component developers; however, it's really an invitation to the dark side of programming. EJB component developers and EJB client application developers should avoid use of the EJBMetaData object.

Chapter 5

Constructing Stateful Session Beans

*W*ith your average automatic teller machine there are some actions that are easily accomplished with a single stroke. Make a deposit. Make a withdrawal. Inquire about the current balance of your account. All are simple questions with simple answers. But there are some actions that require more than one step, such as transferring funds from one account to another. A transfer requires a withdrawal from one account and a deposit into another.

Okay, okay . . . you could make a transfer in a single step and you could use a stateless session bean to perform the task. But assume for the duration of the chapter that you choose not to. That way you'll get an example of a stateful session bean.

In a stateless world — where state (data) is not passed on across multiple client interactions — managing a transfer is difficult because the withdrawal and the deposit have to be coordinated. Stateless session beans aren't effective when it comes to coordinating such actions because each stateless session bean is released from a transaction as soon as it completes its specified operation. When the stateless session bean is released, it loses all memory of what operation it performed and whom it performed the operation for.

On the other hand, stateful session beans are ideally suited for the task of coordinating transactions that require more than one step. Likewise, stateful session beans are appropriate for situations that call for the preservation of information across multiple client interactions. Stateful session beans are *stateful* because they can remember information relevant to a single client between method invocations. Doing so means that, once associated with a client, a stateful session bean belongs to that client until it is destroyed. Stateful session beans aren't pooled and shouldn't be shared by different clients. Some common cases that call for a stateful session bean are

✔ The obvious (and previously stated) funds transfer, which illustrates a stateful session bean's ability to be a coordinator for transactions requiring more than one step

✔ Online shopping carts, which illustrate a stateful session bean's ability to preserve information about items a client has requested across multiple client interactions until the client is ready to "check out"

✔ User profile information, which can be loaded into a stateful session bean and made available to a Web service for the duration of a user's visit to a given Web site

Because the stateful session bean can remember what a client has done from one method invocation to the next, and because it can also track its internal actions between method invocations, stateful session beans are said to preserve *conversational state*.

As you proceed through this chapter, you get a closer look at the stateful session bean lifecycle — which happens to be very different from the lifecycle of the stateless session bean that I discuss in the previous chapter. With the lifecycle knowledge in hand, you proceed to developing a stateless session bean component. In the end, you get a look at how stateful session beans can participate in the transaction lifecycle of a container-managed transaction and examine the numerous interfaces exposed to stateless session beans in the EJB API.

Stateful Session Bean Lifecycle

The key to getting the most out of a stateful session bean is understanding what happens in the lifecycle of a stateful session bean. Basically that means knowing

✔ How and when the stateful session bean gets created

✔ What methods of the stateful session bean are invoked by the EJB container and when they are invoked

✔ How the various states of a stateful session bean work and what causes the stateful session bean to move from one state to another

✔ What your responsibilities as an EJB component developer are in creating a functional stateful session bean component

Open wide — you're about to get this all in one big bite. You can see the entire lifecycle of the stateful session bean in Figure 5-1.

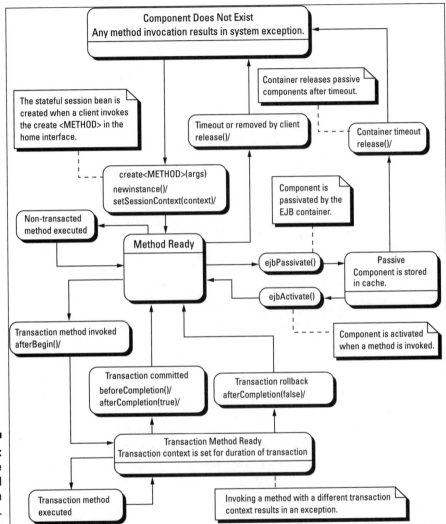

Figure 5-1:
Lifecycle
of a stateful
session
bean.

More! You want more? Well, I guess I could connect a few dots. But before proceeding, take note of the following about Figure 5-1:

- ✔ **This is a Unified Modeling Language (UML) activity diagram.** The diagram is used to illustrate the actions that occur as a stateful session bean transitions from one state to the next.

- ✔ **The rectangular shapes with rounded corners and horizontal lines through them are called state elements.** *State elements* identify the condition an object is in when it is "at rest," or in between actions. There are four states in the diagram: Does Not Exist, Method Ready, Transaction Method Ready, and Passive.

✔ **The capsule shapes are activities.** *Activities* label the actions that are taking place when an object is in transition. Some activities involve several steps. These activities contain internal transitions, which identify each method invoked as the activity is completed.

✔ **The dotted lines are used to connect comment elements to an activity or a state element.** *Comment elements* are used to provide a more detailed explanation of a diagram element.

✔ **With the exception of the create<METHOD>, all the methods identified in Figure 5-1 are available within the context of the session bean class.** As you proceed through the chapter, you'll see more on each method.

Stateful session beans are distinct from their stateless cousins in that one stateful session bean is associated with one client application for the duration of its life. In contrast, stateless session beans can exist without being associated to any client and are shared among many clients throughout their lives. The four basic states in a stateful session bean's existence are

✔ **Does Not Exist:** A stateful session bean is in this state before a `create` method is invoked from the home interface, or after the bean is removed by either the client or the EJB container invoking the bean's `remove` method.

 • Stateful session beans are associated with a client from the time they're created to the time they're destroyed.

 • Stateful session beans are destroyed when a client calls the `remove` method. In addition, the EJB container also expires session beans and removes them automatically.

 • If a client holds a *variable* — a named reference to an object — referring to an EJB object prior to its creation or after its destruction, the value of the variable is `null`. Any method invocation on that variable will throw a system exception.

✔ **Method Ready:** The Method Ready state of a stateful session bean exists after the stateful session bean is created and while it resides in memory between method invocations.

 • The stateful session bean is created when a `create` method is invoked from the bean's home interface. Stateful session beans can define more than one `create` method, and each `create` method can pass different arguments to the EJB container that will represent the bean's initial state.

 • The stateful session bean is assigned a `SessionContext` variable after it's created and before it enters the Method Ready state.

- The Method Ready state is the central resting place for a stateful session bean in its lifecycle. From there, business methods can be invoked on the component, or it can be involved in a transaction, or it can be stored in cache by the EJB container.

- EJB methods that don't have an associated *transaction context* are invoked from the Method Ready state. A transaction context is used by the EJB container to coordinate changes to data and manage access to methods in EJB components.

✔ **Transaction Method Ready:** When a transacted method is invoked on a stateful session bean, it is first added to a transaction context, which raises the bean to the Transaction Method Ready state. From there, the transacted method can be executed, and the transaction can be committed or rolled back. I cover how stateful session beans can interact with transactions later in this chapter in the section "Participating in the Transaction Lifecycle." For now, here's a summary of the steps:

  - A bean is raised to the Transaction Method Ready state when a transacted method is invoked on the bean from its client. Transacted methods are identified in the `ejb-jar.xml` file. In Chapter 14, I cover the definition of transactions in detail.

  - If the stateful session bean class implements the `SessionSynchronization` interface, the `afterBegin` method is invoked on the session bean before it enters the Transaction Method Ready state.

  - After the stateful session bean class enters the Transaction Method Ready state, the transacted method is executed on the bean.

  - Transactions may involve many different EJBs. A stateful session bean will remain in the Transaction Method Ready state for the duration of the transaction.

  - When all the operations of the transacted method are complete — but before the EJB container commits those transactions — the `beforeCompletion` method is invoked. The stateless session bean can use this method to store any state prior to the completion of the transaction.

  - Finally, the `afterCompletion` method is invoked to let the session bean know whether the transaction was successful. If the transaction is not successful, then it is the bean provider's responsibility to restore the original state of the session bean. After this method is invoked, the stateful session bean returns to the Method Ready state.

✔ **Passive:** When a stateful session bean is in the Method Ready state, the EJB container can decide to reduce its memory mode by serializing the session bean and caching it. This process is called *passivation*.

- The container decides when to passivate a stateful session bean; this process should be mostly transparent to an EJB bean developer.

- Before passivation, the container calls a stateful session bean's `passivate()` method. Bean providers can implement operations that clean up the session bean's resources in this method.

- When an EJB client invokes a method on a passive bean, the container is responsible for activating the bean and returning it to the Method Ready state. Before returning to the Method Ready state, the container calls the `activate()` method on the stateless session bean. The bean provider can use this method to restore application resources that were cleaned in the `passivate()` method.

While a stateful session bean is in the Transaction Method Ready state, a system exception will be thrown if you attempt to invoke a method of the session bean that isn't part of the transaction.

Defining Remote Interfaces

Defining the remote interfaces for a stateful session bean holds no more magic than it does for any other type of EJB component. Just remember that the remote interface allows remote computers to gain access to your EJB component. That being said, there are a couple of minor variations in the rules between stateless session beans and stateful session beans, primarily resulting from differences between the lifecycle management associated with each type of session bean and the way each type manages state. The next sections will point out such differences as they arise.

Building the remote home interface

The remote home interface of the stateful session bean provides remote client applications with a gateway to the EJB container through which they can create a stateful session bean component. While stateless session beans are created by a container and only associated with a client when a method is invoked, the stateful session bean is actually created when a client invokes the bean's `create` method in the home interface. In addition, the client can pass arguments to the home interface's `create` methods, which are used to initialize the state of the stateful session bean.

Listing 5-1 illustrates the remote home interface of the ATMTransactionBean, a stateful session bean in the sample banking application that I'm using throughout this book.

Listing 5-1   The ATMTransactionRemoteHome Interface

```
package com.sextanttech.transactions.interfaces;

import javax.ejb.EJBHome;
import java.rmi.RemoteException;
import javax.ejb.CreateException;

public interface ATMTransactionRemoteHome extends EJBHome {

    public ATMTransactionRemote create( String username,
            String password ) throws RemoteException,
    CreateException;

}
```

The ATMTransactionRemoteHome interface illustrates the following important points:

✔ The remote home extends EJBHome, which is the case for all remote home interfaces regardless of the type of EJB component.

✔ The remote home interface is responsible for defining create methods for the stateful session bean. The following rules apply to stateful session bean create methods:

- Each create method name must begin with the prefix **create**, followed by a meaningful suffix appropriate to the EJB component's name. In the case of the ATMTransactionBean, I use the suffix **Transaction**, resulting in the method name createTransaction.

- Stateful session beans can define multiple create methods, which means that each create method needs to have a different signature in order to keep things straight. A method's *signature* is composed of its name and the number and types of arguments defined for the method. That means the name, number of arguments, and type of arguments must be unique for all create methods defined in the remote home interface. Note that the exceptions a method throws and its return value are not part of its signature.

- Objects passed into each create method as well as objects returned from each create method must implement the java.io.Serializable interface.

- Each create method must return a reference to the remote interface for the EJB component.

- Each create method must throw the javax.ejb. CreateException and the java.rmi.RemoteException. The CreateException is invoked by the EJB container when a problem occurs while creating an EJB component. The RemoteException is used to indicate any other system level exception.

Think of the create method as the client application programmer's constructor for a stateless session bean. If you were defining a local component, you could provide different constructors for each type of initial state possible in your component. The same principle applies to creating stateful session beans. Providing multiple create methods is your way of allowing a client programmer to create a stateful session bean component with different types of initial states.

Each create method must have a corresponding ejbCreate method in the session bean class. The corresponding create method must have the prefix **ejb**, followed by the create method name, and must contain the same number and types of arguments in the same order as the create method.

Building the remote interface

The remote interface of the stateless session bean, as with other types of EJB components, defines the business methods that the client can invoke on the EJB component. The client application obtains a reference to the remote interface by invoking a create method in the remote home interface. Thereafter, client applications can invoke bean methods on the stateful session bean through the remote interface.

No special rules apply to the creation of remote interfaces for stateful session beans. Listing 5-2 illustrates the ATMTransactionRemote interface, which defines three business methods for the sample application.

Listing 5-2 The ATMTransactionRemote Interface

```
package com.sextanttech.transactions.interfaces;

import java.rmi.RemoteException;
import javax.ejb.EJBObject;
import com.sextanttech.entities.interfaces.*;
import com.sextanttech.transactions.*;
import java.util.Map;

public interface ATMTransactionRemote extends EJBObject {

    public void transfer( AccountKey sourceAccount,
            AccountKey targetAccount, double amount )
    throws RemoteException, WithdrawException,
            DepositException;

    public void getStatement( AccountKey account, String
            username, String password ) throws
            RemoteException;
    public void deposit( DepositEnvelope dep ) throws
            RemoteException, DepositException;
```

```
public void withdraw( double amount, AccountKey
        accountKey ) throws RemoteException,
        WithdrawException;

double balance( AccountKey accountKey ) throws
        RemoteException;

Map getAvailAccounts() throws RemoteException;
}
```

All remote interfaces must extend the EJBObject interface. In addition, each method defined in the remote interface must include the java.rmi. RemoteException in its throws clause. All support classes used by the remote interface, such as the AccountKey class in Listing 5-2, must implement the java.io.Serializable interface. Finally, the remote interface shouldn't override any methods defined in the EJBObject interface.

Defining Local Interfaces

The local interfaces of a stateful session bean define the methods used by an EJB client located in the same JVM as the EJB component. Local interfaces are available only since the EJB 2.0 specification. While local interfaces provide better performance than remote interfaces, they can't be used by client applications that are located outside the JVM running the EJB container. Consequently, local interfaces are primarily intended for use by EJB components that need to access other EJB components in the same EJB application.

Some EJB containers provide *transparent* support for local method invocation in the remote interface of an EJB component, when it's possible. This support guarantees you the benefit of local method invocation without losing the flexibility of remote method invocation.

Nothing prevents you from developing both local and remote interfaces for an EJB component. Because the amount of additional effort involved in developing both local and remote interfaces is nominal, you may find this to be a practical approach.

Building the local home interface

The local home interface provides a mechanism for EJB client applications to create a new stateful session bean in the EJB container. The local home interface is used to define create methods that can be invoked by the client to create an EJB component. The local home interface for the ATMTransactionBean is defined in Listing 5-3.

Listing 5-3 The ATMTransactionLocalHome Interface

```
package com.sextanttech.transactions.interfaces;

import javax.ejb.EJBLocalHome;
import javax.ejb.CreateException;

public interface ATMTransactionLocalHome extends EJBLocalHome
        {
    public ATMTransactionLocal create( String username,
            String password ) throws CreateException;
}
```

When defining a local home interface for a stateful session bean, adhere to the following guidelines:

- All local home interfaces must be extended from the `javax.ejb.EJBLocalHome` interface. Local interfaces should not override any methods of the `EJBLocalHome` interface.

- Stateful session beans can define multiple `create` methods, unlike the stateless session bean, which can have only one `create` method. The `create` methods must conform to the following rules:

  - Each `create` method name must begin with the prefix **create**, followed by a meaningful suffix appropriate to the EJB component's name. In the case of the `ATMTransactionBean`, I've chosen the suffix **Transaction**.

  - The signature for each `create` method must be unique, meaning that no two `create` methods can have the same name and the same number and type of arguments.

  - Each `create` method must return a reference to the local interface for the EJB component.

  - Each `create` method must include the `javax.ejb.CreateException` in its throws clause. The `CreateException` is invoked by the EJB container when a problem occurs while creating an EJB component.

Because the local home interface doesn't participate in remote method invocation, its methods don't need to throw the `RemoteException`. Likewise, the arguments and return values for each method don't have to be serializable. However, to ensure the maximum flexibility in your application design, my advice is that you ensure that all arguments of the remote home `create` methods implement the `Serializable` interface so that the methods in your local home interface can easily be defined in a remote home interface if one is needed.

Each `create` method defined in a local home interface must have a corresponding `ejbCreate` method in the session bean class. The reason? The EJB container invokes the `ejbCreate` method on behalf of a client's invocation of the `create` method.

Building the local interface

The local interface for a stateful session bean is indistinguishable from a local interface for a stateless session bean. The local interface is simply used to define business methods for a client application to access — if the client application is located in the same EJB container. Remember that local interfaces are available only to local clients, and they can be used only in EJB containers that support the EJB 2.0 specification.

Listing 5-4 defines the local interface for the ATMTransactionBean. This interface is largely identical to its remote cousin. All local interfaces must extend the javax.ejb.EJBLocalObject interface and are used to define business methods accessible to a client application. Local interface business methods do not need to throw exceptions, but can throw application exceptions as needed.

Listing 5-4   The ATMTransactionLocal Interface

```
package com.sextanttech.transactions.interfaces;

import javax.ejb.EJBLocalObject;
import javax.ejb.EJBException;
import com.sextanttech.entities.interfaces.*;
import com.sextanttech.transactions.*;
import java.util.Map;

public interface ATMTransactionLocal extends EJBLocalObject {
    public void transfer( AccountKey sourceAccount, AccountKey
            targetAccount, double amount )
        throws EJBException, WithdrawException,
            DepositException;

    public void getStatement( AccountKey account, String
            username, String password ) throws EJBException;


    public void deposit( DepositEnvelope dep ) throws
            EJBException, DepositException;

    public void withdraw( double amount, AccountKey accountKey
            ) throws EJBException, WithdrawException;

    double balance( AccountKey accountKey ) throws
            EJBException;

    Map getAvailAccounts() throws EJBException;
}
```

TIP

While arguments and return values of remote interface business methods must be serializable, the local interface isn't bound by the same restriction. Nevertheless, to ensure that business methods defined in a local interface can be easily transferred to a remote interface, I recommend that all arguments and return objects implement the `java.io.Serializable` interface.

Creating the Stateful Session Bean Class

At the heart of every stateful session bean is a session bean *class*. The session bean class is the class that implements all the business methods and home interface methods you define for the session bean. From an API perspective, the session bean class of the stateless session bean is identical to the session bean class of a stateful session bean. Here's an overview of the key tasks a stateful session bean developer must perform:

- **The stateful session bean must implement the** `SessionBean` **interface.** The `SessionBean` interface defines lifecycle methods known as *callbacks* that the EJB container invokes at key transitions in a session bean's life. The callback gives an EJB component developer the opportunity to write code that responds to the event in the EJB container that triggered the invocation of the callback method. The following listing shows all the callback methods of the `SessionBean` interface:

  - `SessionBean.setSessionContext(SessionContext)`: This method is invoked by the EJB container after a new instance of the session bean is created. The component developer must store the `SessionContext` object in an *instance variable* — a variable that is scoped to a particular Java object, as opposed to a class variable or a method variable. The `SessionContext` object provides the session bean with access to system services defined in the EJB container, as well as application resources for the EJB application.

  - `SessionBean.passivate()`: The EJB container invokes this method immediately prior to storing a session bean in cache. For stateful session beans, the bean developer is responsible for releasing any instance variables in the session bean that can't be serialized in this method. In addition, scarce resources, such as database connections, should also be released in the `passivate` method.

  - `SessionBean.activate()`: The EJB container invokes this method immediately after restoring a session bean from cache. The bean developer should use this method to restore any instance variables that were released in the `passivate` method.

  - SessionBean.release(): The EJB container invokes this method when a session bean expires and is prepared for garbage collection. As with the passivate method, any scarce resources should be released from the session in this method. In fact, all instance

> variables should be cleaned up and released in this method so that the EJB component can be prepared for the garbage collector.

✔ **The stateful session bean must define an** `ejbCreate` **method for each** `create` **method defined in its home interfaces.** The `ejbCreate` method should have the same signature as the `create` method, with the following exceptions:

   - The `ejbCreate` method has a prefix of **ejb** on the method name.

   - The `ejbCreate` method must have a return type of `void`.

   - The `ejbCreate` method arguments must be serializable if there's a corresponding remote home interface for the `ejbCreate()` method.

✔ **Each business method defined in a remote or local interface for the EJB component must have a corresponding business method implementation in the session bean class.**

Listing 5-5 illustrates a stateful session bean implementing the `SessionBean` interface. As you review the listing, you'll see a few features of this class that distinguish it from a stateless session bean. First, the `ejbCreate` method defines operations used to initialize the application state managed within this bean. Second, note that the application state of this session bean is cleaned up in the `release` method.

Listing 5-5   The ATMTransaction Bean Class

```
package com.sextanttech.transactions.implementations;

import javax.ejb.SessionBean;
import javax.ejb.SessionContext;
import javax.ejb.FinderException;
import javax.ejb.CreateException;
import javax.ejb.EJBException;
import com.sextanttech.entities.interfaces.*;
import com.sextanttech.transactions.interfaces.*;

import com.sextanttech.transactions.*;
import javax.jms.*;
import java.util.Set;
import java.util.Map;
import java.util.Iterator;
import javax.naming.Context;
import javax.naming.InitialContext;
import javax.naming.NamingException;

public class ATMTransactionBean implements SessionBean {

    private SessionContext context;
    private Map availAccounts;
```

(continued)

Listing 5-5 *(continued)*

```
private WithdrawLocalHome withdrawHome;
private DepositLocalHome depositHome;
private AccountLocalHome accountHome;
private AccountHolderLocal accountHolder;

/** Lifecycle method called after a new instance is
 * created.
 */
public void ejbCreate( String username, String password )
       throws CreateException, EJBException {
    /* In the body of this create method, I lookup
     * references to entities associated with the user's
     * identity (username and password). These entities
     * are held in the ATMTransaction bean where they
     * can be referenced in subsequent transactions.
     */
    AccountHolderLocalHome holderHome;
    try {
        Context ctx = new InitialContext();
        holderHome = ( AccountHolderLocalHome )
        ctx.lookup("java:comp/env/ejb/accountHolderEJB");
        this.accountHolder = holderHome.findByIdentity(
        username, password );
        availAccounts = accountHolder.getAvailAccounts();

        accountHome = (AccountLocalHome) ctx.lookup(
        "java:comp/env/ejb/accountEJB" );
        withdrawHome = ( WithdrawLocalHome )ctx.lookup(
        "java:comp/env/ejb/withdrawEJB" );
        depositHome = ( DepositLocalHome )ctx.lookup(
        "java:comp/env/ejb/depositEJB" );
    }
    catch ( Exception e ) {
        throw new CreateException( e.toString() );
    }
    finally {
        holderHome = null;
    }
}


/** Lifecycle method called after activation occurs. */
public void ejbActivate() throws EJBException { }

/** Lifecycle method called before passivation occurs.
 */
public void ejbPassivate() throws EJBException { }

/** Lifecycle method for removing the stateful session
 * bean.
 */
public void ejbRemove() throws EJBException {
```

```
        this.context = null;
        this.accountHolder = null;
    }

    /** Lifecycle method for initializing the session
     * context.
     */
    public void setSessionContext( SessionContext context )
            throws EJBException {
        this.context = context;
    }

    /** This method causes funds to be transferred from one
     * account to another.
     */
    public void transfer( AccountKey sourceAccountKey,
            AccountKey targetAccountKey, double amount )
            throws EJBException, DepositException,
            WithdrawException {
            this.withdraw( amount, sourceAccountKey );
            this.deposit( new DepositEnvelope(amount,
            targetAccountKey));
    }

    /** This method will invoke a message driven bean,
     * causing a statement to be printed.
     */
    public void getStatement( AccountKey account, String
            username, String password ) throws EJBException {
        try {
            InitialContext ctx = new InitialContext();
            QueueConnectionFactory factory = (
            QueueConnectionFactory )ctx.lookup(
            "ConnectionFactory" );
            QueueConnection conn =
            factory.createQueueConnection();
            QueueSession session = conn.createQueueSession(
            false, QueueSession.AUTO_ACKNOWLEDGE );
            Queue defaultQueue = ( Queue )ctx.lookup(
            "queue/testQueue" );
QueueSender sender = session.createSender( defaultQueue );
            MapMessage message = session.createMapMessage();
            message.setString( "username", username );
            message.setString( "password", password );
            message.setLong( "accountId", account.accountId
            );
            message.setLong( "createDate", account.createDate
            );
            sender.send( defaultQueue, message );
        }
        catch ( NamingException e ) {
            throw new EJBException( e );
```

(continued)

Listing 5-5 *(continued)*

```
    }
        catch ( JMSException e ) {
            throw new EJBException( e );
        }
    }

    /** This method returns a list of accounts to the client
     * application.
     */
    public Map getAvailAccounts() throws EJBException {
        return availAccounts;
    }

    public void deposit( DepositEnvelope dep ) throws
            EJBException, DepositException {
        DepositLocal deposit;
        try {
            Context ctx = new InitialContext();
            deposit = depositHome.create();
            deposit.deposit( dep );
        }
        catch ( NamingException naming ) {
            throw new EJBException( naming );
        }
        catch ( CreateException create ) {
            throw new EJBException( create );
        }
        finally {
            deposit = null;
            depositHome = null;
        }
    }

    public void withdraw( double amount, AccountKey
            accountKey ) throws EJBException,
            WithdrawException {
        WithdrawLocal withdraw;
        try {
            Context ctx = new InitialContext();
            withdraw = withdrawHome.create();
            withdraw.withdraw( amount, accountKey );
        }
        catch ( NamingException naming ) {
            throw new EJBException( naming );
        }
        catch ( CreateException create ) {
            throw new EJBException( create );
        }
        finally {
            withdraw = null;
            withdrawHome = null;
        }
    }
```

```
public double balance( AccountKey accountKey ) throws
    EJBException {
AccountLocal account;
double balance = 0.0;
try {
    account = accountHome.findByPrimaryKey(
    accountKey );
    balance = account.getBalance();
}
catch ( FinderException e ) {
    throw new EJBException( e );
}
finally {
    account = null;
}
return balance;
}
}
```

The methods defined in the SessionBean interface provide a means for EJB component developers to respond to important lifecycle events in an EJB container. EJB component developers aren't required to respond to these events, and you may find that many of your session beans don't perform any operations within the methods defined by the SessionBean interface.

There are cases where you will need to perform operations within the methods of the SessionBean interface, however. Two of the most common cases are

✔ **When your EJB component contains an attribute that cannot be serialized:** If attributes in the stateless session bean cannot be serialized, they must be released in the ejbPassivate method. Failure to do so will interfere with an EJB container's ability to cache your session bean. If the EJB container cannot cache your session beans, you'll expose yourself to potential server crashes caused by out of memory errors. Likewise, if you remove an attribute in the ejbPassivate method, you must restore it in the ejbActivate method.

✔ **When your EJB component holds scarce resources in instance variables:** If attributes in the stateful session bean contain resources (such as database connections or other application services) that must be shared between EJB components, they should be released prior to passivation. Releasing such resources should occur in the ejbPassivate method. As in the preceding case, any resources released in passivation must be restored in the ejbActivate method.

If you're working with scarce resources — such as database connections — within a stateful session bean, it may be best to obtain those resources at the beginning of a business method and release them at the end. This tip assumes that you're using a database connection pool, which is an object that provides rapid access to a set of database connections. If you're not using a pool, then you should be (using one, that is).

In addition to responding to activation and passivation events, stateful session beans may need to initialize any system resources they hold prior to business method invocation. System resources can be listed in the ejb-jar.xml file, and accessed through the JDNI ENC or through the SessionContext interface. For more information about accessing JNDI ENC, refer to Chapter 12. For more information about initializing the session context, refer to the upcoming section, "Creating an ejb-jar.xml Entry."

Participating in the Transaction Lifecycle

Stateful session beans can be included in container-managed transactions or can manage their own transactions. If they manage their own transactions, they are said to have bean-managed transactions. I address both transaction topics in greater detail in Chapter 14, which I've devoted entirely to transactions. But a few important highlights deserve attention here.

First, while EJB containers provide a transaction context for stateful session beans, they do not transact the conversational state of the stateful session bean. Conversational state is contained in any attribute of your stateful session bean that tracks information on behalf of a client application. To illustrate, consider the following hypothetical scenario:

1. You write a stateful session bean that counts the number of invocations by a client. If a client invocation fails, it doesn't get counted.

2. When a client invokes the stateful session bean, the count is incremented, and then the operation is performed.

3. If you have an operation that increments the count to 4, after which an operation fails, the EJB container rolls the transaction back. But the EJB container will not deincrement the count attribute. Thus, to remove the failed invocation from the count, you must supply a mechanism that deducts the failed invocation from the count.

The crux of this example is the fact that the count attribute, which is conversational state, is not modified when a transaction fails. Hence, the container does not transact its state and the transaction of state must be managed by the bean provider.

Likewise, if you write stateful session beans that perform operations directly on a database instead of using entity beans, those database operations will not be transacted by the EJB transaction manager. Again, any manual state changes performed by a stateful session bean aren't transacted by an EJB container.

Unlike stateful session beans, entity beans can have interactions with a database transacted by the EJB container. That means that if you perform database operations inside an entity bean, the container will transparently rollback changes in the event that a transaction fails.

Because EJB containers cannot transact the state of a stateful session bean, this task is left to the EJB bean developer. If you have state within a stateful session bean that needs to be transacted, and if your session bean participates in container-managed transactions, you can transact the state of your session bean by implementing the `javax.ejb.SessionSynchronization` interface. The `SessionSynchronization` interface defines three methods that get invoked by the EJB container on a session bean when it is involved in a transacted method invocation:

✔ `SessionSynchronization.afterBegin()`:This method is invoked by the EJB container after the start of a transaction. You can use it to capture state within a session bean that needs to be transacted. Doing so can be pretty complex, and different attributes require different treatment when it comes to capturing state. You can read more about this topic in Chapter 15.

✔ `SessionSynchronization.beforeCompletion()`:This method is invoked by the EJB container before a transaction is completed. Typically, this method is used by a component developer to indicate whether a transaction failed. That vote is cast through the `SessionContext.setRollbackOnly()` method, which tells the container to mark the transaction for rollback.

✔ `SessionSynchronization.afterCompletion(boolean committed)`: This method is invoked by the EJB container immediately after a transaction is finished. The argument tells the EJB component whether the transaction completed successfully or failed. If a transaction fails, the `committed` variable will be `false`. In that case, the component developer should respond by restoring the state of the session bean that was initially captured in the `afterBegin()` method.

The `SessionSynchronization` interface can be used only by stateful session beans that participate in container-managed transactions. Bean-managed transactions cannot use the `SessionSynchronization` interface.

When it comes to implementing transaction support, my advice is, "Never sniff a gift fish." By participating in container-managed transactions, your EJB component will be much simpler to develop and to maintain. Instead of creating special cases where you can't benefit from container-managed transactions, accept the gift of transaction support and design your EJB program to take full advantage of it by using entity beans to manage database interactions.

Creating an ejb-jar.xml Entry

The ejb-jar.xml file defines important information about EJB applications for use by the EJB container and by the EJB client programmer. Chapters 13 and 14 are devoted to a complete investigation of the ejb-jar.xml file. Listing 5-6 illustrates an ejb-jar file entry for a stateful session bean. As you review Listing 5-6, take note of the following points:

- ✔ The entry for a stateful session bean is delimited by the ⟨session⟩ tag.
- ✔ The classes for all the elements of the stateful session beans are identified in the ejb-jar.xml file.
- ✔ The only feature that identifies a stateful session bean as stateful is the ⟨session-type⟩ attribute, which must have the value Stateful.
- ✔ The stateless session bean must indicate the type of transaction management required for the bean component. The ⟨transaction-type⟩ allows two values: Bean for bean-managed transactions, and Container for container-managed transactions.

Listing 5-6   The ejb-jar.xml File

```
<!DOCTYPE ejb-jar PUBLIC '-//Sun Microsystems, Inc.//DTD
          Enterprise JavaBeans 2.0//EN'
          'http://java.sun.com/dtd/ejb-jar_2_0.dtd'>
<ejb-jar>
  <enterprise-beans>
    <session>
      <description>
        This provides a wrapper for ATMTransactions.
      </description>
      <ejb-name>ATMTransactionEJB</ejb-name>
      <home>

            com.sextanttech.transactions.interfaces.ATMTransac
            tionRemoteHome

      </home>
      <remote>

            com.sextanttech.transactions.interfaces.ATMTransac
            tionRemote
      </remote>
      <local-home>

            com.sextanttech.transactions.interfaces.ATMTransac
            tionLocalHome
      </local-home>
      <local>
```

```
             com.sextanttech.transactions.interfaces.ATMTransac
             tionLocal
     </local>
     <ejb-class>

             com.sextanttech.transactions.implementations.ATMTr
             ansactionBean
     </ejb-class>
     <session-type>Stateful</session-type>
     <transaction-type>Container</transaction-type>
   </session>
 </enterprise-beans>
</ejb-jar>
```

Examining Additional API Features

While you've seen the most important classes and interfaces of the stateless session bean, there are several less prominent classes that are accessed through the home and component interfaces of the session bean. Several of these classes can be accessed by the component programmer, and while it may be tempting to make use of these classes — or simply to assume that they're important to client applications — that isn't necessarily so. In the remainder of this chapter, I review the classes you can access in session bean components and assess their importance and value in the context of stateless session beans. A more detailed review, addressing similar points, is provided in Chapter 4.

The EJBHome and EJBLocalHome interfaces

The EJBHome and EJBLocalHome interfaces are respectively extended by the remote home and local home interfaces of an EJB component. The API defined in these interfaces is covered in detail at the end of Chapter 4. To summarize:

✔ The EJBLocalHome interface contains a single remove method, which only applies to entity beans. Invoking the remove method from a session bean of any kind results in a javax.ejb.EJBException.

✔ The EJBHome interface provides access to the EJBMetaData object and the HomeHandle object. The EJBMetaData object is intended for use by software development tools and should not be used within application code.

✔ The `EJBHome` interface also defines two `remove` methods. While it's a good practice to remove stateful session beans when you're finished using them, there is a `remove` method defined in the `EJBObject` and the `EJBLocalObject` interface that's more appropriate for the client programmer to use. Refer to the next section for more information on the `remove` method.

One of the `remove` methods for the `EJBHome` object requires a `primaryKey` argument. This method is for removing entity beans, and it will always throw a `javax.ejb.EJBException` if invoked on a session bean.

The EJBObject and EJBLocalObject interfaces

The `EJBObject` and `EJBLocalObject` are respectively extended by the remote interface and local interface. The remote and local interfaces are collectively referred to as the *component interfaces* because they provide a client view of the EJB component. Because they're extended by the remote and the local interfaces, the methods of the `EJBObject` and `EJBLocalObject` are revealed to client programmers. There are numerous methods within the `EJBObject` and `EJBLocalObject`. While some have value in the context of stateful session beans, several do not. In the following list, I guide you past the risky methods and point out the ones that you'll find useful:

✔ The `EJBLocalObject` defines four methods:

- `getEJBLocalHome()`: This method returns a reference to the `EJBLocalHome` object. Most client applications will not need this method because the `EJBLocalHome` should be obtained prior to creating an `EJBLocalObject`.

- `getPrimaryKey()`: This method is for use with entity beans only. Invoking this method from a session bean will throw an `EJBException`.

- `isIdentical(EJBLocalObject obj)`: This method determines whether the provided `EJBLocalObject` is the same as the object on which it is invoked. If a client programmer encounters a situation where two `EJBLocalObject` references need to be compared for equality, this is the method to do it with. If the method returns `true`, then both objects refer to the same stateful session bean. That means that method invocations from one can change the state of both.

- `remove()`: This method will cause the EJB container to invoke the `ejbRemove` operation on a stateful session bean and then release the session bean class for garbage collection. If you know you no longer need a stateful session bean, invoking the `remove` operation will free memory in the EJB server for other clients.

✔ The `EJBObject` interface defines a parallel set of operations to the `EJBLocalObject` with one addition — the `getHandle()` method. The following differences exist between the `EJBObject` and the `EJBLocalObject`:

- The `getHandle` interface returns a reference to the `Handle` object for this `EJBObject`. The `Handle` can be passed between JVMs and used to re-create a reference to an EJB object in a different JVM. This approach is not recommended because it doesn't ensure that a valid security context is maintained and can result in some unanticipated errors.

- The `isIdentical` method is identical to the `EJBLocalObject`, with the exception that it accepts an `EJBObject` as an argument. The `isIdentical` method is used to determine whether or not two `EJBObject` variables refer to the same `EJBObject`.

After the `remove` operation is invoked on an `EJBObject` or `EJBLocalObject`, the session bean is moved to the Does Not Exist state; refer to Figure 5-1. Any further attempts to invoke methods through the component interface will throw an `EJBException`.

The SessionContext interface

The `SessionContext` interface is assigned to a session bean class when its `setSessionContext` method is invoked by the EJB container. That method is invoked immediately after the `ejbCreate` method is invoked on a session bean. As I reveal at the end of Chapter 4, several methods are defined in the `SessionContext` interface that can be of use to an EJB component. However, most should not be used inside the session bean class because they invite relationship violations between the EJB container and an EJB component.

On the other hand, a stateful session bean has a different lifecycle from the stateless session bean and thus has fewer restrictions on the types that are reasonable for it to perform. Because the `SessionContext` defines methods that aren't valid for the entire lifecycle of a stateful session bean, it's important that you determine whether the methods you intend to invoke are available before using them.

Table 5-1 identifies the methods of the `SessionContext` — and its super interface `EJBContext` — and assesses their value to stateful session bean development.

Table 5-1	Methods of the SessionContext Interface
Method	*Description*
`EJBLocalObject getEJBLocalObject()`	Returns a reference to the `EJBLocalObject`, if one exists.
`EJBObject getEJBObject()`	Returns a reference to the `EJBObject`, if one exists.
`Principal getCallerPrinicipal()`	Provides access to the `Principal` object, which is part of the security API. It's best to let the EJB container handle security considerations and not to access the security API explicitly. That ensures that the application assembler can flexibly manage security when the application is deployed.
`EJBHome getEJBHome()`	Returns a reference to the `EJBHome` object, if one exists.
`EJBLocalHome getEJBLocalHome()`	Returns a reference to the `EJBLocalHome` object, if one exists.
`boolean getRollbackOnly()`	Indicates whether a container-managed transaction is marked for rollback or not. A return value of `true` means the transaction is marked for rollback.
`UserTransaction getUserTransaction()`	For use in implementing bean-managed transactions. Refer to Chapter 15 for more information on this topic.
`boolean isCallerInRole(String roleName)`	Indicates whether a client invocation has a given security role. Not recommended for use by EJB bean developers, for the same reason that programmers shouldn't retrieve the `Principle` object.
`void setRollbackOnly()`	Marks the current container-managed transaction for rollback. For container-managed transactions only.

Table 5-2 takes a closer look at what methods of the `SessionContext` can be invoked through the various API methods of the stateful session bean. The term *Container-Managed Transaction Demarcation* indicates that the EJB container marks the beginning and end of a transaction. *Bean-Managed Transaction Demarcation* means that the bean developer manually marks the beginning and end of a transaction.

Table 5-2	When to Access Methods of the SessionContext	
Bean Method	**Container-Managed Transaction Demarcation**	**Bean-Managed Transaction Demarcation**
constructor	—	—
setSessionContext	SessionContext **Methods:** getEJBHome, getEJBLocalHome	SessionContext **Methods:** getEJBHome, getEJBLocalHome.
ejbCreate, ejbRemove, ejbActivate, ejbPassivate	SessionContext **Methods:** getEJBHome, getEJBLocalHome, getCallerPrincipal, isCallerInRole, getEJBObject, getEJBLocalObject; **Enterprise bean access.**	SessionContext **Methods:** getEJBHome, getEJBLocalHome, get CallerPrincipal, isCallerInRole, getEJBObject, getEJBLocalObject, getUserTransaction; **User Transaction methods; Enterprise bean access.**
business method from component interface	SessionContext **Methods:** getEJBHome, getEJBLocalHome, getCallerPrincipal, getRollbackOnly, isCallerInRole, setRollbackOnly, getEJBObject, getEJBLocalObject; **Enterprise bean access.**	SessionContext **Methods:** getEJBHome, getEJBLocalHome, get CallerPrincipal, isCallerInRole, getEJBObject, getEJBLocalObject, getUserTransaction; **User Transaction methods; Enterprise bean access.**
afterBegin beforeCompletion	SessionContext **Methods:** getEJBHome, getEJBLocalHome, getCallerPrincipal, getRollbackOnly, isCallerInRole, setRollbackOnly, getEJBObject, getEJBLocalObject; **Enterprise bean access.**	N/A. (A bean with bean-managed transaction demarcation cannot implement the SessionSynchronization interface.)
afterCompletion	SessionContext **Methods:** getEJBHome, getEJBLocalHome, getCallerPrincipal, isCallerInRole, getEJBObject, getEJBLocalObject	N/A. (A bean with bean-managed transaction demarcation cannot implement the SessionSynchronization interface.)

Part III
Entity Beans: The Way Things Are

"THE ARTIST WAS ALSO A PROGRAMMER AND EVIDENTLY PRODUCED SEVERAL VARIATIONS ON THIS THEME."

In this part . . .

Entity beans are used to represent business data in an EJB application. This part is entirely devoted to creating entity beans, which can be a complicated task. Never fear — for when you finish with these pages, you'll be ready to overcome all the basic obstacles of creating great entity bean components.

Chapter 6

Entity Beans with Container-Managed Persistence 2.0

● ●

In This Chapter

▶ Discovering the lifecycle of entity beans

▶ Creating a container-managed entity bean with the 2.0 persistence model

▶ Creating entity bean primary keys

▶ Defining entity bean relationships

▶ Describing entity beans in a deployment descriptor

● ●

*F*or me, entity beans are probably the most exciting feature of the EJB 2.0 specification because entity beans are making the notion of a *portable database architecture* — an application design allowing you to switch databases without changing your application — a reality. A database allows your EJB application to maintain a *persistent* copy of data. Persistent data is data stored on a physical device that can be retrieved even after a computer crashes and reboots. For business application developers, databases are a fact of life. Selecting a database is a major investment, and after you've picked your favorite flavor, it's a mind-boggling investment to change. By using entity beans, you have the power to define a data model — illustrating the structure of your data and relationships between different pieces of data — for your application that's completely independent of the underlying database implementation. That means that as the needs of your business evolve, you can switch database implementations with relative ease.

Container-managed persistence (CMP) is the feature of entity bean components that allows you to create portable database solutions. Persistence refers to the process of storing data in an entity bean to a database. CMP entity beans allow an EJB container to define data structures of an entity bean, create the representation of that bean in a database, and manipulate that data within a database. Because the CMP entity bean is completely decoupled from the underlying data structure in a database, switching databases can be as easy as copying data from one database to another and supplying the EJB container with connection information for the new database.

The two models of container-managed persistence are CMP 1.1 and CMP 2.0. CMP 1.1 was defined with the EJB 1.1 specification, and while it's supported in EJB 2.0 containers for backward compatibility, it's significantly different from the updated CMP 2.0 model. In this chapter, I address developing entity beans that make use of the CMP 2.0 model.

A second type of persistence is *bean-managed persistence* (BMP). Developing BMP entity beans is a horse of a different color. If you're looking for more information on developing BMP entity beans, refer to Chapter 8.

Creating an entity bean with container-managed persistence can be divided into five basic tasks:

- ✔ **Create the home or remote home interface for the entity bean.** Entity bean home interfaces have `create` methods, finder methods (for obtaining references to existing entity beans), and *home methods*. Home methods are business methods defined in the home interface of an entity bean.

  The home methods in a home or remote home interface can make changes to sets of entity beans — they apply to groups of a particular kind of entity. For example, you could define a home method named `annualBonus` that provides every employee entity with a 10 percent bonus. Or you could define an `annualBonus` home method, which takes a job title as an argument and only gives the employees with that job title a bonus.

- ✔ **Define a component interface — either a remote or local interface.** The component contains business methods, and getters and setters (more about these in the section "Defining CMP fields") for entity bean fields.

- ✔ **Create a primary key for the entity bean.** The entity bean's *primary key* is a Java object that uniquely identifies the entity bean component. Head to the section "Building a Primary Key Class" for more.

- ✔ **Create the entity bean class.** Entity bean classes include lifecycle methods, just as session beans. They also have CMP fields and container-managed relationship (CMR) fields. CMP fields hold the data an entity bean contains while CMR fields define relationships between entity beans. Finally, the entity bean class defines `ejbSelect` methods, which the business methods use to navigate relationships between entity beans.

- ✔ **Describe the entity bean in the deployment descriptor file.** The deployment descriptor for an entity bean contains a lot more information than the typical session bean because the container collects a lot of information about managing entity bean persistence and relationships through the descriptor.

I detail all five tasks in this chapter. But before I do that, I give you a review of important entity bean features and the entity bean lifecycle, which may help you better understand your responsibilities as an entity bean developer. If you're daunted by entity beans, take my advice. The issue with entity beans isn't that they're overly complex to develop, but that there are so many parts to developing them. To manage that complexity, simply break the development process down into bite-sized pieces, and develop the entity bean in a natural order. I've organized this chapter so that it follows the order that makes most sense to me. Hopefully, you'll find it to be useful.

Entity Bean Features

While session beans are primarily intended for managing workflows and processes, entity beans are intended for managing data. The distinction is essentially the difference between a noun and a verb. Session beans are verbs because they represent actions; entity beans are nouns because they represent the objects actions are taken upon. Entity beans have some special properties and characteristics that you should take into account when you consider using them.

✔ **Each instance of an entity bean can be shared by multiple clients.** By contrast, session beans are private and can't be shared. Thus, if you have to model a process that requires visibility from multiple clients, the process should be implemented with an entity bean. An ideal example of this shared state is a printer queue. Because a printer can print just one document at a time, all clients assigned to a printer should place print jobs in the same queue. The entity bean is an ideal solution for implementing a printer queue.

✔ **Entity beans are persistent.** Information that you store in an entity bean will be stored in a persistent data storage facility, such as a database. Typically, entity beans store persistent data in a database, but that isn't required, so it is possible that an EJB container may choose to store data in another format, such as a file. In terms of persistent storage, the only requirement of entity beans is that the data be capable of surviving a computer crash. Thus, if you need to preserve data beyond a single user session, the entity bean is the appropriate tool for the job.

✔ **The EJB container transacts the state of an entity bean.** If your entity bean is changed in the middle of a transaction, the EJB container will commit the change if the transaction is successful or will rollback the change if the transaction fails. Remember that the session bean doesn't transact state automatically, but the entity bean does. So if you need a relatively simple way to transact the state of some data, the entity bean is the appropriate tool to use.

Lifecycle of an Entity Bean

Entity beans have two different lifecycles. One is the *object lifecycle*, which applies to the use of a particular instance of an entity. The other is the *entity lifecycle*, which applies to the creation, modification, and destruction of an entity. Managing the lifecycle of an entity is a rather complex task. Figure 6-1 provides a generic view of an entity bean's lifecycle.

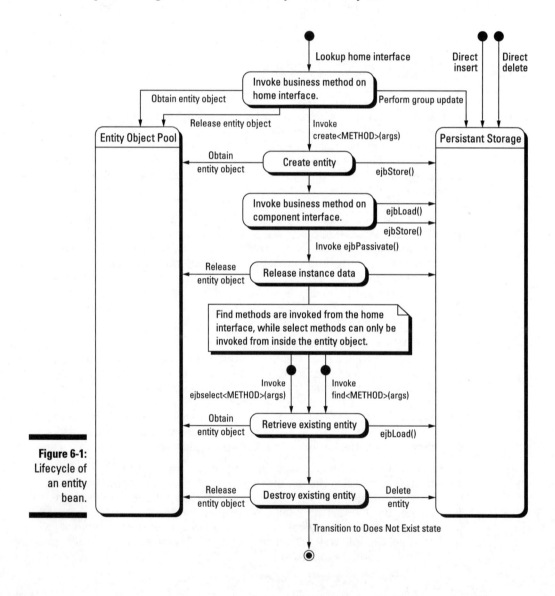

Figure 6-1: Lifecycle of an entity bean.

As you review Figure 6-1, take note of the following points:

- ✔ Because entity beans can have home methods in their home interfaces, it is possible to invoke those methods on entity objects without referring to any particular instance. Home methods behave similar to group updates in a relational database. The operations of the home methods will be applied to any entity that matches the criteria specified in the method's name or arguments.

- ✔ The life of an entity instance begins when it is created. Entities can be created by invoking `create` methods in the home interface. They can also be created by performing a direct insert. With a *direct insert,* entity data is inserted directly into a database without interacting with the EJB container. Direct inserts are typically accomplished with SQL. In either approach, the entity data is stored in the database. But with the `create` method, an entity object is obtained from a pool of objects (kept for performance reasons), the instance data is assigned to the object, and a component interface reference to the object is returned to the client application.

- ✔ When a business method is invoked on an entity through its component interface, any modifications to the entity will apply to that particular instance, and not to other entities of the same class. Depending on parameters specified in the deployment descriptor, data may be loaded from the database prior to a business method invocation.

- ✔ When an entity is idle, the EJB container can passivate it. When the entity is passivated, its instance data is cached, and the entity object is returned to the object pool. When a client invokes a passive entity through its component interface, it is activated by retrieving an entity object from the pool, and restoring the cached data to the object. Depending on the configuration of the deployment descriptor, the entity object may also update its data from the database.

An entity object's cached data isn't necessarily the same as its persistent data stored in a database. It is possible for the two to get out of synch if the database is updated via a direct update while the entity is in a passive state.

- ✔ If you invoke the `remove` method on an entity object, it is permanently deleted — from memory and from the database. Thus, `remove` methods should only be performed when an entity is to be destroyed completely. Executing a `remove` method on an entity object is equivalent to deleting its data from the database. After a `remove` method is committed, the entity is gone forever.

Don't invoke `remove` on an entity object unless you mean to delete it permanently.

Client view of an entity bean

Different features of an entity bean's lifecycle take on different levels of prominence depending on what perspective they're viewed from. The activity diagram in Figure 6-2 illustrates an entity bean's lifecycle from the client application's perspective.

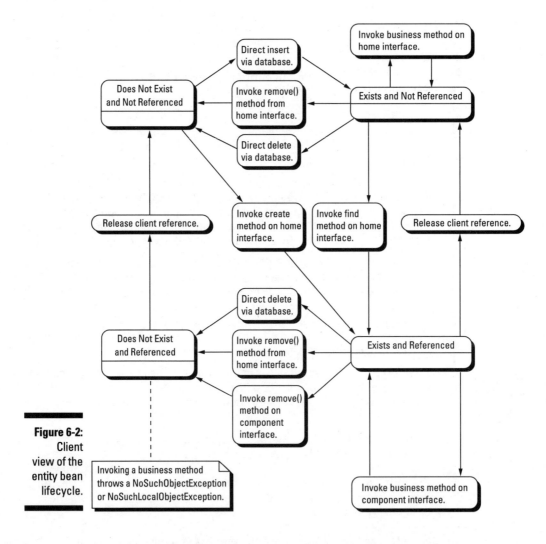

Figure 6-2: Client view of the entity bean lifecycle.

For client applications, there are four different states in an entity bean lifecycle:

✔ **Does Not Exist And Not Referenced:** In this state, the data for an entity bean does not exist in the entity bean or in the database. In addition, there are no references to an entity bean component. This state exists prior to the creation of an entity bean, or after an entity bean is deleted and the reference is released. (A *reference* in this context refers to the reference held by a client application.)

✔ **Exists And Not Referenced:** When an entity bean exists and isn't referenced, it exists in persistent storage but isn't referenced by an instance variable in an application. Entity beans can only achieve this state via a direct insert, or when all client references to the entity have been released.

✔ **Exists And Referenced:** An entity bean exists and is referenced when a reference to the instance is held by a client application. This state is achieved when a client invokes the `create` method on an entity bean's home or remote home interface, or when the client invokes a `find` method on the entity's home or remote home interface.

✔ **Does Not Exist And Referenced:** When an entity bean does not exist, but is referenced, the client application holds a reference to the entity bean but the persistent storage of the entity bean has been destroyed. Three different approaches lead to this state:

- If the entity is referenced by a client, but some unrelated process performs a direct delete against the database, then the entity is destroyed but a reference is still held.

- If the client invokes the `remove` method from the home interface, the reference exists, but the entity is destroyed.

- If the client invokes the `remove` method from the component interface, the reference exists but the entity is destroyed.

If you're familiar with database development, then you'll easily map the operations on an entity bean to standard database operations. A `create <METHOD>` invocation is equivalent to a database insert. A `find<METHOD>` is equivalent to a SQL query. A modification to an entity bean's attributes is equivalent to an update operation. Finally, invoking `remove` on an entity bean is equivalent to a SQL delete statement.

When an entity is in the Does Not Exist And Referenced state, any method invocation on the entity will throw a `NoSuchObjectException` or a `NoSuchLocalObjectException`.

Container view of an entity bean

As with all EJB components, entity bean developers must conform to a development contract that ensures entity beans will work regardless of which EJB container they're deployed to. This contract is best understood when the lifecycle of an entity bean is viewed from the container's perspective. In Figure 6-3, the lifecycle of an entity bean shows three basic states:

- ✔ **Does Not Exist:** In this phase, the entity bean doesn't exist. This is prior to its creation or after its removal. Because an entity bean is stored in a database between uses, executing a `create` operation is equivalent to inserting an entity into the database. Likewise, executing a `remove` method is equivalent to deleting the entity bean.

- ✔ **Pooled:** In this state, the entity doesn't contain any instance data. Instead, it is in an uninitialized state that contains global information applying to the type of an entity. Methods can be performed on pooled entities through their home interfaces, but not through the component interface.

- ✔ **Ready:** In this state, the entity is initialized with instance data. Thus, it moves from an empty shell of an entity to a specific entity instance. Methods can be performed on the entity through both the home and the remote interface. Entity bean instances are moved into a ready state when looked up by the client application, and are retired to the pooled state when not in use.

In the remainder of this chapter, I investigate how to make use of all the lifecycle methods illustrated in Figure 6-3. For now, just focus on what the EJB container does with an entity bean, and when each lifecycle event occurs. The following list walks you through the process:

- ✔ Creating an entity bean object is a precursor to creating an instance of the entity bean. The entity bean object is just an instance of the entity bean class that is not associated with any particular entity data. It's like a template that's waiting to be populated with some real information. This step is used by the EJB container to populate an entity bean pool and not to create instances of any particular entity.

  - The `Class.newInstance` method is used by the EJB container to create instances of the entity object. At this stage, no instance data is associated with the entity bean.

  - After each entity object is created, its `EntityBean.setEntityContext` method is invoked.

  - After the entity context is set, the entity bean object is placed in a pool where it can be accessed and assigned instance data as needed.

- ✔ While in a Pooled state, a client can invoke any method on the entity bean's home or remote home interfaces. While only `create`, `find`, and home methods are exposed to client applications through the home interface, home methods may indirectly invoke an `ejbSelect` method on the entity object.

✔ When a `find` or `create` method is invoked, a reference to an instance of an entity object is returned to the client. With respect to finder methods, the reference may be to an entity that's already in the Ready state, as I explain later. But a `create` method always causes an entity bean object to transition from Pooled state to Ready state.

- With a `create` method invocation, the entity bean executes the specified `ejbCreate` method in the entity object, and subsequently executes an `ejbPostCreate` method. At this stage, a new entity is created, by removing an entity object from the pooled state and assigning instance data to the object.

- When a `find` method is invoked, the container invokes the `ejbActivate` prior to moving the entity to its ready state. Two things can happen when a finder method is invoked. If another client already has a reference to the entity bean that is retrieved by the finder method, then the client receives a reference to that instance. But if no references exist to the entity bean, then the finder method removes an entity bean object from the pool and associates that object with data from the database. Then the reference is returned to the client application.

✔ From its Ready state, a client can invoke any method on an entity bean instance that's defined in the component interface. Clients can invoke business methods on the entity bean, which in turn cause `ejbLoad`, `ejbStore`, and `ejbSelect` methods to be invoked.

- The `ejbLoad` method is invoked after data is loaded into an entity bean from the database.

- The `ejbStore` method is invoked before data is stored to a database from an entity bean.

- The `ejbSelect` methods are used to obtain references to related entity beans from inside the entity bean object.

✔ When an entity bean in Ready state is expired by the EJB container, the `ejbPassivate` method is invoked. An EJB container expires entity components after they have been inactive for a while, which allows the container to reuse entity bean objects. When the entity is passivated, its state is cached, and the entity object is cleaned and returned to the Pooled state. From there, the EJB container can recycle the object and use it for another entity.

✔ If the client application invokes a `remove` method on the entity bean, either through the home or the remote interface, the bean is deleted from the database and its entity object is turned to the Pooled state.

✔ Finally, when a container removes entities from the entity object pool, it first invokes the `unsetEntityContext` method on the entity object. After that, the entity object no longer exists.

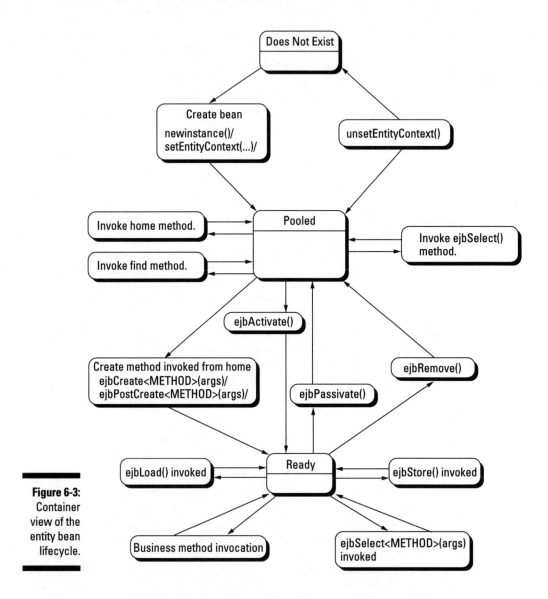

Figure 6-3:
Container
view of the
entity bean
lifecycle.

Creating Entity Bean Home Interfaces

The entity bean home interfaces pack a little heavier punch than their session bean counter parts. That's because, in addition to providing `create` methods, the entity bean also supports *finder methods*, and *home methods*. Home interfaces use the `create` methods of an entity bean to create a new entity bean instance. This is equivalent to inserting a record in a database. On the other hand, *finder methods* are used to look up an existing entity bean. Thus, they correspond to SQL queries. The business methods in a home interface are called *home methods*, which distinguish them from business methods in a component interface. Home methods are performed without the client needing a reference to any particular entity bean.

While it is possible to perform more methods with an entity bean's home and remote home interfaces, the fundamentals of creating the home interface are very similar to the principles of home interfaces for session beans. That's because the entity bean's local home interface must extend the javax.ejb. EJBLocalHome interface, and the entity bean's remote home interface must extend the javax.ejb.EJBHome interface.

In the following subsections, I examine the create methods, finder methods, and home methods in greater detail. Each section is illustrated with examples from the sample ATM application's AccountBean. I use the ATM application as an example to illustrate the creation of different EJB components throughout this book. As you proceed through the sections, refer to Listing 6-1 for a complete AccountRemoteHome interface and Listing 6-2 for a complete view of the AccountLocalHome interface.

Listing 6-1 The AccountRemoteHome Interface

```
package com.sextanttech.entities.interfaces;

import javax.ejb.EJBHome;
import javax.ejb.CreateException;
import javax.ejb.FinderException;
import java.rmi.RemoteException;
import java.util.Date;

public interface AccountRemoteHome extends EJBHome{
    public AccountRemote createAccount(java.util.Date
            createDate, long clientId) throws CreateException,
            RemoteException;

    public AccountRemote createAccount(java.util.Date
            createDate, long clientId, float balance) throws
            CreateException, RemoteException;

    public AccountRemote createAccount(java.util.Date
            createDate, long clientId, double balance) throws
            CreateException, RemoteException;

    public AccountRemote findByPrimaryKey(AccountKey key)
            throws FinderException, RemoteException;

    public AccountRemote
            findByAccountHolderKey(AccountHolderKey key)
            throws FinderException, RemoteException;
```

(continued)

Listing 6-1 *(continued)*

```
    public double getNetWorth(AccountHolderKey key) throws
        RemoteException;

}
```

Listing 6-2   The AccountLocalHome Interface

```
package com.sextanttech.entities.interfaces;

import javax.ejb.EJBLocalHome;
import javax.ejb.CreateException;
import javax.ejb.FinderException;
import java.util.Date;

public interface AccountLocalHome extends EJBLocalHome{
    public AccountLocal createAccount(Date createDate, long
        clientId) throws CreateException;

    public AccountLocal createAccount(Date createDate, long
        clientId, float balance) throws CreateException;

    public AccountLocal createAccount(Date createDate, long
        clientId, double balance) throws CreateException;

    public AccountLocal findByPrimaryKey(AccountKey key)
        throws FinderException;

    public java.util.Collection
        findByAccountHolderKey(AccountHolderKey key)
        throws FinderException;

    public double getNetWorth(AccountHolderKey key);

}
```

Defining create methods

The entity bean developer can define zero, one, or more `create` methods for an entity bean. Each `create` method is prefixed with the term **create** followed by a meaningful name. `Create` methods can take different numbers and types of arguments. Each `create` method typically includes arguments that define all the required data for an entity bean to be created.

While `create` methods don't have to define all the data of an entity bean, supplying as much information as you can to create an entity bean is a good idea — it minimizes the need for multiple method invocations to set attributes of the entity bean. Particularly when working with remote interfaces, the fewer method invocations you make, the faster your EJB application will run.

When defining `create` methods in a home or remote home interface, be sure to adhere to the following rules:

- Each `create` method must return a reference to an entity bean component interface. If the `create` method is in a remote home interface, the return type must be the entity bean's remote interface. If the `create` method is in a local home interface, the return type must be the entity bean's local interface.

- Each `create` method defined in a home or remote home interface must correspond with an `ejbCreate<METHOD>(<args>)` and an `ejbPostCreate<METHOD>(<args>)` in the entity bean class for the component. The `<args>` parameter is a placeholder that must correspond to any arguments you define in the `create` method. If identical `create` methods are defined in both the home and the remote home interface, the EJB container will use the same `ejbCreate` and `ejbPostCreate` methods for both.

- If a remote home interface is defined, all the arguments and the return type of the `create` method must be serializable.

- In the remote home interface, each `create` method must include a `javax.ejb.CreateException` and a `java.rmi.RemoteException` in its `throws` clause. In a local home interface, each `create` method must include a `javax.ejb.CreateException` in its `throws` clause, and can't throw a `java.rmi.RemoteException`. Create methods may also throw arbitrary application exceptions defined by the bean developer.

In the following example, two `create` methods are defined for the `Account` entity bean's remote home interface in the sample ATM application:

```
public interface AccountRemoteHome extends javax.ejb.EJBHome{
    /* This create method creates a new account without a
            balance.*/
    public AccountRemote createAccount( long clientId)
        throws CreateException, RemoteException;

    /* This create method creates a new account with a
            balance.*/
    public AccountRemote createAccount( long clientId,
        float balance) throws CreateException,
        RemoteException;

    /* This create method creates a new account with a large
            balance.*/
    public AccountRemote createAccount( long clientId,
        double balance) throws CreateException,
        RemoteException;

    //... remainder of remote home interface
}
```

The following code sample illustrates corresponding create methods defined in a local home interface:

```
public interface AccountLocalHome extends
        javax.ejb.EJBLocalHome{
    /* This create method creates a new account without a
        balance.*/
    public AccountLocal createAccount( long clientId)
        throws CreateException;

    /* This create method creates a new account with a
        balance.*/
    public AccountLocal createAccount( long clientId,
        float balance) throws CreateException;

    /* This create method creates a new account with a large
        balance.*/
    public AccountLocal createAccount( long clientId,
        double balance) throws CreateException;

    //... remainder of local home interface
}
```

Defining finder methods

Finder methods are used by EJB client applications to locate entity beans that already exist. The entity bean developer must define at least one finder method, but can define more as necessary. Each finder method is prefixed with the term **find** followed by a meaningful name. The mandatory finder method is findByPrimaryKey(Object primaryKey). Given a primary key object, a client application can use the findByPrimaryKey() method to look up an entity with the given primary key. For more about primary keys, check out the later section "Building a Primary Key Class."

In addition to the findByPrimaryKey() method, the home interface can define additional finder methods as necessary. When defining a finder method, you can return either a single entity bean component interface, or a collection of entity bean component interfaces. Finder methods that always return a single component interface are called *single-object finder methods*. Conversely, objects that return a collection of component interfaces are called *multiple-object finder methods*.

Finder methods must conform to the following rules:

- ✔ **All finder methods must be prefixed with the term** find.

- ✔ **All finder methods must throw a** `javax.ejb.FinderException`. Finder methods defined in the remote home interface must also include the `java.rmi.RemoteException` in its `throws` clause. All finder methods may also throw application exceptions defined by the EJB component developer.

- ✔ **For each finder method other than the** `findByPrimaryKey()` **method, the bean provider must supply a corresponding EJB query in the EJB component's deployment descriptor.** For detailed information on the EJB Query Language, refer to Chapter 7.

- ✔ **All finder methods must return a reference to an object implementing a component interface for the EJB component.** If the finder method is located in a remote home interface, the return object must implement the remote interface for the entity bean. If the finder method is located in a local home, the return object must implement the local home interface for the finder method.

- ✔ **When defining a multiple-object finder method, the return value must also implement the** `java.util.Collection` **interface.**

Don't be intimidated by implementing the `java.util.Collection` interface in a multiple-object finder method. Remember that you don't have to implement component interfaces, the EJB container does that for you. Thus, all you have to do is declare that the component interface implements `java.util.Collection`. I provide an example in the upcoming section "Creating Entity Bean Component Interfaces."

If you define a single-object finder method that attempts to return more than one component interface at runtime, the EJB container will throw a `javax.ejb.FinderException`.

Use the semantic difference between single-object finder methods and multiple-object finder methods to your advantage. If you're defining a finder method that must never return more than a single value by design, be sure to use the single-object finder method. Doing so will make your code easier to maintain and debug if the method attempts to return multiple entities. That's because an exception will be thrown, telling you exactly where the problem occurred.

The following sample code illustrates a single-object finder method — `findByPrimaryKey()` — and a multiple-object finder method — `findByAccountHolderKey()`. Note that the return type of all multiple-object finder methods is `java.util.Collection`.

```
public interface AccountRemoteHome extends javax.ejb.EJBHome{
    /* The findByPrimaryKey method is always a single-value
          finder
     * method. All single value methods must return a
          reference to the
     * entity bean's component interface.
     */
    public AccountRemote findByPrimaryKey( AccountKey key)
        throws FinderException, RemoteException;

    /* This is a multiple-value finder method. The method's
          return type
     * is java.util.Collection, but the return object must
          also
     * implement a component interface.
     */
    public java.util.Collection findByAccountHolderKey(
        AccountHolderKey key) throws FinderException,
        RemoteException;

    //... remainder of remote home interface
}
```

The next code sample illustrates the same finder methods defined in a local home interface.

```
public interface AccountRemoteHome extends
        javax.ejb.EJBLocalHome{
    /* The findByPrimaryKey method is always a single-value
          finder
     * method. All single value methods must return a
          reference to the
     * entity bean's component interface.
     */
    public AccountRemote findByPrimaryKey( AccountKey key)
        throws FinderException;

    /* This is a multiple-value finder method. The method's
          return type
     * is java.util.Collection, but the return object must
          also
     * implement a component interface.
     */
    public java.util.Collection findByAccountHolderKey(
        AccountHolderKey key) throws FinderException;

    //... remainder of remote home interface
}
```

In multiple-object finder methods, the `java.util.Collection` interface allows the finder method to return duplicate entity objects. If you don't want duplicate references to entity objects in the return collection, you must write an EJB query that eliminates duplicates. This topic is addressed in greater detail in Chapter 7.

Defining home methods

Home methods are business methods that apply to an entire class of entity objects, rather than to a specific entity instance. With home methods, you can make modifications to an entire class of entities; you can modify members within an entity class identified with home method parameters; or you can generate calculated values from the attributes of multiple entities in a class. When a client application uses home methods to interact with entities, it doesn't receive references to the entities affected by the home method. Instead, home methods simply return the result of the method performed. In the following sample code, a home method is used to calculate the net worth of an account holder:

```
public interface AccountRemoteHome extends javax.ejb.EJBHome{
    /* This home method returns the net worth of an account
            holder
     * given the account holder's ID
     */
    public double getNetWorth(AccountHolderKey key) throws
            RemoteException;
    //... remainder of remote home interface
}
```

If you see a similarity between home methods and the business methods in component interfaces, you're on the right track. In fact, the rules are virtually identical for creating home methods and business methods in component interfaces. Here are the key points to remember:

- For each home method you define, you must create a corresponding method in the entity bean class. The corresponding method must be prefixed with the term **ejbHome**, followed by the name of the home method and the same arguments.

- If you define identical home methods in both a remote home and local home interface, the EJB container will use a single `ejbHome` method in the entity bean class to support both.

- If a home method is implemented in a remote interface, it must include the `java.rmi.RemoteException` in its `throws` clause. If a home method is implemented in a local home interface, it doesn't have to throw an exception. You're free to throw any application exception in a home method.

✔ If a home method is defined in the remote home interface, all the arguments and the return type must be primitive variables, or objects that implement the `java.io.Serializable` interface. A *primitive variable* is a variable of one of Java's primitive data types.

The following sample code illustrates the home method defined in a local home interface:

```
public interface AccountLocalHome extends EJBLocalHome{
    /* This home method returns the net worth of an account
         holder
     * given the account holder's ID
     */
    public double getNetWorth(AccountHolderKey key);
}
```

Creating Entity Bean Component Interfaces

Entity bean component interfaces are essentially the same as their counterparts in session beans. The component interfaces are used to supply access to business methods in an entity bean. While session bean business methods typically perform actions, entity bean business methods are typically used to modify the bean's state by invoking getters and setters on the entity bean attributes. While the business methods of an entity bean are defined in a component interface, all the getters and setters for entity bean attributes are hidden inside the bean. Consequently, client applications using an entity bean are only shown the business methods that can be performed, while the mechanics to implement those methods are hidden inside the entity bean class.

While you can create business methods that retrieve and modify entity attributes one at a time, a preferred approach is to define task-oriented business methods that perform all updates to an entity bean necessary to complete a given task. Likewise, you can retrieve all the attributes of an entity bean with a single method by creating a serializable object that can be initialized inside the entity bean and then returned to the client. These types of methods are typically called *bulk methods* because they reduce the number of method invocations necessary to perform bulk jobs.

Using the local interface

The local interface for an entity bean allows local EJB clients to access the business methods of an entity bean using pass-by-reference methods. Pass-by-reference is much more efficient than pass-by-value, which is the technique used to support remote methods. That's because pass-by-value calls pass *copies* of objects, while pass-by-reference calls pass *references* to objects. Because entity beans are typically accessed only by local clients, the local interface is often a preferred solution. See the sidebar "An argument for local interfaces" (elsewhere in this chapter) for a more detailed explanation.

There's an important side effect of pass-by-reference calls. When an object is passed by reference, changes made to the object are permanent. But when the object is passed by value, changes made are only valid for the duration of the method call. That's because changes impact the copy of the object, not the original object itself.

When defining a local interface, you have only a few simple rules that you must follow:

- ✔ The local interface must extend the `javax.ejb.EJBLocalObject`. The `EJBLocalObject` interface is implemented by the EJB container, and provides client applications with facilities to get the local home for an entity bean, to remove the entity bean from the EJB container and persistent store, and to get the primary key to an entity bean.

- ✔ None of the methods in the local interface are allowed to throw the `java.rmi.RemoteException`. This is common sense because, by definition, the local object is never remote.

- ✔ Business methods in the local interface are free to throw any application exception appropriate as defined by the EJB component developer.

The `javax.ejb.EJBLocalObject` interface already provides a method for getting the primary key of your entity bean. That means you shouldn't define a method to get the primary key class for an entity bean.

When you create a client application with a reference to a local object, you may be tempted to pass that local object to another object. Sharing local interfaces between clients is the programming equivalent of running with scissors — it's dangerous stuff and puts your EJB application at severe risk. The EJB container needs to manage transactions, security, synchronization, and a variety of other services for each individual client application, so each client application that needs to modify an entity bean should do so through its own personal, private, and confidential local interface. There is an exception: If you're accessing an entity bean only to read data, and not to modify it, then it's okay to pass it around.

The sample code in Listing 6-3 illustrates the local interface for the `Account` entity bean in the sample ATM application used throughout this book.

An argument for local interfaces

When an entity bean makes use of local interfaces, it can only be accessed from a local client. That means that they can't be accessed from remote client applications. While the EJB 1.1 specification didn't envision the creation of non-distributed entity beans, the fact of the matter is that, in practice, the vast majority of entity bean clients are local — because entity beans are typically only accessed by session beans or, in EJB 2.0, by message-driven beans.

Unfortunately, supporting remote communication for EJB components requires a lot more overhead than supporting local communication — even when both the client and the EJB component are local to each other. With EJB 1.1, local interfaces weren't an option. The consequence to entity beans was a heavy performance penalty to support remote communication that generally wasn't needed. But with

the release of the EJB 2.0 specification, it is possible to implement local and local home interfaces and thus provide your entity beans with a huge boost in performance.

Are local and local home interfaces right for you? If you only intend to access entity beans from a local source, the answer is a resounding "Yes!" There are some cases where you'll want entity beans to be accessible from remote clients; in these cases, you have to implement the remote interface. Typically, entity beans that are accessed from remote clients are used to manage lookup data. Also, remember that, because of the performance limitations of remote communication, some EJB container vendors have created solutions that automatically support local communication for remote and remote home interfaces when it's possible.

Listing 6-3   The AccountLocal Interface

```
package com.sextanttech.entities.interfaces;

import javax.ejb.EJBObject;
import java.rmi.RemoteException;

public interface AccountLocal extends EJBObject{
    /* Increment the balance on this account. */
    public void debit(double amount);

    /* Deincrement the balance on this account. */
    public void credit(double amount);

    /* Retrieve the balance for this account. */
    public double getBalance();

    /* Get a reference to the account holder for this
            account. This
     * method should be handled with care since the client
            may not have
     * appropriate security privileges to use the
            AccountHolder entity
     * bean.
```

```
      */
   public AccountHolderLocal getAccountHolder(AccountKey
         accountKey);

   /* This method is an alternative to the previous that is
         less
    * risky. Because the method only returns the key, the
         client can
    * lookup the AccountHolder and establish its own private
    * connection to the AccountHolder. While that involves
         more steps
    * in the implementation, it provides better security
         isolation and
    * transactional isolation of the AccountHolder
         reference. This
    * solution also allows the client application to
         determine whether
    * a local interface or a remote interface is best.
    */
   public AccountHolderKey getAccountHolderKey(AccountKey
         accountKey);
}
```

Using the remote interface

The remote interface for an entity bean typically presents the same methods that a local interface can, except that the remote interface also allows remote clients. Because remote interfaces must support remote communication, a couple of extra requirements must be addressed when developing the remote interface. In a nutshell, you must adhere to the following rules:

- ✔ The local interface must extend the `javax.ejb.EJBObject`. The EJBObj`ect interface is implemented by the EJB container and provides client applications with facilities to get the remote home for an entity bean, to remove the entity bean from the EJB container and persistent store, and to get the primary key to an entity bean.

- ✔ All the arguments and return values of a business method in the remote interface must be primitive data types or must implement the `java.io.Serializable` interface. This requirement is necessary so that the values held by the arguments or return value can be transported across a network.

- ✔ Every business method in the local interface must include the `java.rmi.RemoteException` in its throws clause. The EJB container will throw a `RemoteException` to the client application whenever a system-level error occurs during a business method invocation.

- ✔ Business methods in the remote interface are free to throw any application exception appropriate as defined by the EJB component developer.

In Listing 6-4, the `AccountRemote` interface presents the same business methods to client applications as its `AccountLocal` counterpart, but allows remote clients to access the entity bean's resources. There are only a couple of extra requirements in defining the remote interface — I've highlighted the differences in bold.

Listing 6-4   The AccountRemote Interface

```
package com.sextanttech.entities.interfaces;

import javax.ejb.EJBObject;
import java.rmi.RemoteException;

public interface AccountRemote extends EJBObject{
    /* Increment the balance on this account. */
    public void debit(double amount) throws RemoteException;

    /* Deincrement the balance on this account. */
    public void credit(double amount) throws RemoteException;

    /* Retrieve the balance for this account. */
    public double getBalance() throws RemoteException;

    /* Get a reference to the account holder for this
            account. This
     * method should be handled with care since the client
            may not have
     * appropriate security privileges to use the
            AccountHolder entity
     * bean.
     */
    public AccountHolderRemote getAccountHolder(AccountKey
            accountKey) throws RemoteException;

    /* This method is an alternative to the previous that is
            less
     * risky. Because the method only returns the key, the
            client can
     * lookup the AccountHolder and establish its own private
     * connection to the AccountHolder. While that involves
            more steps
     * in the implementation, it provides better security
            isolation and
     * transactional isolation of the AccountHolder
            reference.
     */
    public AccountHolderKey getAccountHolderKey(AccountKey
            accountKey) throws RemoteException;
}
```

Building a Primary Key Class

The *primary key class* for an entity bean is used by the EJB container to uniquely identify an entity bean object. Each EJB object is uniquely identified by its primary key object and the home interface reference. Thus, an instance of a primary key class must be unique within a given home interface. With the primary key object, your client application has the ability to find the entity bean — or (indirectly) to use the key as an argument in an EJB query that finds related entity beans.

The rules for creating a primary key class vary depending upon whether the entity bean takes advantage of container-managed persistence (CMP) or not. In this chapter, I'm dealing specifically with EJB components that participate in CMP. The rules for creating primary keys using the CMP model are

- The primary key class must implement the `java.io.Serializable` interface, which allows the class to be serialized and transported across a network or written to a database.

- The primary key class must include sufficient attributes to establish a unique identity for the entity bean. The attributes used to establish identity in the primary key must also be present in the entity bean class. The deployment descriptor is used to map relationships between an entity bean class's attributes and the attributes of a primary key.

- The attributes in a primary key class are declared `public`, which allows the EJB container to identify and initialize the primary key class attributes. While a primary key class can provide getter methods to retrieve the values of primary key attributes, it shouldn't provide setter methods.

- The primary key class must override the `Object.equals` method. The `equals` method is inherited by all Java objects, and it is used to compare two objects for equality. The details for overriding the `object.equals` method are illustrated in Listing 6-5.

- The primary key class must override the `Object.hashCode()` method. The `hashCode` method is inherited by all Java objects, and is used to obtain a value called a *hash code*. Java uses hash codes to organize objects; thus, a hash code doesn't have to be a unique value — instead it must be *well distributed*, meaning that for any group of objects the value of hash code used to sort those objects is relatively close to their natural order. That may sound complex in theory, but in practice it's quite simple.

- Because the values of a primary key typically don't change after they're created, primary key classes don't generally have setter methods. Instead the values of the class are set in the constructor.

Because Java's primitive type wrapper classes (java.lang.Integer, java.lang.Long, java.lang.Char, and so on) all implement java.io. Serializable, override Object.equals(), and override Object. hashCode(), they're all legal primary keys. If you're looking for a simple primary key, consider using one of these classes for your primary key. Just remember that the object must map to a field in your entity bean class, and be sufficient to uniquely identify the entity bean.

While the attributes of a primary key class are public, that doesn't mean they should be set by anyone. In fact, after a container sets the attributes of a primary key class, the attributes should be considered immutable. Changing primary key attributes after they're created will undermine the client application's ability to interact with an EJB component.

The attributes of an entity bean primary key class must correspond with attributes of the entity bean class.

There are two types of primary keys: single-field primary keys and compound primary keys. *Single-field primary keys* contain only a single field, such as an integer, to identify the primary key. The single-field primary key only maps to a single field in the entity bean class and is the simplest to create, but not by much. And while a single field may be sufficient to establish the uniqueness of an entity bean, sometimes it is necessary to use a compound primary key to get the job done.

Compound primary keys contain multiple fields, the composite of which determine the identity of an EJB component. Each field in a compound maps to a different field in an entity bean class. Overriding the hashCode method for a compound primary key requires a few more steps than the single-field primary key, as does overriding the equals method. The code in Listing 6-5 illustrates the creation of a compound primary key for the Account class.

Listing 6-5   The AccountKey Class

```
package com.sextanttech.entities.interfaces;

public class AccountKey {
    public long createDate;
    public long accountId;

    public AccountKey(long createDate, long accountId) {
        this.createDate = createDate;
        this.accountId = accountId;
    }

    public long getCreateDate() {
        return createDate;
    }

    public long getAccountId() {
```

```
        return accountId;
}

/* This is an example of overriding the equals method in
 * java.lang.Object.*/
public boolean equals(Object obj) {

    /* First determine if the obj parameter is the same
       type as this
     * object using the instanceof operator. If the
       object is null,
     * or not the same type, the two objects are not
       equal.*/
    if(obj == null || obj instanceof AccountKey){
        return false;
    }
    /* If the two objects are equal, you can cast obj to
       an
     * AccountKey to finish the equality test.
     */
    AccountKey other = (AccountKey) obj;
    // The final step is a matter of comparing the
       primary key fields for equality.
    if( this.accountId == other.accountId &&
        this.createDate == other.createDate){
        return true;
    }
    return false;
}

/* This is an example of overriding the Object.hashCode()
       method.*/
public int hashCode() {
    /* A hashCode is derived from the values of fields in
       a class.
     * To get a reasonable hashcode, the easiest approach
       is to
     * convert all fields into a single string, and then
       get the
     * hashcode of that String. The following code
       illustrates this
     * strategy using a StringBuffer class.
     */
    StringBuffer sb = new StringBuffer();

    // append the fields
    sb.append(this.accountId).append(this.createDate);

    // Convert to a String and get the hash code.
```

(continued)

Listing 6-5 *(continued)*

```
        return sb.toString().hashCode();      }

    /* For completeness, I also override the toString method
            to return
     * a meaningful name for this primary key. In this case
            the
     * meaningful value is the accountId.
     */
    public String toString(){
        StringBuffer sb = new StringBuffer();
        sb.append(accountId);
        return sb.toString();
    }
}
```

Constructing the Entity Bean Class

At the heart of every good entity bean component is an entity bean class. The *entity bean class* is a bustling center of activity. While the entity bean class holds the potential for complexity, when you take advantage of container-managed persistence (CMP), the EJB container does most of the work for you. The result is a development task that's largely a process of connecting the dots. In the case of the entity bean, connecting the dots means providing implementations to business methods and home interface methods within the entity bean class. There are seven important tasks to perform when developing an entity bean class:

- ✔ **Implement the lifecycle methods of the** `javax.ejb.EntityBean` **interface.** These methods are invoked by the EJB container at various points in an entity bean's lifecycle, and can be used to respond to their corresponding lifecycle events.

- ✔ **Define the CMP fields for each attribute of the entity bean class.** These fields contain the information that defines the entity bean, such as its primary key and other data that are relevant to the entity that the entity bean models.

- ✔ **Define** `ejbCreate<METHOD>(args)` **and** `ejbPostCreate<METHOD>` `(args)` **methods for each** `create` **method in an entity bean's home interface.** These methods get invoked by the EJB container when their corresponding `create` methods are invoked from a local home or remote home interface.

- ✔ **Define the container-managed relationship (CMR) fields of the entity bean.** These fields determine the relationships between different entity bean components.

✔ **Define the** `ejbSelect<METHOD>(args)` **for the entity bean.** These methods are used by an entity bean to obtain references to other entity bean classes using the EJB Query Language that I cover in Chapter 7. While `ejbSelect<METHOD>(args)` methods can't be published outside the entity bean class, they can be invoked from other methods within the entity bean class.

✔ **Define the** `ejbHome<METHOD>(args)` **for the entity bean class.** There should be one `ejbHome<METHOD>(args)` for each home method defined in an EJB component's remote home or local home interface.

✔ **Define the business methods for the entity bean class.** There should be one business method implementation in the entity bean class for each business method defined in the entity bean's local or remote interface.

In addition to the preceding seven major steps, there are a couple of other small but important tasks applied to all entity beans:

✔ Entity bean classes taking advantage of CMP 2.0 need to be declared `public` and `abstract`. This requirement forces the EJB Container to provide all the implementation code necessary to facilitate CMP and CMR services.

✔ All entity beans must implement the `javax.ejb.EntityBean` interface. The `EntityBean` interface is what makes an entity bean an entity bean.

✔ All entity beans must define a constructor that takes no arguments. This rule is a basic requirement that allows the EJB container to create new instances of the entity bean class using Java's reflection capability.

These three basic requirements are illustrated in the following code snippet from the `AccountBean` class:

```
package com.sextanttech.entities.implementations;

import javax.ejb.EntityBean;

public abstract class AccountBean implements EntityBean {

    public AccountBean() {} // a noargs constructor
}
```

Implementing lifecycle methods

Every entity bean is endowed by its `javax.ejb.EntityBean` interface with certain inalienable lifecycle methods. Lifecycle methods are invoked by an EJB container in response to lifecycle events in an EJB component's lifecycle. These methods are referred to as *callbacks* because they're a way for the EJB container to callback to the entity bean class and provide you with an opportunity to respond to the lifecycle event. Entity beans have seven lifecycle methods:

- ✔ `setEntityContext(EntityContext ctx)`: This method is invoked by the EJB container after an entity bean object is created and before it enters the entity bean pool. In addition to setting the `EntityContext` for this entity bean, you can also use this method to initialize application resources used by the bean instance. For more information on this topic, see the sidebar "Accessing application resources."

- ✔ `ejbLoad`: This method is invoked by the EJB container to synchronize the CMP fields of the entity bean with data from a database. The method is invoked after the data is retrieved from the database. You can use the method to perform calculations based on the data or to prepare the data for use by EJB clients. For example, if you compress data before storing it in a database, you can use the `ejbLoad` method to expand the data so that it's usable by entity bean clients.

- ✔ `ejbStore`: This method is invoked by the EJB container to synchronize the entity bean and an underlying database by storing the data in the entity bean to the database. The method is invoked before the store method takes place and gives you the opportunity to prepare CMP field data in the entity bean for database storage. If, for example, you compress data before it is stored in the database, this method is the place to perform the compression.

- ✔ `ejbPassivate`: This method is invoked by the EJB container before the data in an entity bean is cached. When entity bean data is cached, it is stored in persistent storage, such as in a file on a computer hard drive, and the entity bean class is cleaned and returned to the entity bean pool. You can use this method to prepare data in an entity bean for passivation.

- ✔ `ejbActivate`: This method is invoked by the EJB container after the data from an entity bean is retrieved from cache and restored to an entity bean class. If you've modified the data prior to storage — perhaps compressing or encrypting it — you can use this method to perform the reverse operation so that it's ready for use by a client application.

- ✔ `ejbRemove`: The EJB container invokes this method before it removes an EJB object. In turn, the container only removes an object when a `remove` method is invoked from the client application, either on the local home, remote home, or a component interface for the entity bean. When an EJB object is removed, the instance data is removed from the EJB container and the underlying database. This method gives the EJB component developer the opportunity to respond to the `remove` method before it is completed.

- ✔ `unsetEntityContext`: This method is invoked by the EJB container before an entity bean object is removed from the EJB container. EJB objects are removed from the container when the size of the object pool is reduced, or when an exception is caused during the invocation of a method in the entity bean. When the unsetEntityContext method is invoked, you can assume that all of the attributes associating an entity bean with the state of an entity instance are nullified. Thus, the key purpose for this method is to prepare the entity bean object for garbage collection by dereferencing any application resources that were initialized in the setEntityContext method.

While you have to implement lifecycle methods, you aren't required to perform any operations in any of the lifecycle methods. They're there as a convenience in case you need them. Listing 6-6 illustrates the lifecycle methods implemented by the entity bean class for the AccountBean.

If you have a field in an entity bean that is calculated based on the values of the bean's attributes, then you can calculate the value of the field in the ejbLoad method. Such fields are referred to as *computed fields*. When the ejbLoad method is invoked, that means that the values of your entity bean fields have been set and any calculations necessary to populate the values of computed fields can begin.

Listing 6-6   The AccountBean Lifecycle Methods

```
package com.sextanttech.entities.implementations;

import javax.ejb.EntityBean;
import javax.ejb.EntityContext;

public abstract class AccountBean implements EntityBean {

    /* This attribute stores the EntityContext for the
            duration of the
     * entity bean's life. Is set before instance information
            is
     * associated with an entity bean, and remains after
            instance
     * information is disassociated from the entity bean.
     */
    private EntityContext context;

    public void setEntityContext(EntityContext ctx){
        this.context = ctx; // context is set
    }

    public void unsetEntityContext(){
        this.context = null; // context is nullified
    }

    public void ejbRemove(){} // no operations performed

    public void ejbActivate(){} // no operations performed
```

(continued)

Listing 6-6 *(continued)*

```
    public void ejbPassivate(){} // no operations performed

    public void ejbLoad(){} // no operations performed

    public void ejbStore(){} // no operations performed

    //... Remainder for AccountBean class
}
```

Defining CMP fields

Container-managed persistence (CMP) fields are fields used to manage the state of an entity bean. Any attribute of an entity bean class that describes an instance of the entity is a CMP field. The EJB 2.0 specification defines new rules for implementing CMP fields that are substantially different from the rules in the EJB 1.1 specification. This is also one place where EJB beans using bean-managed persistence (BMP) diverge from the CMP model. The information in this section applies specifically to CMP 2.0 entity beans.

The EJB container provides the implementation for each CMP field by subclassing your entity bean class. To maintain the container's flexibility in implementing these fields, your responsibility as an EJB component developer is simply to define abstract getter and setter methods for each CMP field. Here are the basic rules for CMP fields:

- **Each CMP field must have a getter method and a setter method.** A getter method is a method prefixed with the term **get** followed by the name of the CMP field with the first character uppercased. For example, with the CMP field `accountBalance`, the getter method would be `getAccountBalance`. Likewise, the setter method is prefixed by the term **set** followed by the name of the CMP field with the first character uppercased, as in `setAccountBalance`. The getter method must have a return type that is the same as the CMP field type. The setter method must accept an argument that is the same type as the CMP field.

- **CMP field getters and setters must be declared as** `public` **and** `abstract`, **and can't be declared** `final`. The getter and setter methods are ultimately implemented by the EJB container when the entity bean is subclassed — these requirements support that process.

- **The CMP field name is identified in the entity bean's deployment descriptor.** The field isn't defined in the entity bean class. When the EJB container subclasses the entity bean class, it will supply the CMP field and the getter and setter implementations. So, continuing the previous example, there would be no `accountBalance` field in the class you define. However, when the container subclasses your class it will supply the `accountBalance` field.

✔ **The primary key fields of an entity bean must not be changed after the entity bean is created.** Thus, setters for primary key fields in an entity bean shouldn't be defined in the entity bean's component interfaces.

Accessing application resources

Application resources are utilities provided by you or by third parties. They could be tools or products that facilitate performing tasks that are outside the normal workflow of a business process, but which enable services used throughout the workflow. These services are typically not provided explicitly by the EJB container, and thus must be added into the workflow of your EJB application. Some examples of application resources are JDBC drivers, logging utilities, and software testing utilities.

Making use of application resources in an EJB application requires a few extra steps, but isn't overly difficult. The first task is to register the resource with JNDI ENC so that it can be accessed by your EJB application. I cover this task in Chapter 13. After you've finished that, you can use lifecycle methods to access application resources from within an EJB component. For entity beans, a simple example follows:

```
public abstract class
    AccountBean implements
    javax.ejb.EntityBean{
  private EntityContext con-
text;
  private ResourceType
resource; // A reference to
some resource.
  public AccountBean(){}

setEntityContext(EntityCont
ext ctx){
    this.context = ctx;
    try{
    InitialContext ic = new
InitialContext();
```

```
    Object obj =
ic.lookup("myApplicationRes
ource");
    this.resource =
(ResourceType)
javax.rmi.narrow(obj,

Class.forName("fully.quali-
fied.ResourceType"));
    }
    catch(Exception e){
    /* Handle
javax.naming.NamingExceptio
n for JNDI and
    *
java.lang.ClassCastExceptio
n for RMI narrowing opera-
tion.
    */
    }
}
  public
unsetEntityContext(){
    this.context = null;
    this.resource = null;
}
}
```

Remember that, because entity bean objects are pooled when not in use, references to generic application resources don't have to be released when `ejbPassivate` is invoked or restored when `ejbActivate` is invoked. The opposite is true for stateful session beans because a stateful session bean class isn't pooled during object passivation.

The name of a CMP field is defined in the deployment descriptor, and must be consistent with the naming of the abstract getter and setter methods you define for the field. The getters and setters of CMP fields for the AccountBean class are illustrated in Listing 6-7.

Listing 6-7   CMP Fields of the AccountBean Class

```java
package com.sextanttech.entities.implementations;

import javax.ejb.EntityBean;
import javax.ejb.EntityContext;

public abstract class AccountBean implements EntityBean {

    // Get the balance for this account.
    public abstract double getAccountBalance();

    // Set the balance for this account.
    public abstract void setAccountBalance(double balance);

    // Get the accountId for this account.
    public abstract long getAccountId();

    // Set the accountId for this account.
    public abstract void setAccountId(long accountId);

    // Get the creation date for this account.
    public abstract long getCreateDate();

    // Set the creation date for this account.
    public abstract void setCreateDate(long date);
    //... Remainder of AccountBean class.
}
```

The CMP fields of an entity bean class are defined according to the same rules for simple JavaBeans.

Defining CMR fields

Container-managed relationship (CMR) fields are entity bean fields that maintain the relationships between an entity bean instance and other entity beans. While the actual implementation of a CMR field is quite simple, some science is needed to decide what types of CMR fields to implement. In a nutshell, the CMR fields define relationships between entity beans like foreign keys define relationships between entities in database tables.

CMR fields are a construct of the EJB 2.0 specification, and did not exist in the EJB 1.1 specification. One very important feature of CMR fields is that they can only define relationships between entity beans in the same local context. CMR fields can't be used to define relationships between entity beans that aren't located in the same EJB container.

The first task for defining CMR fields is to decide how this entity bean relates to other entity beans in the EJB application. This process is called *E-R modeling* — Entity-Relationship modeling — and is traditionally the domain of database programmers and database administrators. Defining relationships between entity beans will be a lot easier if you have some background in database development or have done E-R modeling in the past. If you haven't, brush up on the topic and seek the assistance of someone familiar with the process.

You can get off to a good start with E-R modeling by getting *SQL For Dummies*, by Allen G. Taylor (published by Hungry Minds, Inc.). Be sure to pay close attention to the rules of normalization, which are critical to developing quality E-R diagrams.

Even if you have a background in E-R modeling, you'll find that entity bean relationships are different from database relationships. Entity bean relationships are broken into two broad categories: unidirectional relationships and bidirectional relationships.

Unidirectional relationships are entity bean relationships that can only be navigated in one direction. For example, it may be legal to navigate a relationship from an `AccountHolder` to an `Account`, but not from an `Account` to an `AccountHolder`. With unidirectional relationships, the CMR fields are defined in the entity bean class that has the right to navigate the relationship. The class without the right doesn't contain the CMR field.

The second category of CMR relationships is bidirectional relationships. *Bidirectional relationships* can be navigated in both directions; there are no restrictions on navigating the relationship to either participating entity bean. With bidirectional relationships, a CMR field for the relationship is defined for each entity bean that participates in the relationship.

Within the two broad categories of entity bean relationships, there are three types of *cardinality*. Cardinality refers to the number of participants allowed on each side of a relationship. You'll also see the term *multiplicity* used in the context of a relationship's cardinality. While cardinality refers to the number of participants on each side of a relationship, multiplicity applies to the number of participants on one side of the relationship. The three types of cardinality are

✔ **One-to-One relationships:** This type of relationship restricts the number of entity bean instances participating in the relationship to one instance on each side of the relationship. If a relationship is one-to-one, the CMR field used to represent the relationship must be the local interface of the entity bean that this bean is related to. For example, if there were a one-to-one relationship from an `Account` to an `AccountHolder`, the `AccountBean` class would have a CMR field with the `AccountHolderLocal` interface type.

✔ **One-to-Many relationships:** This type of relationship allows a given entity bean instance to be related to many entity bean instances of another entity bean type. The relationship is implemented by creating a CMR field that has a `Collection` type on one side of the relationship, and a CMR field with the type of the local interface on the other side of the relationship. The collection CMR field can be either the `java.util.Set` interface or the `java.util.Collection` interface. In unidirectional relationships, one of the CMR fields in the relationship is not implemented.

✔ **Many-to-Many relationships:** This type of relationship allows entity beans of one type to be related to many instances of an entity bean of another type. Likewise, entity beans of the other type can be related to many entity beans of the first type. The relationship is implemented by creating CMR fields that are a `Collection` type on both sides of the relationship. The collection CMR field can be either the `java.util.Set` interface or the `java.util.Collection` interface. Again, in unidirectional relationships, one of the CMR fields in the relationship is not implemented.

To assist in understanding how CMR relationships work, take a look at Table 6-1. This table illustrates how each type of CMR relationship is implemented, given two hypothetical entity beans: `EntityA` and `EntityB`.

Table 6-1	Understanding Container-Managed Relationships	
Relationship	*EntityA CMR Field Type*	*EntityB CMR Field Type*
One-to-one unidirectional	EntityB local interface type	None
One-to-one bidirectional	EntityB local interface type	EntityA local interface type
One-to-many unidirectional	`java.util.Collection` or `java.util.Set`	None
One-to-many bidirectional	`java.util.Collection` or `java.util.Set`	EntityA local interface type
Many-to-many unidirectional	`java.util.Collection` or `java.util.Set`	None
Many-to-many bidirectional	`java.util.Collection` or `java.util.Set`	`java.util.Collection` or `java.util.Set`

The hard part of working with container-managed relationships is deciding how entity beans should be related to each other. After that decision is made, the easy part is implementing the solution. The actual implementation of a CMR field is roughly the equivalent of implementing a CMP field. The rules are

✔ Bean developers must define abstract getters and setters for the CMR field. The getter is prefixed with the term **get** followed by the CMR field name. The setter method is prefixed with the term **set** followed by the CMR field name.

✔ Setter methods must accept either the local interface type of the related entity bean or a collection interface (either `java.util.Set` or `java.util.Collection`). Getter methods must return the local interface type of the related entity or a collection interface. The type of interface to be used is determined based on the cardinality of the relationship. (If the bean is related to a single entity, the CMR field should be that entity bean's local interface; otherwise it should be a collection.)

✔ The CMR getter and setter methods must be defined as `public` and `abstract`, and can't be `final`. That's because the EJB container will provide the actual implementation of a CMR field in a subclass of the entity bean that you create.

✔ The name and type of each CMR field are defined in the entity bean's deployment descriptor. Name and type of the CMR field defined in the deployment descriptor must be consistent with the abstract getter and setter methods provided for the CMR field in the entity bean class.

When a CMR field type is `java.util.Collection`, it is possible for the CMR field to hold more than one reference to the same entity bean instance. On the other hand, if you use the `java.util.Set` interface, the CMR field can't contain duplicate references to the related entity bean instances. Except when some special case suggests otherwise, a CMR field shouldn't contain duplicate references to the same entity bean instance. Thus, `java.util.Set` is a safe way to prevent duplicate entries in the CMR fields.

The CMR field itself is created by the EJB container and not defined by you directly. All you have to do is define the abstract getter and setter methods, and create an entry for the CMR field in the entity bean's deployment descriptor. Listing 6-8 illustrates the completed CMR getter and setter definitions for the `AccountBean` in the sample ATM application I use throughout the book. In the sample application, the `AccountBean` has a many-to-one relationship with the `AccountHolderBean`. That means that each account holder can have many accounts, but an account can only have one account holder. Consequently the CMR field in the `AccountBean` can only hold a single value of type `AccountHolderLocal`.

Listing 6-8   CMR Fields for the AccountBean Class

```
package com.sextanttech.entities.implementations;

import javax.ejb.EntityBean;
import javax.ejb.EntityContext;
import
          com.sextanttech.entities.interfaces.AccountHolderL
          ocal;

public abstract class AccountBean implements EntityBean {

    /* This is a CMR getter for the AccountBean. There is one
     * AccountHolder for each Account, and many Accounts for
          each
     * AccountHolder.
     */
    public abstract AccountHolderLocal getAccountHolder();

    /* This is a CMR setter for the AccountHolder. There is
          one
     * AccountHolder for each Account, and many Accounts for
          each
     * AccountHolder.
     */
    public abstract void setAccountHolder(AccountHolderLocal
          owner);

    //...And now for the rest of the entity bean class
}
```

Listing 6-9 illustrates the opposite side of the one-to-many relationship between the `AccountHolderBean` and the `AccountBean`. In this case, because the `AccountHolderBean` can hold multiple accounts, the CMR field type is a `java.util.Set`. By using the `Set` interface, I prevent the `AccountHolderBean` from holding duplicate references to `AccountBean` instances. In this case, because both the `AccountHolderBean` and the `AcccountBean` hold CMR references to each other, the relationship is bidirectional.

Listing 6-9   CMR Fields for the AccountHolderBean Class

```
package com.sextanttech.entities.implementations;

import javax.ejb.EntityBean;
import javax.ejb.EntityContext;
import java.util.Set;

public abstract class AccountHolderBean implements
          EntityBean{
    /* This is a CMR getter for the Account bean. There are
          many
```

```
      * Account instances for each AccountHolderBean.
      */
     public abstract Collection getAccounts();

     /* This is a CMR setter for the Account bean. There are
         many
      * Account instances for each AccountHolderBean.
      */
     public abstract void setAccounts(Collection accounts);

     //...And now for the rest of the entity bean class
}
```

Using dependent value classes

Dependent value classes are CMP classes used by an EJB component developer to separate the internal representation of data in an entity bean from meaningful business representations of that data. In Chapter 4, dependent value classes were used to encapsulate the components of a Deposit transaction and a Withdraw transaction. Instead of performing a Deposit with several different arguments, a class called com.sextanttech.transactions.DepositEnvelope was created that contained all the elements necessary to perform a deposit. If desired, this DepositEnvelope class could be passed all the way to an account entity bean, where it would be inspected by the entity bean and used to update the appropriate CMP fields.

Dependent value classes are useful because they allow an EJB component developer to perform business methods with objects that make sense in a business context, while hiding the internal implementation of the objects that perform those business methods. Thus, if the internal definition of an entity bean were to change — perhaps with the renaming of fields or the addition or removal of elements — the entity bean's clients would be unaffected by those changes due to the fact that they used dependent objects to communicate instead of the entity bean's abstract getters and setters.

While the EJB specification is very open with how dependent value objects are implemented, there are a couple of rules to follow; dependent value objects

- Must be declared public
- Shouldn't be used in CMR fields
- Must implement the java.io. Serializable interface

In addition to those requirements, some recommend that dependent objects be *immutable*, which means that their attributes can't be changed after they're set. By following this advice, you wouldn't supply any setter methods inside the dependent value object. The reason for making the dependent value object immutable is that it is a copy of an entity bean's data — not a reference to the data. Thus, changing the attributes of a dependent value object doesn't result in changes to the entity bean from whence it came.

Defining ejbSelect methods

An entity bean's `ejbSelect` methods are abstract method definitions that can be invoked by the entity bean class to perform queries on other entity beans in the EJB container. The `ejbSelect` method is like a private finder method that can be invoked from within an entity bean instance. Hence, you can use `ejbSelect` methods as a shorthand tool for accessing other entity beans. But unlike finder methods, `ejbSelect` methods can also query data from within other entity beans, which means that you can use them to retrieve the values for fields in other entity beans without retrieving the entity beans themselves.

The guidelines for creating `ejbSelect` methods are simple:

- Each `ejbSelect` method must be prefixed with the term **ejbSelect**.

- All `ejbSelect` methods must be declared `public` and `abstract`. As with CMR and CMP fields, the EJB container provides the implementation for an `ejbSelect` method.

- Each `ejbSelect` method is backed by an EJB Query Language query, which is supplied in the entity bean's deployment descriptor. Chapter 7 provides background on writing EJB Query Language queries.

- Each `ejbSelect` method must include the `javax.ejb.FinderException` in its `throws` clause.

- The `ejbSelect` methods must not be defined in an entity bean's component or home interfaces. They're for use only inside the entity bean class.

- The `ejbSelect` methods can return values that correspond to any CMP or CMR field type in the entity bean class.

- Each `ejbSelect` method can return either a single object or multiple objects. If the `ejbSelect` method is a single-object select, the return type should be the local home interface of the selected entity. If the `ejbSelect` method is a multi-object select, the return type should be either a `java.util.Set` interface or a `java.util.Collection` interface.

Because `ejbSelect` methods are used to initialize CMR fields, there should be — at the very least — an `ejbSelect` method defined for each CMR field in the entity bean class. In Listing 6-10, an `ejbSelect` method is defined in the `AccountBean` for use with initializing the `AccountHolder` CMR field. While the number of requirements on a `ejbSelect` field may seem daunting, the actual implementation of the method is simple — as you can see from Listing 6-10.

Listing 6-10 ejbSelect Methods for the AccountBean

```
package com.sextanttech.entities.implementations;

import javax.ejb.EntityBean;
```

```
import javax.ejb.EntityContext;
import
          com.sextanttech.entities.interfaces.AccountHolderL
          ocal;
import com.sextanttech.entities.interfaces.AccountKey;
import java.util.Collection;
import javax.ejb.FinderException;

public abstract class AccountBean implements EntityBean {

    /* This method is a single-value ejbSelect method that
          returns a
     * reference to the AccountHolder that owns this account.
          The
     * method uses the primary key for the Account class as
          an argument
     * so that the EJB QL query can find the corresponding
     * AccountHolder class.
     */
    public abstract AccountHolderLocal
          ejbSelectAccountHolder(
        AccountKey key) throws FinderException;

    //...Remainder of entity bean class.
}
```

When using multi-value `ejbSelect` methods, remember that the type of collection you use may determine whether the collection can return duplicates or not. If you use the `java.util.Collection`, the `ejbSelect` method may contain duplicate entries. On the other hand, the `java.util.Set` collection doesn't allow duplicate entries.

Adding ejbCreate and ejbPostCreate methods

The EJB container uses `ejbCreate<METHOD>(<args>)` and `ejbPostCreate <METHOD>(<args>)` methods to manage the process of creating an entity bean instance. EJB bean developers are responsible for initializing CMP fields with arguments supplied in the `ejbCreate<METHOD>` method. In the `ejbPostCreate<METHOD>`, the entity bean provider is responsible for initializing the values of CMR fields in the entity bean class.

Here are the guidelines to follow when defining these methods:

✔ For each `create` method you define in an entity bean's home interface, you must define corresponding `ejbCreate<METHOD>(<args>)` in the entity bean class. The `ejbCreate<METHOD>(<args>)` method is prefixed with the term **ejbCreate**, followed by the signature for a `create` method in the home interface. For example, given the `create` method `createAccount(long clientId)` in a home interface, you must define an `ejbCreateAccount(long clientId)` method in the entity bean class.

✔ In the `ejbCreate<METHOD>(<args>)`, you can use the arguments of the method and any calculated values to initialize the CMP fields of the entity bean class using the abstract CMP setter methods. At the very least, you must initialize all the CMP fields that are mapped to the primary key of the entity bean instance.

✔ The `ejbCreate` method must be defined as `public` and can't be declared `static` or `final`. It must also include a `javax.ejb.Create Exception` in its `throws` clause.

✔ For each `create` method you define in an entity bean's home interface, you must define a corresponding `ejbPostCreate<METHOD>(<args>)` method in the entity bean class. The `ejbPostCreate<METHOD>(<args>)` method is prefixed with the term **ejbPostCreate**, followed by the signature of a `create<METHOD>(<args>)` method in the home interface. For example, given the `create` method `createAccount( long clientId)` in a home interface, you must define the method `ejbPostCreate Account( long clientId)`.

✔ Using the arguments in the `ejbPostCreate<METHOD>(<args>)` method, the entity bean developer must initialize the CMR fields for the entity bean. There are two simple ways to initialize a CMR field:

   • The first and most direct method is to pass a local interface to the related entity bean into the `create` method for the new entity. Then, during the `ejbPostCreate` method, you can assign the local interface of the related entity to the CMR field by using the appropriate CMR setter.

   • The second method is to pass the primary key of the related entity to the `create` method of the new entity bean. Then, from the `ejbPostCreate` method, invoke an `ejbSelect` method that takes the primary key as an argument and returns a local interface. These can then be assigned to the appropriate CMR field by using the CMR setter method. This technique is illustrated in Listing 6-11.

✔ The `ejbPostCreate` method must be defined as `public` and can't be declared `static` or `final`. It must also include a `javax.ejb.CreateException` in its `throws` clause.

Tying everything back to the example `AccountBean` class, Listing 6-11 illustrates the standard definitions of `ejbCreate` and `ejbPostCreate` methods. Remember that there must be one `ejbCreate` and one `ejbPostCreate` method corresponding to each `create` method in the entity bean's home interface. Because there are three `create` methods in the `AccountBean` class's home interface, there must be three `ejbCreate` methods and three `ejbPostCreate` methods.

If you define both a remote home and a local home interface that contain `create` methods with the same signatures, they will share the same `ejbCreate` and `ejbPostCreate` methods in the entity bean class.

Listing 6-11   The ejbCreate and ejbPostCreate Methods

```
package com.sextanttech.entities.implementations;

import javax.ejb.EntityBean;
import javax.ejb.EntityContext;
import
        com.sextanttech.entities.interfaces.AccountHolderL
        ocal;
import com.sextanttech.entities.interfaces.AccountKey;
import com.sextanttech.entities.interfaces.AccountHolderKey;
import com.sextanttech.util.IdManager;
import java.util.Collection;
import java.util.Date;
import javax.ejb.FinderException;
import javax.ejb.CreateException;

public abstract class AccountBean implements EntityBean {
    public void ejbCreateAccount(AccountHolderKey key) throws
        CreateException {
        Date created = new Date();

        // Create Date CMP field set
        this.setCreateDate(created.getTime());

        // AccountId CMP field set
        this.setAccountId(IdManager.getNewId());

    }

    public void ejbPostCreateAccount(AccountHolderKey key)
            throws
        CreateException{
        try{

            this.setAccountHolder(ejbSelectAccountHolder(key))
            ;
        }
        catch( FinderException e){
            throw new CreateException();
        }
    }

    public void ejbCreateAccount(AccountHolderKey key, float
            balance)
```

(continued)

Listing 6-11 *(continued)*

```
      throws CreateException {

      Date created = new Date();
      // Create Date CMP field set
      this.setCreateDate(created.getTime());

      // AccountId CMP field set
      this.setAccountId(IdManager.getNewId());

      this.setBalance(balance); // Small account balance is
          set
  }

  public void ejbPostCreateAccount(AccountHolderKey key,
          float
      balance) throws CreateException{
      try{

          this.setAccountHolder(ejbSelectAccountHolder(key))
          ;
      }
      catch( FinderException e){
          throw new CreateException();
      }
  }

  public void ejbCreateAccount(AccountHolderKey key, double
          balance)
      throws CreateException {

      Date created = new Date();
      // Create Date CMP field set
      this.setCreateDate(created.getTime());
      // AccountId CMP field set
      this.setAccountId(IdManager.getNewId());

      // Large account balance is set
      this.setBalance(balance);
  }


  public void ejbPostCreateAccount( AccountHolderKey key,
          double
      balance) throws CreateException{
      try{

          this.setAccountHolder(ejbSelectAccountHolder(key))
          ;
      }
```

```
        catch( FinderException e){
            throw new CreateException();
        }
    }
}
```

As you review the code, notice that I've added a special utility class called `IdManager`. This class defines a single `static` method called `getNewId` that returns a new unique ID for the account number. In the case of this application, the internal implementation of the `getNewId` doesn't matter. In the real world, the solution might be rather complex, but I've just made a simple counter for this application. The important consideration is that account IDs should be unique, so it makes sense to have a single class that manages the IDs for all entity beans.

Implementing business methods

As usual, I like to save the best part for last. The business methods in an entity bean class are the methods used by the entity bean's component interface to make modifications to an entity bean, or to retrieve information from the entity bean. Two different categories of business methods are in the entity bean class:

✔ `ejbHome<METHOD>` methods are business methods defined in the entity bean's local home or remote home interfaces. For each home method defined in a home interface, you must define a corresponding `ejbHome<METHOD>` in the entity bean class. The method must be declared `public` and can't be `static` or `final`. Aside from the **ejbHome** prefix, the home method must have the same signature as the home method it corresponds with. While an `ejbHome<METHOD>` can throw application exceptions, it isn't legal to throw a `java.rmi.RemoteException`. Violators will be prosecuted.

✔ Standard business methods are invoked from an entity bean's component interface. The signature of a standard business method must match the signature of the corresponding method defined in the entity bean's component interface. Standard business methods must also be `public`, and can't be declared `static` or `final`. Like the `ejbHome<METHOD>` methods, standard business methods can throw any application exception, but aren't allowed to throw the `java.rmi.RemoteException`.

If a business method or an `ejbHome<METHOD>` encounters a system level error, it can throw a `javax.ejb.EJBException`.

Because business methods are invoked after an entity bean is created — and after all CMP and CMR fields are initialized — they can legally interact with any other method defined in the entity bean class. That includes CMP getters and setters, CMR getters and setters, and `ejbSelect` methods. Basically, business methods have the full resources of the entity bean class at their disposal.

When you retrieve values from CMR fields, it's a good idea to invoke the CMR setter first. That's because while a container will initialize the value of CMR fields, it won't maintain the value after a bean is created. Thus, in order to ensure that the information contained in a CMR field is current and accurate, you should invoke the field's setter before retrieving the field's value. When you invoke a CMR field's setter method, the container will automatically update both sides of the CMR relationship.

In the `AccountBean` class, there are three business methods and one `ejbHome <METHOD>`. The business methods are `debit`, `credit`, and `getBalance`. The `ejbHome<METHOD>` is `ejbHomeGetNetWorth`. In Listing 6-12, these methods are implemented to illustrate the process of implementing business methods.

Listing 6-12   AccountBean Business Methods

```
    package com.sextanttech.entities.implementations;

import javax.ejb.EntityBean;
import javax.ejb.EntityContext;
import
          com.sextanttech.entities.interfaces.AccountHolderL
          ocal;
import com.sextanttech.entities.interfaces.AccountKey;
import com.sextanttech.entities.interfaces.AccountHolderKey;
import com.sextanttech.entities.interfaces.AccountLocalHome;
import com.sextanttech.entities.interfaces.AccountLocal;
import com.sextanttech.util.IdManager;
import java.util.Collection;
import java.util.Date;
import javax.ejb.FinderException;
import javax.ejb.CreateException;

public abstract class AccountBean implements EntityBean {

    /* This method calculates net worth by obtaining the
            balance of
     * each account belonging to the account holder.
     */
    public double ejbHomeGetNetWorth(AccountHolderKey key){
        java.util.Set accounts;
        AccountLocalHome home;
        double netWorth = 0;
        try{
            home = (AccountLocalHome)
            context.getEJBLocalHome();
```

```
                    accounts = home.findByAccountHolderKey(key);
                    java.util.Iterator acct = accounts.iterator();
                    while( acct.hasNext()){
                        netWorth = netWorth +
                    ((AccountLocal)acct.next()).getBalance();
                     }
            }
        catch(java.lang.IllegalStateException e){
            // thrown if there is no LocalHome object.
        }
        catch(javax.ejb.FinderException e){
            // thrown if findByAccountHolder() fails.
        }
        finally{
            // nullify home and local references before
            completing
            accounts = null;
            home = null;
        }
        return netWorth;
    }

/* This method adds the specified amount to the
        balance.*/
public void debit(double amount){
    // note I'm using CMP setters and getters to do the
        job.
    this.setBalance( this.getBalance() + amount);
}

/* This method subtracts the specified amount from the
        balance.*/
public void credit(double amount){
    // note I'm using CMP setters and getters to do the
        job.
    this.setBalance( this.getBalance() - amount);
}
}
```

Before continuing, notice the bold text in Listing 6-12. In that example, I used an `ejbSelect` method to obtain the net worth of an account holder. The `ejbSelect` method offers concise and efficient means for getting values out of entity beans without having to access those objects through their remote or local interfaces. The alternative is to look up the home object accounts through JNDI and then obtain a reference using a finder method.

Because `ejbHome` methods are invoked without creating an entity bean instance, you can't access CMP and CMR fields inside the entity bean class from an `ejbHome` method. That's because CMP and CMR fields are defined by instance data. Consequently the `ejbHomeGetNetWorth` method must obtain `AccountLocal` interfaces in order to calculate the net worth of the account holder.

Describing Entity Beans in the ejb-jar.xml File

While entity beans seem complex, the complexity is a result of the number of tasks required to create an entity bean, rather than the difficulty of any single task. But because entity beans are composed of so many different features, there's a lot more to an entity bean's deployment descriptor than there is to a session bean's deployment descriptors. By breaking the entity bean's deployment descriptor into bite-sized pieces, you can manage the complexity and cover all your bases with ease. The complete deployment descriptor for the Account entity bean illustrated in this chapter is provided in Listing 6-13. As you proceed through definitions of each descriptor element, refer to Listing 6-13 to see the element implemented.

Two important tasks in creating the deployment descriptor are deferred until Chapter 7. Defining CMR relationships is accomplished with an <ejb-relation> element in the deployment descriptor. Also, supplying the EJB QL queries for finder methods and for ejbSelect methods are accomplished in the deployment descriptor with a <select> attribute of the entity bean. EJB QL is the new query language defined for EJB applications and is used to obtain information from an entity bean's persistent storage. In Chapter 7, I describe the finer points of creating EJB QL queries and defining relationships between entity beans.

Listing 6-13   The Account Deployment Descriptor

```
<?xml version="1.0" encoding="UTF-8"?>
<!DOCTYPE ejb-jar PUBLIC "-//Sun Microsystems, Inc.//DTD
          Enterprise
JavaBeans 2.0//EN" "http://java.sun.com/dtd/ejb-jar_2_0.dtd">

<ejb-jar>
  <enterprise-beans>
    <entity>
      <description>This bean holds account
          information.</description>
      <ejb-name>Account</ejb-name>
      <home>
        com.sextanttech.entities.interfaces.AccountRemoteHome
      </home>
      <remote>
        com.sextanttech.entities.interfaces.AccountRemote
      </remote>
      <local-home>
        com.sextanttech.entities.interfaces.AccountLocal
```

```
    </local-home>
    <local>
      com.sextanttech.entities.interfaces.AccountLocal
    </local>
    <ejb-class>
      com.sextanttech.entities.implementations.AccountBean
    </ejb-class>
    <prim-key-class>
      com.sextanttech.entities.interfaces.AccountKey
    </prim-key-class>
    <persistence-type>Container</persistence-type>
    <reentrant>False</reentrant>
    <cmp-version>2.0</cmp-version>
    <abstract-schema-name>Account</abstract-schema-name>
    <cmp-field>
      <description>This is the accountId.</description>
      <field-name>accountId</field-name>
    </cmp-field>
    <cmp-field>
      <description>
        This is the date the account was created.
      </description>
      <field-name>createDate</field-name>
    </cmp-field>
    <cmp-field>
      <description>This is the balance of the
        account.</description>
      <field-name>balance</field-name>
    </cmp-field>
    <query>
      <!-- Details of EJB QL query specified. See Chapter
        7. -->
    </query>
  </entity>
</enterprise-beans>
<relationships>
  <ejb-relation>
    <!-- details of EJB relationships specified. See
        Chapter 7. -->
  <ejb-relation>
</relationships>
</ejb-jar>
```

In Listing 6-13, the text in bold defines the Account entity bean. While this definition of the entity bean is complete, there are additional elements that could be supplied as necessary. In Table 6-2, I describe the purpose of each attribute that you see in Listing 6-13.

Table 6-2 **Attributes of the Entity Bean Deployment Descriptor**

Attribute name	Required	Multiplicity	Parent	Value
`<entity>`	Yes	One per entity bean	`<enterprise-beans>`	Entity bean attributes
`<description>`	No	One	`<entity>`	Text description of entity bean
`<display-name>`	No	One	`<entity>`	Name of entity bean for GUI tools
`<large-icon>`	No	One	`<entity>`	Location and name of icon for GUI tools
`<small-icon>`	No	One	`<entity>`	Location and name of icon for GUI tools
`<ejb-name>`	Yes	One	`<entity>`	Name of EJB component
`<home>`	No	Zero to one	`<entity>`	Fully qualified class name of remote home interface
`<remote>`	No	Zero to one	`<entity>`	Fully qualified class name of remote interface
`<local-home>`	No	Zero to one	`<entity>`	Fully qualified class name to local home interface
`<local>`	No	Zero to one	`<entity>`	Fully qualified class name to local interface
`<ejb-class>`	Yes	One	`<entity>`	Fully qualified class name to entity bean class

Attribute name	Required	Multiplicity	Parent	Value
`<primkey-field>`	No	One	`<entity>`	For CMP single value primary keys — not used with compound primary keys; specifies the name of the primary key field
`<prim-key-class>`	Yes	One	`<entity>`	Defines the primary key class type for simple or compound primary keys
`<persistence-type>`	Yes	One	`<entity>`	`Container` for CMP or `Bean` for bean-managed persistence (BMP)
`<reentrant>`	Yes	One	`<entity>`	`True` or `False`; see sidebar "The grand reentrant" for more details
`<cmp-version>`	No	One	`<entity>`	Either `2.x` or `1.x`; defaults to 2.0 when not specified
`<abstract-schema-name>`	No	One	`<entity>`	Uniquely identifies an entity bean component in a JAR file; used for EJB QL query statements
`<cmp-field>`	No	Zero to many	`<entity>`	Identifies a CMP field in the entity bean
`<description>`	No	One	`<cmp-field>`	Describes the CMP field

(continued)

Table 6-2 *(continued)*

Attribute name	Required	Multiplicity	Parent	Value
`<field-name>`	Yes	One	`<cmp-field>`	Identifies the name of the CMP field
`<query>`	No	Zero to many	`<entity>`	One query is required for each `ejbQuery` and each finder method

While Table 6-2 will help you through most of the requirements in defining a deployment descriptor, I should clarify a couple of additional requirements:

- ✔ While the EJB 2.0 specification doesn't require `<local>`, `<local-home>`, `<remote>`, or `<remote-home>` attributes for an `<entity>` entry, each entity bean must have a local home and local interface or a remote home and remote interface. The specification cannot require you to specify references to classes that don't exist, which is why these fields are optional. But you must define the `<local>` and `<local-home>` attributes if you supply local and local home interfaces, and you must define the `<remote>` and `<remote-home>` attributes if you define remote and remote home interfaces for your entity bean.

- ✔ Although `<cmp-field>` attributes aren't required, they must be specified for each CMP field in an entity bean — if the bean is to benefit from container-managed persistence. If your entity bean participates in CMP, the value for the `<persistence-type>` field must be `Container`.

- ✔ For each CMR field in an entity bean, there must be a `<relationship>` entry defined in the deployment descriptor. I discuss the syntax for `<relationship>` elements in Chapter 7.

- ✔ For each `ejbQuery<METHOD>` and for each `finder<METHOD>` other than `findByPrimaryKey`, there must be a corresponding `<query>` element defined in the deployment descriptor. Check out Chapter 7 for more about the syntax for the `<query>` element.

There are additional entity bean attributes that I didn't define here because I cover them in other parts of the book. You can discover more about defining deployment descriptors for entity beans in the following chapters:

✔ Several entity bean attributes in the deployment descriptor are used for JNDI ENC services. See Chapter 12.

✔ Some entity bean attributes in the deployment descriptor are used to manage security definitions for an entity bean. See Chapter 15.

✔ Many deployment descriptor attributes aren't defined until application assembly time. Some deployment descriptor definitions are specific to transaction management. See Chapter 14.

✔ For your convenience, two chapters focus directly on deployment descriptor topics. See Chapter 11 for a review of the packaging of EJB components and definition of deployment descriptors for EJB providers. See Chapter 13 for a review of the packaging of EJB applications and for the details about attributes of a deployment descriptor that are defined at application assembly time.

The grand reentrant

Just when you thought you understood everything, I go and throw a new concept at you to mix things up. If you're not familiar with the term *reentrant,* you should be. And if you don't want to be familiar with the term, then take my advice and never set the <reentrant> attribute to True. The term *reentrant* refers to whether an entity bean can be invoked twice in the same thread of control. To get to the bottom of reentrance, the review of some basic concepts in Java and EJB development is in order.

To understand the concept of reentrance, take three objects — A, B, and C. Object A starts a thread of execution by invoking a method in object B. Object B continues the thread of execution by invoking a method in object C. If object C then invokes a method in either A or B, the invocation is reentrant because the thread of execution reenters an object that it previously invoked. You'll also see the term *loopback* used in this context. A *loopback* refers to the act of looping back into an object that was previously invoked in the current thread of execution. In many applications, reentrance is used by design to help perform complex computational tasks — but not in EJB applications.

Because EJB components are single-threaded — *single-threaded objects* can be invoked by only one thread of execution at a time — by default, every EJB component can only be invoked by one client application at one time. Each client invocation represents a thread of execution. If one EJB component is invoked, no other client can invoke that EJB component until the first client releases the component.

The issue is that session and entity components are never invoked directly. Instead, they're invoked through a local or remote interface. Because of this indirection, EJB classes never know which client is invoking them; all they know is that they're being invoked. Thus, from an EJB class's point of view, a reentrant invocation appears the same as a multi-threaded method invocation. Multi-threaded invocations are strictly forbidden on all session and entity beans because they can wreak havoc on the internal state of a bean and completely undermine the EJB container's transactional and concurrence management services.

Session beans can never be reentrant, which makes this subject a non-issue. But entity beans are something completely different. While the EJB specification allows entity beans to accept reentrant method invocations, when the <reentrant> attribute is set to True, the EJB bean developer must take responsibility for distinguishing between reentrant invocations and multi-threaded invocations, and the bean developer must throw a system exception, such as the javax.ejb.EJBException when a multi-threaded invocation occurs.

As you might guess, allowing <reentrant> method invocations in an entity bean is beyond the Dummies stage of development. Even experts are daunted by this task. So, the advice of the EJB specification — and my advice — is not to allow <reentrant> method invocations in your entity beans.

Chapter 7

EJB QL and the Abstract Persistence Schema

*O*ne of my favorite new features of the EJB 2.0 specification is EJB Query Language, or EJB QL for short. EJB QL is a language that allows EJB containers to store the data held in entity beans in a database or some other persistent storage. Before diving into this topic, it's important to understand the basic concept of *persistence*, the meaning of the EJB specification's *abstract persistence schema*, and the role of query languages — of which EJB QL is one — in facilitating persistence.

As you proceed through this chapter, you'll come to understand the solution that EJB applications use for managing persistence, and you'll get to see the mechanisms for the EJB Query Language, which is used to find persistent entities. This is quite a trick, considering that at the time you write an EJB application you don't need to know how entity beans are stored, where they're stored, or what brand of container they're stored in. Although managing persistence is complex, most of the complexity is hidden from EJB application developers. As a developer, all you have to do is tell the EJB container what to do. It's the container's job to determine how to do the task you tell it to perform.

This chapter addresses topics specific to container-managed persistence and the EJB 2.0 specification. If you're developing entity beans that used the CMP 1.1 model, this information isn't relevant to you. Instead, refer to Chapter 9. If you're developing entity beans by using bean-managed persistence, refer to Chapter 8.

Defining an Abstract Persistence Schema

In the world of EJB, when an object is persisted, the system stores it in some permanent physical storage medium (usually a database). In EJB applications, for a piece of software to be *persistent,* it must be able to survive a computer shutdown. Entity beans can survive a computer shutdown because they're stored in permanent physical locations. Thus, they are persistent. The trick is that the EJB specification doesn't describe the type of physical storage for entity beans; it just requires that such storage exist.

Not specifying the type of persistent storage that entity beans use is a means of ensuring that EJB applications remain platform independent. But to achieve platform independence, entity beans must have a platform-independent way to store their state to a persistent location. To accomplish that task, the EJB language describes an *abstract persistence schema.*

An *abstract persistence schema* is like a blueprint for software that describes the relationships between entities and how they're stored in a persistent location. EJB applications have an abstract persistence schema because the actual method used to persist entity beans is defined by the EJB container. Thus, the EJB container takes the abstract persistence schema defined by the EJB application developer and turns it into a concrete solution for making entity beans persistent, just as a contractor takes the blueprints for a house and turns it into an actual building. In EJB applications, the abstract persistence schema is defined by a set of XML elements in the EJB application's deployment descriptor.

For an example that's closer to home, an abstract persistence schema is similar to an abstract class in Java. The abstract class can describe what methods and what attributes are contained in the class, but it doesn't supply the actual implementations. Likewise, the abstract persistence schema describes the entities — and relationships between entities — for an EJB application, but doesn't supply an actual persistence solution.

Examining Entity Bean Persistence

Defining entity bean persistence occurs in two phases. First, the entity bean provider defines the abstract persistence schema through the deployment descriptor and the definition of abstract methods in the EJB component. The EJB container takes those abstractions and converts them into a concrete solution, which it is responsible for maintaining. The maintenance of the persistence scheme is governed by the settings of the <commit-option> tags in the deployment descriptor.

Abstract schema names

Abstract schema names are names assigned to entity beans in the deployment descriptor. These names are used as aliases to reference a class of entity beans in an EJB QL (Query Language) query. An *alias* is nothing more than a shorthand term that identifies a class. Persistence schema names are set by using the `<abstract-schema-name>` element of the deployment descriptor for an entity bean, as illustrated in the following example:

```
<ejb-jar>
 <enterprise-beans>
  <entity>
   <ejb-name>AccountEntityBean</ejb-name>
   <abstract-schema-name>Account</abstract-schema-name>
   <!-- rest of AccountEntityBean description-->
  </entity>
 </enterprise-beans>
</ejb-jar>
```

In the preceding example, the `AccountEntityBean` is assigned the abstract schema name of `Account`. Thus, `Account` is an alias for the `AccountEntityBean`.

When you define abstract schema names, remember these important rules:

✔ Abstract schema names must be unique within a given `ejb-jar.xml` file.

✔ Abstract schema names must be valid Java identifiers, which basically means that you need to follow the same rules for abstract schema names that you do for Java class names.

Persistence fields

Persistence fields, or CMP fields, are the fields of an entity bean that hold the entity bean's data. As you can discover in Chapter 6, CMP fields are represented as abstract getter and setter methods in the definition of an entity bean class. Each persistence field of an entity bean is identified in the deployment descriptor by means of the `<cmp-field>` attribute of an entity. The `<cmp-field>` attribute contains an optional `<description>` element, and a mandatory `<field-name>` attribute, as illustrated in the following example:

```
<ejb-jar>
 <enterprise-beans>
  <entity>
   <ejb-name>AccountEntityBean</ejb-name>
   <cmp-field>
```

(continued)

```
     <description>This is the balance of the
          account.</description>
     <field-name>balance</field-name>
     </cmp-field>
     <!-- rest of AccountEntityBean description-->
     </entity>
   </enterprise-beans>
</ejb-jar>
```

Regarding the field name, the EJB specification has a few requirements that you must follow:

- The field name must be a valid Java identifier, which means that it has to follow Java naming rules for class member variables.

- The field name must begin with a lowercase letter.

- The `<field-name>` element must correspond with the abstract getter and setter methods for the CMP field in the entity bean class.

  In the getter and setter methods, the field name must also begin with an uppercase letter. Thus, for the field name `balance`, there must be a method `abstract <fieldType> getBalance()` and an `abstract void setBalance( <fieldType> balance)` method in the entity bean class for the `AccountEntityBean`.

Characteristics of persistence schema relationships

Persistence schema relationships are used to define the relationships between entity beans. Every relationship in the EJB architecture must be between two entity beans. Hence, relationships have two sides; each side of the relationship describes one of the entity beans involved in the relationship. Every relationship is described in the deployment descriptor. An entity bean uses a container-managed relationship (CMR) field to access the entity beans to which it's related. CMR fields hold a reference or collection of references to entities on the other side of the relationship. In every relationship, at least one entity bean in the relationship must have a CMR field defined for that relationship. If only one entity bean in the relationship has a CMR field, that's called a *unidirectional relationship*; if both entity beans have CMR fields, then they're in a *bidirectional relationship*. See the next section for details on the characteristics of unidirectional and bidirectional relationships.

In Chapter 6, I show you that CMR fields are defined via abstract getter and setter methods. The EJB application developer must initialize one side of a CMR relationship during the creation process for an entity bean. This initialization occurs in the `ejbPostCreate<METHOD>()`, which I illustrate in Chapter 6. After one side is initialized, the EJB container takes over and maintains the relationship.

CMR relationships are defined in terms of the local interfaces of the entity beans involved in a relationship. So to participate in CMR relationships, entity beans must conform to the following rules:

- **Entity beans must have a local interface.** If an entity bean doesn't have a local interface defined, it can't participate in a CMR relationship. Therefore, EJB 1.1 specification beans can't have CMR relationships because the EJB 1.1 specification doesn't include local interfaces.

- **Entity beans must be in the same local context, meaning that they have to be part of the same** `ejb-jar` **file.** If two entity beans are located in different `ejb-jar` files, they can't participate in CMR relationships with each other, even if they're deployed to the same EJB container.

While the EJB container is responsible for maintaining entity bean persistence and entity bean relationships, the entity bean developer must initialize entity bean relationships. To do so, the entity bean developer must initialize one side of the relationship by using a CMR setter method, as I demonstrate in Chapter 6. After the first side is initialized, the EJB container can coordinate the initialization of the other side and the maintenance of the relationship.

Unidirectional and bidirectional relationships

An EJB relationship is always composed of two entity bean components. There are two broad categories of entity bean relationships, unidirectional relationships and bidirectional relationships. *Unidirectional* relationships can only be navigated in one direction, which causes one entity bean in the relationship to be hidden from the other. *Bidirectional* relationships are used when each side of a relationship should be accessible to the other.

- **Unidirectional relationships can only be traversed in one direction.** Given two entity beans A and B, a unidirectional relationship allows Bean A to access Bean B, but does not allow Bean B to access Bean A. To access Bean B, Bean A must have a CMR field that contains a reference or collection of references to Bean B. On the other hand, Bean B cannot define a CMR field referring to Bean A. The absence of a CMR field on one side of the relationship makes the unidirectional relationship unidirectional.

- **Bidirectional relationships can be traversed in both directions.** Given entity beans A and B, a bidirectional relationship allows Bean A to access Bean B, and Bean B to access Bean A. In a bidirectional relationship, Bean A and Bean B must define CMR fields that refer to each other. Bidirectional relationships require the presence of CMR fields on both sides of a relationship.

If a relationship is unidirectional, only one of the entity beans in the relationship will have a CMR field with getter and setter methods. Because the relationship must be initialized by the client program, the side without the CMR fields must be created, and then a local interface from that new entity bean must be assigned to a CMR field on the other side of the relationship.

Relationship cardinality

Entity bean relationships are also defined in terms of cardinality. *Cardinality* refers to the magnitude of two sets of values in relation to each other. In an entity bean relationship, each side of the relationship consists of a set of entity beans that may contain zero, one, or many entity bean instances. *Relationship cardinality* is used to tell the EJB container how many entity bean instances it should allow to exist on each side of the relationship. The three types of cardinality that apply to entity bean relationships are one-to-one, one-to-many, and many-to-many.

- ✔ **A one-to-one entity bean relationship can have zero or one entity bean instance on each side of the relationship.** Consider the example of Bean A and Bean B. In a one-to-one relationship, any instance of Bean A can refer to zero or one instance of Bean B while any instance of Bean B can refer to zero or one instance of Bean A.

- ✔ **A one-to-many entity bean relationship can have zero to many entity beans on one side of a relationship for each entity bean on the other side.** If Bean A is in a one-to-many relationship with Bean B, each instance of Bean A can refer to zero to many instances of Bean B, but each instance of Bean B can only refer to a single instance of Bean A. In the real world, a one-to-many relationship is illustrated by the relationship between an account holder and accounts. An account holder can have zero, one, or many accounts.

- ✔ **A many-to-many entity bean relationship can have zero to many entity beans on one side of the relationship referring to zero to many entity bean instances on the other side.** In a many-to-many relationship, a given instance of Bean A can refer to zero or more instances of Bean B; a given instance of Bean B can also refer to zero or more instances of Bean A.

The cardinality of an entity bean relationship is defined in the deployment descriptor under the term `<multiplicity>`. While cardinality refers to the magnitude of each side of a relationship in relation to the other (such as one-to-one or one-to-many), *multiplicity* refers to the magnitude of one side of a relationship (which is just one or many). Each side of the entity bean relationship has its own `<multiplicity>` field. The `<multiplicity>` field can hold the values `one` or `many`.

A CMR field that corresponds to a `<multiplicity>` term of many must be of the type `java.util.Set` or `java.util.Collection`. On the other hand, CMR fields that correspond to a `<multiplicity>` term of one must be of the type of the related entity bean's local interface.

Cascade delete and entity lifecycles

The final way to describe a relationship is in terms of the lifespan of the relationship. Within the bean relationship, you can tell the EJB container to delete all entity beans on the other side of the relationship when the given entity bean is deleted. This feature is called *cascade delete*, which invokes the image of a delete operation cascading from one entity bean to all of its related entity beans. The cascade delete action can only be invoked from an entity bean with a relationship <multiplicity> of one.

Cascade delete operations are necessary where the existence of one entity bean is determined by the existence of another. Thus, given the relationship between an InvoiceHeader entity and an InvoiceDetail entity, the instance of the InvoiceDetail shouldn't exist unless they're related to an instance of the InvoiceHeader. The relationship between an InvoiceHeader and an InvoiceDetail is essential to the existence of the InvoiceDetail. Thus, if the InvoiceHeader instance is deleted, the related InvoiceDetail instances must also be deleted. A cascade delete operation should never be applied to a member in a non-essential relationship.

Defining relationships in the deployment descriptor

The relational aspect of an EJB application's abstract persistence schema is expressed entirely in the deployment descriptor. The <relationships> section of the deployment descriptor, which appears directly after the <enterprise-beans> section, contains all of the relational expressions. I cover the syntax used to describe relationships in the bulleted list that follows. As you examine the syntax, you may find it helpful to refer to the example relationships that I illustrate in the following section.

- ✔ For each relationship in an EJB application, there is a single <ejb-relation> element in the deployment descriptor. This element contains all the information necessary to describe the relationship to the EJB container.

- ✔ Each EJB relationship must include two entity beans. Each entity bean plays a role in the relationship. Hence, each <ejb-relation> element must contain two <ejb-relationship-role> elements. Each <ejb-relationship-roles> element contains all the information necessary to describe one side of an EJB relationship.

- ✔ Each <ejb-relationship-role> identifies one entity bean class in an <ejb-relation>. At the least, the element must identify the entity bean component that it describes and express the multiplicity of that entity bean in the relationship. If the entity bean has a CMR field referring to the other side of the relationship, the CMR field must also be identified. At least one of the `<ejb-relationship-role>` elements must identify a CMR field. The following sublelements are used to describe the `<ejb-relationship-role>`:

- The name of a relationship role is expressed by using the `<ejb-relationship-role-name>` tag. This name can be anything that is meaningful to the entity bean developer. Try to resist using the names of your favorite presidents.

- The cardinality of a relationship is expressed by using the `<multiplicity>` tag. The `<multiplicity>` tag is mandatory and must either have the value of `one` or `many`, which identifies how many of the entity beans represented by the relationship role can be present in the relationship. Thus, if the entity is `Account` and the `<multiplicity>` is `many`, the relationship can have many `Account` bean instances.

- If the entity bean participating in a relationship role is dependent upon the relationship — meaning that there must be an entity bean instance on the other side of the relationship — its dependency is expressed with the `<cascade-delete/>` tag. The `<cascade-delete/>` tag can only be used if the other side of the relationship has a `<multiplicity>` of `one`. The `<cascade-delete/>` tag tells the EJB container that if the bean on the other side of the relationship is deleted, then the entity beans on this side must also be deleted. The `<cascade-delete/>` tag is an *empty tag*, which means that it doesn't contain a value. In the XML language, empty tags are closed with a `/>` character.

The `<cascade-delete/>` tag can only be used in an `<ejb-relationship-role>` if the other `<ejb-relationship-role>` has a multiplicity of `one`. So in one-to-one relationships, either side can specify `<cascade-delete/>`; in one-to-many relationships, on the other had, only the many side can specify `<cascade-delete/>`. Many-to-many relationships can't use the `<cascade-delete/>` feature.

- The `<ejb-relationship-role>` is bound to an entity bean using the `<relationship-role-source>` tag. The `<relationship-role-source>` tag is required and contains a single subelement called `<ejb-name>`. The value of the `<ejb-name>` in the `<relationship-role-source>` tag must be the same as the value of the entity bean's `<ejb-name>` tag in the `<enterprise-beans>` section.

✔ If the entity bean identified in a `<relationship-role-source>` element contains CMR fields for that relationship, the `<relationship-role-source>` element must contain a `<cmr-field>` attribute. The `<cmr-field>` attribute identifies the CMR field. This is accomplished with several subattributes that describe the field, identify the field name, and in the case of fields with a `multiplicity` of `many`, identify the type of the field. The subelements of the `<cmr-field>` are as follows:

- The `<cmr-field>` element can contain a `<description>` element that is used for documentation purposes. The `<description>` element is optional.

- The name of the CMR field is identified in the `<field-name>` subelement. The value of the `<field-name>` element must correspond with the name of the CMR field in the entity bean object. Remember that the entity bean object just defines abstract getters and setters for CMR fields. You can derive the field name from these abstract getters and setters by removing the method prefix (get or set) and making the first character lowercase. Thus, a field with the getter of `getFieldName`, would have the name `fieldName`.

- Finally, if the `<multiplicity>` of the `<ejb-relationship-role>` is many, then the `<cmr-field>` must have a subelement called `<cmr-field-type>` that identifies the type of collection used in the field. The value of the `<cmr-field-type>` element can be either `java.util.Set` or `java.util.Collection`, and must correspond with the return type of the CMR field's getter method in the entity bean class.

The `<cmr-field-type>` element is only used if the `<multiplicity>` of the `<ejb-relationship-role>` is many.

A couple of topics to keep in mind as you use the `<cascade-delete/>` tag are as follows:

- ✔ **The `<cascade-delete/>` tag only applies to the relationship in which it's specified.** In other words, it doesn't cascade beyond the scope of the relationship. Thus, if you want `remove` methods to cascade across multiple relationships, you must specify `<cascade-delete/>` in each relationship.

- ✔ **Cascade delete operations are typically only expressed on one side of a relationship.** For example, a one-to-one relationship in which both sides use the `<cascade-delete/>` tag is possible. While that's syntactically correct, it's very uncommon. To illustrate, it may be reasonable to have a one-to-one relationship between a `Person` and an `Address`, but deleting the `Address` doesn't mean the `Person` should also be deleted. In most applications, however, deleting the `Person` does mean the `Address` should also be deleted. Thus, the cascade delete flows in one direction only.

Illustrating relationship role examples

In the section "Characteristics of persistence schema relationships," I cover all the theoretical mumbo jumbo regarding the definition of relationships in EJB applications. I also give you a solid dose of the syntax for container-managed relationships in the previous section. But if you're like me when I was first exposed to this container-managed relationship business, you're looking for the examples. The proof is in the pudding. In the upcoming sections, you'll see three different examples of container-managed relationships. While they don't cover all the possibilities, they should be enough to get you going on your own. Each example focuses on illustrating the definition of a relationship in the deployment descriptor, but I also show relevant codes in the entity bean instances.

By now you've probably observed that the deployment descriptor can get very long and cumbersome to work with manually. The good news is that most EJB container vendors provide EJB application management tools that make it easier to work with deployment descriptors. Some software development tools also provide this feature. Finally, you can get third-party utilities that help you work with a deployment descriptor. One of those utilities is xdoclet, which you can obtain free at sourceforge.net (`http://sourceforge.net/projects/xdoclet`).

Defining a one-to-one bidirectional relationship

To illustrate the one-to-one bidirectional relationship, I'm using the relationship between an `AccountHolder` and an `AccountHolderAddress`. Granted, in the real world, people can have more than one address, but I'm just glossing over that detail for the purposes of this example. Figure 7-1 illustrates an object diagram that illustrates what the one-to-one relationship looks like when implemented. Note that the entity bean classes aren't directly related to each other. Rather, they're related through references to local interfaces.

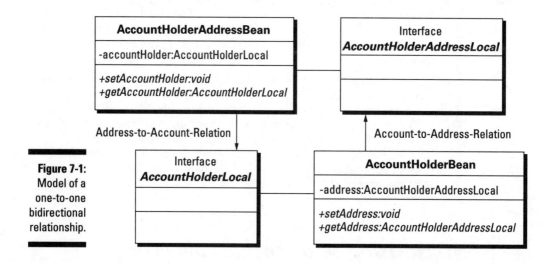

Figure 7-1: Model of a one-to-one bidirectional relationship.

The first task in defining the relationship is to identify the relevant entity beans in the `<enterprise-beans>` section of the deployment descriptor. To define a relationship, we need to know the `<ejb-name>` attribute for each entity bean. The following code snippet defines the `<ejb-name>` tags for my example classes. This is only a partial listing, with the `<ejb-name>` in bold.

```
<ejb-jar>
  <enterprise-beans>
    <entity>
      <ejb-name>AccountHolderEJB</ejb-name>
      ...
    </entity>
    <entity>
      <ejb-name>AccountHolderAddressEJB</ejb-name>
      ...
    </entity>
  </enterprise-beans>
</ejb-jar>
```

The next step is to identify the relationship between the two. You already know that this is a one-to-one bidirectional relationship. I will also be defining the `AccountHolderAddressEJB` as a `<cascade-delete/>` class because I see no reason for preserving an account holder address if the account holder ceases to exist. The relationships section for this relationship is illustrated in Listing 7-1.

Listing 7-1   A One-to-One Bidirectional Relationship

```
<ejb-jar>
  <enterprise-beans>
    ...
  </enterprise-beans>
  <relationships>
<!--The following bold block defines the relationship-->
    <ejb-relation>
<!--The first role is from the AccountHolder perspective.-->
      <ejb-relationship-role>
        <ejb-relationship-role-name>
          AccountHolder-to-Address-Relation
        </ejb-relationship-role-name>
        <!--The multiplicity is one.-->
        <multiplicity>one</multiplicity>
        <relationship-role-source>
          <ejb-name>AccountHolderEJB</ejb-name>
        </relationship-role-source>
        <!--The relationship is bidirectional because each
         side has a cmr-field referring to the other side.-->
        <cmr-field>
          <field-name>address</field-name>
```

(continued)

Listing 7-1 *(continued)*

```
        </cmr-field>
      </ejb-relationship-role>
<!--The second role is from the AccountHolderAddress
        perspective.-->
      <ejb-relationship-role>
        <ejb-relationship-role-name>
          Address-to-AccountHolder-Relation
        </ejb-relationship-role-name>
        <!--The multiplicity is one.-->
        <multiplicity>one</multiplicity>
        <!--cascade-delete indicates this side should be
          deleted if the other side is deleted.-->
        <cascade-delete/>
        <relationship-role-source>
          <ejb-name>AccountHolderAddressEJB</ejb-name>
        </relationship-role-source>
        <!--The relationship is bidirectional because each
          side has a cmr-field referring to the other side.-->
        <cmr-field>
          <field-name>accountHolder</field-name>
        </cmr-field>
      </ejb-relationship-role>
    </ejb-relation>
  </relationships>
</ejb-jar>
```

After this relationship is specified in the deployment descriptor, the entity
bean developer is responsible for defining the abstract accessor methods for
the CMR fields. Because this is a bidirectional relationship, each entity bean
will have CMR fields referring to the other. In Listing 7-1, the CMR field names
are identified for the relationship under the <cmr-field> tags.

Following the conventions required by the EJB specification, the abstract
accessor methods for CMR fields must be prefixed with get and set terms,
followed by the CMR field name with the first character capitalized.
In Listing 7-2, the abstract accessor methods for the AccountHolder are
illustrated. This is a one-to-one relationship, so the CMR field must be a
reference to the local interface of the AccountHolderAddress.

Listing 7-2   CMR Fields for the AccountHolder

```
package com.sextanttech.entities.implementations;

import javax.ejb.EntityBean;
import javax.ejb.EntityContext;
import
        com.sextanttech.entities.interfaces.AccountHolderA
        ddressLocal;

public abstract class AccountHolderBean implements
```

```
EntityBean{

    /** This is the abstract getter method for the address.*/
    public abstract void setAddress(AccountHolderAddressLocal
        addr);

    /** This is the abstract setter method for the address.*/
    public abstract AccountHolderAddressLocal getAddress();

    //... The rest of the AccountHolderBean class.
}
```

To complete the bidirectional relationship, abstract CMR accessors must be defined in the `AccountHolderAddress` class. Because the relationship `<multiplicity>` is `one`, the CMR field type must be the local interface for the account holder. The definitions of the CMR field accessors are shown in bold in Listing 7-3.

Listing 7-3   CMR Fields for AccountHolderAddressBean

```
package com.sextanttech.entities.implementations;

import javax.ejb.EntityBean;
import javax.ejb.EntityContext;
import
        com.sextanttech.entities.interfaces.AccountHolderL
        ocal;

public abstract class AccountHolderAddressBean implements
        EntityBean{

    /** This is the abstract getter method for the
        AccountHolder.*/
    public abstract void setAccountHolder(AccountHolderLocal
        addr);

    /** This is the abstract setter method for the
        AccountHolder.*/
    public abstract AccountHolderLocal getAccountHolder ();

    //... The rest of the AccountHolderAddressBean class.
}
```

Defining a one-to-many unidirectional relationship

Defining a one-to-many unidirectional relationship differs from its one-to-one counterpart in only a couple of aspects. First, because the relationship is unidirectional, only one side of the relationship will define `<cmr-field>` elements. Second, one side of the relationship will have a `<multiplicity>` of `many`. The relationship between an `AccountHolder` and an `Account` can be expressed as a one-to-many unidirectional relationship. Figure 7-2 illustrates how a one-to-many unidirectional relationship appears in a class diagram. Note that because the relationship can only be traversed in one direction, there is only one CMR field.

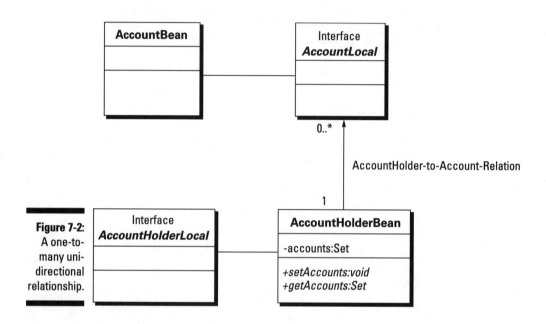

Figure 7-2: A one-to-many uni-directional relationship.

Listing 7-4 shows the deployment descriptor relationship description.

Listing 7-4   One-to-Many Unidirectional Relationships

```
<ejb-jar>
  <enterprise-beans>
    <entity>
      <ejb-name>AccountHolderEJB</ejb-name>
      ...
    </entity>
    <entity>
      <ejb-name>AccountEJB</ejb-name>

      ...
    </entity>
  </enterprise-beans>
  <relationships>
<!--The following bold block defines the relationship-->
    <ejb-relation>
<!--The first role is from the AccountHolder perspective.-->
      <ejb-relationship-role>
```

```
            <ejb-relationship-role-name>
                AccountHolder-to-Account-Relation
            </ejb-relationship-role-name>
<!--The multiplicity is one to indicate only one
            accountHolder for any
    given account.-->
            <multiplicity>one</multiplicity>
            <relationship-role-source>
                <ejb-name>AccountHolderEJB</ejb-name>
            </relationship-role-source>
<!--The relationship is unidirectional because only this side
            has a
    CMR field.-->
            <cmr-field>
                <field-name>account</field-name>
            </cmr-field>
        </ejb-relationship-role>
<!--The second role is from the Account perspective.-->
        <ejb-relationship-role>
            <ejb-relationship-role-name>
                Account-to-AccountHolder-Relation
            </ejb-relationship-role-name>
<!--The multiplicity is many to indicate many accounts per
            account
    holder.-->
            <multiplicity>many</multiplicity>
            <cascade-delete/>
            <relationship-role-source>
                <ejb-name>AccountEJB</ejb-name>
            </relationship-role-source>
        </ejb-relationship-role>
    </ejb-relation>
  </relationships>
</ejb-jar>
```

Because this is a one-to-many relationship, the <cascade-delete/> tag can be used on the many side of the relationship, but it can't be used on the one side of the relationship. In this case, I've applied the <cascade-delete/> tag because it doesn't make sense to preserve account information if an AccountHolder is removed from the application.

This is a unidirectional relationship, so only one set of CMR field accessors is defined. They're located in the AccountHolderBean class and define access to the Account. Because there are many accounts per AccountHolder, the type of the CMR field type must be a Java collection — either java.util.Collection or java.util.Set. Listing 7-5 shows the abstract accessors for the AccountHolder class in bold.

Listing 7-5   Representing a One-to-Many Relationship

```
package com.sextanttech.entities.implementations;

import javax.ejb.EntityBean;
import javax.ejb.EntityContext;
import java.util.Set;

public abstract class AccountHolderBean implements
            EntityBean{

    /** This is the abstract getter method for the account.*/
    public abstract void setAccount(Set account);

    /** This is the abstract setter method for the account.*/
    public abstract Set getAccount();

    //... The rest of the AccountHolderBean class.
}
```

Using the `java.util.Set` collection to represent a CMR relationship prevents duplicate references to entity beans on the other side of the relationship. Using `java.util.Collection` doesn't prevent duplicate relationships.

Defining a many-to-many bidirectional relationship

Defining many-to-many relationships should be a relatively uncommon task. In most applications, the vast majority of relationships will be one-to-many relationships because these relationships are more common in well-designed relational systems. Occasionally, a one-to-one relationship is defined, but that's usually pertaining to some arbitrary business rule. For example, in the real world, a person can have more than one address, but most applications only support a single address for a person.

Many-to-many relationships, on the other hand, are very rare. Because I haven't designed many-to-many relationships into the sample banking application I've used throughout the book, I'm stepping outside the box to illustrate a scenario that's grounded in a medical application. Consider the situation in which you want to suggest possible diagnoses based on the symptoms a patient presents. Each possible diagnosis could have multiple symptoms. In addition, each symptom could have multiple diagnoses. Thus, you have a many-to-many relationship; Figure 7-3 shows this relationship.

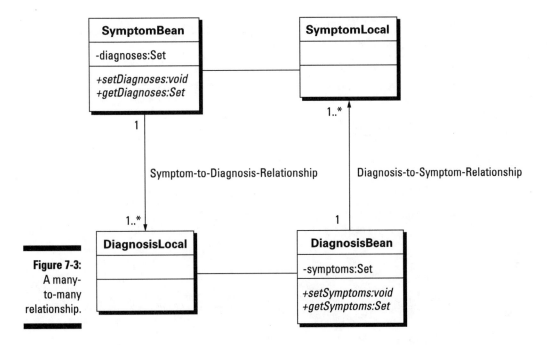

Figure 7-3:
A many-
to-many
relationship.

Listing 7-6 describes the many-to-many bidirectional relationship between
the Symptom and Diagnosis entity beans. Note that both relationship roles
have a <multiplicity> of many, and both sides have CMR fields.

Listing 7-6   A Many-to-Many Relationship

```
<ejb-jar>
  <enterprise-beans>
    <entity>
      <ejb-name>DiagnosisEJB</ejb-name>
      ...
    </entity>
    <entity>
      <ejb-name>SymptomEJB</ejb-name>
      ...
    </entity>
  </enterprise-beans>
  <relationships>
<!--The following bold block defines the relationship-->
    <ejb-relation>
<!--The first role is from the Diagnosis perspective.-->
```

(continued)

Listing 7-6 *(continued)*

```
        <ejb-relationship-role>
          <ejb-relationship-role-name>
            Diagnosis-to-Symptom-Relation
          </ejb-relationship-role-name>
<!--The multiplicity is many to indicate many potential
            symptoms per
    diagnosis.-->
          <multiplicity>many</multiplicity>
          <relationship-role-source>
            <ejb-name>DiagnosisEJB</ejb-name>
          </relationship-role-source>
<!--The relationship is bidirectional because both sides have
            a
    CMR field.-->
          <cmr-field>
            <field-name>symptoms</field-name>
            <cmr-field-type>java.util.Set</cmr-field-type>
          </cmr-field>
        </ejb-relationship-role>
<!--The second role is from the Symptom perspective.-->
        <ejb-relationship-role>
          <ejb-relationship-role-name>
            Symptom-to-Diagnosis-Relation
          </ejb-relationship-role-name>
<!--The multiplicity is many to indicate many possible
            diagnoses per
    symptom.-->
          <multiplicity>many</multiplicity>
          <relationship-role-source>
            <ejb-name>SymptomEJB</ejb-name>
          </relationship-role-source>
<!--The relationship is bidirectional because both sides have
            a
    CMR field.-->
          <cmr-field>
            <field-name>diagnoses</field-name>
            <cmr-field-type>java.util.Set</cmr-field-type>
          </cmr-field>
        </ejb-relationship-role>
      </ejb-relation>
    </relationships>
</ejb-jar>
```

Because the Diagnosis-Symptom relationship is many-to-many, the `<cascade-delete/>` tag can't be used on either side of the relationship. In addition, both of the CMR fields must be Java Sets.

Entity bean matchmaking

Entity beans weren't put on this planet to be alone. In fact, when you define an entity bean with a CMR field, it naturally desires to be in a relationship with another entity bean. I guess you could say that if an entity bean has multiple CMR fields, it has a natural drive to participate in multiple relationships, potentially at the same time. While an EJB container will maintain a relationship after it's initialized, it doesn't know which entities to match with which. Your responsibility, as a programmer, isn't to question these natural desires, but to support them. You play the role of entity bean matchmaker.

For a relationship to exist, the relationship must be initialized by the EJB client. Only one side of a relationship must be initialized in the client program. After the one side is initialized, the EJB container can finish the job by initializing the other side for you.

You can use any of several techniques to initialize a CMR relationship. Some are simple while others can be simple or complex. The technique you use depends on the cardinality and directionality of the relationship in question. I've summarized the options available to you in Table 7-1.

In Table 7-1, each entity bean is described both by the ⟨multiplicity⟩ of its CMR field and by the availability of its CMR accessors. If the CMR ⟨multiplicity⟩ is one, this entity refers to a single entity instance on the other side of the relationship. If the ⟨multiplicity⟩ is many, the entity refers to many entity instances on the other side of the relationship. If CMR accessors are available, this entity can initialize the relationship internally. If the CMR accessors aren't available, the relationship must be initialized from the other side. The Initialization Strategy column in Table 7-1 suggests techniques to use when initializing the relationship.

Table 7-1		Strategies for Initializing Relationships
CMR Multiplicity	*CMR Accessors Available*	*Initialization Strategy*
one	Yes	Pass related entity's local interface to `create` method or pass related entity's primary key to `create` method and select using an `ejbSelect` method. If this relationship is initialized after creation, the initialization can be implemented inside a business method.

(continued)

Table 7-1 *(continued)*

CMR Multiplicity	CMR Accessors Available	Initialization Strategy
many	Yes	Pass a collection of related references to the `create` method or pass a value that can be used in a parameterized `ejbSelect` method to select a collection of related local interfaces. If this entity is already created, new relations can be added from a business method by using the CMR getter to obtain a reference to the CMR field, and then invoking the `Collection.add` or `Collection.addAll` method to add local interfaces to the relationship.
one	No	Create the entity. The client program should obtain a local reference or the primary key for the entity and pass that reference to the `create` method or a business method of the related entity, according to the guidelines outlined in the first two rows of this table.
many	No	Create the entity. The client program should obtain a local reference or the primary key for the entity and pass that reference to the `create` method or a business method of each related entity, according to the guidelines outlined in the first two rows of this table.

Invoking a CMR setter method always has the effect of replacing a relationship if one already exists. Thus, in CMR fields with a multiplicity of many, if you want to add to an existing collection of relationships, you must first obtain the collection by using the CMR getter method and then invoke the `Collection.add` or `Collection.addAll` method to add the new related entity.

Remember that a CMR field with a multiplicity of many can contain either a `Collection` of local interfaces or a `Set`. If the `Collection` is used, it is possible for the CMR field to have duplicate entries. If you were to initialize both sides of a CMR relationship using the `Collection.add` or `Collection.addAll` technique, the result would be duplicate references for all the added relationships. I really can't think of any case where a duplicate entry in a CMR field is a good idea, so my advice is to avoid double initialization.

Because adding new entities to an existing relationship with a multiplicity of many can be complex, I illustrate the technique by using the sample banking application that I use throughout this book. In this scenario, the Account Holder can have many Account entities, but each Account can have only a single AccountHolder. In addition, the Account doesn't have CMR accessors to the `AccountHolder`. So, when a new `Account` is created for an existing `AccountHolder`, the relationship must be initialized in the `AccountHolder` bean. Listing 7-7 illustrates the code of the `AccountHolderBean` that adds an account to the `AccountHolder`. As you can see, the `Collection.add` method is used. Look for the bold code.

Listing 7-7   Adding Relationships to a CMR Field

```
package com.sextanttech.entities.implementations;

import javax.ejb.EntityBean;
import javax.ejb.EntityContext;
import java.util.Set;
import com.sextanttech.entities.interfaces.AccountLocal;

public abstract class AccountHolderBean implements
            EntityBean{

    /** This is the CMR getter.*/
    public abstract Set getAccounts();

    /** This is the CMR setter.*/
    public abstract void setAccounts(Set accounts);

    /** In this business method a new account is added.*/
    public void addNewAccount(AccountLocal account){
        // First obtain a reference to the CMR field
        Set accounts = getAccounts();
        // Next add the new account to the field.
        accounts.add(account);
    }
    //...Rest of entity bean class code.
}
```

Listing 7-8 illustrates the client code that implements this process. Note that because the `addNewAccount` method accepts a local interface, it must be invoked from a local client. An alternative that can be invoked from a remote client is to pass the primary key to the new account, and have the `AccountHolder` obtain a reference using an `ejbSelect` method with the primary key as an argument. Look for the bold code.

Listing 7-8   Client Code for Adding CMR Relations

```
package com.sextanttech.client;

import
            com.sextanttech.entities.interfaces.AccountHolderL
            ocal;
import
```

(continued)

Listing 7-8 *(continued)*

```
com.sextanttech.entities.interfaces.AccountHolderLocalHome;

import com.sextanttech.entities.interfaces.AccountLocal;
import com.sextanttech.entities.interfaces.AccountLocalHome;
import com.sextanttech.entities.AccountData;

public class AddAccountExample{

    private AccountHolderLocalHome holderHome;
    private AccountHolderLocal holder;
    private AccountLocalHome accountHome;
    private AccountLocal newAccount;

    public void CreateAccount(AccountData data){
        /*...In initialization code, obtain a reference to
            the
         * AccountHolderLocal interface and an
            AccountLocalHome
         * interface.
         */
        // Now create the new account.
        newAccount = accountHome.createAccount(data);
        // the local interface returned by the account is
            passed to the account holder's addAccount()
            business method.
        holder.addAccount(newAccount);
        // The relationship is initialized.
    }
}
```

Discovering the Syntax of EJB QL

Prior to the EJB 2.0 specification, there was no standard way for entity beans to manage the process of retrieving data from a persistent storage such as a database. EJB Query Language — or EJB QL for short — was created in the EJB 2.0 specification to address this lack of standards. EJB QL is based on Structured Query Language (SQL) and is very similar to it. There are some distinctions though. In the remainder of this chapter, I introduce you to the role EJB QL plays in entity beans and explore the syntax of this important innovation.

Defining query methods

EJB QL is used to implement query methods. *Query methods* are methods that are implemented using a query written in EJB QL. There are currently two kinds of query methods: finder methods and `ejbSelect` methods. Finder methods — which are written in the remote home and local home interfaces — are used to look up entity bean instances. The `ejbSelect` methods — which are written inside the entity bean class — can look up entity bean instances or retrieve data within an entity bean instance. While the finder methods of an entity bean are accessible to client applications through the home interface, `ejbSelect` methods are hidden inside the entity bean class and must not be exposed to entity bean clients. They are for internal use only.

EJB QL statements can only return a single value or a collection of values of the same type. That should make sense to you because the result of each query must be passed through the query method that implements it. Java language requires that each function can only return a single value, so the same rule must be applied to EJB QL statements.

Queries for finder methods

Listing 7-9 illustrates examples of some finder methods in the `Account` entity bean. While the `findByPrimaryKey` method is standard and implemented by the container, all the remaining finder methods are custom. `findByPrimaryKey` methods aren't implemented with EJB QL, but custom finder methods are.

Listing 7-9 Finder Methods in AccountLocalHome

```
package com.sextanttech.entities.interfaces;

import javax.ejb.EJBLocalHome;
import javax.ejb.CreateException;
import javax.ejb.FinderException;
import java.util.Date;

public interface AccountLocalHome extends EJBLocalHome{
    // default findByPrimaryKey method is required.
    public AccountLocal findByPrimaryKey(AccountKey key)
        throws FinderException;

    // This is a custom, requiring an EJB QL statement.
    public java.util.Set findByAccountHolder(long clientId,
        long
        createDate) throws FinderException;

    //... rest of AccoutLocalHome interface
}
```

The `findByAccountHolder(long clientId, long createDate)` method defined in Listing 7-9 must be implemented with an EJB QL query. The query is supplied inside the deployment descriptor, using the `<query>` element. A query element must be defined for each query method in an entity bean. The `<query>` element is nested inside the `<entity>` tag for the entity bean and maps the query to its corresponding method in the entity bean component. See the example in Listing 7-10.

Listing 7-10   The <query> Element

```
<ejb-jar>
 <enterprise-beans>
  <entity>
   <ejb-name>AccountEntityBean</ejb-name>
   <!--Rest of entity bean description.-->
   <query>
    <description>
     This method finds accounts for a given account holder.
    </description>
    <query-method>
     <method-name>findByAccountHolder</method-name>
     <method-params>
      <method-param>long</method-param>
      <method-param>long</method-param>
     </method-params>
    </query-method>
    <ejb-ql>
     SELECT owner.accounts
     FROM AccountHolder owner
     WHERE owner.clientId = ?1 AND owner.createDate = ?2
    </ejb-ql>
   </query>
  </entity>
 </enterprise-beans>
</ejb-jar>
```

As you can see from Listing 7-10, the `<query>` tag has four main parts:

- `<description>`: This is an optional attribute used to describe the purpose of the tag.

- `<query-method>`: This attribute describes characteristics of the query method that the query applies to. The EJB container uses this tag to map the input parameters of the method to the query as well as the result of the query back to the method. It contains the following features:

  - `<method-name>`: This attribute identifies the name of the method this query applies to.

  - `<method-params>`: An attribute that identifies the number and types of parameters of the method identified in the method name. Each parameter is nested in a `<method-param>` subelement that identifies the parameter type.

- `<result-type-mapping>`: This optional attribute can only be used if the query method is an `ejbSelect<METHOD>` that returns references to entity objects. The element determines whether the result will be a local interface or a remote interface to the entity object. The default value is `Local`, so it isn't required when a query is meant to return local interfaces. To return remote interfaces, the attribute must specify `Remote`.

✔ <ejb-ql>: This attribute contains the EJB QL statement. The EJB QL statement must be a legal statement for the corresponding method in the entity bean. That basically means that the parameters of the query method must be convertible to the query statement and that the return value of the query statement must be convertible to the return type of the query method. If the source object can be converted to the target object following the standard conventions of Java casting, then it is *convertible*.

Finder methods can only return component interfaces referring to the entity beans that they're defined in. For example, any finder method defined in an Account entity can only return references to Account component interfaces. It can't return references to any other type of entity.

Queries for ejbSelect methods

The EJB 2.0 specification introduces a new kind of method in the entity bean class called an ejbSelect method. These methods cannot be defined in the home or component interfaces of an entity bean — that is, they can't be accessed directly by a client program. Yet, because any method implementation in the entity bean class can invoke an ejbSelect method, your client applications can benefit from the powerful query capabilities of the EJB QL by invoking the ejbSelect method from inside a business method implementation. Listing 7-11 shows how that power can be employed, by defining an ejbSelect method and showing the method invoked by an ejbHome method. Using the ejbSelect method the ejbHome method is able to rapidly calculate the net worth of an AccountHolder. See the bold code.

Listing 7-11   Using ejbSelect Methods

```
package com.sextanttech.entities.implementations;

import javax.ejb.EntityBean;
import javax.ejb.EntityContext;
import javax.ejb.FinderException;
import java.util.Set;
import java.util.Iterator;
import com.sextanttech.entities.interfaces.AccountLocal;

public abstract class AccountBean implements EntityBean {

    /** This is the home method that invokes the ejbSelect()
            method.*/
    public double ejbHomeGetNetWorth(AccountHolderKey key){
        Collection balances = this.ejbSelectNetWorth(
            key.getClientId(), key.getCreateDate());
        Iterator i = balances.iterator();
        double sum = 0.0;
        while(i.hasNext()){
            sum += ((Double)i.next()).doubleValue();
        }
```

(continued)

Listing 7-11 *(continued)*

```
        return sum;
    }

    /** This finder method returns a reference to an
            AccountHolder.*/
    public abstract AccountHolderLocal
            ejbSelectAccountHolder( long
        clientId, long createDate) throws FinderException;

    /** This finder method returns the net worth of an
            account
     * holder.
     */
    public abstract double ejbSelectNetWorth(long clientId,
        long createDate) throws FinderException;
}
```

One feature that distinguishes `ejbSelect` methods from their finder method counterparts is that `ejbSelect` methods don't have the same constraints on their return values. The `ejbSelect` methods can return any type of value that is defined in the abstract schema and are allowed to obtain component references to any entity bean defined in the EJB application.

The implementation of the `<query>` element in the deployment descriptor is virtually identical for finder and `ejbSelect` methods. Listing 7-12 illustrates the implementation of the `ejbSelectNetWorth` query statement.

Listing 7-12   A Query for an ejbSelect Method

```
<ejb-jar>
 <enterprise-beans>
  <entity>
   <ejb-name>AccountEntityBean</ejb-name>
   <!--Rest of entity bean description.-->
   <query>
    <description>
     This method finds accounts for a given account holder.
    </description>
    <query-method>
     <method-name>ejbSelectAllBalances</method-name>
     <method-params>
      <method-param>long</method-param>
      <method-param>long</method-param>
     </method-params>
    </query-method>
    <ejb-ql>
     SELECT accts.balance
     FROM AccountHolder owner, IN(owner.accounts) accts
     WHERE owner.clientId = ?1 AND owner.createDate = ?2
```

```
    </ejb-ql>
   </query>
  </entity>
 </enterprise-beans>
</ejb-jar>
```

For you SQL gurus out there, after a summary review of this EJB-QL state-ment, you may note that the job it performs could be made simpler with the benefit of a set operation, such as `SELECT SUM(accts.balance)`. Unfortunately, EJB QL doesn't support SET operations — yet. I'm hopeful that this feature will be supported in the next release.

EJB QL fundamentals

The following code snippet illustrates the basic structure of an EJB QL statement:

```
SELECT [DISTINCT]{<single_valued_path_expression> |
    OBJECT( <identification_variable>)}
FROM <identification_variable_declaration>
[WHERE <conditional_expression> ]
```

If you're tempted to utter a heartfelt, Charlie Brown-ish "Good grief!" after seeing this bit of code, I feel for you. To make things easier, I'll break this state-ment down a little. The first thing you should note is that the statement is made up of three clauses: a `SELECT` clause, a `FROM` clause, and a `WHERE` clause. The `SELECT` and `FROM` clauses are required while the `WHERE` clause is optional.

The keywords for EJB QL statements — such as the terms `SELECT`, `FROM`, and `WHERE` that I mentioned before — are case insensitive, which means they can be written in upper- or lowercase, or any combination of the two. For clarity, I like to write all keywords in uppercase to set them off from the rest of the statement.

The following list spells out how the three clauses work within EJB QL:

- ✔ **The EJB container actually reads the `FROM` clause first, as it contains all of the variable declarations for the statement.** Using the `FROM` clause, the EJB container obtains references to all entity beans that are in the scope of the statement. An entity bean is in scope if it's identified in the `FROM` clause and it has been persisted — meaning it has been stored to a database — by the EJB container.

- ✔ **The `WHERE` clause identifies conditional expressions, which are used to limit the range of values that can be returned by the select state-ment.** This cause is executed second and is used to eliminate entities that are in the scope of the statement but which don't satisfy criteria of the conditional expressions.

- **The SELECT clause identifies the return value of the statement.** A return value can either be a single entity bean attribute — which is called a *single-valued path expression* — or a reference to the local or remote interface for the entity bean — which is called an *identification variable.* EJB QL statements can return a single value or a collection of values.

The return type of a statement is converted to the return type of its corresponding query method by the EJB container.

In the rest of this chapter, I provide you with all the information you need to make sense of EJB QL statements. But I clarify a few elements up front:

- **EJB QL statements return a single value or a collection of values.** If the return value is a single value, it can be either the component interface of an entity bean instance or the value of a CMP field in an entity bean. If the value is a collection, its type is either `java.util.Collection` or `java.util.Set`. A collection value is always a collection of component interfaces.

- **EJB QL statements defined in `ejbSelect` methods can return any type that's defined in the abstract persistence schema.** The `ejbSelect` method can return the value of a CMP field, the value of a CMR field, or the component interface to any entity bean within the scope of the select statement. The return value of the `SELECT` clause in the statement must be convertible to the return value of the `ejbSelect` statement. The EJB container is responsible for performing the actual conversion.

Declaring EJB QL variables

EJB QL makes use of entities and attributes of entities throughout a statement. These entities are referenced through *identification variables.* Identification variables are declared in the `FROM` clause of an EJB QL statement. Each identification variable has a type — which corresponds to a type defined in the abstract persistence schema — and an identifier — which is the variable name. Consider the following `FROM` clause:

```
FROM Account acct
```

This clause declares an identification variable `acct`, which is the type of `Account`. `Account`, in this case, happens to be the value of the `<abstract-schema-name>` for the `AccountEntityBean`. As you might recall from the beginning of this chapter, each entity bean that's used in an EJB QL query must have an `<abstract-schema-name>`.

Identification variables are case insensitive, so the identifiers `acct`, `Acct`, `ACCT`, and `AcCt` all identify the same variable. For readability's sake, I always write identification variables in lowercase.

Identification variables must follow the following naming rules:

- ✔ An identification variable can't be the same as an `<abstract-schema-name>` defined anywhere in the deployment descriptor.

- ✔ An identification variable can't be the same as an `<ejb-name>` declared anywhere in the deployment descriptor.

- ✔ An identification variable can't be the same as any reserved word in EJB QL.

In addition to these guidelines, the EJB specification recommends that an identification variable not be the same as any reserved word in SQL. This approach is recommended so that existing EJB QL statements will be compatible with future releases of the EJB QL specification. Reserved words are the words in any language that have special meaning in the context of that language.

There are many reserved words in SQL, so I recommend picking up an SQL reference such as *SQL For Dummies*, 4th Edition, by Allen G. Taylor (and published by Hungry Minds, Inc.).

Identification variables are declared from left to right in the `FROM` clause. After an identification variable is declared, it can be used in other identification variable declarations, as shown in the following:

```
FROM AccountHolder owner, IN(owner.accounts) accts
```

The first identification variable, `owner`, is declared to be of the type `AccountHolder`. In the next declaration, the `IN` operator gets a reference to all the accounts in the `owner` entity and stores the accounts in the `accts` variable. `owner.accounts` is a reference to the CMR field `accounts` in the `AccountHolderBean`.

Using EJB QL path expressions

Path expressions are references to the CMP or CMR fields of an identification variable. For example, the expression `owner.accounts` is a path expression that refers to the CMR field `accounts` in the identification variable `owner`. In EJB QL, the *root* (the first term in the expression) of every path expression is an identification variable. A period, called a *navigation operator*, is used to reference an attribute of the identification variable. Every path expression must terminate with either a single-valued attribute or a collection-valued attribute. Here are some examples:

- ✔ A CMR field with a `<multiplicity>` of `one` is a single-valued attribute.

- ✔ A CMR field with a `<multiplicity>` of `many` is a collection-valued attribute.

> ✔ A CMP field can be either a single-valued attribute or a collection-valued attribute, depending on the Java type of the CMP field. If the type is a Java collection, then it's a collection-valued attribute. Otherwise, it's a single-valued attribute that evaluates to the Java type of the CMP field.

It's illegal for a path expression to reference to a *multi-valued attribute*. A multi-valued attribute is a group of attributes that aren't contained in a collection. The following example is a multi-valued attribute:

```
owner.accounts.balance
```

In this example, balance is a single-valued attribute for each account to which it belongs. But, because the `accounts` attribute is a collection, the balance of each account is a separate value. The expression yields a different value for each account in the collection, which makes the expression evaluate to a multi-valued attribute.

To prevent the creation of multi-valued attributes, remember that the only place a collection-valued attribute can be used is at the end of a path expression. If you use a collection-valued attribute at any other position except the end of a path expression, you will generate an illegal multi-valued attribute.

Variable variations in EJB QL

There are actually two different kinds of variables in EJB QL: *range variables* and *collection member variables*. The distinction between the two types of variables is the way they're declared. Range variables are declared by using `<abstract-schema-name>` values for their types. `AccountHolder owner` is a range variable declaration because `AccountHolder` is an `<abstract-schema-name>` for the `AccountHolderEntityBean`.

On the other hand, collection member variables are declared by making references to CMR fields inside an entity bean. To declare a collection member variable, you must employ a *path expression*, which references a CMR or CMP field of an entity bean by using a *dot operator notation*. `owner.accounts` is a path

expression, for example. The `owner` is the range variable while the period — the *dot* — is a *navigation* operator. The `accounts` attribute is a reference to a CMR field of the `AccountHolderEntityBean`. As a single expression, `owner.accounts` is a path expression that navigates from an owner to the accounts of the owner.

The expression `IN(owner.accounts)` `accts` declares a collection member variable called `accts`. This is a collection member variable because the `accounts` attribute is a collection of accounts that belongs to (or is a member of) the `owner` range variable. Collection member variables will always have a path expression used to declare their type.

Not all CMR fields are collection-valued attributes. If you have a CMR field with a multiplicity of one, you can navigate across the CMR relationship in a path expression to obtain the value of an attribute on the other side of the relationship. Because the multiplicity of an AccountHolder to an AccountHolderAddress is one, the following path expression is legal:

```
owner.address.street
```

Creating a simple EJB QL query

In its simplest form, an EJB QL query statement selects single values or objects from a particular kind of entity. That means there are no joins (that is, the FROM clause only contains a single entity) and no WHERE clause. The result may be a component interface to the selected entity, a CMR field, or a CMP field. Simple queries with no joins can return single values or collections of values. The following query illustrates an EJB QL query that returns all the component interfaces for the Account beans:

```
SELECT DISTINCT OBJECT(acct)
FROM Account acct
```

This simple query illustrates a couple of syntax elements that are often used in the SELECT clause of a query statement.

- ✔ The DISTINCT keyword tells the EJB container to eliminate any duplicate references in the results. Because the previous statement returns a collection of values, it is possible for the collection to have duplicates if it is mapped to a java.util.Collection object in the query method. By using the keyword DISTINCT, duplicates are prevented.

- ✔ The OBJECT operator must enclose any identification variable in the SELECT clause that isn't part of a path expression. In the previous example, acct is the identification variable, and it isn't used in a path expression, so it must be enclosed in the OBJECT operator.

If the return value of a query's select method is a java.util.Set, the DISTINCT operator will automatically be applied to the result of the query, whether the term is used in the query or not. Yet, even with returning a java.util.Set, I recommend that you use the DISTINCT keyword wherever the intention of the query is to return a collection of results with no duplicates. This clearly indicates to other programmers that duplicates aren't allowed in the results of the query.

In the next query, a path operator is used to return all the balances for all the accounts.

```
SELECT acct.balance
FROM Account acct
```

In this example, note that the DISTINCT keyword isn't used. Because it's legitimate for two accounts to have the same balance, and I want to know the balances of all accounts, my return should be a collection that allows duplicates. Also note that the OBJECT operator isn't used. The result of this query is a path expression. The result is the values of all the balance attributes of the AccountEntityBean class, and would be returned as a java.util.Collection. If you refer back to the Account class, you'll see that the balance attribute is a primitive data type, which means that it can't be added to a collection without being converted to its Java object representation. The EJB container is responsible for performing this task.

Because the result of the previous query isn't a component interface, it is only legal to use that query in an ejbSelect method.

In the final example following, the query uses a path expression to navigate to the CMR field of the Account entity bean, returning a reference to the account holder. While the return value of this field is a component interface, it doesn't require an OBJECT operator because the SELECT clause expression is a path expression.

```
SELECT acct.accountHolder
FROM Account acct
```

Defining join expressions

A *join expression* is an expression that joins two entities by navigating the relationship between them. In EJB QL, the join expression is implemented by using the IN operator to reference the CMR field of an entity bean. For example, given that Account and AccountHolder are related, the two can be joined to traverse the relationship. Thus, it is possible to navigate from an AccountHolder to an Account. An IN operator receives a reference to a CMR field as a parameter, and it returns a reference to the members of the CMR field, a process shown in the following code:

```
FROM AccountHolder owner, IN(owner.accounts) accts
```

In this example, you see the accounts CMR field is passed to the IN operator. The operator returns a reference to the collection of Account objects held in the CMR field, resulting in a traversal of the relationship.

EJB QL identification variables are joined by using a *Cartesian product*, meaning that every attribute in the FROM clause is joined to every other attribute in all possible combinations. In the previous example, a Cartesian product is formed by joining all instances of AccountHolder with all instances of accounts that have an owner. To remove results from the Cartesian product, you must provide a WHERE clause.

Defining conditional expressions

Conditional expressions are defined in the WHERE clause of a select statement. Because conditional expressions can be composed of other conditional expressions, the WHERE clause can easily become the most complex of the clauses in the EJB QL select statement. There are many different kinds of conditional expressions, and some have special rules that govern their use.

Conditional expressions can be composed into larger conditional expressions by using the boolean operators AND, OR, or NOT. Thus, it's very easy to create complex expressions in the WHERE clause of an EJB QL statement.

The following list identifies all the different kinds of conditional expressions:

- **boolean expressions:** Boolean expressions are composed of a left value and a right value that are compared using comparison operators such as =, >, >=, <, <=, and <>. The result of a boolean expression is a boolean TRUE, FALSE, or UNKNOWN.

- **BETWEEN expressions:** BETWEEN expressions are used to determine whether a given value is between two numeric values. The numeric values must be literal values of the types int, long, float, or double. The syntax for a BETWEEN expression is

```
numeric_argument [NOT] BETWEEN numeric_literal AND
        numeric_literal
```

The value of the first numeric_literal must be less than the value of the second numeric_literal.

- **IN expressions:** IN expressions determine whether a given string value is within a set of String constants. For example, you can determine whether an address is within a particular state by using the following IN expression:

```
address.state IN( 'AZ', 'NM', 'CA').
```

The IN operator contains as many string literals as necessary, but each string literal must be separated by a comma. String literals can be surrounded by single or double quotes in EJB QL.

- **LIKE expressions:** `LIKE` expressions determine whether a string value matches a pattern value. The syntax for a `LIKE` expression is

```
string_value [NOT] LIKE string_pattern
```

The string pattern is a literal string with pattern characters and escape characters. The pattern characters are % — which stands for any sequence of characters — and _ — which stands for any single character. The escape character is the \, which causes a pattern character to be evaluated as part of the literal string instead of being evaluated as a special character. The following `LIKE` expression evaluates to `TRUE` because the left side of the expression matches the pattern expressed on the right side.

```
"This is my _example" LIKE "T___s%/_exam%"
```

- **NULL comparison expressions:** `NULL` comparison expressions are used to determine whether the value of a single value variable is `NULL` or not. Because `NULL` values are unknown, they can't be used in typical comparison operations. To work around that, the `NULL` operator is supplied to determine whether an attribute is `NULL` or not. `NULL` comparison expressions can only be performed on single valued path expressions. The syntax is

```
single_valued_path_expression IS [NOT] NULL.
```

- **EMPTY collection expressions:** The `EMPTY` collection expression is the collection's counterpart to the `NULL` comparison expression. Under normal circumstances, a collection can be part of a query even if it doesn't have values. To determine whether or not a collection has values, the `EMPTY` collection expression is used. The expression syntax is

```
collection_value_path_expression IS [NOT] EMPTY.
```

- **Collection MEMBER expressions:** The collection `MEMBER` expression is used to determine whether a given attribute is a member of the specified collection. The syntax for this expression is

```
{single_valued_navigation | identification_variable |
        input parameter}
    [NOT] MEMBER [OF] collection_value_path_expression
```

The single-valued navigation attribute is a path expression that references a CMR field.

- **Functional expressions:** Several string and math functions are available for use in creating EJB QL queries. I cover these expressions in the upcoming section "Using built-in functions."

In the `WHERE` clause, collection value path expressions can only be used in `EMPTY` collection expressions or collection `MEMBER` expressions. All other path expressions must evaluate to a single value.

Creating conditional queries by example

Because there are so many different kinds of conditional expressions, I've provided this section so that you can see examples of different conditional expressions and their impact on the result of a query. As you review these query examples, you can refer to the Entity-Relationship diagram in Figure 7-4. This diagram shows the entities as defined in the abstract schema as well as their relationships to each other.

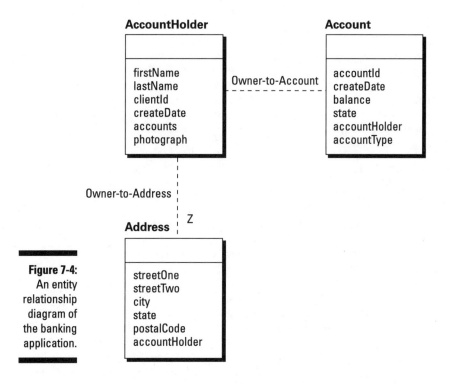

Figure 7-4: An entity relationship diagram of the banking application.

In the first example, the goal of the query is to obtain all account holders who have accounts. Because some account holders may not have accounts, the result of this query can be achieved with the use of an `EMPTY` collection expression on the `accounts` CMR field of the `AccountHolderEntityBean`. The resulting query is as shown here:

```
SELECT OBJECT(owner)
FROM AccountHolder owner
WHERE owner.accounts IS NOT EMPTY
```

In the next example, the goal of the query is to retrieve all account holders with last names that start with the characters "Sch". You can't perform an equality operation in this case; that would require that all account holders' last names be exactly "Sch". Thus, a LIKE operator is used to perform a pattern match, resulting in the following query:

```
SELECT OBJECT(owner)
FROM AccountHolder owner
WHERE owner.lastName LIKE "Sch%"
```

In the next example, the goal of the query is to obtain all account holders who have an account with a balance greater than 5000.00 — I'm thinking of sending them all a special promotional offer. This query is a little more complex because it requires a *join* — using the IN expression — to get the desired result. Remember that a join expresses a relationship between two entities in the FROM clause of an EJB QL statement. Because an owner can have more than one account with a balance greater than 5000.00, and because I only want to get one result per owner, I use the DISTINCT expression to eliminate duplicates. The final query is as follows:

Using the XML CDATA sections for queries

As you know, EJB QL queries are written in an EJB application's deployment descriptor, which is an XML document. XML documents are structured by using tags that are delimited by ⟨ and ⟩ characters. Because these characters have special meaning in the XML language, they can't be used in the value of an XML attribute. Thus, the following XML attribute will generate an error when the document is parsed:

```
<ejb-ql>
   SELECT DISTINCT OBJECT(owner)
   FROM AccountHolder owner,
     IN(owner.Accounts) accts
   WHERE accts.balance > 5000.00
</ejb-ql>
```

The problem is the use of the greater-than symbol (⟩) in the select statement. Because this is a special character, it can't appear in the value of an XML tag. The good news is that XML has a special escape element that can be used to tell an XML parser that the content inside the tag is data and not an XML tag. This special tag is called the *CDATA section*. Any time you need to write something in an XML document that contains characters that have special meaning, such as the ⟨ and ⟩ characters, you can enclose the content inside a CDATA section, which will ensure that the XML parser reads the content properly. Here's an example of the CDATA section applied to the preceding query. I've highlighted the syntax for the CDATA section in bold.

```
<ejb-ql>
   <![CDATA[SELECT DISTINCT
   OBJECT(owner)
   FROM AccountHolder owner,
     IN(owner.Accounts) accts
   WHERE accts.balance >
     5000.00]]>
</ejb-ql>
```

```
SELECT DISTINCT OBJECT(owner)
FROM AccountHolder owner, IN(owner.Accounts) accts
WHERE accts.balance > 5000.00
```

Next, I modify the previous query so that it returns owners whose accounts have a balance between 2000 and 5000. This statement calls for the BETWEEN expression. The resulting query is

```
SELECT DISTINCT OBJECT(owner)
FROM AccountHolder owner, IN(owner.Accounts) accts
WHERE accts.balance BETWEEN 2000.00 AND 5000.00
```

Sometimes a query requires multiple expressions in the WHERE clause. If I targeted the promotion in the previous query to residents of a particular state, I'd have to add another join to obtain the account holders' addresses, and then limit the results to those account holders residing in the specified states. I target the promotion to the residences of Washington, Oregon, and California. That gives me the opportunity to use the IN expression in the WHERE clause. The resulting query is

```
SELECT DISTINCT OBJECT(owner)
FROM AccountHolder owner
    , IN(owner.Accounts) accts
    , IN(owner.Address) addr
WHERE accts.balance BETWEEN 2000.00 AND 5000.00
    AND addr.state IN('OR','WA','CA')
```

All of the identification variables are automatically joined in the FROM clause. The WHERE clause then limits the results by the criteria expressed in each conditional expression. Thus, the previous statement says, "First, get me all the owners, their addresses, and their accounts. Next, I want to throw out all the owners with accounts that are less than 2000.00 and greater than 5000.00. After that, I want to throw out all owners who don't reside in Oregon, Washington, or California. Finally, return the remaining owners." The second AND expression in the WHERE clause requires that both the left conditional expression and the right conditional expression evaluate to TRUE for the whole conditional expression to be TRUE.

In my next example, I establish a hypothetical scenario. Suppose that, because of technological advancements, the video cameras in ATM machines are able to compare the appearance of a person at an ATM with a photograph of the person in a database and match the identity of the two as part of a security measure. That requires the addition of a field in each account holder's entity bean to store the photo data. I need to retrieve all the customers who haven't yet had their pictures taken so that I can send them a notice to come into a branch office and have a picture taken for the new security feature. This query calls for the use of a NULL value expression, which will retrieve all the account holders without a photograph. I create the following EJB QL query:

```
SELECT DISTINCT OBJECT(owner)
FROM AccountHolder owner
WHERE owner.photograph IS NULL
```

Performing queries that evaluate the membership of an entity can be used to generate new promotional material. Suppose that my banking business occasionally needs to send notices to all account holders who have a particular kind of account. In this case, I use the parameterized query syntax to create a reusable query for generating mailing lists, regardless of what kind of account I need at any given time. By passing in the type of account required, I can change the results of the query at runtime. Here's the resulting query:

```
SELECT DISTINCT OBJECT(owner)
FROM AccountHolder owner, Account acct
WHERE acct.type = ?1
    AND owner.accounts MEMBER OF acct
```

In the preceding example, a parameter is supplied that identifies the type of account to include in the mailing list. I address the parameter syntax in greater detail in the upcoming section "Creating parameterized EJB QL queries."

Using built-in functions

While EJB QL offers a few built-in functions that can be used to manipulate the values of attributes in a WHERE clause, the choices are rather dismal. Always an optimist, I think that just means that there's plenty of room for improvement in future releases. The functions are limited to string functions and mathematical functions. The choices for string functions are

- ✔ CONCAT(<string>, <string>): This function takes the second String and appends it to the first String, producing a single String as a result.

- ✔ LENGTH(<string>): This function evaluates a string and returns the number of characters in the string as an int.

- ✔ LOCATE(<string1>, <string2> [, <startPosition>]): Similar to the LIKE operation, this function returns the int position of first occurrence of string1 inside string2. The optional startPosition is an int value that tells the container which character in string2 should be used as a starting point. Note that the start position is 0 based, meaning that the first character in the string is located at position 0 and the last character is located at String.length() - 1. This rule is derived from the Java language rules regarding String objects — not the rules of the underlying database.

✔ SUBSTRING(<string>, <startPostion>, <length>): This function returns a string sliced out of the string argument. The returned string begins with the character in the int startPosition specified, and is the length specified in the <length> argument. Thus, SUBSTRING("A sample", 2, 4) returns the value samp.

Perhaps the most stunning oversights in the category of string functions are UPPER and LOWER, which convert the case of characters in strings so that you can perform comparisons that are case independent. If you're disappointed with the selection of string functions, just wait till you see the options in the arithmetic category:

✔ ABS(number): Returns the absolute value of a number, regardless of whether it's an int, float, or double.

✔ SQRT(double): Returns the square root of a double number.

Creating parameterized EJB QL queries

I like to save the best for last, and after a bit of a letdown with the functional expressions topic, the good news is that EJB QL hasn't overlooked the powerful features of parameterized queries. Parameterized queries take the arguments of a query method and insert them into a query at runtime. The process for inserting the parameters is very similar to the process that's followed for SQL:

✔ **Parameters are identified in an EJB QL query statement by their numeric position in the parameter list of the query method.** The first parameter in a method is assigned to position 1, the second position to position 2, and so on.

✔ **To reference a parameter in a query, you first type a question mark (?), followed by the number of the parameter you want to use.** Thus, if you want to use the first parameter of a query method in an EJB QL statement, you would type ?1 in the position where you want the parameter to appear.

In the following example, an ejbSelect method defines two input parameters, indicated in bold:

```
public abstract Set ejbSelectAllBalances(long clientId,
    long createDate) throws FinderException;
```

These parameters are then identified in the deployment descriptor. The clientId attribute is parameter ?1, and the createDate is parameter ?2:

```
<query-method>
 <method-name>ejbSelectAllBalances</method-name>
 <method-params>
  <method-param>long</method-param>
  <method-param>long</method-param>
 </method-params>
</query-method>
<ejb-ql>
 SELECT accts.balance
 FROM AccountHolder owner, IN(owner.accounts) accts
 WHERE owner.clientId = ?1 AND owner.createDate = ?2
</ejb-ql>
```

The EJB QL query assigns the first parameter to the first conditional expression identified with the ?1 placeholder in the WHERE clause, and the second parameter to the conditional expression identified with the ?2 in the WHERE clause. Input parameters can only be used in the WHERE clause of an EJB QL query. In addition, there are some other constraints:

- ✔ The number of distinct input parameters in an EJB QL statement can't exceed the number of parameters identified in the corresponding query method. The EJB QL statement isn't required to use all of the parameters supplied in the corresponding query method.

- ✔ Input parameters can only be used on one side of a comparison expression. It isn't legal to compare two input parameters to each other in an EJB QL statement.

- ✔ When using input parameters in collection membership expressions (that is, MEMBER OF expressions), the input parameter can only be used on the left side of the expression.

You can pass references to local interfaces or remote interfaces as input parameters.

Chapter 8

Constructing Entity Beans with Bean-Managed Persistence

*I*n Chapter 6, I address the creation of entity beans that use container-managed persistence. Container-managed persistence (CMP) is a relatively simple approach to creating, retrieving, and modifying data within entity beans. Most of the complexity associated with the storage and retrieval of data is managed by the container. But not all applications need — or should take advantage of — features offered by container-managed persistence. To provide the application developer with more control over the persistence process, the EJB specification also defined a persistence process known as *bean-managed persistence*.

Bean-managed persistence (BMP) requires EJB bean developers to implement all the methods for creating, finding, and modifying entity beans. This approach gives developers more control over the persistence process. That control is necessary in cases where the CMP model cannot effectively manage persistence. For example, if you need to access data in a legacy application that is not a database, then you have to use bean-managed persistence.

Aside from managing persistence, entity beans with bean-managed persistence and container-managed persistence are mostly the same. In this chapter, you discover the distinctions between container-managed persistence (CMP) and bean-managed persistence as well as finding the information that you need to create entity beans that use bean-managed persistence. My advice is that before you dive into creating BMP entity beans, get comfortable with using the CMP model. If you read Chapter 6 on CMP entity beans and Chapter 7 on the abstract persistence schema, you'll be a leg up when tackling this topic.

Using bean-managed persistence requires some knowledge of SQL and the Java Database Connectivity (JDBC) API. I provide an introduction to JDBC in this chapter, but if you need assistance with SQL, I recommend getting a copy of *Complete SQL Handbook* by James R Groff and Paul N. Weinberg and published by Osborne.

When you use bean-managed persistence, the EJB application doesn't define an *abstract persistence schema*, that handy feature used by the container to allow entity beans to both be aware of relationships with each other and to query each others' data using the EJB QL language. (For more on the abstract persistence schema, see Chapter 7.) If BMP doesn't define an abstract persistence schema, however, this means that you can't use EJB QL and that you can't define query methods in entity beans (a rather large drawback to BMP entity beans, in my opinion).

Understanding Bean-Managed Persistence

There's no great magic to understanding entity beans with bean-managed persistence. The key distinguishing element between working with bean-managed persistence, as opposed to working with container-managed persistence, is that the bean developer is responsible for implementing all the database interactions, which means that

✔ **The bean developer is responsible for obtaining and releasing database connections.** The database connection allows the entity bean to communicate with a database, which is essential for creating, retrieving, modifying, and deleting entities in the database.

✔ **The bean developer must provide implementations to all methods where the entity bean interacts with a database.** This is a key difference between bean-managed persistence and container-managed persistence. In container-managed persistence, the bean developer defines abstract methods and the container implements them.

Deciding to use bean-managed persistence has important consequences that you should consider *before* you start developing an EJB application. That's because even though you *can* mix the approaches within an application, if more than a small percentage of your entity beans use BMP, then you're not going to get much value out of the CMP framework. See the upcoming sidebar "Mixing BMP and CMP entities" for more information.

When you make use of bean-managed persistence, you need to write code that interacts with a database directly, using the Java Database Connectivity

(JDBC) API. Although both types of persistence (container-managed and bean-managed) use JDBC, with container-managed persistence you don't have to write the JDBC statements — the container does that for you.

If you choose to use bean-managed persistence, you'll have to understand how to use JDBC to interact with a database. There are two JDBC APIs on the market: JDBC 2.0 and JDBC 3.0. JDBC 2.0 is the dominant paradigm as of the writing of this book, but JDBC 3.0 will be implemented rapidly because of the demand for its powerful features. Here's a brief overview:

✔ **JDBC 2.0:** This API is defined in the `java.sql` package and is implemented by database vendors and third-party software vendors for each database flavor that interacts with Java. To interact with JDBC 2.0, you register the database driver with your application by using JNDI, and then you invoke the following statements in the `java.sql` package to interact with the database:

- `java.sql.DriverManager.getConnection`: This method obtains the `java.sql.Connection` object for a particular database.

- `java.sql.Connection`: This object is used to create SQL statements that interact with a database. Through the `Connection` object, you can create a `Statement`, `PreparedStatement`, or `CallableStatement`.

- `java.sql.Statement`: This object is used to invoke SQL statements that don't have parameters. `Statement.executeQuery` is used to execute SQL `SELECT` statements, and returns a `java.sql.ResultSet` object that contains the results of the statement.

  `Statement.executeUpdate`: This object is used to execute SQL `INSERT`, `UPDATE`, or `DELETE` statements. It returns an `int` specifying the number of rows affected by the statement.

- `java.sql.PreparedStatement`: This object is used to invoke SQL statements that have parameters. The `PreparedStatement` object has a number of setter methods that are used to set the values of parameters in a `SELECT` statement. After parameters are set, `PreparedStatement.executeQuery` is used to invoke a SQL `SELECT` statement, or `PreparedStatement.executeUpdate` is used to invoke an `INSERT`, `UPDATE`, or `DELETE` statement.

- `java.sql.CallableStatement`: This object is used to invoke stored procedures in a database. The `CallableStatement` object has methods for setting the values of parameters and methods for registering out parameters, which are parameters that are passed out of a stored procedure. `CallableStatement.executeUpdate` is used to execute the stored procedure.

- `java.sql.ResultSet`: This object contains the results of a SELECT statement. You can navigate through a ResultSet, reading the values of data that are returned from a database. When executing SELECT for update statements, you can also change the values of the ResultSet and store them back to the database. One of the major disadvantages of the ResultSet is that the Connection to the database must be kept open as long as the ResultSet is in use. Because connections are expensive resources, applications developed in JDBC 2.0 typically copy the results of a result set into another object, and then release the ResultSet and close the database connection.

- ✔ **JDBC 3.0:** This API is defined with enterprise applications in mind. Two major packages are included in the JDBC 3.0 API. The `java.sql` package, which is largely the same as the JDBC 2.0 API, is included as a service for database interactions. In addition, the `javax.sql` package is included to provide enterprise application features. The `javax.sql` package has three major improvements over JDBC 2.0:

  - **JDBC 3.0 has built-in connection pooling support.** Connection pools are critical services for enterprise applications because they allow system administrators to manage the number of connections opened to a database and share those connections between users, virtually eliminating the runtime cost of creating and destroying connections. In applications that use JDBC 2.0, a connection pool is typically obtained from a third-party vendor.

  - **JDBC 3.0 has built-in support for distributed transactions.** Because EJB applications are distributed applications, distributed transaction support simplifies interactions between the EJB container and the database.

  - **JDBC 3.0 provides an extension to the** `java.sql.ResultSet` — `javax.sql.CachedRowSet` — **which can be navigated without holding a connection to a database.** That allows application developers to invoke SELECT statements and release a database connection while continuing to work with the results of the query. This feature is another performance booster for enterprise applications.

An entity bean can access a JDBC connection by defining a resource reference (`<resource-ref>`) inside its deployment descriptor. A resource reference defined in an entity bean is abstract; it doesn't map to an actual data source. When an EJB application is deployed, the deployer is responsible for mapping actual data sources to resource references. This approach decouples the entity beans from actual data sources.

For a simple approach to accessing data sources inside an entity bean, follow these steps:

1. **Define a resource reference to the entity bean in the deployment descriptor.**

Each entity bean must have its own resource reference for a data source. The definition of a simple resource reference is illustrated in the following code. For a detailed description of the <resource-ref> tag, check out Table 8-2 at the end of this chapter.

```
<ejb-jar>
  <enterprise-beans>
    <entity>
      <bean-name>AccountHolderBMP</bean-name>
      <resource-ref>
        <description>Data source for account
         holder</description>
        <res-ref-name>jdbc/AcctHolderDatabase</res-ref-
         name>
        <res-type>javax.sql.DataSource</res-type>
        <res-auth>Container<res-auth>
      </resource-ref>
    </entity>
  </enterprise-beans>
</ejb-jar>
```

2. **After a <resource-ref> is defined, reference the resource inside your EJB.**

   The simplest approach, but not the best, is to define a method inside your EJB class for accessing a connection, such as the following getResourceConnection method:

```
public Connection getResourceConnection throws
        SQLException {
    try{
        Context ctx = new InitialContext;
        DataSource ds = (DataSource)
            ctx.lookup("java:comp/env/bankingDB");
        return ds.getConnection;
    }
    catch(NamingException ne){
        throw new SQLException(ne.getMessage);
    }
}
```

The approach illustrated previously isn't ideal because you end up having to write the same code over and over in every class that you create that interacts with a database. For that reason, many developers abstract database methods out of the classes that use them and provide a set of utility classes that have generic support for obtaining connections, constructing statements, executing statements, and returning results. When you already have such a set of classes constructed, you can use them from any object to invoke any type of statement you can imagine without writing a lot of duplicate code.

Defining utility classes for database interaction is beyond the scope of this book. I've implemented a number of classes for my own use that provide these services. They're packaged with the sample ATM application I use in this book, which you can find on the Web at www.dummies.com/extras/ejbfd. These classes are serviceable for JDBC 2.0 drivers but are obsolete for JDBC 3.0 implementations. If you'd like to take a closer look at my utilities for database interaction, investigate the source code for the com.sextanttech.sql package in the sample ATM application.

Chapter 12 illustrates the process for including a JDBC driver in your EJB application. If you can obtain a JDBC 3.0 driver for the database used by your EJB application, then do so. The advantages of JDBC 3.0 drivers over their JDBC 2.0 predecessors are substantial.

While you must implement the database interactions with bean-managed persistence, the EJB container can still manage all other services, including concurrency management, transaction management, and security.

By implementing direct access to the database, you get access to the JDBC API for database transaction management. Remember that persistence management and transaction management are different, and that the EJB container handles transactions for you. You should never use the transaction services in JDBC for EJB applications, because doing so undermines the integrity of container-managed transactions. Even if you're managing your own transactions, there is a separate Transaction API provided with the EJB framework that you should use for transaction management.

When to Use Bean-Managed Persistence

Bean-managed persistence isn't for everyone. As the EJB architecture makes advances, there are sure to be features available in container-managed persistence that cannot be implemented for entity beans that use bean-managed persistence. Thus, when you choose to use bean-managed persistence, you automatically limit some of the flexibility of your entity beans.

One key factor that should figure prominently in your choice of using bean-managed persistence is how you intend to administer your database. Remember that each entity bean is backed by records in a database and that — traditionally, at least — database administration isn't a topic for application developers. Most enterprises hire database administrators that manage database instances and provide a variety of other services, including managing database security, performance tuning, backup and recovery, and other administration issues. Currently, Java doesn't provide the type of robust interface that database administrators need to perform these tasks.

Because the container-managed persistence model doesn't provide the robust tools that database administrators need to do their work, it's likely that organizations that employ database administrators won't be jumping on the container-managed persistence bandwagon quickly. If your enterprise employs database administrators, using bean-managed persistence allows your database administrators to keep control of the database and have the fine-grained control over its creation, structure, and administration to which they're accustomed. Thus, bean-managed persistence makes a good choice for that environment. If you don't have database administrators, you may find that container-managed persistence — while not as powerful — is easier to implement and manage than the bean-managed persistence approach.

Another important consideration when choosing between bean- and container-managed persistence is whether or not your business has an existing database. If you already have a relational database that you'd like to access from Enterprise JavaBeans, then you may not be interested in many of the container-managed persistence features. You'll probably also want more control over accessing and working with the existing data in your database. That makes bean-managed persistence a good solution.

On the other hand, if you're creating a new EJB application and you don't have an existing database — or if you're redefining your database schema — you'll probably find that container-managed persistence offers you an easy way to break away from dependence on a particular database architecture and design a solution that can be easily migrated to a variety of different database vendor solutions, depending on the needs of your business.

 Container-managed persistence sacrifices control in exchange for flexibility. That means that container-managed persistence solutions tend to be more flexible, whereas you can retain more control over your persistence solution and your database implementation by using a bean-managed persistence solution. And as the J2EE architecture continues to evolve, the addition of features to support administration of databases is practically a certainty.

 If you're developing applications for an application solution provider, and those solutions need to work in a variety of database architectures, then using container-managed persistence will offer you the most flexibility for adapting your solutions to different database architectures.

The Bean-Managed Entity Bean Lifecycle

The lifecycle of entity beans with bean-managed persistence is largely the same as that of entity beans with container-managed persistence. This should not come as a surprise, given that they're both entity bean components and that their external behaviors are virtually identical. The key distinction is that entities with bean-managed persistence cannot have ejbSelect methods. That's because ejbSelect methods require the use of EJB QL, which is not supported by BMP. Figure 8-1 illustrates the various activities and states in the life of an entity bean with bean-managed persistence.

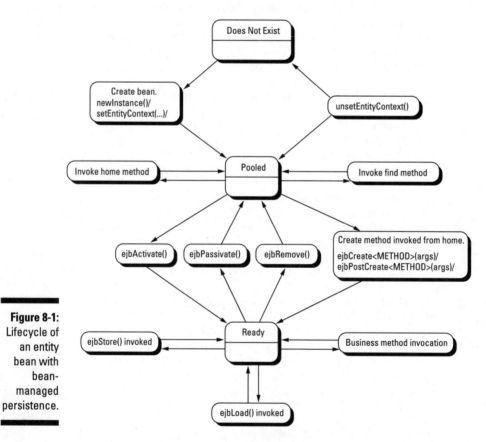

Figure 8-1: Lifecycle of an entity bean with bean-managed persistence.

Figure 8-1 illustrates three states of the entity bean: Does Not Exist, Pooled, and Ready. Activities, depicted as bubbles between the states, cause the entity bean to transition in the direction of the arrows. The following points are distilled from the diagram in Figure 8-1:

Mixing BMP and CMP entities

When using bean-managed persistence (BMP), you're embarking on a significantly different architecture from the container-managed persistence (CMP) model. The decision to use bean-managed persistence should be made as you design your application and is dependent on numerous factors, including performance and feasibility considerations. In some cases, you may encounter scenarios where some entities have to use bean-managed persistence while others do not. Container-managed persistence can handle storing and retrieving entities from a JDBC data source, but if you're storing entity data in some other type of data source, you'll be required to use bean-managed persistence.

If some entities can use container-managed persistence while others have to use bean-managed persistence, you'll find yourself debating whether or not to use both approaches in the same application. Here are some scenarios to consider:

✔ If you have two different data sources with no direct relationship between the two, then you could use a BMP solution with one source while using a CMP solution for the other. For example, you may have one data source that's a JDBC data source and uses container-managed persistence, and the other may be some legacy application or a third-party application interface that requires bean-managed persistence. Because there's a clean separation between the use of container-managed persistence and bean-managed persistence, using both in the previous scenario shouldn't be a problem.

✔ If you're dealing with a single data source and using both bean- and container-managed persistence, then you may encounter undesired complexities. For starters, while CMP beans can manage relationships automatically, BMP beans must manage relationships manually. If you encounter scenarios where CMP beans are related to BMP beans, modeling the solution in your EJB application will rapidly become complex. This scenario may not justify using both bean- and container-managed persistence. You'd simply use BMP for all beans.

✔ The choice to use both container- and bean-managed persistence may come down to a question of practicality from a development perspective. If you find that a significant portion of your entity beans are using a bean-managed persistence model, then doing them all in the same model may just be easier. The fact of the matter is that once you implement a few entity beans using bean-managed persistence, you'll be proficient with the approach. At that stage, switching between the models may be more trouble than it's worth.

In the sample ATM application that I've developed throughout this book, my preference is to use container-managed persistence because a) it simplifies the management of the persistence process and b) there's nothing about the sample application that would compel me to use BMP.

✔ **Entity bean objects are in the Does Not Exist state before they're created and after they're destroyed.** The creation and destruction of entity bean objects doesn't correspond with the insertion of and deletion of data in a database. When entity bean objects are created, they aren't associated with data and thus can be destroyed without deleting data.

✔ **An entity bean instance is created by first invoking the** `Object.newInstance` **method and then the** `EntityBean.setEntityContext` **method.** The `newInstance` method creates the entity bean object. The `setEntityContext` method provides the entity bean with resources for interacting with the EJB container as well as for obtaining other application resources.

✔ **After an entity bean instance is created, it's typically placed in a pool where it can be obtained and used in an EJB application. Each type of entity bean has its own pool.** That means that for every entity bean you create, if the EJB container supports entity bean pools, it will create a pool to store entity bean objects of that type. When in the Pooled state, an entity bean still doesn't have business data associated with it, but it can be used by an EJB application to invoke finder methods, home methods, and `create` methods.

   • **Finder methods are used to look up existing entity beans and return their component interfaces.** When you need to obtain a reference to an entity that's already created, you must use a corresponding finder method. In BMP, each finder method must be implemented by the entity bean provider using an SQL query.

   • **Home methods are business methods that can impact multiple entity bean instances and which can be performed without the client obtaining a component interface.** For example, if you need to perform a group update on a number of entities, you can define a home method to perform the task. The home methods must be implemented by the bean provider using an SQL query.

   • `Create` **methods are methods that are used for creating new entities.** If you're defining a new entity, you must use an appropriate `create` method. Invoking a `create` method will cause an entity bean to transition from the Pooled state to the Ready state.

✔ **When an application invokes a business method on an entity bean using its component interface (either the local or remote interface), the entity bean transitions to the Ready state.** When in the Ready state, an entity bean has instance data associated with it, and it's held in memory. If a particular instance of an entity bean already exists in the Ready state, the EJB container will use that object rather than obtaining another. Thus, entity bean objects in the Ready state can be shared by many EJB client applications, which is the reason why EJB client applications always have a consistent view on the data of entity bean instances.

✔ **The entity bean transitions from the Ready state to the Pooled state via the** `EnityBean.ejbPassivate` **method.** The `ejbPassivate` method is invoked by the EJB container after a predefined period of inactivity. The predefined period of inactivity is actually a configuration issue that is set by the administrator of the EJB container. At this stage, the EJB container no longer needs to hold the entity bean instance data in memory. When an entity bean is passivated, its data is cached, and the entity bean object is returned to the Pooled state.

- ✔ **The entity bean transitions to the Ready state via a `create` method or an `EntityBean.ejbActivate` method.** The `ejbActivate` method is invoked by the EJB container when it needs to restore the cached state of an entity bean to an entity object. When invoked, the cached data is restored to an entity object that's obtained from the Pooled state. The `ejbActivate` method is the inverse operation of the `ejbPassivate` method.

- ✔ **The entity bean loads data from a database when its `ejbLoad` method is invoked.** The EJB container invokes the `ejbLoad` method when the entity needs to initialize or restore its internal data from a database. This initialization process can occur prior to the invocation of a business method, or when a transaction rollback occurs and the entity bean has to return to the state defined before the beginning of the transaction. The entity bean developer can implement the `ejbLoad` method and provide a mechanism for obtaining the state of an entity bean from the database and storing it in the entity bean. Alternatively, instance data of an entity bean can be loaded directly from the database at the beginning of a business method invocation.

- ✔ **When an entity bean needs to store its state to the database, it invokes the `ejbStore` method.** The `ejbStore` method is invoked by the EJB container according to a schedule determined by the EJB container. The entity bean developer can implement the `ejbStore` method and provide a mechanism for writing the state of the entity bean to an underlying database. The EJB container will invoke `ejbStore` whenever it needs to store an entity bean's state to the database.

- ✔ **The EJB container invokes the `ejbRemove` method when the instance data of an entity bean is deleted from the database.** When the `ejbRemove` method is invoked, the instance data for an entity bean is deleted from the database and the entity bean object transitions to the Pooled state. After a `remove` operation is committed, the entity bean ceases to exist. The entity bean developer is responsible for writing the code for the `ejbRemove` method.

When you delete a record from a relational database, it also affects dependent records. To correctly execute the delete, you must remove all the affected records. Otherwise, you'll create *orphan records* — subordinate records that depend on a deleted master record. Correctly processing these deletions is known as performing a cascade delete. While container-managed persistence provides a simple mechanism for managing cascade delete operations, bean-managed persistence does not. Most database systems have built-in features that prevent orphan records from being created and which automatically manage the cascade delete process. The database administrator is responsible for defining rules that manage delete operations.

When cascade delete operations aren't handled properly, it is possible for the database to end up with *orphan records*, which are data unrelated to anything. Orphan records are dangerous — if the primary key of a deleted record ever gets reused in a new record on the same table, orphan records of the deleted record will be associated to the new record, resulting in serious data corruption.

If you take a close look at Figure 8-1, you'll notice that there is no clear transition from a Pooled state to a Ready state when finder methods are invoked on an entity bean. Invoking a finder method doesn't cause a bean to transition to a Ready state, but it does return a component interface to the client application. When the client application invokes a business method on a component interface, the EJB container first determines whether the entity bean needs to be transitioned to the Ready state or an instance of that entity is already in the Ready state. If the client application invokes a business method on an entity bean instance after the instance's ejbRemove method is invoked, the business method invocation will fail.

Figure 8-2 illustrates another view of the entity bean lifecycle displayed from the perspective of the client application.

Figure 8-2 refers to the states of entity bean instance data, not the entity bean object lifecycle. In this diagram, Does Not Exist means that the instance data isn't defined and doesn't have any bearing on the state of an entity bean object. The Referenced state refers to whether an entity bean instance is referenced by a client application — that is, whether or not the client application has a component interface referring to the entity bean instance. In Figure 8-2, you can see four states:

- ✔ **Does Not Exist and Not Referenced:** An entity in this state isn't defined in the EJB container or in an underlying database. This state exists either prior to the creation of an entity or after the entity is removed and its client reference is released. In other words, the entity is either just a twinkle in the EJB container's eye or it's dead.

- ✔ **Does Not Exist and Referenced:** An entity in this state does not exist in the EJB container, and is not defined in the database, yet is referenced by a variable in a client application. The client's reference is held in a variable that was created prior to the removal of the entity bean. This state only exists after an entity is removed, but prior to the client application releasing the reference.

- ✔ **Exists and Referenced:** The Exists and Referenced state exists after an entity is created and before it's removed, and while a client application holds a reference to the entity bean. This state can exist after a client application invokes a create method or a finder method. At both points, the entity is defined in a) the database; b) the EJB container; or c) both. Remember, this doesn't necessarily mean that an entity bean object is in the Ready state, just that the client has a reference to this entity and that it's defined either in the database or in the EJB container.

✔ **Exists and Not Referenced:** This state exists after a client application has created an entity bean and before the entity is removed. In this state, no client applications hold references to the entity.

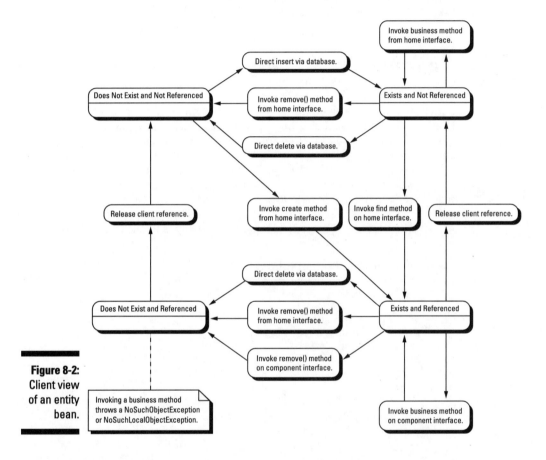

Figure 8-2:
Client view
of an entity
bean.

Coding Entity Beans with Bean-Managed Persistence

The entity bean with bean-managed persistence contains all the same ingredients as its container-managed counterpart. Hence, you still need to define a primary key for the entity bean, the entity bean's home interfaces (local home and/or remote home), the component interfaces (remote and/or local) and the entity bean class. For the most part, the process is identical to what I describe in Chapter 6. The key distinctions are apparent inside the entity bean class, which requires more coding to implement the persistence schema for the entity bean. In this section, I create a new account holder entity bean called `AccountHolderBMPBean` for the sample ATM project I've used throughout this book. You can download the sample project from the Web at www.dummies.com/extras/ejbfd. I've also created an AccountHolderBean that uses container-managed persistence. The two have identical functionality, and you can compare the code to see the key distinctions between these CMP and BMP entity beans.

Defining the primary key

All entity beans have a primary key, which is used to uniquely identify an entity bean within a given home object. The primary key can correspond to a single field or multiple fields in the entity bean class. You can define the primary key to be a Java object wrapper for one of Java's primitive types — such as java.lang.Integer or java.lang.Long — or you can define a composite primary key by creating a custom object that has an attribute for each element of the primary key. Each attribute in the primary key must correspond to a persistence field in the entity bean. In the case of the AccountHolderBMPBean, I've defined a composite primary key called AccountHolderKey. The code for my primary key is illustrated in Listing 8-1.

Listing 8-1   The AccountHolderKey Class

```
package com.sextanttech.entities.interfaces;

public class AccountHolderKey {
    private long clientId;
    private long createDate;

    public AccountHolderKey {
    }

    public AccountHolderKey(long clientId, long createDate )
        {
        this.clientId = clientId;
        this.createDate = createDate;
    }

    public long getClientId {
        return clientId;
    }

    public long getCreateDate {
        return createDate;
    }

    public boolean equals(Object o){
        if (o instanceof AccountHolderKey) {
            AccountHolderKey otherKey = (AccountHolderKey)o;
            return (clientId == otherKey.clientId &&
            createDate ==
```

```
            otherKey.createDate);
      }
    else return false;
  }

  public int hashCode{
    return String.valueOf(clientId).hashCode +
      String.valueOf(createDate).hashCode;
  }
}
```

As you review the code in Listing 8-1, take note of the following points:

✔ Two attributes define the `AccountHolderKey`: `clientId` and `createDate`. Because both attributes are elements of the primary key, they must have corresponding persistence fields in the entity bean class. That means you must define a `clientId` field and a `createDate` field in the entity bean.

✔ This primary key class overrides the `equals` method and the `hashCode` method. All custom primary key classes must override both of these methods to provide appropriate implementations for the primary key class. The purpose of the `equals` method, as the name suggests, is to perform a calculation to determine whether this object is identical to another object of the same type. The purpose of the `hashCode` method is to assist with organizing the primary key class. The easiest way to generate a `hashCode` is to create a string from each attribute in the class and return the sums of the `hashCode` values of those `String` objects.

 The primary key of the entity bean class should include all the fields of the primary key defined for the corresponding table in the database. In this case, the primary key of the database record for an account holder includes the `createDate` and the `clientId`.

Defining the home interfaces

The home interfaces of an entity bean with bean-managed persistence have the same form and function as home interfaces in the container-managed entity bean. The three types of methods defined in the home interfaces are

✔ `create` **methods:** At the very least, an entity bean must have one `create` method. `Create` methods must receive sufficient information about an entity bean to create a new instance of the entity.

✔ **finder methods:** Finder methods are used to look up existing instances of a given entity bean. You can define as many finder methods as you need for looking up entity beans. At the very least, you must define the `findByPrimaryKey` method. This method should accept an instance of the primary key of an entity bean as an argument and return the component interface to that entity bean. For entity beans with bean-managed persistence, the finder method must return one of the following objects:

- **A component interface:** If the finder returns only a single entity, such as findByPrimaryKey, the finder method must return a reference to the component interface of the entity bean. If invoked from a remote home interface, the finder method should return a remote interface. If invoked from the local home interface, the finder method should return a local interface.

- **An enumeration:** When the finder method can return more than one entity, the component interface can be returned as a java.util.Enumeration. This method allows multiple component interfaces to be returned, but it's no longer a recommended approach because it differs from the EJB 2.0 implementation of container-managed persistence.

- **A collection interface:** If the finder method can return multiple entities, the finder method should return a java.util. Collection containing all the component interfaces. Identical to the rule for finder methods of entity beans using container-managed persistence, this is now the recommended approach.

✔ **home methods:** Home methods are business methods that impact groups of entity beans. For example, a home method could be used to generate statements on accounts or to calculate interest income on interest bearing accounts. Because home methods are specific to the application you're developing, you're free to define as many or as few home methods as you need to fulfill the requirements of your application.

In practice, there's virtually no difference between home interfaces that use bean-managed persistence entities and those that use container-managed persistence entities. The reason for this is that the key differences are only apparent inside the entity bean class. The local home interface must extend the EJBLocalHome interface, and the remote home interface must extend the EJBHome interface. Listing 8-2 illustrates the AccountHolderBMPLocalHome interface.

Listing 8-2   AccountHolderBMPLocalHome Interface

```
import javax.ejb.CreateException;
import javax.ejb.FinderException;


public interface AccountHolderBMPLocalHome extends
        EJBLocalHome {
    AccountHolderBMPLocal createAccountHolder( String
            firstName,
        String lastName, String emailAddress) throws
            CreateException;
```

```
AccountHolderBMPLocal findByPrimaryKey(AccountHolderKey
        key) throws
    FinderException;
}
```

Defining component interfaces

Client applications access the business methods of an entity bean through its component interface. There are two types of component interfaces — the local interface and the remote interface. The local interface gives clients local access to an entity bean, meaning that the client application must be located in the same EJB container as the entity bean itself. The local interface must extend the `javax.ejb.EJBLocalObject` interface. The remote interface gives remote client applications access to the entity bean and must extend the `javax.ejb.EJBObject` interface.

Local interfaces for entity beans with bean-managed persistence must adhere to the same rules as those for entity beans with container-managed persistence.

The local interface provides access to business methods in an entity bean. The bean provider may also define the setter methods of persistence fields of an entity bean through the component interface. Because an entity bean is used as a repository for data, defining the setter and getter methods of entity bean fields allows client programs to make changes to the entity bean's state. In Listing 8-3, the `AccountHolderBMPRemote` interface illustrates an example of a remote interface.

Listing 8-3   AccountHolderBMPRemote

```
package com.sextanttech.entities.interfaces;

import javax.ejb.EJBObject;
import java.rmi.RemoteException;

public interface AccountHolderBMPRemote extends EJBObject {
  String getEmailAddr();

  void updateAcctHolder(AcctHolderState state);
}
```

While it isn't illegal for clients to invoke entity bean field getters and setters through the component interface, it may not be the most efficient solution. In a popular alternative scenario, a business method is defined that accepts an object containing all the values that need to change. This type of method is called a *bulk setter* because it contains all the attributes necessary to set any value in an EJB component. By passing an object that contains all the data necessary to update an entity bean, I can perform updates on all changed fields in a single operation instead of invoking multiple setters on an entity bean class. This approach improves efficiency substantially, particularly when used through the remote interface. The `updateAccountHolder` method in Listing 8-3 is an example of a bulk setter method.

Creating the entity bean class

Entity beans with bean-managed persistence are probably the least magical of enterprise bean components. While the EJB container still performs some services for you, as the bean provider your development responsibilities are expanded substantially. Table 8-1 compares the responsibilities involved in creating bean-managed persistence beans versus the responsibilities involved in creating container-managed persistence beans.

Table 8-1	Responsibilities of the Bean Developer	
Task	*Container-Managed Persistence*	*Bean-Managed Persistence*
Create persistence fields	Define abstract getter and setter methods.	Define public fields with concrete getter and setter methods.
Define `create` methods	Use abstract setters to initialize persistence fields.	Initialize persistence fields and insert entity bean data into persistent storage.
`ejbLoad` method	No action required.	Provide implementation of model for loading data from persistent storage; set all persistence fields.
`ejbStore` method	No action required.	Provide implementation of model for updating persistent storage from all persistence fields in entity bean.
finder methods	Define abstract `ejbFinder` method and EJB QL query.	Define concrete `ejbFinder` method that implements query and returns primary key objects corresponding to each entity found in query.
`ejbRemove` method	No action required.	Provide implementation of model for deleting entity from persistent storage.

The entity bean class for an EJB must conform to the following rules:

✔ The class must be declared `public` and cannot be declared `abstract` or `final`.

✔ The class must implement the `javax.ejb.EntityBean` interface. The `EntityBean` interface defines standard methods that must be present in every entity bean class. The container uses the methods of the `EntityBean` interface to manage the lifecycle of each entity bean.

✔ The entity bean class must declare a public constructor that takes no arguments.

✔ The class must not define the `finalize` method. The `finalize` method is a special operation that prepares a class for destruction. The EJB container is responsible for managing the destruction process for entity bean classes, so bean developers shouldn't attempt to override the EJB container functionality by defining their own `finalize` methods.

Listing 8-4 illustrates an entity bean with a *stub implementation* of the `EntityBean` interface. A stub implementation is a class that both implements the method of an interface and defines the default operations that should be performed when the methods are invoked. As you proceed through the subsequent sections, you'll see examples for implementing each of the key methods that bean developers must override for entity beans with bean-managed persistence.

Listing 8-4   An Entity Bean Class Stub

```
public class AccountHolderBMPBean implements EntityBean {

    private EntityContext context; // entity context

    public AccountHolderBMPBean { } // empty constructor

    // the remaining methods are specified in the EntityBean
            interface.
    public void setEntityContext(EntityContext ctx) {
        this.context = ctx;
    }

    public void unsetEntityContext {
        this.context = null;
    }
    public void ejbRemove throws EJBException { ... }

    public void ejbActivate { }

    public void ejbPassivate { }

    public void ejbLoad throws EJBException{ ... }
```

(continued)

Listing 8-4 *(continued)*

```
    public void ejbStore throws EJBException { ... }

    public void ejbRemove throws EJBException { ... }
}
```

Defining persistence fields

For entity beans with bean-managed persistence, the rules for defining persistence fields may surprise you. Although one of the most important principles of object oriented design is hiding the internal representation of data, you'll have to break this rule when creating an entity bean class because all the persistence data in an entity bean must be declared as `public`. In addition, standard accessor methods are also defined for getting and setting the persistence field values. You shouldn't worry too much about declaring entity bean fields `public`. That's because clients can only access entity beans through the component interface, so while persistence fields are `public` the client applications never see them.

To create a persistence field:

✔ **Define a public member variable to hold the value of the field.** For the `AccountHolderBMPBean` class, an example of a persistence field is

```
    public String lastName;
```

✔ **Define public getter and setter methods for the persistence field.** For the `lastName` field, the getter and setter methods are

```
    public void setLastName(String lastName){
        this.lastName = lastName;
    }

    public String getLastName{
        return this.lastName:
    }
```

Listing 8-5 illustrates the definition of the persistence fields in the `AccountHolderBMPBean`. Note that the `photograph` field is a `String`. For an explanation, read the sidebar "Working with Blobs and Clobs."

Listing 8-5   Example Persistence Fields

```
package com.sextanttech.entities.implementations;

import javax.ejb.EntityBean;

public class AccountHolderBMPBean implements EntityBean {
```

```
public String firstName;
public String lastName;
public long clientId;
public long createDate;
public String photograph;
public String emailAddress;

public String getFirstName{ return firstName; }

public void setFirstName(String firstName){
    this.firstName = firstName;
}

public String getLastName{ return lastName; }

public void setLastName(String lastName){
    this.lastName = lastName;
}

public long getClientId{ return clientId; }

public void setClientId(long clientId){
    this.clientId = clientId;
}

public long getCreateDate{ return createDate; }

public void setCreateDate(long createDate){
    this.createDate = createDate;
}

public String getPhotograph{ return photograph; }

public void setPhotograph(String photograph){
    this.photograph = photograph;
}

public String getEmailAddress{ return emailAddress; }

public void setEmailAddress(String emailAddress){
    this.emailAddress = emailAddress;
}
}
```

Working with Blobs and Clobs

Many popular database engines don't support two new data types known as *Blobs* (Binary Large Objects) and *Clobs* (Character Large Objects). Blobs are typically used to store large binary objects, such as pictures or audio files, whereas Clobs are typically used to store very large character documents in a database. Both are given special treatment in Java. In Java, the `java.sql.Blob` data type doesn't actually contain binary data. Instead, it contains a logical pointer that tells the JVM where in the database the binary data associated with a Blob can be found. The same principle applies to the `java.sql.Clob` data type.

Because both Java `Blob` and `Clob` objects don't have internal representations of their data, they're only valid for the duration of a transaction in which they're created. This poses special problems with EJB applications, where the state of an entity bean shouldn't be dependent upon the transactional context. In fact, support for Blobs and Clobs in EJB applications is inconsistent, and in many cases nonexistent.

So, what do you do if your enterprise application needs to work with image files, audio files, and large character documents? The simplest solution is to not store these documents and files in a database. Instead, create a database table that holds a URL to the location of the document or file and store it on a file server. When your application needs to access the file, it can obtain the `String` URL to the file from the database and use that URL to obtain a reference to the desired file from the file server. Files can be accessed using the `java.io.FileInput Stream` object. Note that EJBs should not work with input streams because they undermine the container's ability to properly manage an entity bean object. When working with files, pass the URL to your client application and have the client application access it directly.

Beware of creating your own Blob and Clob data types that hold data internally. Both Blob and Clob objects can potentially contain massive volumes of data. It's not unrealistic to expect that a database Blob or Clob could consume several megabytes of your computer's memory if you tried to load it into an object, and if you loaded more than a few of these objects into memory you could encounter some very serious performance problems.

Implementing create methods

After you've defined the entity bean persistence fields, you should be ready to undertake defining the `create` method. The rules for `create` methods with entity beans are slightly different from those for `create` methods in container-managed persistence. Here's the formula:

- ✔ For each `create<METHOD>` defined in an entity bean's home interface, you must define an `ejbCreate<METHOD>` and an `ejbPostCreate<METHOD>` in the entity bean class.

- ✔ In the `ejbCreate<METHOD>`, first initialize all the persistence fields from the method parameters. Next, you must insert the entity bean's persistence field data into a database inside the method. This is typically accomplished through JDBC.

✔ With bean-managed persistence, the `ejbCreate<METHOD>` must define the primary key of the entity bean and return the primary key from the method.

✔ Use the `ejbPostCreate<METHOD>` to initialize any entity-specific resources for your entity bean prior to its first use. While the `ejbPostCreate<METHOD>` is required, the method is typically empty. You may recall that the `ejbPostCreate<METHOD>` is used to initialize CMR fields in a container-managed entity bean. Because entity beans with bean-managed persistence don't have CMR fields, the role of the `ejbPostCreate<METHOD>` is less prominent.

In Listing 8-6, I illustrate the `ejbCreateAccountHolder` and `ejbPostCreateAccountHolder` for the `AccountHolderBMPBean` class. The `ejbCreate<METHOD>` makes use of the `getResourceConnection` method illustrated in the section "Understanding Bean-Managed Persistence" at the beginning of this chapter. The bold text illustrates the pieces of code that are used to create a new `AccountHolder` entity.

Listing 8-6   Creating an Entity Bean

```
public class AccountHolderBMPBean implements EntityBean {

    private static final String CREATE_CUSTOMER =
        "INSERT INTO customer " +
        " (firstName, lastName, emailAddress, createDate) " +
        "VALUES " +
        " (?,?,?,?)";

    private static final String GET_CLIENT_ID =
        "SELECT clientId " +
        "FROM customer " +
        "WHERE firstName = ? " +
        "    AND lastName = ? " +
        "    AND emailAddress = ? " +
        "    AND createDate = ?";

    public AccountHolderKey ejbCreateAccountHolder(String
            firstName, String lastName, String emailAddress)
            throws CreateException, EJBException{
        Connection conn = null;
        PreparedStatement ps = null;

        this.firstName = firstName;
        this.lastName = lastName;
        this.emailAddress = emailAddress;
        Calendar now = Calendar.getInstance;
        this.createDate = now.getTime.getTime;

        try{
```

(continued)

Listing 8-6 *(continued)*

```
            conn = this.getResourceConnection;
            ps = conn.prepareStatement(this.CREATE_CUSTOMER);
            ps.setObject(1, this.firstName);
            ps.setObject(2, this.lastName);
            ps.setObject(3, this.emailAddress);
            ps.setObject(4, new
        java.sql.Date(this.createDate));
            ps.executeUpdate;
            return this.initClientId(conn);
    }
    catch(SQLException e){
        throw new CreateException(e.getMessage);
    }
    finally{
        try{
            if(ps != null) ps.close;
            if(conn != null) conn.close;
        }
        catch(SQLException e){
            throw new EJBException;
        }
    }
}

public void ejbPostCreateAccountHolder throws
    CreateException, EJBException{
    // Write your code here
}

private AccountHolderKey initClientId(Connection conn)
    throws SQLException {
    PreparedStatement ps;
    ResultSet rs;
    ps = conn.prepareStatement(this.GET_CLIENT_ID);
    ps.setObject(1, this.firstName);
    ps.setObject(2, this.lastName);
    ps.setObject(3, this.emailAddress);
    ps.setObject(4, new java.sql.Date(this.createDate));
    rs = ps.executeQuery;
    if(rs.first){
        this.clientId =  rs.getLong(1);
        return new AccountHolderKey(this.clientId,
        this.createDate);
    }
    if(rs != null) rs.close;
    if(ps != null) ps.close;
    throw new SQLException;
}
}
```

Listing 8-6 is a big chunk of code that illustrates several techniques I like to apply when developing my EJB applications. Take note of the following points:

- ✔ **My SQL statements are defined in** `private static final String` **variables.** I do that because the statement itself shouldn't change over the life of the entity bean; so only one copy is needed for all entity bean classes. Defining a SQL statement in its own static variable makes it easier to find and maintain, and it represents a more efficient use of memory because static attributes are shared by all instances of a class.

- ✔ **The** `ejbCreateAccountHolder` **method, a** `finally` **clause, is used to release resource connections.** The `finally` clause is used to hold code that should always be executed, even if code in the `try` block throws an exception. Because database resources are precious and expensive to maintain, they should be released as soon as they're no longer needed.

- ✔ **The primary key of the entity object is obtained in a separate method,** `initClientId`. I defined a separate method to obtain the ClientId because, unlike the other persistence fields, the client ID is created by the database. Thus, it cannot be provided by the invoker of the `create` method. Most databases have their own facilities for generating sequences of primary key values. If the primary key creation is deferred to a database, then the database becomes the single source for all primary keys. Primary keys must be managed by the database if data in the database is manipulated without using the EJB architecture (that is, through direct inserts). The `initClientId` method is a helper method for the entity bean class. It isn't a business method because it has no public interface. I declare the method `private` so that it can only be accessed from inside the entity bean class.

Implementing ejbFind<METHOD> methods

When using bean-managed persistence, each finder method in the entity bean must be implemented by the entity bean developer. Each finder method provides the entity bean client with a reference to either a single component interface, or a collection of component interfaces for the entity bean. For each `find<METHOD>` defined in the home interface, a corresponding method called `ejbFind<METHOD>` must be defined in the entity bean class. While the finder method in the home interface of an entity bean returns component interfaces, the `ejbFind<METHOD>` returns the primary keys of the entity beans found in the method invocation. The EJB container is responsible for converting the primary keys into component interfaces and returning those interfaces through the `find<METHOD>` in the home interface.

If you define the same finder method in both a remote home and a local home interface, the method is implemented with the same `ejbFind<METHOD>` in the entity bean class. For example, both local home and remote home interfaces must define a `findByPrimaryKey` method that accepts the primary key of the entity bean as an argument. Both methods can be implemented with a single `ejbFindByPrimaryKey` method in the entity bean class.

Each `ejbFind<METHOD>` must be implemented according to the following guidelines:

- Each `ejbFind<METHOD>` must correspond to a `find<METHOD>` located in the local home and/or remote home interface.

- Each `ejbFind<METHOD>` must be declared `public` and cannot be `abstract` or `final`.

- Each `ejbFind<METHOD>` must return either a single primary key or a collection of primary keys. Finder methods returning a single primary key are called *single-object finders* while finder methods returning a collection of primary keys are called *multi-object finders*. The collection of primary keys returned by a multi-object finder implements either a `java.util.Collection` interface or a `java.util.Enumeration` interface. As of EJB 2.0, the `java.util.Collection` interface is preferred because it's more consistent with the specification for container-managed persistence.

- Each `ejbFind<METHOD>` must throw a `javax.ejb.FinderException` and can also throw application exceptions as necessary in your EJB application.

If you're creating an `ejbFind<METHOD>` that has to be compatible with EJB 1.1 compliant servers, the finder method must return a `java.util.Enumeration` interface.

Inside each `ejbFind<METHOD>`, you must supply the code for retrieving entities from a database. You can use the parameters provided to the finder method to help you find the necessary entities. In Listing 8-7, I provide implementations for two `ejbFind<METHOD>` methods:

- `ejbFindByPrimaryKey(AccountHolderKey key)`: This method illustrates the process for defining a single-object finder. Note that the method accepts a primary key as a parameter and returns the same primary key as a result. That may seem to be an unnecessary operation . . . but it's not. The method must still verify that the record corresponding to the primary key exists. For single-object finders, the method should throw a `javax.ejb.ObjectNotFoundException` if an entity isn't found. The `ObjectNotFoundException` is a subclass of the `FinderException`, which means that it doesn't have to be listed separately in the `throws` clause of the method signature.

- `ejbFindByLastName(String lastName)`: This method illustrates the process for defining a multi-object finder. Notice that the method returns a `java.util.Collection` object, rather than a primary key object. Inside this method I must create the `Collection` and assign all primary keys that are returned from the persistent data source. Note that multi-object finders do not throw an `ObjectNotFoundException` when no objects are found. Instead, multi-object finders should return an empty `Collection` object when no object is found.

The bold text in Listing 8-7 illustrates the creation of primary key objects for the AccountHolderBMPBean. Finder methods must return primary keys to the EJB container so that it can construct instances of the entity beans identified by those keys.

Listing 8-7   Implementing ejbFind<METHOD> Methods

```
public class AccountHolderBMPBean implements EntityBean {

    private static final String FIND_BY_PK =
        "SELECT clientId, createDate " +
        "FROM customer " +
        "WHERE clientId = ? " +
        "    AND createDate = ?";

    private static final String FIND_BY_LAST_NAME =
        "SELECT clientId, createDate " +
        "FROM customer " +
        "WHERE lastName = ? ";

    public AccountHolderKey
            ejbFindByPrimaryKey(AccountHolderKey key) throws
            FinderException {
        Connection conn = null;
        PreparedStatement ps = null;
        ResultSet rs = null;

        try{
            conn = this.getResourceConnection;
            ps = conn.prepareStatement(this.FIND_BY_PK);
            ps.setLong(1, key.getClientId);
            ps.setDate(2, new
            java.sql.Date(key.getCreateDate));
            rs = ps.executeQuery;
            if(rs.next){
                return key;
            }
            else throw new ObjectNotFoundException("Entity
            does not exist.");
        }
        catch(SQLException e){
            throw new FinderException(e.getMessage);
        }
        finally{
            try{
                if(rs != null) rs.close;
                if(ps != null) ps.close;
                if(conn != null) conn.close;
            }
            catch(SQLException e){
```

(continued)

Listing 8-7 *(continued)*

```
                       e.printStackTrace;
                }
            }
        }

        public Collection ejbFindByLastName(String lastName)
                throws FinderException {
            Connection conn = null;
            ResultSet rs = null;
            PreparedStatement ps = null;

            try{
                conn = this.getResourceConnection;
                ps =
                conn.prepareStatement(this.FIND_BY_LAST_NAME);
                ps.setObject(1, lastName);
                rs = ps.executeQuery;
                ArrayList keys = new ArrayList;
                while(rs.next){
                    AccountHolderKey key = new AccountHolderKey(
                        rs.getLong(1), rs.getDate(1).getTime);
                    keys.add(key);
                }
                return keys;
            }
            catch(SQLException e){
                throw new FinderException(e.getMessage);
            }
            finally{
                try{
                    if( rs != null) rs.close;
                    if( ps != null) ps.close;
                    if( conn != null) conn.close;
                }
                catch(SQLException e){
                    e.printStackTrace;
                }
            }
        }
    }
```

Implementing ejbLoad methods

The ejbLoad method in an entity bean is used to load data into the persistence fields from the database. The EJB container invokes the ejbLoad method on an entity bean each time it wants to refresh the state of the entity. The EJB container gets to decide when to invoke the ejbLoad method, but it's the bean developer's responsibility to implement the ejbLoad solution in an entity bean with bean-managed persistence.

Aside from `ejbCreate<METHOD>` methods, the `ejbLoad` method should be the only method that initializes persistence data from a database. Furthermore, the `ejbLoad` method should not be invoked from any method inside the entity bean. Failure to observe this rule may cause your entity bean to enter an invalid state in the middle of a transaction. The `ejbLoad` method is for the exclusive use of the EJB container. Ours is not to wonder why; ours is but to do or die.

Fortunately, the `ejbLoad` method is a relatively simple method to implement. Listing 8-8 illustrates a basic implementation of an `ejbLoad` method. The method executes a `SELECT` statement using JDBC, and then sets the value of each persistence field using the results of the statement. The bold lines of code in Listing 8-8 illustrate the point where results are extracted from the `SELECT` statement to reset the persistence fields in the entity bean. Notice that I don't change the fields that are part of the primary key. Primary key fields should never change, so there's no point in resetting them in an `ejbLoad` operation.

Listing 8-8   An ejbLoad Example

```
public class AccountHolderBMPBean implements EntityBean {

    private static final String LOAD_CUSTOMER =
        "SELECT clientId, firstName, lastName, " +
        "    emailAddress, photograph, createDate " +
        "FROM customer " +
        "WHERE clientId = ? " +
        "    AND createDate = ?";

    public void ejbLoad throws EJBException{
        Connection conn = null;
        PreparedStatement ps = null;
        ResultSet rs = null;

        try{
            conn = this.getResourceConnection;
            ps = conn.prepareStatement(this.LOAD_CUSTOMER);
            ps.setLong(1, clientId);
            ps.setObject(2, new
        java.sql.Date(this.createDate));
            rs = ps.executeQuery;
            if(rs.next){
                this.firstName = rs.getString(1);
                this.lastName = rs.getString(2);
                this.emailAddress = rs.getString(3);
                this.photograph = rs.getString(4);
            }
```

(continued)

Listing 8-8 *(continued)*

```
            }
        catch(SQLException e){
            throw new EJBException(e);
        }
        finally{
            try{
                if(rs != null) rs.close;
                if(ps != null) ps.close;
                if(conn != null) conn.close;
            }
            catch(SQLException e){
                throw new EJBException;
            }
        }
    }
}
```

Implementing ejbStore methods

The `ejbStore` method is used by the EJB container to save the state of an entity bean to a database. As with the `ejbLoad` method, the `ejbStore` method is for use exclusively by the EJB container. The container invokes this method whenever it needs to and it should never be invoked by any method inside the entity bean. Listing 8-9 illustrates a basic solution of the `ejbStore` method that writes all persistence data in an entity bean to the database when it's invoked.

Listing 8-9   An ejbStore Example

```
public class AccountHolderBMPBean implements EntityBean {

    private static final String STORE_CUSTOMER =
        "UPDATE customer " +
        "SET firstName = ? " +
        "    lastName = ? " +
        "    emailAddress = ? " +
        "    photograph = ? " +
        "WHERE clientId = ? " +
        "    AND createDate = ?";

    public void ejbStore throws EJBException {
        Connection conn = null;
        PreparedStatement ps= null;

        try{
            conn = this.getResourceConnection;
            conn.setAutoCommit(false);
            ps = conn.prepareStatement(this.STORE_CUSTOMER);
            ps.setObject(1, this.firstName);
            ps.setObject(2, this.lastName);
```

```
            ps.setObject(3, this.emailAddress);
            ps.setObject(4, this.photograph);
            ps.setLong(5, this.clientId);
            ps.setObject(6, new
        java.sql.Date(this.createDate));
            if( ps.executeUpdate != 1){
                conn.rollback;
                throw new EJBException("Invalid update row
        count on
                    customer.");
            }
        }
    catch(SQLException e){
        throw new EJBException(e);
    }
    finally{
        try{
            if(ps != null) ps.close;
            if(conn != null) conn.close;
        }
        catch(SQLException e){
            throw new EJBException(e);
        }
    }
    }
}
```

 Unlike the `ejbLoad` method, the bean developer has more flexibility in defining the mechanics of the `ejbStore` method. The only requirement of the
behavior for the `ejbStore` method is that any data that has been changed
since the last `ejbLoad` statement must be written to the database.

There is a *design pattern* called snapshot that can be used effectively to tune
the performance of an entity bean's interaction with a database. A design pattern is a standard formula for developing a solution to a typical software
problem. The snapshot pattern is a formula for copying the state of an object
and storing it for use at a later time. This solution is valuable, because it
allows you to compare the variables of an entity bean with their snapshot
before they are stored. If the variables haven't changed, then you don't have
to store them.

Taking advantage of the snapshot pattern is relatively simple; just follow
these steps:

1. **Be sure to create a copy of the persistence field data each time that an
   `ejbCreate<METHOD>` is invoked, in addition to initializing persistence
   fields with entity bean data.**

   The copy is called the snapshot and is nothing more than a picture of
   the data prior to any changes.

2. **Replace the old snapshot with a new snapshot of the data supplied from the database each time the `ejbLoad` method is invoked.**

   This keeps the snapshot current and consistent with the database.

3. **Compare each persistence field to the corresponding element in the snapshot each time the `ejbStore` method is invoked.**

   If a persistence field and its snapshot are the same, the field doesn't need to be updated in the database. If they're different, the field must be included in an update statement.

4. **To update, you have to build the update statement each time `ejbStore` is called, including only the fields that change in the update.**

   Handling the update is the most difficult part of the snapshot pattern. If no fields change, an update isn't necessary.

Implementing ejbRemove methods

The `ejbRemove` method is used by the entity bean when an entity bean instance should be deleted from the database. Each entity bean instance is responsible for managing its own removal. That means that an entity bean should only remove itself from the database when its `ejbRemove` operation is invoked. Client applications invoke a remove operation on the entity bean by invoking the `remove` method on the entity bean's component interface or home interface.

With container-managed entity beans, the `ejbRemove` method is supplied to give an EJB developer the opportunity to respond to the `remove` method invocation. For example, the bean developer may want to make a log entry indicating the entity is being destroyed. With bean-managed persistence, the bean developer is responsible for implementing the `remove` operation. Thus, in an entity bean with bean-managed persistence, the developer must perform the actual `delete` operation that removes the entity bean. Listing 8-10 illustrates the implementation of an `ejbRemove` method for bean-managed persistence.

Listing 8-10   An ejbRemove Example

```
public class AccountHolderBMPBean implements EntityBean {

    private static final String DELETE_CUSTOMER =
        "DELETE FROM customer " +
        "WHERE clientId = ? " +
        " AND createDate = ?";

    public void ejbRemove throws EJBException {
        Connection conn = null;
```

```
            PreparedStatement ps = null;
            try{
                conn = this.getResourceConnection;
                ps = conn.prepareStatement(this.DELETE_CUSTOMER);
                ps.setLong(1, clientId);
                ps.setObject(2, new java.sql.Date(createDate));
                if(ps.executeUpdate != 1){
                    throw new EJBException("Invalid delete row
            count.");
                }
            }
            catch(SQLException e){
                throw new EJBException(e);
            }
            finally{
                try{
                    if(conn != null) conn.close;
                    if(ps != null) ps.close;
                }
                catch(SQLException e){
                    throw new EJBException(e);
                }
            }
        }
    }
```

The bold text in Listing 8-10 illustrates the portion of code that manages the
delete operation. The PreparedStatement.executeUpdate method is used
to invoke the delete operation. This method returns the number of rows
deleted. Because each ejbRemove method should only remove a single row,
I test the result of the executeUpdate method to ensure that the change
count is one. Any other result is invalid and results in an EJBException.

Defining the Deployment Descriptor

Having assembled all the components of the entity bean with bean-managed
persistence, it's time to create a deployment descriptor entry for this entity
bean. The deployment descriptor for an entity bean using bean-managed persistence is only slightly different from its container-managed counterpart. In
fact, because the persistence services are implemented by the bean developer, the deployment descriptor is actually simpler. Consequently, the
deployment descriptor doesn't have to specify EJB QL queries for ejbSelect
and finder methods, and there are no container-managed relationships to
define. The descriptor is left to perform the following tasks:

✔ **Identify the name of the entity bean and its interfaces and classes.**
These include the primary key class, component interfaces, home interfaces, and the entity bean class.

  ✔ Specify that the persistence service is bean-managed.

  ✔ Identify the data source used for the entity bean persistence services.

  ✔ Identify whether the entity bean is reentrant or not. *Reentrant entities*
    are entities that can be invoked more than once in the same thread of
    execution. For a complete description of reentrant entity beans, see
    Chapter 6.

Listing 8-11 illustrates the XML deployment descriptor for the
AccountHolderBMP entity bean that I describe in this chapter. Refer to
Table 8-2 for a listing of each attribute and the allowed values in the
deployment descriptor for an entity bean with bean-managed persistence.

Listing 8-11   A Deployment Descriptor

```
<?xml version="1.0" encoding="UTF-8"?>

<!DOCTYPE ejb-jar PUBLIC "-//Sun Microsystems, Inc.//DTD
          Enterprise
JavaBeans 2.0//EN" "http://java.sun.com/dtd/ejb-jar_2_0.dtd">

<ejb-jar>
 <enterprise-beans>
  <entity>
   <description>
    This is an account holder bean with bean managed
          persistence.
   </description>
   <ejb-name>AccountHolderBMP</ejb-name>
   <home>
    com.sextanttech.entities.interfaces.AccountHolderBMPHome
   </home>
   <remote>

          com.sextanttech.entities.interfaces.AccountHolderB
          MPRemote
   </remote>
   <local-home>

          com.sextanttech.entities.interfaces.AccountHolderB
          MPLocalHome
   </local-home>
   <local>
    com.sextanttech.entities.interfaces.AccountHolderBMPLocal
   </local>
   <ejb-class>

          com.sextanttech.entities.implementations.AccountHo
          lderBMPBean
   </ejb-class>
   <prim-key-class>
```

```
      com.sextanttech.entities.interfaces.AccountHolderKey
    </prim-key-class>
    <persistence-type>Bean</persistence-type>
    <reentrant>False</reentrant>
    <resource-ref>
     <description>Data source for account holder</description>
     <res-ref-name>jdbc/AcctHolderDatabase</res-ref-name>
     <res-type>javax.sql.DataSource</res-type>
     <res-auth>Container<res-auth>
    </resource-ref>
   </entity>
</enterprise-beans>
</ejb-jar>
```

Table 8-2		Deployment Descriptors for BMP Entities		
Attribute name	*Required*	*Multiplicity*	*Parent*	*Value*
<entity>	Yes	One	<enterprise-beans>	Entity bean attributes.
<description>	No	One	<entity>	Text description of entity bean.
<display-name>	No	One	<entity>	Name of entity bean for GUI tools.
<large-icon>	No	One	<entity>	Location and name of icon for GUI tools.
<small-icon>	No	One	<entity>	Location and name of icon for GUI tools.
<ejb-name>	Yes	One	<entity>	Name of EJB component.
<home>	No	Zero to one	<entity>	Fully qualified class name of remote home interface.
<remote>	No	Zero to one	<entity>	Fully qualified class name of remote interface.

(continued)

Table 8-2 (continued)

Attribute name	Required	Multiplicity	Parent	Value
`<local-home>`	No	zero to one	`<entity>`	Fully qualified class name to local home interface.
`<local>`	No	zero to one	`<entity>`	Fully qualified class name to local interface.
`<ejb-class>`	Yes	One	`<entity>`	Fully qualified class name to entity bean class.
`<prim-key-class>`	Yes	One	`<entity>` Defines the primary key class type for simple or compound primary keys.	
`<persistence-type>`	Yes	One	`<entity>`Bean for bean-managed persistence (BMP).	
`<reentrant>`	Yes	One	`<entity>`	`True` or `False`. See Chapter 6 for more details.
`<resource-ref>`	Yes	One or more	`<entity>`	Resource ref subelements.
`<description>`	No	One	`<resource-ref>`	Describes the resource reference.
`<res-ref-name>`	Yes	One	`<resource-ref>`	The name assigned to the resource.
`<res-ref-type>`	Yes	One	`<resource-ref>`	The fully qualified class name of the resource.

Attribute name	Required	Multiplicity	Parent	Value
`<res-auth>`	Yes	One	`<resource-ref>`	`Container` for container-managed authentication or `Bean` for bean-managed authentication.
`<res-sharing-scope>`	No	One	`<resource-ref>`	`Sharable` if connections to this resource can be shared with other beans; `Unsharable` if they cannot. The default value is `Sharable`.

Part IV

Expressing Yourself with Message-Driven Beans

The 5th Wave   By Rich Tennant

"What I'm looking for are dynamic Web applications and content, not Web innuendoes and intent."

In this part . . .

Message-driven beans (MDBs), the latest addition to the EJB framework, allow the implementation of processes that can run autonomously from a client application. If you need to build large reports, generate monthly statements, or close the books on your accounts for the month or the year, you'll have to run some computer processes that could take hours or even days. By using MDBs, you'll be able to run those processes without tying up a client computer. To discover more about MDBs and the Java Messaging Service, read on.

Chapter 9

Discovering Java Messaging Service

*T*he Java Messaging Service (JMS) is Java's standard API for creating messaging applications. JMS applications allow client applications and server applications to perform actions in parallel, instead of serially. The key distinction between JMS applications and the EJB components that I've discussed so far is that when a client invokes a JMS service, it can continue to perform operations without waiting for a response from the consumer of the message, whereas the session and entity bean components must respond to the client before it can proceed.

As the following list makes clear, there are three important roles in every JMS application:

✔ **The message producer:** In EJB applications, the message producer is the client of the EJB application. The client doesn't connect directly to an enterprise bean. Instead, it connects to a messaging service provider and delivers the message to that provider. In the following pages, you'll discover how message producers create messages, connect to a service provider, and deliver messages.

✔ **The messaging service:** For messaging to exist, the application developer must create a JMS service. The messaging service is a JMS server that can host a variety of JMS applications. Each application is composed of a set of objects called *administered objects*. Administered objects are so named because they're administered by the JMS service. JMS application developers create their applications by creating administered objects and then deploying them to the JMS server.

Creating administered objects is outside the scope of this book. Throughout this chapter, you see how to connect to administered objects and send messages to them. If you need a good reference on creating JMS applications, check out *Java Messaging Service*, written by Richard Monson-Haefel and David Chappell and published by O'Reilly.

✔ **The message consumer:** In an EJB application, the message consumer is a message-driven bean. The good news about message consumers is that the EJB container manages all the interactions between the consumer and the messaging service provider. Instead of working out how to connect to and receive messages from the server, you can focus on what to do in response to a message delivery. I've devoted Chapter 10 to the topic of creating message-driven beans.

Messaging services are powerful because they provide an intermediary that decouples the message producer and the message consumer. In a messaging service, the message producer connects to the messaging service provider and delivers a message. The service provider says, "Thanks, I got your message." The message producer is then free to move on and perform other tasks. Meanwhile, depending on the type of service in use, the message consumer can either connect to the server at a later, undetermined time or can retain an active connection to the server. When the messaging service provider gets around to it, it delivers the message to the message consumer, which then says, "Thanks, service provider, I got the message," and then goes about its business of doing whatever it is that message consumers do with messages. Note that the message producer doesn't have to wait around for the message consumer to receive a message before it goes about its business. That's important to distributed applications because any one of hundreds of things could go wrong, either causing a delay in delivery of a message or the loss of a message entirely.

Understanding the JMS Architecture

The fundamentals of JMS are pretty easy to grasp. Six core interfaces define a JMS service in the most generic sense. These interfaces are independent of any particular style of messaging service, which means that they can be extended to implement messaging services that support different messaging models. The core interfaces are

✔ `javax.jms.Connection`: This interface defines a connection between a client application and a JMS server. The `Connection` object provides a variety of services associated with the delivery and receipt of messages from a JMS server. These services include the assignment of a unique ID to the client application, the ability to start and stop message delivery, and the ability to disconnect from the JMS server.

✔ `javax.jms.ConnectionFactory`: This interface creates `Connection` objects, which enable communication between a JMS server and a client application. Factory objects of all kinds are used to assemble other complex objects. Factory objects are convenient for hiding the details of how an object is created. In addition, factory objects may provide other hidden services, such as resource pooling. A JMS provider must implement the `ConnectionFactory` for each type of JMS service that it provides.

✔ `javax.jms.Destination`: This interface is one of the administered objects of the JMS provider and contains an address to a particular messaging venue. Multiple client applications can connect to a `Destination` to send and receive messages. The `Destination` is like a mail sorting room — messages come in from `MessageProducer` objects, where they can be held temporarily and/or delivered to a `MessageConsumer`.

✔ `javax.jms.Session`: This interface represents an active channel of communication between a client application and a JMS provider. A `Session` provides a number of services including the creation of `MessageProducer` and `MessageConsumer` objects, the creation of `Message` objects, the administration of transactions, and the delivery and acknowledgement of messages. `Session` objects are obtained from the `Connection` object.

✔ `javax.jms.MessageProducer`: This interface represents a *client handle* — an object that provides clients with access to some resource — to a specific `Destination` object. Client applications use this handle to send messages to the `Destination`. `MessageProducer` objects are created for a specific `Destination` by the `Session` object. The client then obtains new `Message` objects from the `Session`, sets the content of the `Message` object, and delivers the message using a `MessageProducer`.

✔ `javax.jms.MessageConsumer`: This interface represents a client handle to a specific `Destination`. Client applications use this handle to receive messages from the `Destination`. The `MessageConsumer` object is created for a specific `Destination` by the `Session` object.

From those six basic interfaces, the JMS architecture creates *subinterfaces* that support two different types of messaging — point-to-point (PTP) and publish/subscribe (or pub/sub for short):

✔ **PTP messaging results in the delivery of a message from the** `MessageProducer` **to a specific** `MessageConsumer`. When using PTP messaging, the destination is represented as a queue of messages. The message producer adds messages to the end of the queue, and the message consumer removes messages from the front of the queue. Once removed, the messages are gone forever.

✔ **The pub/sub model of messaging is similar to what you experience if you've ever subscribed to a list server.** In pub/sub messaging, message producers publish messages to a destination, which is referred to as a *topic*. After it's published, the destination routes the messages to all interested subscribers. Depending on the configuration of the pub/sub model, the destination can temporarily hold messages for a subscriber that isn't currently logged on.

The interfaces for the pub/sub model and the PTP model are illustrated in Table 9-1.

Table 9-1	Core JMS Interfaces	
Parent Interfaces	*PTP Interfaces*	*Pub/Sub Interfaces*
ConnectionFactory	QueueConnectionFactory	TopicConnection Factory
Connection	QueueConnection	TopicConnection
Destination	Queue	Topic
Session	QueueSession	TopicSession
MessageProducer	QueueSender	TopicPublisher
MessageConsumer	QueueReceiver, QueueBrowser	TopicSubscriber

Producing JMS Messages

Only a couple of simple steps are necessary to produce JMS messages. I cover each step in detail in the following subsections. To summarize, the process goes as follows:

1. **A** ConnectionFactory **is obtained by using the Java Naming and Directory Interface (JNDI) to look up the JMS provider's** ConnectionFactory. The JMS provider should have some documentation indicating what the JNDI name for the ConnectionFactory is as well as the type of ConnectionFactory used.

2. **A** Destination **is obtained using JNDI to look up the** Destination **name.** Remember that a Destination object is an administered object that is provided by the developer of the JMS application. The JMS application developer must register the name of the Destination in JNDI and identify the type of Destination object in use.

3. **Using the** `ConnectionFactory`**, a** `Connection` **is obtained to the JMS provider.** Initially, message delivery is blocked on the `Connection` until the `Session` is properly initialized.

4. **Passing the** `Destination` **obtained in Step 2 as an argument, the** `Connection` **is used to create a** `Session` **with the** `Destination` **object.**

5. **Using the** `Session`**, a** `MessageProducer` **is created.** The `MessageProducer` manages the actual delivery of messages to the specified `Destination`. At this point, you're ready to start creating and delivering messages.

6. **A new** `Message` **object is obtained from the** `Session` **object using one of the factory methods for creating messages.** This message is subsequently populated with content.

7. **The** `Message` **object is delivered to the** `Destination` **through the** `MessageProducer` **object.**

Connecting to a Queue

Listing 9-1 illustrates the implementation of the general steps for creating a connection to a `Queue`. In the `sendMessage` method defined in Listing 9-1, the JMS client performs the following steps:

1. **Obtains a** `QueueConnectionFactory`**.**

2. **Obtains a reference to the desired** `Queue`**.**

3. **Creates a** `QueueConnection` **with the** `QueueConnectionFactory`**.**

4. **Obtains a** `QueueSession` **from the** `QueueConnection`**.** The `QueueConnection.getQueueSession` method takes two arguments. The first is `boolean` and indicates whether or not the session should be transacted. If a `Session` is transacted, mail delivery operations are required to either succeed completely or to fail completely. The second argument identifies the acknowledgement mode. Because our client applications are focusing on sending messages, the acknowledgement mode isn't consequential.

5. **Obtains a** `QueueSender` **from the** `QueueSession`**.** After you've completed this step, you're ready to start delivering messages.

Note that I have included a `finally` clause in the listing that closes my JMS resources when they're no longer in use. This is an important step because resources that are left open are still active and can't be garbage collected. Failure to close resources can result in memory leaks in your application.

Listing 9-1   Creating a Queue Connection

```java
public void sendMessage(String userName, String password) {
    QueueConnection conn = null;
    QueueSession session = null;
    QueueSender sender = null;

    try{
        // First obtain the Connection Factory.
        Object obj = context.lookup("jms/FactoryName");
        QueueConnectionFactory factory =
            (QueueConnectionFactory)
            PortableRemoteObject.narrow(obj,
            Class.forName("javax.jms.
            QueueConnectionFactory"));

        // Next obtain the Destination.
        obj = context.lookup("jms/QueueName");
        Queue destination = (Queue) PortableRemoteObject.
            narrow(obj,
            Class.forName("javax.jms.Queue"));

        // Now it's time to make the connection.
        conn = factory.createQueueConnection(userName,
            password);
        conn.stop(); // blocks the delivery of messages on
            this connection.

        // Once connected it's time to create a session.
        session = conn.createQueueSession(true,
            Session.AUTO_ACKNOWLEDGE);

        // Now you're ready to create the sender.
        sender = session.createSender(destination);
    }
    catch(NamingException e){
        // A JNDI lookup operation failed.
        e.printStackTrace();
    }
    catch(ClassNotFoundException e){
        // A PortableRemoteObject.narrow operation failed.
        e.printStackTrace();
    }
    catch(JMSException e){
        // A messaging failure occurred.
        e.printStackTrace();
    }
    finally{
        try{
            sender.close();
            session.close();
```

```
        conn.close();
    }
    catch(JMSException e){ e.printStackTrace(); }
    }
}
```

Connecting to a Topic

Listing 9-2 illustrates the implementation of the general steps for creating a connection to a `Topic`. In the `sendMessage` method defined in Listing 9-2, the JMS client performs the following steps:

1. **Obtains a** `TopicConnectionFactory`.

2. **Obtains a reference to the desired** `Topic`.

3. **Creates a** `TopicConnection` **with the** `TopicConnectionFactory`.

4. **Obtains a** `TopicSession` **from the** `TopicConnection`. The `TopicConnection.getTopicSession` method takes two arguments. The first is `boolean` and indicates whether or not the session should be transacted. Transacted sessions require mail delivery operations to either succeed completely or to fail completely. The second argument identifies the acknowledgement mode, which is only relevant if you intend to receive messages over the `Connection` (as opposed to just sending messages).

5. **Obtains a** `TopicPublisher` **from the** `TopicSession`. After you've completed this step, you're ready to start delivering messages.

Mirroring my practice in Listing 9-1, I've included a `finally` clause in Listing 9-2 that closes JMS resources when they're no longer in use. Failure to close resources can result in memory leaks in your application.

Listing 9-2   Creating a Topic Connection

```
public void sendMessage(String userName, String password) {
    TopicConnection conn = null;
    TopicSession session = null;
    TopicPublisher publisher = null;

    try{
        // First obtain the Connection Factory.
        Object obj = context.lookup("jms/FactoryName");
        TopicConnectionFactory factory =
            (TopicConnectionFactory)
             PortableRemoteObject.narrow(obj,
              Class.forName("javax.jms.
               TopicConnectionFactory"));
```

(continued)

Listing 9-2 *(continued)*

```
        // Next obtain the Destination.
        obj = context.lookup("jms/TopicName");
        Topic destination = (Topic) PortableRemoteObject.
            narrow(obj,
                Class.forName("javax.jms.Topic"));

        // Now it's time to make the connection.
        conn = factory.createTopicConnection(userName,
            password);
        conn.stop(); // blocks the delivery of messages on
            this connection.

        // Once connected it's time to create a session.
        session = conn.createTopicSession(true,
            Session.AUTO_ACKNOWLEDGE);

        // Now you're ready to create the publisher.
        publisher = session.createPublisher(destination);
    }
    catch(NamingException e){
        // A JNDI lookup operation failed.
        e.printStackTrace();
    }
    catch(ClassNotFoundException e){
        // A PortableRemoteObject.narrow operation failed.
        e.printStackTrace();
    }
    catch(JMSException e){
        // A messaging failure occurred.
        e.printStackTrace();
    }
    finally{
        try{
            // Released all resources.
          publisher.close();
          session.close();
          conn.close();
        }
        catch(JMSException e){ e.printStackTrace(); }
    }
}
```

Creating and sending JMS messages

The first task in defining a messaging service is determining the structure of the message to be delivered. This should make sense because the producer and consumer of a message must understand how to read and interpret the message's contents. A message itself has three distinct components:

✔ **The header:** The header contains a number of fields that describe meta information about the message. Message header fields include the message ID, which identifies this message; the correlation ID, which identifies the previous message in a thread of messages; and the message priority, which may have some impact on the speed at which a message is delivered.

✔ **Message properties:** Unique to an application domain, you can define message properties to help with organizing and describing messages. You can use message properties, for example, to define some criteria for sorting or ranking messages. What's more, a message consumer can accept or refuse delivery of messages based on their properties as well as the values of their header fields.

✔ **The message body:** The message body is where the content of your message is placed. JMS defines five different types of messages, each capable of holding a different kind of body content. The rules for message properties and the header are the same for all types of JMS messages; the only distinction is the type of content held in the message's body. The different types of JMS messages are

- `javax.jms.BytesMessage:` A `BytesMessage` contains a stream of encoded bytes. The producer must add the stream of bytes to the message, which then gets delivered to the consumer of the message. The consumer must then read the bytes and interpret them. `BytesMessages` do not contain Java primitive bytes, although you might assume that fact from the name. If you need to pass a stream of Java primitive bytes, use the `StreamMessage`.

- `javax.jms.MapMessage:` A `MapMessage` has a body that's a set of name/value pairs. The `MapMessage` is a good choice for most EJB purposes, where a message will likely deliver a number of arguments to a message-driven bean, which will map the method arguments to a local method invocation of another EJB component.

- `javax.jms.ObjectMessage:` An `ObjectMessage` has a body that's a serializable Java object. The message producer creates an instance of the object and adds it to the message body. The message consumer retrieves the message from the body of the message and uses it to perform some task. An `ObjectMessage` can contain a JavaBean, which has getters and setters for the object properties, or it could contain a dependent value object for an entity bean.

- `javax.jms.StreamMessage:` A `StreamMessage` message can hold a stream of Java primitive byte values. The stream allows the message consumer to read potentially large amounts of data from a file or across a network connection.

- `javax.jms.TextMessage`: The `TextMessage` has a body of the type `java.lang.String`. The content of the `TextMessage` is a `String` value, and it's the closest to what you might expect for a traditional e-mail message. The purpose envisioned for `TextMessage` objects is the delivery of XML-based messages. Because an XML document is just a `String` of characters with special XML element delimiters, you can deliver an XML-formatted message as a `String`. The message consumer must then parse the message and interpret the meaning of its contents.

After you've selected the type of message you want to send, the process of creating and sending the message is relatively simple. I'll illustrate it using the `MapMessage`, which is probably a good choice for many JMS messages marked for delivery to EJB message-driven-beans. The reason I like the `MapMessage` is that it can hold a variety of named arguments that the message-driven bean can then extract and use to invoke local operations in the EJB container.

Regardless of the type of message you choose, you must obtain an instance of the message from the `Session` object. The code for a `MapMessage` is

```
MapMessage message = session.createMapMessage();
```

The `Session` object provides a different `create` method for each type of message. The name of each `create` method follows the syntax convention of `create<MessageType>` where `MessageType` identifies the type of message you want to create.

After you have the `MapMessage`, you need to initialize the body of the message. In my example, I'm creating some fields in the body that contain a `clientId`, `createDate`, and `emailAddress`. The code to accomplish this task is

```
message.setLong("clientId", 123456781);
message.setObject("createDate", new Date().getTime());
message.setString("emailAddress",
          "feedback@sextanttech.com");
```

When working with the message, you can also initialize properties of a message or modify attributes in the message header. The properties of a message and the attributes of the message header can be used by a message consumer to select only those messages that have the properties and settings the consumer is interested in. This capability allows you to have several message consumers that subscribe to the same `Topic` or `Queue`, but only retrieve messages from the `Topic` or `Queue` that contain properties that interest them. There are numerous methods in each type of message for working with the message header and properties. For more information on the available methods, refer to the Java documentation. In the following example, I adjust a message header attribute that indicates that the message is urgent:

```
message.setJMSPriority(9); // the highest priority
```

When this message is delivered, I could have a special message consumer that only handles high priority messages so that they can be handled quickly without having to wait for low priority messages to be completed. There are many header attributes in JMS messages, and you can define as many properties as you want. I recommend referring to the Java documentation that comes with the J2EE SDK and is downloadable from Sun Microsystems at http://java.sun.com.

The final task is delivering the message. The message is delivered via your MessageProducer object. The code is virtually identical, regardless of whether you're delivering the message to a Topic or to a Queue. When sending messages to a Queue, you should use the QueueSender.send method. When delivering messages to a Topic, you should use the TopicPublisher. publish method. I've illustrated both approaches in the following code:

```
//Sending a message to a queue
sender.send(message);

// Publishing a message to a Topic
publisher.publish(message);
```

Chapter 10

Creating Message-Driven Beans

● ●

In This Chapter

▶ Discovering the lifecycle of message-driven beans

▶ Creating a message-driven bean

▶ Defining the deployment descriptor for message-driven beans

● ●

Message-driven beans are EJB components that listen for messages published on a Java Messaging Service Server (JMS Server). In Chapter 9, I examine the principles of JMS as they apply to creating EJB applications with message-driven beans. The following points from Chapter 9 are relevant to this chapter:

- ✔ **Client applications send messages to a message-driven bean via a JMS server.** The message a client sends must implement the `javax.jms.Message` interface. This interface provides a set of methods that can be used to create and retrieve message properties. The client application uses properties to store attributes that a message-driven bean must retrieve to perform operations.

- ✔ **JMS messages are delivered to a JMS server from the client application.** Because the client never has a direct reference to the message-driven bean, it can continue to perform other actions as soon as the message is delivered to the JMS server. Because the actions of the client application are not synchronized with the actions of the message-driven bean, the two can perform tasks in parallel. The ability for two tasks in an application to be performed in parallel is called *asynchronous processing*.

- ✔ **Message-driven beans are message listeners.** They listen for messages that are posted to a JMS server. In fact, the JMS server can store messages for message-driven beans, even if the message-driven bean is not listening. As soon as the message-driven bean starts listening, the JMS server will start delivering any messages it has stored. Because message-driven beans are never directly accessed by a client application, they don't have home or component interfaces. Thus, you only need to create a single class for a message-driven bean.

Message-driven beans are useful for performing tasks in which the client application doesn't need to know the result of the task. By using message-driven beans, you can make your applications run faster because the client doesn't have to wait for a response from the EJB server when it delivers a message to the JMS server. Consequently, the client application can continue to perform tasks in parallel to the EJB container that is executing the message-driven beans.

Message-driven beans aren't for use in all scenarios. First off, a JMS server will not guarantee that messages are delivered in any particular order. If your client application needs to have messages processed in a particular order, you're probably better off using session beans, which are synchronous and can thus guarantee an order to method invocations. Second, message-driven beans are stateless, so if you need to preserve state between method invocations, you must use stateful session beans.

One important benefit of using message-driven beans is that the EJB container provides all the plumbing necessary for message-driven beans to process messages concurrently. The result is a multithreading environment that provides a substantial improvement in performance.

Lifecycle of Message-Driven Beans

The lifecycle of a message-driven bean is similar to that of a stateless session bean. Message-driven beans are created by the EJB container and pooled in a Method Ready state. Message-driven beans in a Method Ready state are ready to respond to messages delivered by the JMS server. As the JMS server receives messages for message-driven beans, it sends them to the EJB container. The EJB container removes a message-driven bean from the pool and sends the message to it. As soon as the message-driven bean is finished processing the message, it's returned to the pool, where it waits for the next method invocation. Figure 10-1 illustrates the lifecycle of the message-driven bean, showing when each lifecycle method is invoked.

Message-driven beans only have a single method that responds to JMS server invocations, the onMessage method. The Method Ready state gets its name from the fact that the onMessage method is the one that needs to be ready for messages from the JMS server.

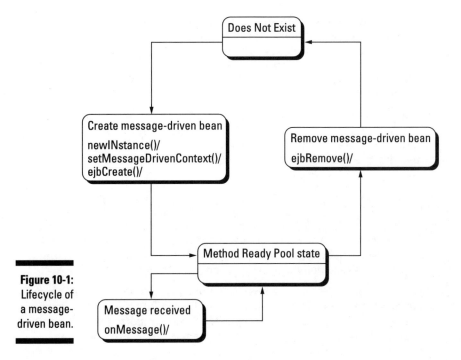

Figure 10-1:
Lifecycle of
a message-
driven bean.

The following activities comprise a message-driven bean's lifecycle:

- When the EJB container is started, message-driven beans are created. The creation process proceeds in the following order:

    1. Each bean is created using the `Class.newInstance` method.

    2. The `setMessageDrivenContext` method is invoked on the message-driven bean. The `setMessageDrivenContext` method is implemented from the `javax.ejb.MessageDrivenBean` interface, which every message-driven bean must implement.

    3. The `ejbCreate` method is invoked on the message-driven bean. The bean developer must supply one `ejbCreate` method with no arguments for a message-driven bean. This method is the place where EJB component developers can initialize any resources that are used by the message-driven bean during method invocations.

- After it's created, the message-driven bean is placed in a pool of beans that are available to process messages delivered by a JMS server. While in the pool, the message-driven bean is said to be in a *method ready state*, which means it's ready to handle method invocations.

✔ As each messaged is delivered, the EJB container takes a random bean from the container and uses it to process the message. The message is delivered by invoking a message-driven bean's onMessage method, passing the message as a parameter. The onMessage method is implemented from the javax.jms.MessageListener interface, which all message-driven beans must implement.

The onMessage method receives a Message object as a parameter, which is similar to a java.util.Map. Attributes can be set by the client application, and the message-driven bean extracts those attributes by invoking the Message.getAttribute method and passing the name of the attribute as an argument.

✔ After a message-driven bean finishes processing a message, it's returned to the method ready pool. Message-driven beans are stateless, which means that a client application isn't guaranteed that the same message-driven bean will process two consecutive messages. In fact, because message-driven beans can process multiple messages in parallel, the order of message delivery isn't guaranteed either.

✔ When a message is to be removed by the EJB container, its ejbRemove method is invoked. This method should be used by the bean developer to release any application resources that were initialized in the bean's ejbCreate method. After the ejbRemove method is invoked, the message-driven bean ceases to exist. The ejbRemove method is invoked any time a runtime exception is thrown in the message-driven bean.

Although under normal circumstances the ejbRemove method is invoked when a bean is about to be destroyed, a couple of scenarios are possible where this may not occur. First, if an EJB container crashes, the ejbRemove method will not be invoked. Second, if a system error is thrown from the message-driven bean to the container, the ejbRemove method is automatically invoked by the container. Primarily because of the latter case, the EJB spec recommends that EJB application developers create some mechanism which periodically searches for and removes unused application resources.

The Message-Driven Bean Class

Message-driven beans are different from any other entity bean because they don't have home or component interfaces. Message-driven beans don't need these interfaces because they don't participate in *RMI communication,* a process that allows applications on different computers to talk directly to each other. Therefore, there is never a need for a message-driven bean to present an interface to a remote client. That makes the creation of message-driven beans a lot simpler than their session bean and entity bean brethren. Here are the basic requirements for each message-driven bean class:

✔ The message-driven bean must implement the `javax.ejb.MessageDrivenBean` interface. This interface defines two methods: `setMessageDrivenContext` and `ejbRemove`.

✔ The message-driven bean must implement the `javax.jsp.MessageListener` interface. This interface defines one method: `onMessage`.

✔ Each message-driven bean must have one `ejbCreate` method that takes no arguments. This method is invoked by the EJB container after a message-driven bean is created and before it's provided to the method ready pool. The bean developer should use this method to initialize any application resources that the message-driven bean needs during method invocations.

✔ Message-driven bean classes must be declared `public` and cannot be declared `final` or `abstract`. The message-driven bean class must not override the `finalize` method.

✔ Each message-driven bean class must declare one constructor that is `public` and takes no arguments.

In addition to these requirements, message-driven bean classes can define as many helper methods as are needed to perform the task of the bean. *Helper methods* are internal methods that are invoked from within the `onMessage` method.

Message-driven beans are strictly forbidden to throw application exceptions from their `onMessage` methods. This rule is prescribed because of the behavior of a JMS server. If an exception is thrown from an `onMessage` method, the JMS server will attempt to redeliver the message. This could lead to an infinite loop of method invocations that generates errors. Thus, any application exception generated inside a message bean must be handled by the message bean before it finishes processing the `onMessage` method invocation.

The `onMessage` method is the only way to invoke a message-driven bean. For clarity, each message-driven bean should be created to perform a single kind of task. This design consideration will help keep the message-driven bean simple and easier to maintain.

Listing 10-1 illustrates a message-driven bean that is used to create an account statement and send it to an account holder's e-mail address. This scenario is appropriate for the message-driven bean because the client does need to know the outcome of the delivery. Besides, if you requested a statement from an ATM machine be delivered to your e-mail address, you wouldn't want to wait around for some computer to generate the statement and deliver it before you got your ATM card back. The asynchronous nature of message-driven beans makes them ideal for performing labor-intensive tasks, such as generating reports.

Listing 10-1   The GenerateStatementBean Class

```
package com.sextanttech.messages;

import javax.ejb.MessageDrivenBean;
import javax.jms.MessageListener;
import javax.ejb.MessageDrivenContext;
import javax.ejb.EJBException;
import javax.ejb.CreateException;
import javax.jms.Message;
import javax.jms.MapMessage;
import javax.jms.JMSException;
import com.sextanttech.entities.interfaces.AccountHolderKey;
import com.sextanttech.entities.interfaces.
          AccountHolderLocalHome;
import com.sextanttech.entities.interfaces.AccountHolderLocal;
import com.sextanttech.entities.interfaces.AccountKey;
import com.sextanttech.entities.interfaces.AccountLocalHome;
import com.sextanttech.entities.interfaces.AccountLocal;
import com.sextanttech.util.AcctStatement;
import javax.naming.InitialContext;
import javax.naming.Context;
import javax.mail.*;
import java.util.Date;
import javax.rmi.PortableRemoteObject;

import java.util.Properties;

public class GenerateStatementBean implements
          MessageDrivenBean, MessageListener {
    private MessageDrivenContext ctx;

    public GenerateStatementBean() {
        // the public noargs constructor
    }

    public void setMessageDrivenContext( MessageDrivenContext
        context ) {
        ctx = context; // store the context in an instance
        variable
    }

    public void ejbCreate() {
        // initialize application resources
    }

    public void ejbRemove() throws EJBException {
        this.ctx = null;
        // release any application resources declared in
        ejbCreate()
    }
```

```
public void onMessage( javax.jms.Message msg ) {
    // declare local ejb references
    AccountHolderLocal owner;
    AccountHolderLocalHome ownerHome;
    AccountLocal acct;
    AccountLocalHome acctHome;
    try {
        // retrieve properties from the message
        MapMessage message = ( MapMessage )msg;
        String username = ( String )message.getString(
        "username" );
        String password = ( String )message.getString(
        "password" );
        AccountKey accountKey = new AccountKey(
        message.getLong( "createDate" ), message.getLong(
        "accountId" ) );
        // Initialize local home interfaces
        Context context = new InitialContext();
        ownerHome = ( AccountHolderLocalHome )context.
        lookup( "java:comp/env/ejb/accountHolderEJB" );
        acctHome = ( AccountLocalHome )context.lookup(
        "java:comp/env/ejb/accountEJB" );
        // find the necessary entity beans to perform
        this task.
        owner = ownerHome.findByIdentity( username,
        password );
        acct = acctHome.findByPrimaryKey( accountKey );
        String statement = this.buildClientStatement(
        acct );
        String[] emailAddress = {owner.getEmailAddr()};
        this.sendStatement( emailAddress, statement );
    }
    catch ( Exception e ) {
    }
}

public String buildClientStatement( AccountLocal acct ) {
    return "Bank error in your favor, collect $200.00.";
}

public void sendStatement( String[] emailAddress, String
        statement ) {
    // JavaMail solution provided in Sample application
        online.
}
}
```

Notice that the only instance variable declared is the `MessageDrivenContext` variable. Because message-driven beans are stateless, only application resources and the `MessageDrivenContext` should be held in instance variables. Any variables that are message-specific should be method scope variables to the `onMessage` method — that is, declared inside the `onMessage` method.

As you can see from the example in Listing 10-1, there's very little to do in the typical message-driven bean other than to implement your business process.

The MessageDrivenContext Examined

As with other EJB components, message-driven beans are executed in a context. The context is used to present some information to the message-driven bean about its state and to give the message-driven bean access to EJB container resources. Typically, message-driven bean implementations will not make heavy use of the application context. No references to the MessageDrivenContext appear in my simple example except when it's initialized and when the ejbRemove method is invoked. Here's an overview of the methods defined in the MessageDrivenContext and their purposes:

- getRollbackOnly: This method returns a boolean value indicating whether the transaction in which the message-driven bean is participating will be rolled back. This method is accessible only in message-driven beans where the message-driven bean participates in container-managed transactions.

- setRollbackOnly: This method tells the container to mark the current transaction for rollback. The method is only accessible to message-driven beans participating in container-managed transactions. You could use this method to force a transaction rollback in the event that you encounter an application error in the onMessage method.

- getUserTransaction: This method is only accessible to message-driven beans with bean-managed transactions. Bean-managed transactions are manually maintained by the EJB developer. They aren't recommended for the faint of heart because managing transactions isn't a beginner's task. Besides, one of the primary benefits of EJB containers is transaction management, so why throw that away? This method returns a javax.transaction.UserTransaction object, which provides access to transaction management services.

- getCallerPrinciple: This method is inherited from EJBContext and is for use with session beans and entity beans only. Message-driven beans can't use this method because the management of security on message-driven beans is different from other EJB components.

- isCallerInRole: Inherited from the EJBContext. Like getCallerPrinciple, this method is for session beans and entity beans only.

- getEJBHome: Welcome to the Land of Oz. There is no home for a message-driven bean. Don't use this method.

- getEJBLocalHome You're not in Kansas anymore. There are no home interfaces for a message-driven bean, so get used to it and don't use this method.

As you can see, most of the methods in the MessageDrivenContext interface have no place in message-driven beans. The fact that they're even present illustrates that the developers of the EJB specification didn't envision a place for asynchronous EJB invocations when they created the EJB 1.1 specification.

Deployment Descriptor Elements for Message-Driven Beans

As with all other EJB components, message-driven beans are blessed with a deployment descriptor. This descriptor is used to tell the EJB container about the characteristics of each message-driven bean in an EJB application. It's with information from the deployment descriptor that the EJB container can dynamically create new instances of the message-driven bean and make use of them in an application context.

Because message-driven beans must interact with a JMS server, there are several properties of the JMS server that must be initialized in the message-driven bean's deployment descriptor. Listing 10-2 displays the deployment descriptor entry for the GenerateStatementBean that I present earlier in the chapter; refer to Listing 10-1.

Listing 10-2   A Message-Driven Bean Descriptor

```
<ejb-jar>
  <enterprise-beans>
   <message-driven>
      <description>This message-driven bean will send email
         messages.</description>
      <ejb-name>GenerateStatementEJB</ejb-name>
      <ejb-class>com.sextanttech.messages.
         GenerateStatementBean</ejb-class>
      <transaction-type>Container</transaction-type>
      <acknowledge-mode>Auto-acknowledge</acknowledge-mode>
      <message-driven-destination>
        <destination-type>javax.jms.Queue</destination-type>
      </message-driven-destination>
   </message-driven>
  </enterprise-beans>
</ejb-jar>
```

The attributes of a message-driven bean entry in a deployment descriptor can be broken into three broad categories:

✔ **Elements used to describe the message-driven bean class.** Table 10-1 contains a listing of all these attributes. You should find most of them familiar because they're also used in other types of EJB components.

✓ **Elements used to describe features of the JMS service provider that apply to this message.** This information is necessary so that the EJB container can initialize the services on the JMS server for the message-driven bean. I examine each of the JMS elements in detail in the upcoming sections.

✓ **Elements that make references to any other EJB application resources that might be needed as part of the message-driven bean's context.** I further examine the elements that perform these services in Chapter 12.

Table 10-1		Attributes of the <message-driven> Tag
Attribute	*Optional*	*Description*
<description>	Yes	An optional text description of the purpose of the bean.
<display-name>	Yes	An optional name that can be displayed in a deployment tool.
<small-icon>	Yes	An optional icon that can be displayed in a deployment tool.
<large-icon>	Yes	An optional icon that can be displayed in a deployment tool.
<ejb-name>	No	Identifies the unique name of the EJB in this application.
<ejb-class>	No	Identifies the fully qualified class name for this message-driven bean.
<transaction-type>	No	Determines whether the bean will have container-managed transactions or bean-managed transactions; the two allowed values are Container and Bean.
<message-selector>	Yes	Narrow the scope of which messages will be accepted by a message-driven bean. See "Understanding message selectors."

Attribute	Optional	Description
`<acknowledge-mode>`	Yes	Used to tell the JMS server that the EJB container has received and is processing the message. See "Acknowledging message delivery."
`<message-driven-destination>`	Yes	Tells the EJB container what kind of messaging service to employ. The two options are `javax.jms.Topic` and `javax.jms.Queue`. See "Setting a message delivery model."
`<env-entry>`	No	Typically set during EJB application assembly or deployment. See Chapter 12.
`<ejb-ref>`	Yes	Identifies a reference to the remote home interface of another entity bean. See Chapter 12.
`<ejb-local-ref>`	Yes	Identifies a reference to the local home interface of another entity bean. See Chapter 12.
`<security-identity>`	Yes	Describes the security semantics of an EJB application and isn't typically set until application assembly or deployment. See Chapter 17.
`<resource-ref>`	Yes	Describes access to an external resource, such as a JDBC driver or a third-party application. See Chapter 14.
`<resource-env-ref>`	Yes	Describes access to an application resource registered with JDNI ENC. See Chapter 13.

Understanding message selectors

The `<message-selector>` tag is a special tag that applies only to message-driven beans. This tag can be used to limit the kinds of messages that a message-driven bean will accept based on attributes of the message. For example, using the message select element, you could run two versions of a message-driven bean with different interfaces at the same time. You do this by setting an attribute of the message indicating which version the message is and then by creating a `<message-select>` entry in the deployment descriptor that specifies which version of a message should be accepted.

The syntax of the message selector attribute is based on the conditional criteria used in the `WHERE` clause — the clause of an SQL statement used to express conditional selection criteria — of SQL-92 select statements. (SQL-92 is the most current release of the specification for the SQL language.) A complete discussion of the `WHERE` clause semantics for SQL is beyond the scope of this book, but just so I don't leave you completely hanging, let me give you a taste of message selector attribute syntax. To specify a version number for a message, the client simply sets an attribute of the message, as in the following example:

```
Message msg = session.createMessage;
msg.setFloatProperty("version", 1.0);
```

The `<message-select>` can be used to select version 1.x messages using the following conditional expression:

```
<message-selector>
 <![CDATA[version >= 1.0 AND version < 2.0]]>
<message-selector>
```

Sometimes a message selector expression will contain characters — such as the < and > characters — that have special meaning in XML. To prevent XML from misinterpreting those characters, you must enclose the expression in a CDATA section, which is shown in bold in the previous example.

The conditional criteria expressed in a `<message-selector>` tag can become quite complex. If you're going to make use of this attribute, it pays to have a good understanding of JMS technology. One excellent resource of this topic is *Java Messaging Service*, written by Richard Monson-Haefel and David Chappell and published by O'Reilly.

Acknowledging message delivery

When a JMS server delivers a message, it's good practice to let the server know that you've received the message. If the server doesn't get a response, it will assume that the message delivery failed and will deliver the message again. Usually that's not a good idea. That's why there's an `<acknowledge-mode>` tag, which tag is used to specify which kind of acknowledgment should be delivered to the JMS server. The two possible values for the `<acknowledge-mode>` tag are

- ✔ **Auto-acknowledge:** This mode tells the EJB container that it should notify the JMS server of a successful message delivery as soon as possible after the message has been assigned to a message-driven bean instance. Because it ensures a rapid response to the message server, this is the safest option. Rapid response means the JMS server won't send the message again, typically a good idea.

- ✔ **Dups-ok-acknowledge:** This mode tells the EJB container that it can send an acknowledgement message to the JMS server whenever it gets around to it. You can assume, as the name implies, that duplicate `Message` objects will be delivered if you use this approach. Consequently, your EJB application must provide special processing logic that handles duplicate message delivery properly.

If you're using container-managed transactions, then the EJB container will override any choice you specify for `<acknowledge-mode>` and make the mode `Auto-acknowledge`. Thus, when using container-managed transactions, you don't have to define the `<acknowledge-mode>` attribute.

Setting a message delivery model

The message delivery model addresses the type of message solution that should be employed by the JMS container to deliver messages to the EJB container. This information is supplied in the `<message-driven-destination>` tag, which identifies the type of messaging service that should be used for this message-driven bean. The type of messaging service is expressed in a subelement called `<destination-type>`. The `<destination-type>` element has two possible values:

- ✔ `javax.jms.Queue`: A message queue is like a line of messages that get delivered in the order that they're added to the queue. `Message` objects are added to the end of the line by message producers. Message consumers remove `Message` objects from the front of the line. This model is often referred to as *point-to-point communication* because a given `Message` only comes from a single source and goes to a single message listener. Although there can be multiple listeners that consume messages from a `Queue`, each `Message` is only consumed once.

- ✔ `javax.jms.Topic`: A message topic is like a container that contains a bunch of unordered messages. Each message gets delivered but in no particular order. `Topics` are processed in a publish/subscribe model. Any client with something to say on a `Topic` must publish to it. Any interested listener to a `Topic` must subscribe. Because message-driven beans are message listeners, they are referred to as subscribers when they interact with a `Topic`. The publish/subscribe model allows multiple publishers and multiple subscribers to exist in the same `Topic`. In this model, each message delivered to a `Topic` by a publisher is distributed to all the subscribers in the `Topic`.

Although a `Topic` delivers a `Message` object to each subscriber, each message-driven bean is considered to be a single subscriber. Thus, although you have a pool of each kind of message-driven bean listening for messages from a `Topic`, only one `Message` will be delivered to a single instance in that pool. The behavior of `Topics` is influenced by the `<subscriber-durability>` element in a message-driven bean's deployment descriptor. The `<subscription-durability>` tag must be included in the `<message-driven-destination>` tag if the destination type is a `Topic`. There are two allowed values for the `<subscription-durability>` element:

- **Durable:** `Durable` subscriptions are able to survive a crash of an EJB container. If the container were to go down, the `Topic` would not deliver messages until the container was back online.

- **NonDurable:** `NonDurable` subscriptions are intended for scenarios where a subscriber doesn't want to receive messages that are delivered while the subscriber is offline. What that means is that if the EJB container were to crash, any message delivered to a non-durable subscription would be lost forever.

The `<subscription-durability>` should not be used if the `<destination-type>` is `javax.jms.Queue`.

Selecting the type of `Topic` you want the `Message` to use doesn't make it a done deal. This is simply a cue to the application deployer that indicates what kind of message service should be used. The deployer is responsible for mapping the `<message-driven-destination>` to an actual JMS server `Topic` or `Queue`. That process is typically accomplished with deployment tools provided by a specific EJB application server vendor, but is beyond the scope of this book.

Part V
Putting It All Together

The 5th Wave   By Rich Tennant

"THIS SECURITY PROGRAM WILL RESPOND TO THREE THINGS:
AN INCORRECT ACCESS CODE, AN INAPPROPRIATE FILE REQUEST,
OR SOMETIMES A CRAZY HUNCH THAT MAYBE YOU'RE JUST
ANOTHER SLIME-BALL WITH MISAPPROPRIATION OF SECURED
DATA ON HIS MIND."

In this part . . .

A lot of miscellaneous tasks are involved with creating an EJB application that you'll need to know in order to finish your application. In this part, by discovering what you need to know to package EJB applications, prepare EJB applications for deployment, implement support for transactions, and implement some simple EJB client application components, you'll literally be putting it all together.

Chapter 11

Deploying EJBs for Bean Providers

*I*n every EJB application, there are two separate but collaborating pieces: the application itself — composed of EJB components, interfaces, and support classes — and the system that runs EJB components. The application provides all the services that apply to the domain for which it's developed. Banking applications perform banking tasks, insurance applications implement insurance business processes, sales systems provide sales support and management, and so on. Under each of these applications, the EJB container provides a consistent set of services, including

✔ **Transaction management:** Most business applications need to implement transactions to ensure that activities performed by the application don't fail and leave business data in an invalid state. In a transaction, all the operations must succeed or the changes made to the data must be undone.

✔ **Security management:** Security ensures that applications only allow access to authorized users and that applications provide different levels of access to users with different roles. For example, a human resource director should have broader access to HR information than a human resource staff member.

✔ **Resource management:** The system needs to coordinate access to EJB components from their clients. This process includes the creation of resource pools and caching of entity beans.

The system is the host of an EJB application. Because the system and the application are developed separately, the system needs a way to discover the contents of the EJB application and the services it needs. This interface between the EJB application and the system that supports it is the *deployment descriptor*. The deployment descriptor is an XML document that describes both the contents of an EJB application as well as the services that the application needs from the container. The two types of elements in a deployment descriptor are

- ✔ **Structural information:** The structural information in a deployment descriptor tells the EJB container about the contents of the EJB application. Structural information includes the following types of information:

  - **The EJB components of the application:** These include the session beans, entity beans, and message-driven beans in the application.

  - **The resources used by EJB components:** Resources describe references between entity bean components as well as references to external resources.

- ✔ **Assembly information:** The assembly information in an EJB application describes the services needed by an EJB application from the EJB container. Assembly information describes the following kinds of information in an EJB application:

  - **Transactional semantics:** Transactions are sets of operations that must all succeed or all fail as a group.

  - **Security services:** Security features in an application include the definition of users, roles, and security permissions for EJB components as well as the methods within those components.

Generally, it's safe to say that EJB developers are responsible for defining the structure of an EJB application while application assemblers are responsible for defining the assembly information. This should be common sense because most structural information is essential to an EJB container's ability to run the application. Thus, to perform the most basic unit testing — testing each component in isolation to ensure that it works properly — on an application, the bean provider must define structural information in the deployment descriptor.

On the other hand, assembly information may not be known until an application is ready for deployment. Security rules, for example, are often defined in the context of the environment in which an application runs, not in the context in which the beans were developed. Obviously, if a bean developer doesn't know the security rules, defining them in the deployment descriptor is more difficult.

In this chapter, I cover the required information and conventions associated with defining elements of the deployment descriptor that pertain to an application's structure. Near the end of the chapter, I show you the (really quite simple) steps required to actually package the EJB application.

Several features of the deployment descriptor aren't covered in this chapter. First, the abstract persistence schema — which is actually more closely related to entity beans and the CMP 2.0 architecture — receives thorough coverage in Chapter 7. Defining resources for EJB components gets its due in Chapter 12, and application assembly information is addressed in greater detail in Chapter 13. Transactions — a huge topic — are covered in Chapter 14. Finally, the subject of security receives treatment in Chapter 15.

If your EJB application makes use of the CMP 2.0 architecture, then the abstract persistence schema is part of the structure of the EJB application and must be described by the bean developer.

A Review of XML Fundamentals

The deployment descriptor in an EJB application is an XML file. You don't have to know a lot about XML to create a deployment descriptor, but it helps to have some basic rules down. First, XML files are similar to HTML files; they're documents that have information organized into a tag-based structure. Each tag contains some information about the document. In HTML, tags describe how a browser should display a document. For example, the `<BODY>` tag in HTML contains the body of the HTML document. In XML, tags are used to describe information. To illustrate, the XML tag `<entity>` describes information about an entity bean. All XML documents exhibit the following characteristics:

✔ **The XML document begins with a version tag that identifies the version of the XML language the document uses as well as the character encoding of the document.** The version tag is mandatory and must appear in the XML document before any white space or other tags. That means no spaces or tabs can appear before the version tag. The following code sample illustrates a version tag:

```
<?xml version="1.0" encoding="UFT-8"?>
```

✔ **Following the version tag, an XML document may contain a reference to a document called a DTD, or Document Type Descriptor.** A *DTD* is a document used by engineers to describe the elements allowed in an XML document, their structure, the allowed values in each element, and the meaning of each element. EJB deployment descriptors have a DTD document that defines the elements used to describe EJB applications.

An XML parser uses the DTD document to check your XML file and to make sure that it's defined properly. The EJB applications that I cover in this book make use of the EJB 2.0 specification, which has its own DTD. The following tag is the reference to the DTD that must appear in all EJB deployment descriptors for EJB 2.0 applications:

```
<!DOCTYPE ejb-jar PUBLIC
   "-//Sun Microsystems, Inc.//DTD Enterprise JavaBeans
      2.0//EN"
   "http://java.sun.com/dtd/ejb-jar_2_0.dtd">
```

✔ **The content of an XML document is described after the reference to the DTD.** The content of an XML document is organized in a hierarchy of tags. There can be only a single root tag in an XML document, and all other tags are nested within the root tag. The tags describing the content of an XML document are expressed in two formats, as follows:

- **Value tags:** Value tags are XML tags that contain some value. A value tag has an opening tag, followed by a value, then a closing tag. The value tag may also define various attributes that are expressed inside the opening tag. The following code sample illustrates a value tag:

```
<ejb-name>AccountEntityBean</ejb-name>
```

  The opening tag is delimited with less-than and greater-than symbols and contains the name of the tag, like this: `<ejb-name >`. The closing tag is the same as the opening tag, with the exception that a forward slash is placed after the less-than symbol, like this: `</ejb-name >`. The body of the tag is all the content between the opening tag and the closing tag — indicated in bold.

- **Empty tags:** Empty tags are tags that don't contain a value or a closing tag. Instead, the empty tag is expressed with a single tag that ends with a `/>` symbol. The following code sample illustrates an empty tag:

```
<use-caller-identity/>
```

An XML attribute is like an attribute in an HTML element. The XML tags used in EJB applications don't contain attributes, so you don't really need to worry about using them. XML tags and the values they contain are case-sensitive. By convention, EJB application XML tags are all expressed in lowercase. If the tag specifies a range of values, those values are initial-capped by convention.

The EJB Deployment Descriptor

Two major versions of EJB deployment descriptors are currently in circulation. The EJB 1.1 deployment descriptor describes the structure and assembly of EJB applications built to the EJB 1.1 specification. The EJB 2.0 deployment descriptor adds a number of tags that are necessary to describe the additional features of EJB 2.0 applications. While EJB 2.0-compliant EJB containers are required to support EJB 1.1 applications, EJB containers that haven't been upgraded to support the 2.0 specification won't support EJB 2.0 deployment descriptors.

Every EJB deployment descriptor must be named `ejb-jar.xml`.

This book focuses on developing EJB applications that conform to the 2.0 specification. Thus, when selecting an EJB container, you should use support for the EJB 2.0 specification as a selection criteria. Leading EJB container vendors — including IBM's WebSpere, BEA's WebLogic, and the open source JBoss Application Server — are good places to start looking.

The root element of an EJB deployment descriptor is `<ejb-jar>`. All tags must be nested inside the `<ejb-jar>` tag. Within the `<ejb-jar>` tag are three subelements:

- ✔ `<enterprise-beans>`: This tag contains descriptive information about the EJB components in an EJB application. When an entity bean needs to make references to external resources, system resources, and other entity beans, those resources are described in this section. This chapter focuses on all the elements in the `<enterprise-beans>` tag.

- ✔ `<relationships>`: This tag describes the relationships between entity beans using the container-managed relationship support for EJB 2.0 applications. The second half of Chapter 7 is entirely devoted to describing the elements in the `relationships` section of the deployment descriptor.

- ✔ `<assembly-descriptor>`: This tag is used to describe assembly information for an EJB application. While bean providers may supply some assembly information, application assembly is a responsibility that primarily falls on the application assembler's shoulders. The two major elements of application assembly are describing transactions and describing security. Chapter 14 addresses transaction support, and Chapter 15 addresses EJB application security.

The `<enterprise-beans>` tag contains descriptions for each kind of enterprise bean that can be defined in an EJB application. It has three subelements: `<session>` for session beans, `<entity>` for entity beans, and `<message-driven>` for message-driven beans. Session, entity, and message-driven beans share several XML tags in common. I describe these general tags here:

- ✔ **Logical name:** Every EJB component has a logical name that identifies the name by which each bean is referenced in the rest of the deployment descriptor. The logical name is contained in the `<ejb-name>` tag. It must be unique for the scope of the `ejb-jar` file in which the component is packaged. The `<ejb-name>` tag is a subelement of the `<session>`, `<entity>`, and `<message-driven>` tags.

- ✔ **Enterprise bean class:** The enterprise bean class is the class that implements all the business methods and lifecycle management methods of the EJB component. This class must be identified by the `<ejb-class>` tag. The `<ejb-class>` must have the fully qualified class name of the EJB class. The `<ejb-class>` tag is a subelement of the `<session>`, `<entity>`, and `<message-driven>` tags.

- ✔ **Component interfaces:** Session and entity beans also can have both local and remote component interfaces. The EJB container needs to know which classes implement the component interfaces for the session and entity beans. The `<remote>` tag is used to identify a remote interface and must contain the fully qualified class name of the remote interface (if one exists). The `<local>` tag is used to identify a local interface and must contain the fully qualified class name of the local interface (if one exists).

An EJB component doesn't have to have both remote and local interfaces, but it must have one or the other. The exception to this rule is message-driven beans, which can't have remote or local interfaces. For entity beans and session beans, you can have both local and remote interfaces. For each component interface, the deployment descriptor must define a corresponding home interface for an enterprise bean.

- ✔ **Home interfaces:** Home interfaces can be defined for session and entity beans. The local home interface provides local access to the enterprise bean while the remote home interface provides remote access to the enterprise bean. The local home interface is identified by the `<local-home>` tag in the deployment descriptor. The remote home interface is identified by the `<home>` tag in the deployment descriptor.

- ✔ **Transaction type:** Every enterprise bean component has a `<transaction-type>` tag. The `<transaction-type>` tag is used to describe whether the enterprise bean's transaction service is managed by the bean or by the EJB container. The two allowed values for the `<transaction-type>` tag are `Bean` (for bean-managed transactions) and `Container` (for container-managed transactions).

Bean-managed transactions can be very complex and are certainly beyond the scope of an entry-level EJB programmer. This book doesn't cover the implementation of bean-managed transactions.

- ✔ **Description:** Each EJB component can have an optional description tag that describes the purpose of the EJB component. The description element is demarcated by the `<description>` tag, which should include documentation about the purpose of the EJB component.

- ✔ **Build tool tags:** There are several optional tags in each enterprise bean used to provide additional information for build tools. *Build tools* provide a graphical interface for creating EJB applications. One example utility that you can use to build EJB applications is xdoclet, available at `http://sourceforge.net/projects/xdoclet`. Build tool tags are used to improve the presentation of enterprise beans in the build tool's user interface.

- `<display-name>`: This tag identifies the name under which the enterprise bean component should be displayed in a build tool.

- `<large-icon>`: This tag identifies the path to a 32 pixel by 32 pixel icon used to display the enterprise bean. The image must be in either a JPEG or GIF format.

- `<small-icon>`: This tag identifies the path to a 16 pixel by 16 pixel icon used to display the enterprise bean. The image must be in either a JPEG or GIF format.

As you proceed through the chapter, you'll come across examples of these general tags when I deal with specific bean types.

Describing Session Beans

Aside from the general tags that I identify in the preceding section, the session bean has only one mandatory tag that's unique for session beans: the `<session-type>` tag. The `<session-type>` tag identifies whether the session bean is a stateless session bean or a stateful session bean. There are two allowed values for this tag: `Stateless` (for stateless session beans) and `Stateful` (for stateful session beans). You can see the complete listing for a stateless session bean in the bold text of Listing 11-1.

Session beans may optionally make use of environmental entries for application support classes, resource references to external resources, and other EJB components. All three topics are covered in Chapter 12.

Listing 11-1   Session Bean Descriptor

```
<?xml version="1.0" encoding="UFT-8"?>
<!DOCTYPE ejb-jar PUBLIC
  "-//Sun Microsystems, Inc.//DTD Enterprise JavaBeans
        2.0//EN"
  "http://java.sun.com/dtd/ejb-jar_2_0.dtd:>

<ejb-jar>
 <enterprise-beans>
  <session>
   <description>
    This bean manages the deposit process.
   </description>
   <ejb-name>DepositEJB</ejb-name>
```

(continued)

Listing 11-1 *(continued)*

```
    <home>
      com.sextanttech.transactions.interfaces.DepositRemoteHome
    </home>
    <remote>
      com.sextanttech.transactions.interfaces.DepositRemote
    </remote>
    <local-home>
      com.sextanttech.transactions.interfaces.DepositLocalHome
    </local-home>
    <local>
      com.sextanttech.transactions.interfaces.DepositLocal
    </local>
    <ejb-class>
      com.sextanttech.transactions.implementations.DepositBean
    </ejb-class>
    <session-type>Stateless</session-type>
    <transaction-type>Container</transaction-type>
  </session>
 <enterprise-beans>
</ejb-jar>
```

Describing Entity Beans

Entity beans are the most complex of EJB components — a fact reflected by the number of XML elements required to describe each EJB component. In addition to the standard tags that I identify in the prior section "The EJB Deployment Descriptor," EJB components must describe the persistence model employed by the entity bean component. The specialized elements of the entity bean component are

- `<persistence-type>`: This tag defines whether the entity bean component uses container-managed persistence or bean-managed persistence. The `<persistence-type>` tag must contain the value `Container` (for container-managed persistence) or `Bean` (for bean-managed persistence).

- `<cmp-version>`: This tag identifies the container-managed persistence version to use for the entity bean that uses container-managed persistence. This tag only applies when the `<persistence-type>` tag has a value of `Container`. The default value for the tag is `2.x`. If defining an application that uses CMP 1.1, the value should be `1.x`.

✔ `<cmp-field>`: This tag is used to identify the name of each persistence field in an EJB component. This tag should only be supplied for entity beans that utilize container-managed persistence. The tag should be repeated for each `<cmp-field>` in the entity bean. The `<cmp-field>` tag can have two subelements:

- `<description>`: An optional tag that provides some documentation about the purpose of the field.

- `<field-name>`: A required tag that identifies the field name of the `<cmp-field>`. Remember that with container-managed persistence, the entity bean class must define abstract getter and setter methods that have the names `get<field-name>` and `set<field-name>` where `<field-name>` is the value of this tag.

✔ `<primkey-field>`: This is an optional tag that identifies the field of an entity bean used for its primary key. A primary key field must hold a value that is unique across all entity bean objects of a given EJB component. This tag is used if the primary key of the entity bean is one of its CMP fields. If an entity bean class implements a compound primary key — meaning the key is composed of two or more CMP fields — the `<primkey-class>` element must be used to identify the class holding the primary key. The `<primkey-field>` value must be the name of the `<field-name>` tag that is used as the primary key.

✔ `<primkey-class>`: The `<primkey-class>` tag identifies the name of the primary key class for an entity bean when the entity bean has a compound primary key. The value of the `<primkey-class>` element must be the fully qualified class name of the class that implements the entity bean's primary key. Remember that the fields of the primary key class must be declared `public`, and they must have the same names as their corresponding persistence fields within the entity bean class. The `<primkey-class>` tag can be used for both bean-managed and container-managed persistence.

For entity beans with container-managed persistence, either the `<primkey-class>` or the `<primkey-field>` element must be specified in the deployment descriptor.

✔ `<reentrant>`: Reentrance describes whether an entity bean can be invoked twice in the same thread of execution. The `<reentrant>` tag may have one of two values: `True` if the bean supports reentrant invocations and `False` if it doesn't support reentrant invocations. Generally speaking, entity beans aren't allowed to be reentrant. However, there are cases where you may want a reentrant entity bean.

In brief, the issue with reentrance is that an EJB container cannot typically tell whether the same thread has invoked an entity bean twice or an entity bean has been invoked twice by two separate client invocations in the same transaction context. It's always illegal for a client to invoke an entity bean twice from the same transaction context. Thus, if the `<reentrant>` tag is set to `True`, the bean developer must write code to prevent two client invocations in the same transaction context. For more information on this topic, see the sidebar "The grand reentrant" in Chapter 6.

✔ `<query>`: The `<query>` tag is used to define the EJB QL query for an entity bean's finder and `ejbSelect` methods. I explain the `<query>` tag in detail in Chapter 7, where I address the entity bean abstract persistence schema and the EJB QL language.

Describing persistence can be a topic in and of itself. If you're using the Container-Managed Persistence 2.0 model (CMP 2.0), be sure to read Chapter 7, which provides a complete specification of the CMP 2.0 abstract persistence schema and the EJB Query Language. Both topics are essential to understanding and defining a deployment descriptor that supports CMP 2.0. Listing 11-2 illustrates a complete entity bean description (shown in bold) in a deployment descriptor.

Listing 11-2   The Entity Bean Descriptor

```
<?xml version="1.0" encoding="UTF-8"?>
<!DOCTYPE ejb-jar PUBLIC "-//Sun Microsystems, Inc.//DTD
          Enterprise
JavaBeans 2.0//EN" "http://java.sun.com/dtd/ejb-jar_2_0.dtd">

<ejb-jar>
  <enterprise-beans>
    <entity>
      <ejb-name>AccountEJB</ejb-name>
      <home>
        com.sextanttech.entities.interfaces.AccountRemoteHome
      </home>
      <remote>
        com.sextanttech.entities.interfaces.AccountRemote
      </remote>
      <local-home>
        com.sextanttech.entities.interfaces.AccountLocalHome
      </local-home>
      <local>
        com.sextanttech.entities.interfaces.AccountLocal
      </local>
      <ejb-class>
        com.sextanttech.entities.implementations.AccountBean
```

```
            </ejb-class>
            <persistence-type>Container</persistence-type>
            <prim-key-class>
              com.sextanttech.entities.interfaces.AccountKey
            </prim-key-class>
            <reentrant>False</reentrant>
            <cmp-version>2.x</cmp-version>
            <abstract-schema-name>Account</abstract-schema-name>
            <cmp-field>
              <description>This is the accountId. </description>
              <field-name>accountId</field-name>
            </cmp-field>
            <cmp-field>
              <description>This is the timestamp for account
                  creation.</description>
              <field-name>createDate</field-name>
            </cmp-field>
            <cmp-field>
              <description>This is the balance of the account.
                </description>
              <field-name>balance</field-name>
            </cmp-field>
            <cmp-field>
              <description>Name of account, such as "Primary
                  checking".</description>
              <field-name>accountName</field-name>
            </cmp-field>
            <query>
              <!-- Details of EJB QL query specified. See Chapter
                  7. -->
            </query>
          </entity>
      </enterprise-beans>
  <ejb-jar>
```

Entity beans can make use of several different types of resources, including local and remote references to other EJB components, references to environmental resources of the EJB application, and references to external and system resources. For more on accessing resources in an EJB application, see Chapter 12.

An application assembler or deployer should map the persistence fields and relationship fields of an entity bean to an actual data source before the application is deployed. Believe it or not, the EJB specification doesn't specify how this is done. Instead, the solution is left to an implementation decision for the vendor. Typically an EJB application vendor will provide documentation or a GUI application to assist in performing this task. Thus, you should consult the documentation of an EJB vendor's implementation to discover how persistence fields get mapped to data sources.

Describing Message-Driven Beans

The deployment descriptor entry for a message-driven bean is different from that of a session or entity bean, primarily because message-driven beans receive instructions through a JMS server, rather than through component interfaces. The message-driven bean must therefore describe the JMS server to use, rather than describing home and component interfaces. The following list identifies all the XML elements unique to message-driven bean deployment descriptors:

✔ `<message-selector>`: This tag is defined as part of the JMS specification. A *message selector* is a form of query that narrows the types of messages that the message-driven bean can receive. The query is roughly equivalent to the `WHERE` clause of an SQL statement, minus the `WHERE` keyword. Using the `<message-selector>` tag requires some specialized knowledge of JMS systems and is outside the scope of this book. The `<message-selector>` element is optional and has the selector query as a value.

For more information on JMS, refer to *Java Messaging Service,* written by Richard Monson-Haefel and David Chappell and published by O'Reilly.

✔ `<acknowledge-mode>`: This tag determines whether the message-driven bean uses the JMS-defined `Auto-acknowledge` mode, or the `Dups-ok-acknowledge` mode when acknowledging the receipt of a message. If the value is `Auto-acknowledge`, the EJB container must send an acknowledgement of message delivery as soon as possible to the JMS server. If `Dups-ok-acknowledge` is specified, the EJB container can send an acknowledgement whenever it wants to.

If a JMS server doesn't receive acknowledgement of a message delivery within a certain time frame, it will deliver the message again. Message-driven beans with `Dups-ok-acknowledge` must be designed to handle the receipt of multiple copies of the same message. The safe play for the `<acknowledge-mode>` is to always use the `Auto-acknowledge` mode.

✔ `<message-driven-destination>`: This tag identifies the type of JMS message service that should be used when delivering messages to this message-driven bean. The service type is identified by a subelement of `<message-driven-destination>` called `<destination-type>`. There are two types of services: topic services and queue services. In addition to the two types of services, a topic can have two types of subscriptions: a durable subscription and a non-durable subscription. The durability of a topic indicates whether a subscription to a topic will survive a crash of the EJB container. The durability of the topic is specified using the `<subscription-durability>` tag, which has a default value of `Durable`.

- **If the messaging service should conform to a publish/subscribe paradigm, the topic service should be used.** In the publish/subscribe paradigm, a topic can have many subscribers who all receive delivery on the messages that are published to the topic. This service is identified by specifying the value `javax.jms.Topic` as the value of the `<destination-type>` element. By default, a topic subscription is `Durable`. If you want a subscription to be non-durable, the `<subscription-durability>` tag must have the value `NonDurable`.

- **If the messaging service should be implemented on a point-to-point protocol, then the queue should be used.** In the point-to-point protocol, there is only one publisher of messages and one subscriber. The delivery is from one point to another. The messages are loaded into a queue as they're delivered. When the subscriber is interested in receiving messages, it removes the messages from the queue one at a time. This is similar to the way e-mail works. For queue message services, the `<destination-type>` element must have the value `javax.jms.Queue`. There should be no `<subscription-durability>` tag when the queue is used.

Listing 11-3 contains an example of a message-driven bean declaration in a deployment descriptor.

Listing 11-3   A Message-Driven Bean

```
<?xml version="1.0" encoding="UTF-8"?>
<!DOCTYPE ejb-jar PUBLIC "-//Sun Microsystems, Inc.//DTD
          Enterprise
JavaBeans 2.0//EN" "http://java.sun.com/dtd/ejb-jar_2_0.dtd">

<ejb-jar>
 <enterprise-beans>
  <message-driven>
   <ejb-name>GenerateStatementEJB</ejb-name>
   <ejb-class>
    com.sextanttech.messages.GenerateStatementBean
   </ejb-class>
   <transaction-type>Container</transaction-type>
   <message-selector></message-selector>
   <acknowledge-mode>Auto-acknowledge</acknowledge-mode>
   <message-driven-destination>
    <destination-type>javax.jms.Topic<destination-type>
    <subscription-durability>Durable< subscription-durability>
   </message-driven-destination>
  </message-driven>
 </enterprise-beans>
</ejb-jar>
```

When an EJB application makes use of message-driven beans, the JMS service must be described elsewhere. JMS servers don't just magically appear. Typically, it's the responsibility of the application assembler to map a message-driven bean to an actual JMS server. The solution for mapping a message-driven bean to a JMS server isn't specified in the EJB specification.

Packaging an EJB Application

After you write the code for an EJB application and complete the deployment descriptor, you're ready to package the application. *Packaging* an application is a process whereby you build a single archive file — like a ZIP file — that contains all the Java classes and a deployment descriptor of an EJB application. To prepare for packaging the EJB application, follow these basic steps:

1. **Create a build directory for your EJB application.** A *build directory* is a location that you use to organize the EJB application directories and files. On my computer, my build directory name is `c:\build`.

2. **In the build directory, create a directory with the same name as your EJB application.** In my sample project, I'm calling the application bankingapp. Thus, I create a directory called `c:\build\bankingapp`. The `bankingapp` directory is the root directory for my banking application. In Java, this root directory is called the *default package*.

3. **In the default package directory, create another subdirectory called** `meta-inf`. The `meta-inf` directory contains meta information about the EJB application. The deployment descriptor is the meta information for an EJB application, so it should be placed in the `meta-inf` directory.

4. **Finally, copy all of the class files from your EJB application into the default package directory.** Class files that are included in a specific package should be placed in the default package. All other files should be located in a subdirectory of the default package directory with a name that corresponds to the class file's package structure. For example, the class `AccountHolderBean.class` is located in the following package:

```
com.sextanttech.entities.implementations.
        AccountHolderBean.class
```

Thus, for my computer, the file `AccountHolderBean.class` should be located at:

```
C:\build\bankingapp\com\sextanttech\entities\
        implementations\AccountHolderBean.class
```

After you've organized your project according to the preceding guidelines, you're ready to package your EJB application. For comparison purposes, Figure 11-1 illustrates the organization of my build directory for the `bankingapp` sample project. I've placed a rectangle around all the directories that are included in the application.

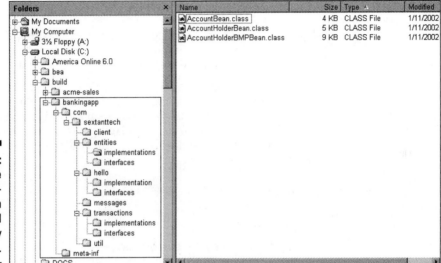

Figure 11-1: The banking-application build directory structure.

Now it's time to package the application. Most EJB container vendors will supply a build tool that helps you create the deployment descriptor and to build an application package for deployment. But if you don't have access to such tools, I cover all you need to know here. I make my build using a tool called JAR (Java Application archive) that's distributed with the Java 2 Standard Edition. The JAR tool builds an application archive field, and you can use it to build EJB applications. The EJB application should be named the same as the default directory of the application. Creating the `jar` file with the JAR tool is pretty straightforward; just follow these steps:

1. **Start by launching a DOS command prompt.**

   On most Windows computers, all you need to do is choose Start⇨Run, type the command **command** in the Open field of the dialog box that appears, and click OK. That should open a DOS window.

2. **Change directories to your application's default package directory.**

   In my computer, I accomplish this step by typing **cd c:\build\bankingapp** and pressing the Enter key.

   Now you're ready to build your application.

3. **Build your application by typing the following command:**

```
jar cfv <application-name> <include-files>
        <include-directories>
```

In this example:

- `<application-name>` is the name of your application and should end with a `.jar` extension. My application name is `bankingapp.jar`.

- `<include-files>` are the individually listed files that should be included in the root of the EJB application. If you followed the build directions in Steps 1-3, this option isn't necessary.

- `<include-directories>` is either a group of directories or a directory wild card specification that points to the directories you want included in your `jar` file. If you're in the build directory, this tag should be replaced with the default package directory of your EJB application, followed by a `\*.*` wildcard operator. In my application, this value is `*.*`.

After you type in a complete `jar` command — such as

```
jar cfv bankingapp.jar *.*
```

and then press Enter, a whole bunch of messages should whiz by that start with something like `adding:` followed by some filename. When the `jar` program is finished, the command prompt returns. Figure 11-2 shows my command prompt after I've run the `jar` command.

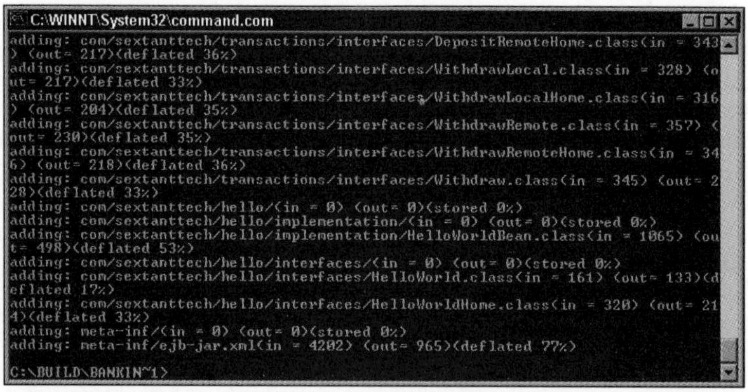

Figure 11-2:
The building of an EJB application.

To verify that the `jar` file was built, simply type **dir** in the DOS window and press Enter. You should see a file with the same name as your EJB application. If you do, you're finished! Almost. . . .

From the command line, you can type the command **jar tvf <file-name>** to view the contents of a `jar` file. You can also use a ZIP compression utility (such as WinZip) to view the contents of a `jar` file. But you can't use a ZIP compression utility to build a `jar` file because the `jar` program adds a special file called a *manifest* that's used by Java programs to investigate the contents of `jar` files. If you ever need to add anything to a `jar` file, be sure to use the `jar` utility so that the manifest is properly updated.

Building a Client Application Archive

Remember that you distribute an EJB application to two possible audiences: the EJB server, which has to have all the classes of your EJB application, and the client, which ruins — I mean runs — your application. The client application can use the same `jar` file that you build for the server, but by convention you shouldn't distribute the server application to a client. Instead, you should create a smaller `jar` file that contains only the home and component interfaces as well as the support classes that the client needs to work with your application. The client will need the following classes to run your EJB application:

- ✓ **Utility classes:** If you've created any utility classes such as bulk operation objects — which update multiple attributes of an entity bean object at a time — the client will need the class files for those objects.

- ✓ **Primary key classes:** The client needs to be able to get a reference to the primary key of an entity bean, so all entity bean primary key classes should be distributed to the client.

- ✓ **Home interfaces:** The client needs the `.class` files for home interfaces so that it can look up session and entity beans.

- ✓ **Component interfaces:** The client needs the `.class` files for component interfaces so that it can obtain references to session and entity beans in your application.

- ✓ **Deployment descriptor:** The client needs the deployment descriptor so that it knows the abstract names to use for remote and component interfaces.

Although the EJB specification allows for the creation of a `client-jar` file that contains the information previously identified, it doesn't say exactly how the `client-jar` file should be constructed, which classes should be included, and what the format for the client's deployment descriptor should be. Consequently, each EJB container vendor is free to come up with its own solution for packaging EJB client applications. Be sure to consult your EJB container vendor's documentation to see the precise solution for creating a `client-jar` file.

Chapter 12

Registering Application Resources with JNDI

In This Chapter

▶ Reviewing Java Naming and Directory Interface (JNDI)

▶ Accessing system resources

▶ Defining environmental resources

▶ Referencing other EJB components

*O*ne of the challenges of programming in Enterprise JavaBean (EJB) applications is that an EJB component may need to make references to application resources — such as other EJB components or utility objects — that aren't available until after the application is deployed. Such resources are often referred to as *runtime resources* because they are defined when the application is running, rather than when it's coded. The problem is that you need to make references to runtime resources when you code an EJB component, even if you don't know the names of the classes providing those resources until runtime. For example, an EJB application may need to use a JDBC driver to get access to a database, but the actual driver may not be supplied until the EJB component is prepared for deployment. Thus, the EJB component developer may not know the exact name of the driver or how to create a reference to that driver.

Early attempts to employ the Psychic Friends Network for assistance in identifying runtime resources proved to be unreliable. Thus, Java engineers came up with a new solution to the problem. Because the resource name may not have been known when the program was developed, instead of accessing a resource inside the code for an EJB program, they instead created an alias to the type of resource needed and then referenced the alias inside the EJB component.

This alias is called a *JNDI name*, short for *J*ava *N*aming and *D*irectory *I*nterface name. The alias is like a plug on a power cord. When the resource is defined at deployment time, the alias is mapped to the resource like a power cord is connected to an outlet. The result is that the EJB application — perhaps a desk lamp in my hypothetical scenario — can be designed and built without access to the power outlet that it will ultimately be plugged into.

Actually, the JNDI upon which JNDI names are based existed before EJB applications, but the idea was adapted a little to conform with the needs of EJB components. In standard JNDI services, a directory is created with resources, each of which has a string alias and a type — the Java class name for the resource — that can be looked up in the application's CLASSPATH. A JNDI directory doesn't actually map to a directory on a hard drive; instead, it serves as a logical directory used to organize JNDI resources in memory. Applications can look up resources in the directory and retrieve a reference to the resource. Thus, the application doesn't need to know exactly how to refer to the resource; instead it needs to know the JNDI name for the resource.

In EJB applications, each EJB component has its own private naming context, which is like a logical partition for JNDI resources. This partition is called the JNDI Enterprise Naming Context (JNDI ENC), and each EJB component has its own private JNDI ENC. The JNDI ENC is the directory service that provides aliases for resources that EJB components need to do their jobs. The actual resources and aliases of the JDNI ENC are defined inside the EJB application's deployment descriptor. As an EJB component developer, you can create logical references to resources needed by your EJB components in the JNDI ENC. These references allow you to get access to the resource inside your EJB component without knowing the exact name of the resource or where it comes from.

When the EJB application is assembled by an application assembler, the assembler will connect your JNDI ENC references to actual resources in the EJB application. Thus, an EJB component can be created by someone who knows absolutely nothing about the runtime environment of the EJB application and only knows about the types of resources that his or her EJB component needs.

Runtime resources are part of the environment of an EJB program. Environment refers to the context in which an application runs and includes all the services and resources that the application has access to.

In this chapter, you discover how to define JNDI ENC resources in the deployment descriptor and also see a simple example for referring to a JNDI ENC resource in an EJB component. There are five types of JNDI ENC resource tags in an EJB deployment descriptor:

✔ **Environment entries:** Reference objects that hold what's known as *environmental information* for use in an EJB component. Environmental information is information that can be configured after an EJB component is deployed — information that, when configured, will adjust an EJB component's behavior. For example, a banking application might define a minimum credit score for someone wanting to open a credit card account. That credit score could be defined in an environment entry called MIN_CREDIT_SCORE. As a component developer, you know that a credit card applicant must have a MIN_CREDIT_SCORE to get a credit card, but the actual threshold of the MIN_CREDIT_SCORE can change over time. By defining MIN_CREDIT_SCORE as an environmental entry, you allow the application's behavior to be configured at runtime without changing any source code. An EJB component can then obtain the MIN_CREDIT_SCORE value from its JNDI ENC each time that it needs to perform some task that calls for that value.

✔ **EJB local references:** Define the alias that an EJB component uses to refer to another EJB component through its local home and local interfaces. An EJB accesses these resources by looking up the specified resource name using JNDI.

✔ **EJB remote references:** Define the alias that an EJB component uses to refer to another EJB component through its remote home and remote interfaces. An EJB accesses these resources by looking up the specified resource name using JNDI.

✔ **Resource references:** Define an alias that an EJB component uses to refer to some resource outside the EJB application. The resource could be an external e-mail application or a legacy application.

✔ **Resource environment references:** Define aliases that EJB components can use to refer to environment resources that are administered inside the EJB application's environment. Such resources could include an internally administered Java Messaging Service (JMS) server or JDBC driver connection pool. EJB applications look up these resources through JNDI.

Defining Environment Resources

Environment resources are resources for particular EJB components that can store information that is global to that type of component. For example, different types of bank accounts may have different monthly fees. In addition, these fees may change over time. An EJB component that represents a bank account needs a flexible way to identify the fee and charge it to the customer. The monthly fee could be defined as an application resource, which allows it to be changed periodically without changing the EJB components code. Defining a monthly fee inside the application code is asking for trouble because changing it could prove very difficult and expensive. An environment resource is intended to hold information that an EJB component needs to refer to, but that can change periodically.

The information held inside an environment entry must be represented as a Java object wrapper corresponding to one of the primitive types in the Java language. That means that any type of character or number defined in Java can be represented in an environment reference. The legal types for environment references are `java.lang.Boolean`, `java.lang.Byte`, `java.lang.Character`, `java.lang.Double`, `java.lang.Float`, `java.lang.Integer`, `java.lang.Long`, `java.lang.Short`, and `java.lang.String`.

Many argue that an environment entry should be able to hold a date. There is no primitive date type in Java, but you can get around that issue in a couple of ways. First, you can store the date as a `String` and parse it inside your EJB application. The second method is to determine the `Long` value of your date and store the `Long` value in the environment reference.

Environment resources can be defined inside `<session>`, `<entity>`, and `<message-driven>` tags in an EJB application's deployment descriptor. Each EJB defines its own environment entries, and they aren't shared between different EJB components. The environment entry is defined inside an `<env-entry>` tag. I describe each element in the environment entry in the following list:

- `<env-entry>`: The outermost tag of an environment entry, the `<env-entry>` tag groups all the attributes pertaining to the environment entry. Each EJB component can define zero, one, or more `<env-entry>` tags.

- `<description>`: An optional tag, `<description>` defines the purpose of the environment entry. I highly recommend providing a precise definition for every environment entry that you create.

- `<env-entry-name>`: This tag identifies the logical name of the environment entry. The EJB component will look up each environmental entry that you define using its logical name.

- `<env-entry-type>`: This identifies the type of the environment entry object. It must be one of the objects identified in the second paragraph of this section — `Boolean`, `Byte`, `Character`, `Double`, `Float`, `Integer`, `Long`, `Short`, or `String`.

- `<env-entry-value>`: This identifies the value of the environment entry object. It must be legal for the type of the environment entry.

Listing 12-1 illustrates an example of the minimum credit card score environment entry, shown in bold.

Listing 12-1   An Environment Entry

```
<?xml version="1.0" encoding="UTF-8"?>
<!DOCTYPE ejb-jar PUBLIC "-//Sun Microsystems, Inc.//DTD
           Enterprise
JavaBeans 2.0//EN" "http://java.sun.com/dtd/ejb-jar_2_0.dtd">

<ejb-jar>
 <enterprise-beans>
  <session>
   <ejb-name>CCApplicationEvaluatorBean<ejb-name>
   <env-entry>
    <description>
     This is the minimum credit score for a platinum card.
    </description>
    <env-entry-name>PLATINUM_MIN_CREDIT_SCORE</env-entry-name>
    <env-entry-type>java.lang.Integer</env-entry-type>
    <env-entry-value>660</env-entry-value>
   </env-entry>
  </session>
 </enterprise-beans>
</ejb-jar>
```

For information on referring to an environmental resource, see the last section in this chapter, "Using JNDI to Look Up a Resource."

Defining EJB Local References

EJB local references are references to other EJB objects in an application through the other EJB object's local home and local interfaces. If you want to use the local interface of another EJB object inside your EJB component, you must define an EJB local reference in your deployment descriptor.

If you want to refer to an EJB component through a remote interface, refer to the next section, "Defining EJB Remote References."

EJB local references are defined using the `<ejb-local-ref>` tag, which can be nested inside an `<entity>`, `<message-driven>`, or `<session>` tag. In the following list, I define each element in the `<ejb-local-ref>` tag:

✔ `<ejb-local-ref>`: This element contains all the information needed to make a reference to another EJB component through its local interface. Each EJB component can define zero, one, or more `<ejb-local-ref>` tags.

✔ `<description>`: This is an optional description of the EJB component referred to. The element doesn't have to be included, but providing a description is good practice.

- ✔ `<ejb-ref-name>`: This is the alias by which your EJB component will look up the EJB identified in this reference. The reference name should be unique within the context of the EJB component. (That is, no two `<ejb-local-ref>` tags should have the same value for the `<ejb-ref-name>` in a given EJB component.) Typically, the `<ejb-ref-name>` is either a name that makes sense to you or the same as the name of the referred EJB component's home interface. By convention, `<ejb-ref-name>` starts with an **ejb/** to indicate that the resource is an EJB component.

- ✔ `<ejb-ref-type>`: This attribute indicates whether the EJB referenced is an entity bean or a session bean. The allowed values are `Session` for session beans and `Entity` for entity beans.

- ✔ `<local-home>`: This attribute identifies the fully qualified class name to the referenced EJB's local home interface.

- ✔ `<local>`: This attribute identifies the fully qualified class name to the referenced EJB's local interface.

- ✔ `<ejb-link>`: This attribute can be used if an EJB local reference links to another EJB component defined inside this EJB-JAR file. This is typically the case for EJB local references. If this attribute is used, it should contain the value of the `<ejb-name>` attribute for the referenced EJB component.

Listing 12-2 illustrates an example of an EJB local reference entry to another EJB component. I've included the `<ejb-link>` element for the purposes of this example. Note that the value is the same as the referred entity's `<ejb-name>`.

Listing 12-2   An EJB Local Reference

```xml
<?xml version="1.0" encoding="UTF-8"?>
<!DOCTYPE ejb-jar PUBLIC "-//Sun Microsystems, Inc.//DTD
           Enterprise
JavaBeans 2.0//EN" "http://java.sun.com/dtd/ejb-jar_2_0.dtd">

<ejb-jar>
 <enterprise-beans>
  <session>
   <ejb-name>DepositBean</ejb-name>
   <ejb-local-ref>
    <ejb-ref-name>ejb/local/accountEJB</ejb-ref-name>
    <ejb-ref-type>Entity</ejb-ref-type>
    <local-home>
      com.sextanttech.entities.implementations.
          AccountLocalHome
    </local-home>
    <local>
      com.sextanttech.entities.implementations.AccountLocal
    </local>
    <ejb-link>AccountEJB</ejb-link>
```

```
    </ejb-local-ref>
   </session>
   <entity>
     <ejb-name>AccountEntityBean</ejb-name>
   </entity>
  <enterprise-beans>
</ejb-jar>
```

Defining EJB Remote References

Referring to an EJB component through its remote interface is similar to the process for referring to an EJB component through its local interface. The distinction lies in the fact that remote references refer to the EJB component's remote home and remote interfaces instead of its local home and local interfaces. The remote reference for an EJB component is defined in the `<ejb-ref>` tag in the deployment descriptor. In the following, I describe the syntax for the tag:

- ✔ `<ejb-ref>`: This tag contains all the information needed to make a reference to another EJB through its remote interface. Each EJB component can define zero, one, or more `<ejb-ref>` tags.

- ✔ `<description>`: This is an optional description of the EJB component referred to. The element doesn't have to be included, but providing a description is good practice.

- ✔ `<ejb-ref-name>`: This is the alias by which your EJB component will look up the EJB identified in this reference. The reference name should be unique within the context of the EJB component. (That is, in a given EJB component, no two `<ejb-ref>` tags can have the same value for the `<ejb-ref-name>`.) Typically the `<ejb-ref-name>` is either a name meaningful to you or the same as the name of the referred EJB component's home interface. By convention, `<ejb-ref-name>` starts with an **ejb/** to indicate that the resource is an EJB component.

- ✔ `<ejb-ref-type>`: This attribute indicates whether the EJB referenced is an entity bean or a session bean. The allowed values are `Session` for session beans and `Entity` for entity beans.

- ✔ `<home>`: This attribute identifies the fully qualified class name to the referenced EJB's remote home interface.

- ✔ `<remote>`: This attribute identifies the fully qualified class name to the referenced EJB's remote interface.

- ✔ `<ejb-link>`: This attribute can be used if an EJB local reference links to another EJB component defined inside this EJB-JAR file. If this attribute is used, it should contain the value of the `<ejb-name>` attribute for the referenced EJB component.

Listing 12-3 illustrates the definition of a remote reference to an EJB component in bold.

Listing 12-3   An EJB Remote Reference

```
<?xml version="1.0" encoding="UTF-8"?>
<!DOCTYPE ejb-jar PUBLIC "-//Sun Microsystems, Inc.//DTD
          Enterprise
JavaBeans 2.0//EN" "http://java.sun.com/dtd/ejb-jar_2_0.dtd">

<ejb-jar>
 <enterprise-beans>
  <session>
   <ejb-name>DepositBean</ejb-name>
   <ejb-ref>
    <description>Account to deposit funds into.</description>
    <ejb-ref-name>ejb/remote/AccountEJB</ejb-ref-name>
    <ejb-ref-type>Entity</ejb-ref-type>
    <home>
     com.sextanttech.entities.interfaces.AccountRemoteHome
    </home>
    <remote>
     com.sextanttech.entities.interfaces.AccountRemote
    </remote>
    <ejb-link>AccountEJB</ejb-link>
   </ejb-ref>
  </session>
  <entity>
   <ejb-name>AccountEntityBean</ejb-name>
  </entity>
 <enterprise-beans>
</ejb-jar>
```

You may wonder why a remote reference isn't named `<ejb-remote-ref>` to distinguish it from an `<ejb-local-ref>`. The reason is that the EJB 1.1 specification contained no local references, so that meant that the `<ejb-ref>` was the only tag in town and that there wasn't a need to distinguish between two types of EJB references. Consequently, the syntax for making a remote reference is a holdover from the EJB 1.1 specification.

Defining External Resource References

External resources include references to applications and utilities defined outside the scope of the present EJB application. A common feature of all external resources is that they can't be managed from the context of the EJB application. There are many possibilities for external resources in an EJB application, including the following:

✔ **A JDBC data source:** Most EJB systems will use a database to manage the persistence of entity bean attributes, which means that the JDBC database driver needs to be defined as a resource to each EJB component.

✔ **An e-mail system:** Perhaps your EJB application is designed to send alerts to system administrators when a certain type of error occurs. Perhaps an e-mail is sent to a security expert when some unauthorized access attempt is made. Or perhaps your application sends an e-mail to clients when they overdraft their accounts. There are many opportunities to make use of e-mail in an EJB application — to do so you need to create an external resource reference to the e-mail service used by your EJB component.

✔ **Integration to a legacy system:** Many EJB applications may be nothing more than an enterprise application that directs messages to some legacy system. If so, you'll need to have resources that allow your EJB application to communicate with that legacy system. These resources are probably classes or drivers that provide a set of methods for interfacing with the legacy system. Getting access to the classes and drivers requires making a reference to the external resource.

✔ **Business-to-business communication:** Perhaps your EJB system automatically orders new stock when inventory for an item falls below a certain level. Business-to-business integration requires that some communication medium exists between you and your vendor. If the vendor publishes code for establishing such connections, you can refer to it by defining an external resource reference.

External resources are defined in the deployment descriptor using the ⟨resource-ref⟩ element. The following list identifies the elements of an external resource reference and each element's purpose:

✔ ⟨resource-ref⟩:This element groups all the elements that describe an external resource of the EJB component.

✔ ⟨description⟩: Use this element to provide some documentation about the purpose of the external resource. Although this element isn't required, I highly recommend that you take a little time to document each external resource. It is an especially good idea to use the ⟨description⟩ tag to identify the JAVADOC that documents the interfaces, classes, and exceptions of the external resource.

✔ ⟨res-ref-name⟩: This is the logical name by which the external resource will be identified inside the EJB component for which it's defined. You'll use the name to look up the resource through JNDI.

By convention, resources are placed in a directory that applies to the type of resource they represent. For example, all JDBC drivers used by your application should have their ⟨res-ref-name⟩ tags prefixed with jdbc/ to indicate that they're JDBC drivers. E-mail servers are prefixed with `email/`, XML document parsers are placed in the `xml/` directory, and so on. The directory names are optional but help to organize different types of resources.

✔ `<res-type>`:This is the fully qualified class name of the resource obtained by this reference. For example, a JDBC data source could have the values `java.sql.Driver` or `javax.sql.DataSource`, depending on which version of JDBC is used.

✔ `<res-auth>`: This attribute indicates whether the EJB container or the code inside the EJB component will handle security authentication for the resource. There are two possible values: `Container` for container-managed authentication, and `Application` for application-managed authentication. If `Container` is specified, the application deployer is responsible for providing the authentication information for the resource. If `Application` is specified, the authentication code must be supplied by the bean developer. It's generally a good practice to use `Container` authentication because the management of authentication to various data sources is an administrative issue and not a software development issue.

✔ `<res-sharing-scope>`: An optional tag, `<res-sharing-scope>` indicates whether the specified EJB component can share the resource with other EJB components that it calls. The default value for this element is `Sharable`, indicating that this resource has a public scope and can be shared by other EJB components. The value `Unsharable` tells the EJB container this resource has a private scope and cannot be shared with other EJB components.

The `<res-sharing-scope>` only applies to EJB components that called the EJB component which has the `<resource-ref>` tag. Even if the `<res-sharing-scope>` is `Sharable`, the resource cannot be shared by EJB components that are not called by the EJB component for which the tag is defined.

Listing 12-4 illustrates (in bold) the implementation of a `<resource-ref>` tag for a JDBC data source. The resource manager is a `javax.sql.DataSource` class, which makes this resource a JDBC 3.0 database driver. The resource reference is `Sharable`, meaning that this resource can be shared with other EJB components that are called by this component.

Listing 12-4   Defining an External Resource

```
<ejb-jar>
  <enterprise-beans>
    <entity>
      <bean-name>AccountHolderBMP</bean-name>
      <resource-ref>
        <description>Data source for account holder</
            description>
          <res-ref-name>jdbc/AcctHolderDatabase</res-ref-name>
```

```
        <res-type>javax.sql.DataSource</res-type>
        <res-auth>Container<res-auth>
        <res-sharing-scope>Sharable</res-sharing-scope>
    </resource-ref>
  </entity>
 </enterprise-beans>
</ejb-jar>
```

Defining Local Resource References

Local resource references are references to resources that are defined and administered by the EJB application. Because these resources are local, the EJB component that uses them has a special trusted privilege, which means that the resource doesn't have to define authentication and sharing rules. Determining what resources are part of your EJB application's environment must be done after you've selected the EJB container that you plan to deploy to. Many EJB containers have local JMS servers. They may also have a mail server and define additional local resources that your application can use. When making use of these local resources, you should define local resource references for them.

The deployment descriptor's tag for a local resource reference is `<resource-env-ref>`, and the syntax for each local resource reference is illustrated in the following list:

- ✔ `<resource-env-ref>`: This element contains all the elements that define a local resource.

- ✔ `<description>`: This is an optional documentation element that should be used to describe the purpose of the resource.

- ✔ `<resource-env-ref-name>`: This element identifies the logical name of the resource, which will be used inside the EJB component to refer to the resource.

- ✔ `<resource-env-ref-type>`: This element identifies the Java type that's associated with this resource reference and should be the fully qualified class name of the resource reference.

Listing 12-5 illustrates (in bold) the XML code used to define a local resource reference. Local resource references can be defined inside the `<session>`, `<message-driven>`, and `<entity>` attributes.

Note that the `<message-driven>` element has a separate attribute for identifying the type of JMS server that it subscribes to. When using a resource reference for a JMS server, you should be defining a resource you want to send messages to. If you'd like to receive messages from a JMS server, create a message-driven bean instead. Message-driven beans don't need to define a resource reference for the JMS server that they subscribe to.

Listing 12-5   Defining a Local Resource Reference

```
<?xml version="1.0" encoding="UTF-8"?>
<!DOCTYPE ejb-jar PUBLIC "-//Sun Microsystems, Inc.//DTD
          Enterprise
JavaBeans 2.0//EN" "http://java.sun.com/dtd/ejb-jar_2_0.dtd">

<ejb-jar>
 <enterprise-beans>
  <entity>
   <description>
    This is an account holder bean with bean-managed
          persistence.
   </description>
   <ejb-name>AccountHolderBMP</ejb-name>
   <resource-env-ref>
    <description>
     This is a JMS server that sends alerts to an account
     representative when an Account Holder's account is
          overdrawn.
    </description>
    <resource-env-ref-name>jms/CustomerService</resource-env-
          ref-name>
    <resource-env-ref-type>javax.jms.Topic</resource-env-ref-
          type>
   </resource-env-ref>
  </entity>
 </enterprise-beans>
</ejb-jar>
```

As with other types of resources, local resources can be assigned to different directories. For example, the JMS resource defined in Listing 12-5 is assigned to the directory `jms/`, which corresponds to the directory for all Java Messaging Service resources. Assigning a resource to a directory helps to organize them into meaningful groups. It's not required, but convention dictates that each resource be assigned to a meaningful directory.

Using JNDI to Look Up a Resource

After you define the resources in an application, you're ready to make use of those resources in your EJB component. Resources are accessed from inside the EJB component class by using the Java Naming and Directory Interface, or JNDI. JNDI is really easy to use. Here are the fundamentals for accessing any EJB resource:

1. **Obtain the JNDI context by using the** `javax.jndi.LocalContext` **class.**

   The statement is

   ```
   javax.jndi.Context context = new javax.jndi.LocalContext();
   ```

2. **Look up any resource defined in the context (which includes all the resources defined for the type of EJB component you're working with) using the** context.lookup **method.**

All the environment entries for an EJB component are stored under the context java:comp/env, so if you wanted the entire environment of the EJB component, the code would be as follows:

```
javax.jndi.Context myContext = (Context)
    context.lookup("java:comp/env");
```

3. **After the** myContext **variable is defined, look up specific environment entries within that variable.**

For example:

```
javax.sql.DataSource ds = (DataSource)
   context.lookup("jdbc/AcctHolderDatabase");
```

Alternatively, you can skip Step 2 and move directly to extracting a resource from the context object, as I illustrate in the following example:

```
javax.sql.DataSource ds = (DataSource)
    context.lookup("java:comp/env/jdbc/
        AcctHolderDatabase");
```

4. **The return value of the** Context.lookup **method is a** java.lang. Object, **which you'll notice I have to cast — convert the object type — to the type of the object identified in the object's resource entry.**

There's a catch with casting and EJB applications. If you're looking up a remote resource, such as a remote EJB reference, you must perform the cast by using the java.rmi.ProtableRemoteObject.Narrow method. Here's an example of casting a remote object that uses the PortableRemoteObject.narrow method:

```
Object obj = context.lookup("java:comp/env/ejb/
        AccountHolder");
AccountHolderRemoteHome holderHome =
        (AccountHolderRemoteHome)
  PortableRemoteObject.narrow( obj, Class.forName(
   "com.sextanttech.entities.interfaces.
        AccountHolderRemoteHome"));
```

Note in the previous example that the narrow method takes two arguments; the first is the object that needs to be cast, and the second is the Class that the object should be cast to. The Class can be obtained by calling the static method Class.forName and supplying the string name of the class as an argument. These two arguments are identified in the bold text.

Chapter 13

Assembling EJB Applications

• •

In This Chapter

▶ Examining the build and deployment process

▶ Kicking off with a simple deployment

▶ Cross-referencing to fundamental application assembly tasks

▶ What happens where the sidewalk ends

• •

*I*n the beginning of this book, I provide you with a brief review of some of the different responsibilities of EJB application developers. EJB bean suppliers are responsible for actually coding EJB components as well as for describing those components in a deployment descriptor. In Parts II, III, and IV, I explore the process of coding EJB components. In Chapter 11, I lead you through a detailed analysis of describing EJB components. In Chapter 12, I cap it all off with an investigation of JNDI, which bean providers use to describe the resources accessed by the EJB components they develop.

At this stage, you're moving beyond the realm of EJB development and getting into the realm of EJB application assembly. It's a good idea to take off your EJB bean developer hat for a little while because you're not in Kansas anymore. Assembling and deploying EJB applications requires a different frame of mind. That's why the EJB specification makes a distinction between an EJB bean provider, an EJB application assembler, and an EJB application deployer. The three roles are (briefly) defined as follows:

✔ **Bean provider:** When you're wearing this hat, your responsibility is to both create EJB components and describe those components in the deployment descriptor. Bean providers focus on one EJB component at a time. They build the component, they describe the component, and they move on to the next component. A bean provider is concerned only with the big picture of an EJB application insofar as it affects the internal implementation of the EJB component that he or she is working on right now.

✔ **Application assembler:** The application assembler takes a wider perspective on an EJB application. As the name implies, the application assembler is responsible for assembling the different components of any EJB application together in a single unit. The bean provider doesn't accomplish this task because the focus of the bean provider is the implementation and description of a single EJB component. The application assembler is left to provide the connective tissue that connects different EJB components and also has the task of describing the features of the EJB application as a whole. When the application assembler is finished, the view of what an EJB application does and how it should work is mostly in place . . . but not entirely.

✔ **Application deployer:** The deployer of an EJB application shares some of the responsibilities of the application assembler, but must have not only a global perspective on the internal mechanics of an EJB application, but also a grasp of how the internal mechanisms of the EJB application interact with the services provided by the EJB container. For example:

- The deployer needs to verify that the application assembler's task is complete.

- The deployer needs to assess the assembler's description of the EJB application and ensure that it doesn't conflict with any other applications that are deployed to the EJB container. Any conflicts must be corrected.

- Finally, the application assembler must map the services demanded by the EJB application to the services of the EJB container. This is perhaps the most demanding task of all because each EJB container has a unique and proprietary format for hooking the EJB application into the EJB container services.

As long as you're defining EJB components and assembling EJB applications, you're working with a standardized technology specification — all coding and assembly tasks for EJB applications are standard. But when you reach the deployment phase, each EJB container vendor is allowed to pursue a different course. That means there is no single standard for deploying an EJB application to an EJB container. It also means that this book cannot be your only guiding light as you reach the stage of deploying your application. Thus, although I'll give you some pointers and show you a simple deployment, you'll have to consult with the documentation provided with the EJB container you choose to get the details on deploying EJB applications.

An application deployer is like a database administrator for a database engine — the task is truly that complex. Although many people can wear the hats of both the EJB component provider and the application assembler, it is a rare bird that can throw the deployer hat into the mix. A deployer must have specialized knowledge of the EJB container's services, configuration, and administration. It is my view — and the view of the EJB specification —

that the bean developer on your team shouldn't try to take on the tasks of a deployer. Your team can benefit from a new — and highly specialized — set of eyes.

This word of advice is directed at all you Information Technology (IT) managers out there — you can hire as many contractors as you want to develop your EJB components, but you must have a deployer on staff. Think of a deployer as you would a database administrator. The deployer and the database administrator both have the responsibility of loading changes to their products into a test environment, ensuring that they work, and then loading them into the production environment. When those responsibilities aren't needed, both a deployer and a database administrator can focus on support, maintenance, and administrative tasks. For an EJB deployer, those tasks might include monitoring and tuning performance of the EJB container and granting security clearance to various users of the EJB application. The task is easily a full-time job.

Deploying a Sample EJB Application

As you approach your first deployment of an EJB application, I think it's a good idea to start out with something that's very simple and work your way up to more complex programs. Deploying a simple program allows you to get familiar with the EJB container-specific technology and ensures that you can focus on deployment issues — without having to worry about whether or not any problems you encounter are a result of coding or deployment errors.

I acquired this wisdom by trying to deploy a complex application the first time I worked with the BEA WebLogic Server. After three days of messing around, I applied the KISS principle (Keep It Simple, Stupid) and was able to get an EJB application deployed in a couple of hours. From there, I was able to incrementally add more complexity to my programs. By incrementally adding complexity to the program, you'll be able to isolate any problems you encounter and overcome them.

To assist with breaking into a simple deployment, I've provided a simple Hello World EJB application, available with the source code from this book on the Web at www.dummies.com/extras/ejbfd. The Hello World application includes a single EJB stateless session bean. The session bean's only purpose is to print the message "Hello World!" You'll see this message if the application is successfully deployed; if it isn't, you'll get some kind of indication about what went wrong. Listing 13-1 illustrates the remote home interface for the Hello World application. Listing 13-2 illustrates the remote interface for the application. Listing 13-3 shows the session bean class that generates the Hello World message. Finally, Listing 13-4 shows the deployment descriptor that goes with the application.

Listing 13-1   The HelloWorldRemoteHome Interface

```
package com.sextanttech.hello.interfaces;

import javax.ejb.EJBHome;
import javax.ejb.CreateException;
import java.rmi.RemoteException;

public interface HelloWorldRemoteHome extends EJBHome {
    HelloWorld create() throws RemoteException,
            CreateException;
}
```

The HelloWorldRemoteHome interface provides a single create method that helps the client application obtain a reference to the EJB component.

Listing 13-2   The HelloWorldRemote Interface

```
package com.sextanttech.hello.interfaces;

import javax.ejb.EJBObject;

public interface HelloWorldRemote extends EJBObject {
    String helloWorld() throws java.rmi.RemoteException;
}
```

The HelloWorldRemote interface has a single method that returns the message "Hello World!" to the client application.

Listing 13-3   The HelloWorldBean Class

```
package com.sextanttech.hello.implementation;

import javax.ejb.SessionBean;
import javax.ejb.SessionContext;
import javax.ejb.CreateException;
import javax.ejb.EJBException;
import java.rmi.RemoteException;

public class HelloWorldBean implements SessionBean {
    SessionContext context;

    public void ejbActivate() {} // no opp

    public void ejbPassivate() {} // no opp

    public void ejbRemove() {} // no opp
```

```
    public void setSessionContext(SessionContext context) {
        this.context = context;
    }

    public String helloWorld() { return "Hello World!"; }

    public void ejbCreate() throws CreateException,
        EJBException {} // no opp
}
```

The bean class is the ultimate in simplicity, with only a single business method that returns the literal value "Hello World!"

Listing 13-4   The HelloWorld Deployment Descriptor

```
<?xml version="1.0" encoding="UTF-8"?>

<!DOCTYPE ejb-jar PUBLIC "-//Sun Microsystems, Inc.//DTD
            Enterprise JavaBeans 2.0//EN" "http://java.
            sun.com/dtd/ejb-jar_2_0.dtd">

<ejb-jar>
  <enterprise-beans>
    <session>
      <ejb-name>HelloWorldEJB</ejb-name>
      <home>
        com.sextanttech.hello.interfaces.HelloWorldRemoteHome
      </home>
      <remote>
        com.sextanttech.hello.interfaces.HelloWorldRemote
      </remote>
      <ejb-class>
        com.sextanttech.hello.implementation.HelloWorldBean
      </ejb-class>
      <session-type>Stateless</session-type>
      <transaction-type>Container</transaction-type>
    </session>
  </enterprise-beans>
</ejb-jar>
```

Finally, you define the deployment descriptor, which contains only the bare-essential information needed to describe the HelloWorldEJB component and should be specified by the EJB bean provider. The only missing piece of this application that a deployer must specify is the JNDI name for this EJB component. Declaring the JNDI name for the component is different for each type of EJB container that you choose to deploy to. In this example, I'm deploying the EJB application to a JBoss Application server. When using JBoss, you have to create a separate XML file called jboss.xml, which identifies the EJB component and supplies a JNDI name for the component. The source code is illustrated in Listing 13-5.

Listing 13-5   The Source Code for the jboss.xml File

```
<?xml version="1.0" encoding="UTF-8"?>

<jboss>
  <enterprise-beans>
    <session>
      <ejb-name>HelloWorldEJB</ejb-name>
      <jndi-name>ejb/HelloWorldEJB</jndi-name>
    </session>
  </enterprise-beans>
</jboss>
```

In essence, the code in Listing 13-5 tells the JBoss EJB container to take the
EJB component named HelloWorldEJB and register it with a JNDI directory
under the name ejb/HelloWorldEJB. After JBoss has performed that task,
any application with access to the JBoss JNDI directory can look up the
ejb/HelloWorldEJB name and retrieve an instance of the
HelloWorldRemoteInterface.

The final task to preparing this sample application is writing a test program
that will run it. In Listing 13-6, I provide a sample main method that can be
used to invoke the HelloWorldEJB component.

Listing 13-6   Invoking the HelloWorldEJB

```
package com.sextanttech.hello.interfaces;

import javax.ejb.*;
import javax.naming.*;
import com.sextanttech.hello.interfaces.*;
import javax.rmi.*;
import java.rmi.*;

public class Client {
  public static void main(String[] argv) {
    HelloWorldRemote hello = null;
    try{
      System.out.println("getting initial context");
      Context context = new InitialContext();
      System.out.println("retrieving HelloWorldRemoteHome
          from context.");
      Object obj = context.lookup("ejb/helloWorldEJB");
      System.out.println("casting obj to HelloWorldRemoteHome
          Interface.");
      HelloWorldRemoteHome home = (HelloWorldRemoteHome)
        PortableRemoteObject.narrow(obj,
        Class.forName( "com.sextanttech.hello.interfaces.
          HelloWorldRemoteHome"));
```

```
        System.out.println("Retrieving HelloWorldRemote
            Interface.");
        hello = home.create();
        System.out.println("The message of the day is " + hello.
            helloWorld());
    }
    catch(CreateException e){
        e.printStackTrace(System.out);
    }
    catch(RemoteException e){
        e.printStackTrace(System.out);
    }
    catch(NamingException e){
        e.printStackTrace(System.out);
    }
    catch(Exception e){
        e.printStackTrace(System.out);
    }
    finally{ hello = null;}
    }
}
```

In Listing 13-6, the following tasks are performed:

- ✔ The client application starts by retrieving the JNDI initial context, which is enclosed in the InitialContext object. The JNDI context has a reference to the HelloWorldEJB under the name ejb/HelloWorldEJB — this is assigned to the context when the EJB container executes the context of the jboss.xml file.

- ✔ The main method uses that JNDI name to retrieve an instance of the remote home interface for the EJB component.

- ✔ The remote home interface is then used to retrieve an instance of the remote interface.

- ✔ Finally, the remote interface is invoked to print the message "Hello World!" If all goes according to plan, the message "The message of the day is Hello World!" is printed out to the console running the main method.

This application is bundled into a jar file — called, appropriately enough, HelloWorldEJB.jar — and you can find it at www.dummies.com/extras/ ejbfd. It's ready to deploy; to see it work, all you need to do is download it and drop it into the EJB container.

With minor modifications, this program can run on any EJB container. The only change that needs to be made involves replacing the jboss.xml file with the container-specific deployment descriptor extension. All you need to do is ensure that the EJB component is registered under the JNDI name ejb/HelloWorldEJB.

Figure 13-1 illustrates the structure of my HelloWorld application after I've compiled all my classes and created the `ejb-jar.xml` file and the `jboss.xml` file. Note that the `jboss.xml` file is placed in the same directory as the `ejb-jar.xml` file. Even if you're deploying to a different EJB container, you'll place the deployment descriptor extension for that EJB container in the `META-INF` directory.

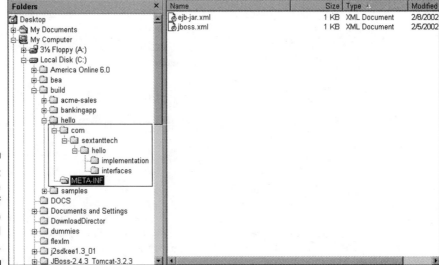

Figure 13-1:
The structure of the Hello World application.

After I've got my EJB application in the build directory, I'm ready to create a `jar` file. I describe the steps for this process at the end of Chapter 11; you can review them there to get the blow-by-blow steps of creating a `jar` file. For the Hello World application, after I have everything set up according to the instructions in Chapter 11, I execute the `jar` command, as follows:

```
C:\build\hello>jar cvf  helloWorldEJB.jar com META-INF
```

That tells the `jar` program to build a `jar` file called `HelloWorldEJB.jar` that contains all the contents of the `com` and `META-INF` directories. The `jar` command is executed from my `hello` directory — if you refer to Figure 13-1, you'll see that the `com` and `META-INF` directories are subdirectories of the `hello` directory.

The final phase of this simple deployment is to copy the `helloWorldEJB.jar` file and deploy it to the JBoss application server. Figure 13-2 illustrates the directory structure of the JBoss application server. On my computer, I have JBoss 3.0.0 alpha installed. Notice that the `Deploy` directory is open. To deploy the `helloWorldEJB.jar` file to JBoss, simply paste the file into the `Deploy` directory.

Folders		Name △	Size	Type	Modified
⊟ 🖳 Local Disk (C:)	▲	🗀 Default		File Folder	2/5/2002 5:42 PM
├ ⊞ 🗀 America Online 6.0		🗀 farm		File Folder	11/20/2001 11:05 PM
├ ⊞ 🗀 bea		🗀 lib		File Folder	11/20/2001 11:06 PM
├ ⊞ 🗀 build		📄 deploy.txt	1 KB	Text Document	11/20/2001 11:05 PM
├ 🗀 DOCS		📄 ejb-management.jar	5 KB	Executable Jar File	11/20/2001 11:05 PM
├ ⊞ 🗀 Documents and Settings		📄 helloWorldEJB.jar	5 KB	Executable Jar File	2/8/2002 3:13 PM
├ ⊞ 🗀 DownloadDirector		📄 hsqldb-default-service.xml	5 KB	XML Document	11/20/2001 11:05 PM
├ ⊞ 🗀 dummies		📄 j2eedeployment-service.xml	3 KB	XML Document	11/20/2001 11:05 PM
├ 🗀 flexlm		📄 jbossmq-service.xml	9 KB	XML Document	11/20/2001 11:05 PM
├ ⊞ 🗀 j2sdkee1.3_01		📄 jms-service.xml	3 KB	XML Document	11/20/2001 11:05 PM
├ ⊞ 🗀 JBoss-2.4.3_Tomcat-3.2.3		📄 jmx-ejb-adaptor.jar	12 KB	Executable Jar File	11/20/2001 11:05 PM
├ ⊟ 🗀 jboss-3.0.0alpha		📄 mail-service.xml	2 KB	XML Document	11/20/2001 11:05 PM
│ ├ ⊞ 🗀 admin					
│ ├ 🗀 bin					
│ ├ 🗀 client					
│ ├ ⊞ 🗀 conf					
│ ├ ⊞ 🗀 db					
│ ├ ⊟ 🗀 deploy					
│ │ ├ ⊞ 🗀 Default					
│ │ ├ 🗀 farm					
│ │ └ 🗀 lib					
│ ├ ⊞ 🗀 lib					
│ ├ 🗀 log					
│ └ ⊞ 🗀 tmp					
├ ⊞ 🗀 jdk1.3	▼				

Figure 13-2:
The JBoss
directory
structure.

Running the Hello World Application

After you deploy the `HelloWorldEJB.jar` file, you're ready to run it. Running the application occurs in two phases. First, you have to launch JBoss. To get JBoss started on a Windows computer, just follow these simple steps:

1. **From the Start menu, choose the Run command and type** command **in the dialog box that appears.**

   Click OK to continue. At this point, a DOS window should appear.

2. **In the DOS window, change directories so that you're in the** bin **directory of the JBoss application's home.**

   The home is the root directory of your JBoss installation. On my computer, the `bin` directory is located at `C:\JBoss-3.0.0alpha\bin`. (You can see it in Figure 13-2.)

3. **After you're in the** bin **directory, type the command** run.bat **and press Enter.**

   If your JBoss installation is correct, you'll see a number of messages as it initializes its services. Near the end, you should see the message, `"J2EE application: file:/C:/jboss-3.0.0alpha/deploy/ helloWorldEJB.jar is deployed successfully."` Your message might be a little different depending on where you installed the JBoss Application Server.

After you've started the JBoss application server, you're ready to start the client program. For this example, the client program is located in the helloWorldEJB.jar file. To make this task easier, I've supplied a special batch file called helloWorld.bat that properly executes the Hello World application. You'll have to modify the batch file so that all of the path references are correct for your computer. In the batch file, you'll see the following (very long) command:

```
java -classpath %JBOSS_DIST%\client;
    %JBOSS_DIST%\client\auth.conf;
    %JBOSS_DIST%\client\concurrent.jar;
    %JBOSS_DIST%\client\gnu-regexp.jar;
    %JBOSS_DIST%\client\jaas.jar;
    %JBOSS_DIST%\client\jboss-client.jar;
    %JBOSS_DIST%\client\jboss-common-client.jar;
    %JBOSS_DIST%\client\jboss-j2ee.jar;
    %JBOSS_DIST%\client\jbossmq-client.jar;
    %JBOSS_DIST%\client\jbosssx-client.jar;
    %JBOSS_DIST%\client\jboss-system-client.jar;
    %JBOSS_DIST%\client\jcert.jar;
    %JBOSS_DIST%\client\jndi.jar;
    %JBOSS_DIST%\client\jnet.jar;
    %JBOSS_DIST%\client\jpn-client.jar;
    %JBOSS_DIST%\client\jsse.jar;
    %JBOSS_DIST%\client\jndi.properties;
    %JBOSS_DIST%\server\default\deploy\helloWorld.jar;
    com.sextanttech.hello.interfaces.Client
```

You'll need to modify this batch file so that each path is correct for your computer. This batch file is set up for a Windows-based computer. If you have a Unix computer, you'll need to change the backslashes to forward slashes. After you set that up, you're ready to rock and roll; just follow these simple steps to run the client application:

1. **From the Start menu, choose Run and type** command **in the dialog box that appears; click OK to continue.**

   This starts up a second DOS window, which you'll use to run the client program.

2. **In the second DOS window, change directories so that you're located in the directory containing the** helloWorld.bat **file.**

   On my computer, that directory is C:\build\hello. You can see an example in the top-left corner of Figure 13-3.

3. **After you're in the right directory, type the command** helloWorld.bat.

   You should see the output shown in the main section of Figure 13-3.

Figure 13-3:
The output
of the Hello
World EJB
application.

The Final Stages

After you've successfully deployed a simple EJB application, you can start to add additional features and extend the application's functionality. EJB applications benefit from a number of standard services provided by the EJB container. To enhance the power of your EJB application, explore the following chapters:

✔ **Chapter 12 provides you with additional information about registering JNDI resources for use in your EJB application.** The information in Chapter 12 will allow you to reference additional resources that you define inside and outside your EJB application. Remember that your EJB container still has to map the JNDI references in your EJB application to actual resources. Mapping JNDI names to actual resources is an EJB container-specific problem, so you'll have to consult the documentation for your EJB container to get the answers.

✔ **Chapter 14 reviews the implementation of transactions in EJB applications.** This is a must-read for serous EJB application developers. You'll discover how to declare transactions for your EJB applications. Again, you'll need to consult your EJB container vendor documentation for certain extensions to the transaction service.

✔ **Chapter 15 addresses implementing security in EJB applications.** In Chapter 15, you'll see the syntax for declaring security roles and granting roles access to EJB components and methods in those components. To complete the security service, you'll have to map the security roles you declare — using the rules in Chapter 15 — to a security service in your EJB container. The EJB container manages the definition of users and passwords, creation of user groups, and granting of security roles to those user groups.

✔ **Finally, Chapter 16 introduces you to the techniques you'll use to access an EJB application from a remote client, such as a JSP application.** You'll review some tricks you can use to attach a user interface to your EJB application.

Remember that, in this phase of EJB application development, you're beginning to move out of the realm of the EJB specification and into vendor-specific issues. In other words, the sidewalk ends here. But don't sweat it too much — most vendors are pretty good about supplying documentation with their applications, so you should be able to pick up where this book leaves off and fit the final pieces of the puzzle together without too much difficulty.

Chapter 14

Implementing EJB Transaction Support

. . . .

In This Chapter

▶ Reviewing the key concepts of transactions

▶ Discovering transaction behaviors for EJB applications

▶ Exploring the semantics of EJB transactions

. . . .

*T*hroughout this book you'll find a lot of references to the role of transactions in EJB applications. In most of those references, I advise you not to worry about transactions because the EJB container takes care of transaction services for you. But, if you're like me, you worry anyway. You might be asking yourself how the EJB container knows what type of transactions to implement. You might be wondering whether coding an EJB component in the wrong way will undermine transactional services. You might even be wondering what the heck a transaction is anyway. If you've been asking yourself these questions, then this chapter is for you.

In the following pages, you'll discover the basic principles that define transactions, you'll get to see what types of transactional services are supported by EJB containers, and you'll also see what you need to do to tell the EJB container how you want transactional services implemented. But before I get into that, I hope that this simple fact will put your mind at ease: **You do not need to implement transactions yourself; all you need to do is tell the EJB container how you want transactions to be implemented.** You do that by using simple XML declarations to describe the transaction in the deployment descriptor of your EJB application. All the code is supplied by the EJB container. So, the long and short of it is this: Using transactional services in EJB applications is relatively simple.

There are two ways that implementing transactional services can go wrong. The first occurs if you start manually tinkering with the transactional services through the code in your EJB program. Such tinkering isn't guaranteed to lead you astray, but it increases the risk of things going wrong. The second way is if you tell the EJB container to perform the wrong kind of transactional service. You can prevent the latter problem by understanding both the mechanics of EJB transactions as well as the implications of each transactional declaration you make. This chapter provides you with the information you need to work around the latter problem.

Reviewing Transaction Fundamentals

What the heck is a transaction anyway? In the simplest sense, a transaction spans a chain of method invocations, ensuring that the changes made by those methods all succeed or all fail as a group. For example, if you were to transfer funds between two bank accounts, the code might look something like the following pseudocode:

```
boolean transferFunds(int funds, Account source, Account
          dest){
    return (withdrawFunds(int funds, Account source) &&
          depositFunds(int funds, Account dest));
}
```

In the preceding example, there are three method invocations: transferFunds, withdrawFunds, and depositFunds. For a transfer to complete successfully, all three operations must succeed without a hitch. But if any one of the operations fails, then they should all fail. To make sure that they all succeed or fail as a group, all three methods would be included in a single transaction.

Keeping things simple, a *transaction* is a set of operations that must all succeed or all fail as a group. Each transaction has a boundary, or logical marker, which is often referred to as a *transaction demarcation*. The boundaries are like bookends on a set of operations. At the beginning, a logical marker is set that indicates that the following activities are part of a transaction. At the end of these operations is another marker. If all the operations between these two bookends succeed, then the whole group is said to be committed. When a transaction is *committed*, all the changes that the transaction made are permanently etched into stone. But if any one of the operations inside a transaction fails, then all operations within the transaction are rolled back. When a *rollback* occurs, all the changes made by a transaction are restored to the way they were before the transaction started.

Transactions exist to achieve some basic goals, which are described as the ACID properties of transactions. ACID is an acronym for *A*tomic, *C*onsistent, *I*solated, and *D*urable. I describe each of these properties following:

✔ **Atomic:** *Atomic* means indivisible. A transaction is a single, complete unit of work that cannot be subdivided into other complete units of work. That doesn't mean that a transaction can't span more than a single method call. Just as atoms described in physics have sub-particles, transactions can have sub-components. A transaction can span several method calls in different objects, but all those methods *as a group* must perform a single task, no less and no more. An example is a transfer of funds from one account to another. It involves two steps — withdrawing funds from the source account and depositing funds into the target account. Both steps taken together are an atomic unit of work. Either taken on its own doesn't constitute a transfer of funds.

✔ **Consistent:** *Consistent* means the operation of a transaction cannot generate more nor less than the sum of its parts. This pertains to any data that is manipulated by a set of transacted operations. To use the transfer example again, if I transfer $400.00 from one account, the debit to the target account had better balance with the credit to the source account. If, after completing the transfer, the source account has the same amount of money and the target account has $400.00 more money, then the data is inconsistent. If this inconsistency occurred inside a transaction, the Consistent rule requires that the transaction be rolled back.

A main goal of transactions is not the redoing of failed operations, but rather the restoration of the underlying data to a consistent state when it becomes inconsistent. This is achieved by restoring the values of the underlying data to where they were prior to the beginning of the transaction.

✔ **Isolated:** *Isolated* means that a transaction occurs without interference from outside sources. In a real world environment, it's possible to have many requests to view and change the same data at the same time. A transaction has to ensure that all of these requests do not interfere with each other. If, for example, I start with a balance of $200.00 in my bank account and try to carry out two concurrent transactions, both of which are meant to withdraw $200.00, the transaction should force one to occur first and the second to wait — a process known as *blocking* — until the first is completed. After the first transaction is completed, the second transaction gets a new view of the data — showing that my new balance is zero dollars — and the second transaction subsequently fails.

✔ **Durable:** *Durable* refers to the persistence of transacted changes. To say that something is durable means that a change made by a transaction must be permanently written to some physical device, such as a database located on a hard drive, before the transaction completes successfully. This device, no matter what it is, must be able to preserve that data **even if the system crashes and all memory is erased.** A hard drive can accomplish that task, as can a database so long as no physical damage is inflicted on the device. The memory of a computer cannot be durable because memory is transient, and it gets erased every time the computer reboots.

One of the most important things to keep in mind about transactions is that they aren't intended to be used for building faster, glitzier systems. They are all about managing risk and preserving the integrity of data. Thus, although transactions may incur significant operating expenses in terms of runtime performance, they're an essential cost of business and they can save a lot of money in the event that things go wrong (and invariably they do). Writing an EJB application that doesn't use transactions is flirting with disaster.

You aren't absolved from implementing a proper database design just because your EJB application supports transactions. An EJB application doesn't know anything about the internal rules of a database, including the database's primary key fields, relationships, referential integrity rules, rules on null values for specific columns, and the like. In order to ensure that the EJB transactions properly enforce a database's rules, you must define those rules inside the database using SQL.

Examining EJB Transactions

In Enterprise JavaBean applications, there are two models for transaction implementation: container-managed and bean-managed. Bean-managed transactions are entirely controlled by the EJB component developer and are significantly more complex than container-managed transactions. Implementing bean-managed transactions isn't an entry-level task, and that's why you won't find it covered in this book. Instead, you'll get a close look at the more manageable task of implementing container-managed transactions.

Message-driven beans and session beans can have either container-managed or bean-managed transactions, but entity beans can have only container-managed transactions.

In container-managed transactions, the EJB container defines the actual transaction. The transaction is constructed based on rules that you specify in the deployment descriptor for the EJB container. As I discuss in the previous section, a transaction is a sequential set of method invocations that performs a task. In EJB applications, your job is to specify the transactional behavior of each method in an EJB component. The behavior is specified with EJB elements called *transactional attributes*. Transactional attributes describe the transactional behavior of methods listed in the home or component interfaces of session and entity beans, and in the onMessage method of the message-driven bean.

Transactional attributes aren't used on all methods and objects in your EJB application, but they must be specified for the following methods:

- **Session and entity beans:** Transactional attributes must be specified on the home and component interfaces for session and entity beans. In addition, all methods of the direct and indirect superinterfaces of the component and home interfaces — the interfaces that your home and component interfaces are extended from — must have transactional attributes, with the exception of the following:

  - For session beans, methods of the `javax.ejb.EJBObject` and `javax.ejb.EJBLocalObject` can't have transactional attributes in the deployment descriptor.

  - For entity beans, the methods `getEJBHome`, `getEJBLocalHome`, `getHandle`, `getPrimaryKey`, and `isIdentical` of the component interfaces can't have transactional attributes. The methods `getEJBMetaData` and `getHomeHandle` of the home interfaces can't have transactional attributes.

- **Message-driven beans:** Only the `onMessage` method of the message-driven bean must have a transactional attribute. No other methods can have transactional attributes.

There are six types of attributes:

- `NotSupported`: This attribute indicates that the method being invoked doesn't support external coordination of transactions. Your EJB components should only use this attribute if they access some external resource that doesn't support remote coordination of transactions. For example, you may need to invoke an operation on some legacy system that doesn't provide access to its transactional system, or which doesn't have a transactional system. In that case, the EJB container cannot possibly manage the transaction.

- `Required`: This attribute tells the EJB container that a transaction is required for this method. If the container hasn't yet started a transaction, it will start a new transaction when it encounters this attribute. If it already has started a transaction, then it will include a method with the `Required` attribute in the existing transaction.

- `Supports`: This attribute indicates that the method in question supports transactions, meaning that if the container has an existing transaction, it will add the method to the transaction. But if it doesn't have an existing transaction, then it won't create a new transaction for this method.

✔ RequiresNew: This attribute indicates that the method in question must have a new transaction. Regardless of whether there's an existing transaction or not, when the container encounters a method with the RequiresNew transactional attribute, it will create a new transaction for the method.

✔ Mandatory: This attribute indicates that the container must include this method in an existing transaction. If there is no existing transaction, then the container must generate an exception. When a container attempts to invoke a method with the Mandatory attribute and there is no existing transaction, the container throws the following exception:

```
javax.transaction.TransactionRequiredException
```

✔ Never: This attribute indicates that the designated method can never be included in a transaction. If the method is invoked and there is an existing transaction, the container will throw a javax.rmi.RemoteException object for remote clients or a javax.ejb.EJBException object for local clients.

The EJB container loads these rules with your EJB application. Then, when a method is invoked, the EJB container applies the transactional behavior associated with each attribute to the method as it is invoked. To illustrate, consider the three methods of a transfer: transferFunds, depositFunds, and withdrawFunds. In the deployment descriptor, I might declare the following rules:

✔ transferFunds requires a new transaction, so I specify RequiresNew because a transfer is an atomic operation that typically isn't a member of larger operations.

✔ depositFunds and withdrawFunds require transactions, but they don't necessarily have to be new ones. Consider that a withdrawal or a deposit can occur outside the context of a transfer. In all contexts, deposits and withdrawals should be transacted, but they shouldn't have their own transactions if they're part of a transfer. Thus, I use the Requires attribute for each.

When the container encounters these methods, it will start a transaction on the invocation of the transferFunds and add the withdrawFunds and depositFunds invocations to that transaction. In addition, if it encounters either withdrawFunds or depositFunds outside the context of a transaction, it will create a new transaction for those methods.

Rules constrain the use of different types of transactional attributes. As a matter of common sense, you can't apply a Never attribute to a method invoked from a method that requires a transaction. The two are diametrically opposed declarations. In addition, Table 14-1 shows the types of attributes allowed on methods in different EJB components.

Table 14-1	Support for Transactional Attributes		
Attribute	**Session Beans**	**Entity Beans**	**Message-Driven Beans**
NotSupported	Yes	Optional	Yes
Required	Yes	Yes	Yes
Supports	Yes	Optional	No
RequiresNew	Yes	Yes	No
Mandatory	Yes	Yes	No
Never	Yes	Optional	No

In Table 14-1, the methods of an EJB component that support a given transactional attribute have the value Yes, and those that don't support the transactional attribute have the value No.

The Optional attribute means that the transactional attribute can optionally be supported by the EJB container vendor. To determine whether the transactional attribute is supported, you must consult your container vendor's documentation. Bear in mind, however, that even if the container does support those attributes, by using them you cause your EJB application to be non-portable, which means that it isn't guaranteed to run on another EJB container.

One of the biggest challenges of working with container-managed transactions is understanding the implications of using each transactional attribute within the context of different transactions that a method participates in. To illustrate, if you have a method that is invoked in two or more transactions (such as the depositFunds or withdrawFunds methods of previous examples), you must specify an attribute that provides the appropriate behavior and works in the context of all the transactions. In large applications — with lots of transactions — a lot of attention to detail is required to ensure that you identify all the possible transactions a method is involved in, and select the appropriate transactional attribute for all the transactions.

When deciding which transactional attribute to apply to a method, trace the execution path of each invocation of that method. The *execution path* shows the chain of methods that lead to a particular method invocation as well as the methods that follow it. The EJB container has the ability to define different transactions along each execution path. As you choose the transactional attribute, make sure that it works in the context of each execution path. To discover more about the implications of each choice you make, refer to the upcoming section "EJB Transaction Behavior."

EJB transaction syntax

For each session and message-driven bean that you develop, you must specify whether the bean has container-managed or bean-managed transactions. You accomplish this with the <transaction-type> attribute, which allows the values Container or Bean. Entity beans don't have a <transaction-type> attribute because they're always container-managed. If the <transaction-type> attribute of your EJB component is set to Container — or if you create an entity bean — then you must supply information about the transactional attributes for all the methods in the bean.

The transactional attributes for a bean are declared in the <assembly-descriptor> section of the deployment descriptor using the attribute <container-transaction>. An EJB component with container-managed transactions can have multiple <container-transaction> elements — one for each type of transactional attribute that applies to the EJB component. Thus, if an EJB component has some methods that use the transactional attribute RequiresNew and some methods that use the transactional attribute NotSupported, then the EJB component must have two <container-transaction> entries. The following syntax is used for each <container-transaction> element:

- ✔ <description>: This is an optional subelement of <container-transaction> that provides some documentation. Although I am normally an advocate of populating description elements, this element seems extraneous to me because the purpose of the <container-transaction> element is clearly identified in the <trans-attribute> element that I define at the end of this list.

- ✔ <method>: Each <container-transaction> element can have multiple <method> subelements. Each <method> subelement identifies a method of the EJB component that uses the specified <trans-attribute> (defined next). All method entries must be methods from the same EJB component.

- ✔ <trans-attribute>: This subelement of <container-transaction> identifies the specific transactional attribute that applies to all of the methods identified by <method> elements. The value of this element should be one of the transactional attributes that I describe in the previous section.

The <method> subelement of <container-transaction> has many subelements of its own. These subelements — which I identify and define in the following list — describe the method in more precise detail:

- ✔ <description>: This is an optional attribute that documents the purpose for marking the method with the specified transactional attribute. In addition to documenting the reason for using the attribute, you might also consider identifying the different execution paths that this method is used for. Doing so will assist others in understanding your choice and maintaining the EJB application.

✔ **<ejb-name>:** This identifies the <ejb-name> for the EJB component to which this method belongs. The value of this attribute must correspond to the <ejb-name> of a component identified in the <enterprise-beans> section of the deployment descriptor. Remember that although each <method> element has its own <ejb-name> element, all the <method> elements of a given <container-transaction> must identify the same EJB component.

✔ **<method-intf>:** If the same method name is used in more than one of the EJB component's interfaces, you can use this attribute to clarify which interface you're referring to. For example, if you define the same business method in both the remote and local interfaces for an EJB component, you can identify which interface you want this <method> element to apply to. The value of this element should be the fully qualified class name of the interface. *Note:* This is an optional element. If you don't specify a <method-intf> for a method that's defined in two interfaces, the <method> entry will be applied to both methods.

✔ **<method-name>:** This identifies the name of the method that the <method> element applies to. The value of this element can be a wildcard character *, in which case the <method> element is applied to all methods in all interfaces of the EJB component. Otherwise, it must identify the name of a method, such as withdrawFunds or depositFunds. More on the use of the wildcard character * follows.

✔ **<method-params>:** If your EJB component defines overloaded methods, you can identify which overloaded method a <method> element refers to by using the <method-params> element. An *overloaded method* occurs when you have several methods with the same name and different parameter lists. *Note:* This element is optional. If you don't specify the <method-params>, the <method> entry will apply to all methods that have the same <method-name>.

Each <method-params> contains a list of <method-param> elements. Each <method-param> element identifies the fully qualified type name of a parameter for the identified element.

Three strategies for defining transactions

Using the syntax that I describe in the previous section, there are three strategies that you can apply to define the transactional attributes in an EJB component. These strategies control the range of methods in an EJB component that are effected by the transactional attribute:

✔ **In the first strategy, the wildcard character * is used, which applies the specified transactional attribute to all methods of the EJB component.** This strategy uses a single `<method>` element with the wildcard character * used for the `<method-name>` value.

✔ **The second strategy applies the transactional attribute to a specific method name.** This strategy provides a different `<method>` element for each method that should have the specified transactional attribute. The name of the method is given as the value of the `<method-name>` element. This strategy overrides the behavior of the first strategy. Consequently, you can use the wildcard character * as a catchall approach for all the methods of an EJB component and then override the transactional attribute assigned in the wildcard character * by using the second strategy to assign a different transactional attribute to a specific method.

✔ **The third strategy narrows the application of the transactional attribute to a specific method with a specific set of parameters.** This strategy is implemented by specifying a specific method name in the `<method-name>` element and then identifying the parameters for that method in the `<method-params>` element. This strategy will override both of the previous strategies.

You can modify all three preceding strategies by using the `<method-intf>` element, which will narrow the behavior of the transaction attribute to the interface you specify. Thus, if you used the * to apply behavior to all methods and specified the class for the local home interface by using the `<method-intf>` element, the behavior of the transactional attribute would be applied to all methods of the local home interface.

The code in Listing 14-1 illustrates the definition of transactional attributes, applying the principles that I've described so far. This code meets the fundamental requirements for implementing the balance transfer transaction that I describe earlier in this chapter. The bold text in Listing 14-1 highlights the relevant tags for declaring transactional attributes.

Although you can override transactional attributes by assigning a different transaction using a narrower scope, you should never specify two transactional attributes for a single method by using the same scope.

Listing 14-1   Declaring Transactional Attributes

```
<ejb-jar>
  <enterprise-beans>
    <session>
      <ejb-name>DepositBean</ejb-name>
      ...
    </session>
    <session>
      <ejb-name>WithdrawBean</ejb-name>
      ...
```

```
    </session>
    <session>
      <ejb-name>ATMTransactionBean</ejb-name>
      ...
    </session>
    <entity>
      <ejb-name>AccountEntityBean</ejb-name>
      ...
    </entity>
</enterprise-beans>
<assembly-descriptor>
  <container-transaction>
    <description>I start by initializing all methods in the
        ATMTransactionEJB
      so that they require a transaction. This is a default
        initialization that ensures
      that all methods in the bean have some transaction
        attribute.
    </description>
    <method>
      <description>This assignment applies to all methods.
        </description>
      <ejb-name>ATMTransactionEJB</ejb-name>
      <method-name>*</method-name>
    </method>
    <trans-attribute>Required</trans-attribute>
  </container-transaction>
  <container-transaction>
    <description>In this declaration I override the default
        behavior of
      the previous declaration, forcing transfers to have a
        new transaction context.
    </description>
    <method>
      <description>
        This assignment overrides the default "Required"
        attribute.
      </description>
      <ejb-name>ATMTransactionEJB</ejb-name>
      <method-name>transfer</method-name>
    </method>
    <trans-attribute>RequiresNew</trans-attribute>
  </container-transaction>
  <container-transaction>
    <description>This sets the default value for all
        deposits.</description>
    <method>
      <description>Another wildcard declaration.
        </description>
      <ejb-name>DepositEJB</ejb-name>
      <method-name>*</method-name>
    </method>
```

(continued)

Listing 14-1 *(continued)*

```
        <trans-attribute>Required</trans-attribute>
    </container-transaction>
    <container-transaction>
      <description>This sets the default value for all
          withdraws.</description>
      <method>
        <description>Another wildcard declaration.
          </description>
        <ejb-name>WithdrawEJB</ejb-name>
        <method-name>*</method-name>
      </method>
        <trans-attribute>Required</trans-attribute>
    </container-transaction>
    <container-transaction>
      <description>
        This sets the default value for all the account bean.
      </description>
      <method>
        <description>Another wildcard declaration.
          </description>
        <ejb-name>AccountEJB</ejb-name>
        <method-name>*</method-name>
      </method>
        <trans-attribute>Required</trans-attribute>
    </container-transaction>
  </assembly-descriptor>
</ejb-jar>
```

A lot is going on in Listing 14-1, so take a moment to review the following highlights:

- ✔ **The beginning of the deployment descriptor declares a number of EJB components, including the beans involved in our transfer transaction.** With respect to the declaration of transactional attributes, the most important feature of the ⟨enterprise-beans⟩ section is the ⟨ejb-name⟩ declarations. In addition, you may find the interface names for each EJB component useful if you need to use the ⟨method-intf⟩ element in your transactional declaration.

- ✔ **In the ⟨assembly-descriptor⟩ section of the deployment descriptor, you'll find the transactional attribute declarations for each EJB component involved in our transaction.** Note that you do not have to assign transactional attributes to EJB components until the application is deployed, but if you assign a transactional attribute to any method in an EJB component, you must then assign transactional attributes to all the methods in that component. Thus, the wildcard operator is very convenient for initializing the transactional attributes of all methods.

> ✔ **In the sample transactional attribute declarations, I've initialized all EJB components that are involved in a transfer transaction by using the wildcard operator.** In addition, because a transfer must have its own transaction context, the second `<container-transaction>` element overrides the default transactional attribute for the `ATMTransactionBean`, applying a `RequiresNew` attribute to the `transfer` method.

EJB Transaction Behavior

Grasping how different transactional attributes are applied to a transaction context is probably about as difficult as describing it. The best way to achieve an understanding is to visualize it. In this final section, the implications of using transactional attributes are illustrated visually so that you can see the effect they have on the behavior of the EJB container's transactional management service. The diagrams in this section are provided by Marc Fleury, Chief Technology Officer and Founder of JBoss Group, LLC, and come from the JBoss Application Server training manual, which is used in its excellent week-long, instructor-led class.

Although I hope my book is taking you a long way toward discovering all that EJB applications have to offer, each application server on the market has a slightly different twist on configuration, deployment, and administration of EJB applications. Thus, I highly recommend taking a class that focuses on your application server of choice. For more information about JBoss training, visit the JBoss Web site at `www.jbossgroup.com`.

In each of the following diagrams, the flow of execution passes through several EJB components. Each component is identified by its type and the transactional attribute that's applied to it. There are several key points that are identified by the numbered bubbles. To see what happens at the key point, refer to the corresponding number in the lists following each diagram. These examples, beginning with Figure 14-1, illustrate the successful flow of a transaction.

1. **At Position 1, the first method of an EJB component is invoked.** The transactional attribute is `Required`, which causes a new transaction to be defined. Note that the outer transaction boundary labeled "Transaction 1" defines the scope of this new transaction. The new transaction is defined because a transaction isn't yet available. If a transaction were already established, a new transaction wouldn't be defined.

2. **At Position 2, a method on Entity A is invoked.** This method is labeled with the `Supports` attribute. Because Entity A supports a transaction, the context from the calling session bean is used. Because a transaction context is supplied, the entity bean will invoke its `ejbLoad` method when added to this transaction context. This causes the state of the entity bean to be synchronized with the database, which is necessary to ensure consistency during the transaction invocation.

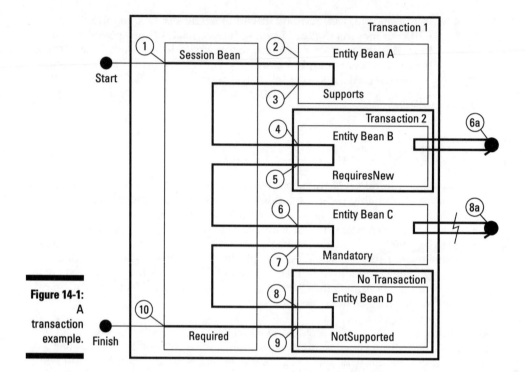

Figure 14-1:
A
transaction
example.

3. **At Position 3, the method invoked on Entity A is completed.** Because Entity A is added to the existing transaction context, it will not commit its changes until the entire transaction is completed at Step 10. Thus, the EJB container doesn't invoke any transactional methods at Position 3.

4. **At Position 4, the session bean invokes Entity B.** Entity B is marked with a RequiresNew attribute, which means it must have its own transaction. The EJB container will implement this feature by suspending the existing transaction and starting a new transaction for Entity B. At Position 4, the new transaction — labeled "Transaction 2" — begins, which causes Entity B to invoke its ejbLoad method.

   The EJB specification doesn't require EJB containers to support nested transactions. That means that Transaction 2 is completely separate from Transaction 1. If Transaction 2 fails, it will not cause Transaction 1 to fail. If Transaction 1 fails after invoking Transaction 2 and if Transaction 2 committed, Transaction 2 will remain committed. Container vendors may optionally support nested transactions, but the behavior isn't stated in the EJB specification.

5. **At Position 5, the work of Entity B is completed.** Entity B is the only bean in the context of Transaction 2. Because Position 5 marks the end of Transaction 2, all the changes made in Transaction 2 are committed. This is accomplished by invoking the ejbStore method on Entity B,

causing changes to the entity to be written to the database. After the work is committed, Transaction 2 goes out of scope and the work of Transaction 1 resumes.

6. **At Position 6, Entity C is invoked, with the transactional attribute of** `Mandatory`. The `Mandatory` attribute indicates that there must be an existing transaction or Entity C will throw a `javax.transaction.TransactionRequiredException`. Lucky for us, Transaction 1 already exists. Thus, the work of Entity C is added to Transaction 1. At Position 6, the `ejbLoad` method of Entity C is invoked to ensure a consistent state between the entity and the database as work in the transaction begins.

6a. **At this point, another client invokes a method on Entity B from a different transaction context.** Because Transaction 2 on Entity B is already completed, the work initiated from Position 6a can proceed, even though Transaction 1 hasn't finished. An entity bean will be isolated and all other method invocations will be blocked until the transaction it is included in is finished. After its transaction is completed, it can continue to service other method invocations from other client applications.

7. **At Position 7, the work of Entity C is completed.** Because Transaction 1 isn't ready to commit, the changes to Entity C are preserved in the entity bean, but not written to the database.

8. **At Position 8, Entity D with a transactional attribute of** `NotSupported` **is invoked.** The `NotSupported` attribute requires the EJB container to suspend the work of Transaction 1 and proceed to perform changes in Entity D without the context of a transaction.

Recall from earlier in this chapter that the EJB container isn't required to implement the `NotSupported` attribute for entity beans. In fact, it's unusual that such an attribute would be used in an entity bean. Because JBoss doesn't have any hard and fast rules for how to treat entity beans that don't support transactions, it implements them like it would a `RequiresNew` attribute. Thus, the `ejbLoad` method for Entity D is invoked at Position 8. This behavior isn't strictly enforced and other EJB containers may behave differently. Be sure to consult your vendor's documentation to determine whether the vendor supports the optional transactional attributes for entity beans. If the vendor does support those optional attributes, be sure to read the vendor's documentation on what the expected behavior is for each optional attribute.

8a. **Now a third client application attempts to invoke Entity C from yet another transaction context.** The work of Entity C is isolated in Transaction 1. Because Transaction 1 isn't yet complete, all other client invocations are blocked out of Entity C. The same principle would apply for Entity A if it were invoked while Transaction 1 is in progress. When a client invocation is blocked, that means that the client has to wait until the transaction is finished. After that point, the client invocation proceeds as normal.

9. **Position 9 marks the end of the work for Entity D.** Because the JBoss application server treats NotSupported as a separate transaction for entity beans, it now invokes the ejbStore method for Entity D. After ejbStore is invoked, the method returns to the session bean and to the context of Transaction 1. Note that if Transaction 1 were to fail at this point, the changes made in Entity B and Entity D would remain committed while the changes in Entity A and Entity C would be rolled back.

10. **Position 10 marks the end of the work performed in the session bean and the end of the scope of Transaction 1.** As a result, Transaction 1 is committed at this point, meaning that the ejbStore operation is invoked on Entity A and on Entity C, causing the changes to be written to the database.

In Figure 14-2, the behavior of the Never attribute is illustrated.

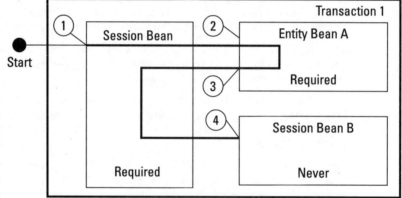

Figure 14-2:
Another transaction example.

1. **In Position 1, the first Session Bean is invoked with a transactional attribute of** Required. This causes the creation of Transaction 1, to which the method invocation for the first session bean is added.

2. **Entity Bean A is invoked with an attribute of** Required. Because Transaction 1 already exists, Entity Bean A is added to the transaction. Its ejbLoad method is invoked so that the state between the bean and the database is consistent.

3. **Now the work of Entity Bean A is completed.** No special operation is performed here, though, because Transaction 1, which Entity Bean A belongs to, hasn't yet completed.

4. **Finally, the first session bean invokes Session Bean B.** Session Bean B has a transactional attribute of `Never`, which means that it can never be part of an transaction and that, if it's invoked from a transaction context, it must throw an exception. This raises a `javax.ejb.EJBException` if the first session bean invoked it from a local interface, or `java.rmi.RemoteException` if the first session bean invoked it through a remote interface.

   If an application exception (which isn't a subclass of the `java.lang.RuntimeException`) is thrown, Transaction 1 isn't rolled back unless the exception handling code in the first session bean explicitly tells it to. But both `EJBException` and `RemoteException` are runtime exceptions, which means that the EJB container will roll back Transaction 1. Because of the rollback, the `ejbLoad` method on Entity Bean A will be invoked again. This causes the state of the database to be restored to Entity Bean A, in effect restoring the original values of Entity Bean A.

If you encounter an application exception from which you can't successfully recover, you can force a rollback to occur by invoking the `setRollbackOnly` method. You can invoke the `setRollbackOnly` method from the `EntityContext` for entity beans, the `SessionContext` for session beans, or the `MessageContext` for message-driven beans. Remember that the `setRollbackOnly` method can only be invoked from EJB components with container-managed transactions.

Chapter 15

Creating Secure EJB Applications

• •

• •

*I*n *Field of Dreams* we learn, "If you build it, they will come." That principle is very apt for developing distributed applications, only the "they" are more likely to be hackers — rather than a bunch of angelic baseball heroes — who will attempt to bring your system to a standstill. An effective security solution isn't only your defense against invasion but is also your means of recovery. While security systems can keep unwanted visitors out, hackers can always find loopholes. So your security system should also monitor activity in the system — to keep an eye on intruders and audit changes to any critical files or data that your system contains. That allows you to restore critical data to its original state in the event that it's manipulated by a malicious user. There are three key goals that all security solutions should address:

✔ **Authenticate and authorize users:** Authentication is the process of ensuring that a user is who she claims to be, typically via a username and password. Authorization is used to determine whether an authenticated user has the right to perform specific actions or access specific resources in an application. Authentication and authorization are closely related because authorization means nothing unless you're sure that a user is who he claims to be. Likewise, just because you know who a user is doesn't mean he should be able to do anything he wants in your application.

✔ **Encrypt data:** Data encryption aims to protect confidential information while it is being transported across an unsecured medium, such as a network or the Internet. When you transport data across a network, it isn't protected by the security mechanisms that exist at its source and destination. By encrypting the data, you conceal its meaning.

✔ **Audit:** No security solution is complete without some form of auditing function. Auditing is simply tracking who does what in your system and when they do it. Auditing is your friend when your security is breached. It's the solution that allows you to identify what the unauthorized user has done and — if the solution has been well-defined — enables you to go back and undo the changes that an unauthorized user may have made.

Security experts would add a number of other aims into a holistic vision of the role for security, but the preceding three are essential components for a complete security system.

The traditional problem with security products is their complexity. As an application programmer, it's hard to understand both the business domain as well as all the latest and greatest security products. Security is an issue for specialists and experts, not for your typical application programmer. Consequently, you should not make security an integral part of your application design. That advice may seem counterintuitive because security is so important. The point is that security is *not* an application domain problem; it is a *system development* and *system administration problem*. Security is primarily the responsibility of EJB container providers and the people who administer containers to manage security. Instead of hard coding a security system into your application, security should be a service that your application benefits from — and which can be changed without redesigning or rebuilding the application. So, as a developer of EJB components, you should be aware of how the EJB security model works, primarily so that you don't accidentally write code that undermines the integrity of the EJB container's security framework.

The good news is that the EJB architecture treats security as a system-level issue and, as a result, requires EJB container vendors to implement a *security framework* for EJB applications. The security framework is a declarative framework that you can control through your EJB application's deployment descriptor; you tell the EJB container what kind of security rules to apply, and it provides them for you. It really doesn't get much simpler than that. The only problem is that the language of security systems is often so obscure that it's almost as if this part of the specification was run through an obfuscation algorithm. (*Obfuscators* change variable names and function names in a program into meaningless mumbo-jumbo so that it becomes impossible to read.) This chapter guides you through the process of making sense of security semantics and also illustrates the elegant simplicity of the EJB security architecture.

EJB Applications and Role-Based Security

The basic premise of EJB security is that security is a *system service* that can be applied to any application. Because security is treated as a service, it is abstracted out of the design of the business processes for your application and is dealt with separately. One benefit of this approach is that you don't have to devote a lot of energy to security considerations while designing your EJB components. But more importantly, because the security service is separate, you can enhance the security service without redesigning your EJB application.

The security architecture of EJB applications is modeled after a *role-based security architecture*, a security model that assigns roles to users and allows them access to software services based on their roles. Role-based security is primarily concerned with user authentication. It doesn't address the goals of auditing or encryption, but because role-based security assigns identities to users, you can implement an auditing solution by accessing the security credentials of users inside your EJB application. I address the topic of auditing at the end of this chapter, in the section "Auditing User Activity."

Here are the basic principles of role-based security:

- ✔ **Each user of a system must be uniquely identified.** The user's identity is referred to as the *security identity*, which is usually confirmed through the use of a username and a password. In the case of ATM transactions, users are identified by IDs stored in their ATM cards as well as by PIN numbers they enter into the ATM machine. The process of identifying a user is called *authentication*.

- ✔ **A user is assigned one or more security roles that pertain to his or her responsibilities within an application.** A *security role* identifies under a single heading both a logical type of user as well as the security privileges that the user has. For example, a user could have a security role of "HR Team Member," which carries with it the security privileges granted to any HR team member.

  Note: A user can have more than one security role because a single person can perform more than one logical type of task. For example, a user could be assigned a "Basic User" role — giving that user the same level of access granted all users — and an "HR Team Member" role that adds the privileges of a human resources employee.

✔ **Each security role is assigned a set of method permissions that are necessary for people in a particular role to perform their responsibilities.** A *method permission* is a declaration that a certain set of methods within an EJB component can be executed by the specified security role. When a user is granted a specific security role, that user has permission to invoke all the methods associated with that security role. And when the role is revoked, the user no longer has access to those methods.

✔ **When a user invokes a method, the user's identity and roles are passed together to the method.** The identity of a user in combination with his or her associated roles are referred to as a *security principle*. When a method is invoked, the security principle of the *caller* (also known as the invoker of the method) is used to verify security. If the security principle has permission to invoke the method, the method invocation proceeds. But if the security principle isn't authorized, then a `java.lang.SecurityException` is thrown.

✔ **A method may propagate the security principle of the caller to subsequent method invocations, or it can have its own security principle that's used for subsequent method invocations.** If the security principle is propagated, the identity and rights of the caller are applied to subsequent method invocations. This is referred to as using the caller identity. In some cases, a method will perform tasks that a user couldn't otherwise access. In these cases, the method is assigned its own security principle, which it uses for subsequent method invocations. The process of replacing a caller principle with a method's principle is called *principle delegation*.

Assigning methods their own security principles can be useful if you want to ensure that users can only access your EJB application through a few tightly managed gatekeeper EJB components. By giving the gatekeepers a unique security principle, you allow users to access underlying EJB components through the gatekeeper component, but you never expose the security requirements for your underlying components to the outside world.

To give a method its own security principle, you define a `<run-as>` tag in the deployment descriptor, which identifies the new security principle. When the `<run-as>` element is used, the security principle of the caller is replaced with the new security principle for all subsequent method invocations.

✔ **The security principle — and the roles contained within a security principle — can be obtained programmatically inside an EJB component.** Both the caller's security principle and the security roles in that principle are stored in the `javax.ejb.EJBContext` object. This is the parent object of the context object defined for each type of EJB component (`SessionContext` for session beans, `EntityContext` for entity beans, and `MessageContext` for message-driven beans). If a method is run using the caller identity, the security principle and security roles of the caller are presented. If, however, the ⟨run-as⟩ attribute is specified for a method, then that method and subsequent methods can only retrieve the principle assigned in the ⟨run-as⟩ element. More information about programmatic access to security roles and principles is available at the end of this chapter in the section "Auditing User Activity."

In most cases, the security principle of a caller is propagated throughout a system. That allows the system to audit the activities of the caller, regardless of what operations are performed. When the security principle of a caller is replaced using the ⟨run-as⟩ element, all users that invoke the given method are blurred into the identity associated with that method. Consequently, their individual actions become more difficult to track.

Accessing the security principle and method permissions for the purpose of performing programmatic security authentication isn't advisable. Hard coding references to specific security roles and principles undermines the flexibility of the EJB framework. The EJB specification's primary reason for providing access to a caller's security principle is to enable application-level auditing. Under special circumstances, this access also allows application developers to implement extensions to the security framework.

The EJB specification doesn't define the process for identifying application users and assigning security roles to users. This topic is deferred to the vendors of EJB containers. To discover more on this topic, consult with the vendor documentation for your EJB container.

The Syntax of EJB Security

Defining the security framework for an EJB application requires coordination between the developers of EJB components, those who assemble EJB applications, and the deployers of the EJB applications. In many cases, all three roles are filled by a single person (which makes the communication process easier). That isn't always the case, however, so the deployment descriptor provides mechanisms for the people in these three roles to communicate to each other. Ultimately, it's the responsibility of the EJB application deployer to ensure that the security framework is well defined.

The security framework is defined in the EJB application's deployment descriptor. There are four basic tasks that must be performed when the security framework is defined. The following list covers these four basic tasks while introducing some of the key elements in the deployment descriptor that support the tasks. I cover each task in detail in the subsequent sections.

✔ **If EJB component developers make hard-coded references to security roles inside the bean code, they must tell the application assembler and deployer what the security roles are.** The deployment descriptor supports this responsibility with the `<security-role-ref>` tag, which identifies a reference to a security role inside the code of an EJB component.

✔ **The application assembler and the deployer are responsible for defining security roles.** These are the logical roles that apply to the domain that's using an application. Security roles are defined using a `<security-role>` element that names and describes the role. Multiple `<security-role-ref>` elements can be linked to a single security role by adding a `<role-link>` element to the `<security-role-ref>`. This allows the application assembler and deployer to apply a consistent naming scheme to security roles, regardless of the source of the EJB components and their `<security-role-ref>` names.

✔ **The application assembler and deployer may also define the security identity to be applied to an EJB component.** This is how an application assembler can specify whether an EJB method should use the principle of its caller or its own principle. When a method uses its own principle, the deployment descriptor contains a `<run-as>` tag that links the method to a specific security role defined in the previous step.

✔ **The application deployer is responsible for mapping security roles to specific method permissions.** This task is accomplished using the `<method-permission>` element. In addition, the deployer can determine whether a specific method should use the security principle of its caller or its own security principle.

Identifying hard-coded security roles

When describing an EJB component in the deployment descriptor, the component developer must identify any explicit references made to security roles in the component. A component developer can make explicit references to security roles to extend the security framework, but explicit references aren't required to make use of the standard EJB security service. The EJB container will automatically check a security principle based on information you supply in the deployment descriptor to ensure that it contains the security roles required of a method in the deployment descriptor.

The methods of the EJB framework that allow you to access security information inside an EJB component are intended for non-standard *extensions* to the security service. You should only need to use these extensions if you're working on applications where security is a central concern of the application domain. Examples of such security extensions that could be necessary include EJB applications containing classified government information and healthcare products. In cases where custom security services aren't needed, it's best not to muck around with the security methods inside an EJB component.

If your application does make explicit references to security roles, you can identify those references using the `<security-role-ref>` tag. The `<security-role-ref>` tag is a subelement of either the `<entity>` or `<session>` elements, meaning that `<security-role-ref>` elements can be used in either entity beans or session beans.

While message-driven beans allow explicit references to security roles in the source code, they don't allow the definition of a `<security-role-ref>` element. The security principal of a method-driven bean invocation is managed by the JMS server that delivers a message — and not the EJB container. To avoid a lot of pain and agony, don't define explicit references to security roles in message-driven beans.

The `<security-role-ref>` element includes the following subelements:

- ✔ `<description>`: An optional element, you can use `<description>` to define the role of and identify the purpose of the `<security-role-ref>` element.

- ✔ `<role-name>`: Containing the name of the role referenced in the EJB component code, the `<role-name>` identified here must be identical to the role name that you use in code.

- ✔ `<role-link>`: This is an optional element that the application assembler or application deployer can use to link the role you specify in your code to some abstract security role defined in a `<security-role>` element. The value of the `<role-link>` element must be the value of a `<role-name>` in one of the `<security-role>` elements for the deployment descriptor.

Listing 15-1 illustrates the definition of a `<security-role-ref>` in the deployment descriptor for an EJB application. See the bold text.

Listing 15-1   A <security-role-ref> Element

```
<ejb-jar>
 <enterprise-beans>
  <session>
   <description>This bean manages the deposit process.
          </description>
   <ejb-name>DepositBean</ejb-name>
   ...
   <security-role-ref>
    <description>
     This role is required for all users of the deposit bean.
```

(continued)

Listing 15-1 *(continued)*

```
      </description>
      <role-name>depositor</role-name>
      <role-link>account-holder</role-link>
    </security-role-ref>
  </session>
</enterprise-beans>
<assembly-descriptor>
  <security-role>
    <description>
      This is the role applied to all banking customers.
    </description>
    <role-name>account-holder</role-name>
  </security-role>
</assembly-descriptor>
</ejb-jar>
```

In the listing, a `<security-role-ref>` element identifies the fact that, in the `DepositBean`, a hard-coded reference is made to a security role called `depositor`. The application assembler has linked this role to a `<security-role>` called `account-holder`. The link states that the `account-holder` is a `depositor` and should thus have the security permissions of a `depositor`. The `account-holder` security role is defined in the `<security-role>` tag, also illustrated in Listing 15-1. To discover more on creating `<security-role>` tags, continue to the next section.

Specifying security roles

When an EJB application is assembled, the application assembler can define the security roles that are appropriate for the users of the application. Security roles identify logically related sets of users and identify the types of operations they can perform. Security roles are defined with the `<security-role>` element, which is used in the `<application-assembly>` section of the deployment descriptor. The `<security-role>` element contains the following subelements:

✔ `<description>`: An optional subelement that describes the role

✔ `<role-name>`: Identifies the name of the security role

Ultimately, the application assembler or deployer should link every `<security-role-ref>` to an actual security role. Even if the `<security-role-ref>` name is identical to the name of a security role to which it applies, the `<role-link>` element must be used to link the two together. Listing 15-2 illustrates the definition of some security roles for the banking application.

Listing 15-2   Defining <security-role> Elements

```
<ejb-jar>
  <enterprise-beans>
    ...
  </enterprise-beans>
  <assembly-descriptor>
    <security-role>
      <description>
        This is the role applied to all banking customers.
      </description>
      <role-name>account-holder</role-name>
    </security-role>
    <security-role>
      <description>
        This is the role applied to bank tellers.
      </description>
      <role-name>bank-teller</role-name>
    </security-role>
    <security-role>
      <description>
        This is the role applied to customer service reps.
      </description>
      <role-name>customer-service</role-name>
    </security-role>
  </assembly-descriptor>
</ejb-jar>
```

In Listing 15-2, you see that there are three security roles defined for the sample ATM application I've used throughout this book. Each role is identified and referred to by its <role-name> tag. The implication of defining these three different roles is that users who possess those roles will have different security constraints applied to their access in the ATM application.

Defining security identities

A *security identity* defines whether an EJB component will have the security identity of its caller or whether it will use its own security identity. If the identity of the EJB component is inherited from its caller, the security credentials of the EJB component's caller must be valid for all the EJB components it calls. If the credentials of the caller aren't valid, then a java.lang. SecurityException will be thrown. But if a bean defines its own identity, then its identity replaces the identity of the caller, which is called *principal delegation*.

At this point, I have to gripe a little about the use of the term "security identity." In this context, the security identity refers to the "security principle," which is the combination of the *identity* and *roles* of a caller. Just remember that security identity is not the same as a user id.

A `SecurityException` is a runtime exception, which means that any transaction that is in progress will be rolled back when it's thrown.

Security identities are generally defined by the application assembler or the application deployer. They are defined using the `<security-identity>` element of an EJB component's description in the deployment descriptor. That means they can be defined inside the `<entity>`, `<message-driven>`, or `<session>` elements of the deployment descriptor. *Note:* The `<security-identity>` element is optional. By default, the security identity (that is, security principle) of an EJB component is inherited from its caller.

The subelements of the `<security-identity>` attribute are

- ✔ `<description>`: This is an optional element that can be used to describe the reason for the assignment of a security identity.

- ✔ `<use-caller-identity/>`: This is an empty tag that tells the EJB container to use the identity of the caller. (Remember that the caller identity is equivalent to its security principle.) When specifying this element, the application assembler is specifically saying that the caller identity must be used. Essentially, this is a stronger statement than allowing a bean to default to the use of the caller identity.

- ✔ `<run-as>`: This attribute is an alternative to the `<use-caller-identity/>` attribute. You use the `<run-as>` tag to assign a new security identity to a method, as opposed to using the caller identity. You can't use both the `<run-as>` and the `<use-caller-identity/>` attributes in the same `<security-identity>` element. This element is used to identify the security role that should be applied to all methods that are invoked from this EJB component. The `<run-as>` element has two subelements:

  - `<description>`: Once again, this is another optional opportunity to describe the reason for the `<security-role>` assigned with the `<run-as>` element.

  - `<role-name>`: This attribute identifies the role name to use for the `<run-as>` attribute. The `<role-name>` must correspond to the value of a `<role-name>` in a `<security-role>` tag.

Listing 15-3 illustrates the declaration of two different `<security-identity>` elements in bold. The first requires the EJB component to use the caller's identity while the second defines a different security identity for the EJB component.

Listing 15-3   Defining <security-identity> Elements

```
<ejb-jar>
 <enterprise-beans>
  <session>
    <description>This bean manages the withdraw process.
          </description>
    <ejb-name>WithdrawBean</ejb-name>
    ...
    <security-identity><use-caller-identity/></security-
          identity>
  </session>
  <session>
    <description>
      This provides a wrapper for ATMTransactions of all
          kinds.
    </description>
    <ejb-name>ATMTransactionBean</ejb-name>
    ...
    <security-identity>
      <run-as>
        <description>
          When an ATM transaction is emulated by a customer
            service rep,
          it should use the identity of a banking customer.
        </description>
        <security-role>account-holder</security-role>
      </run-as>
    </security-identity>
  </session>
 </enterprise-beans>
 ...
<ejb-jar>
```

Declaring method permissions for security roles

The final task that EJB application assemblers and deployers must undertake is the task of defining *method permissions* for each security role. When a method permission is assigned to a security role, all users with the associated security role are allowed to invoke the specified method. Assigning method permissions for security roles is very similar to assigning transaction attributes to methods. (See Chapter 14 for more on EJB transactions.)

Method permissions can only be assigned for methods that are defined in the home or component interfaces of an EJB component. Method permissions are assigned using the <method-permission> element, which is located in the <assembly-descriptor> section of the deployment descriptor. The subelements of the <method-permission> element are

✔ `<description>`: This is an optional attribute that describes the reason for including the specified methods in the method permission.

✔ `<role-name>`: You can include multiple `<role-name>` elements in a `<method-permission>` element. The value of each `<role-name>` element must correspond to the role name of a `<security-role>` element. When a `<role-name>` is specified for a method permission, **all** the methods identified in the method permission can be invoked by a user with **any** of the specified roles.

✔ `<unchecked/>`: This empty tag can be used instead of specifying `<role-name>` elements in a method permission. When the `<unchecked/>` element is applied, all the specified methods aren't included in security authentication. The behavior of the `<unchecked/>` attribute will always override the behavior of any other method permission rule. Thus, you should use the `<unchecked/>` element with extreme caution.

✔ `<method>`: You can define multiple `<method>` elements for each method permission. Each `<method>` element can identify a set of methods within a single EJB component. All the methods identified in a specific `<method>` tag will be accessible to all the security roles identified in the `<method-permission>` element. A `<method>` element has the following subelements:

  • `<description>`: This is an optional documentation element.

  • `<ejb-name>`: This element identifies the EJB component in which this set of methods is defined. The value of this element must correspond to the value of an `<ejb-name>` defined elsewhere in the deployment descriptor.

  • `<method-intf>`: An optional element that identifies which interface the specified methods are contained in, its value must be the fully qualified class name of an interface in the EJB component with the given EJB name.

  • `<method-name>`: The `<method-name>` tag identifies the method or set of methods from the EJB component that the given method permission applies to. As you will see, there are three ways — referred to as *styles* in the EJB specification — in which a `<method-name>` can be identified. Those styles include the use of the wildcard character * to assign a `<method-permission>` to all methods in the specified EJB component, the use of the name of the method, or the use of the name and a specified set of method parameters.

  • `<method-params>`: An optional element, `<method-params>` is used to identify a specific method with a specific set of parameters. This element can't be used if the `<method-name>` element contains a wildcard operator.

There are three styles for assigning method permissions:

- ✔ **Use a wildcard * operator to assign specific method permissions to all the methods of an EJB component.** The wildcard * operator is used as the value of a `<method-name>` element, as follows:

```
<method-name>*</method-name>
```

This assignment is for making broad brushstroke-type assignments. This technique can be used to grant permission to access all methods in an EJB component to one or more security roles.

- ✔ **Assign method permissions to specific method names in an EJB component by specifying the method name in the method permission.** If the specified method exists in multiple interfaces of the EJB component, the method permission will apply to all methods in all interfaces. If the method is *overloaded* — meaning that there are two or more methods with the same name and different arguments — the method permission will apply to all the overloaded methods with the specified name. Method permissions are assigned to specific method names using the following syntax:

```
<method-name>method1</method-name>
<method-name>method2</method-name>
<method-name>method3</method-name>
```

- ✔ **The application assembler or deployer can specify a method permission for a specific method name with a specific set of parameters.** When this style is used, only the method with the specified set of parameters receives the method permission assignment. If the method with the specified set of parameters exists in more than one interface of the EJB component, the method permission is applied to all occurrences of the method in all the component's interfaces. The method permission is assigned to a specific method with a set of parameters using the following format:

```
<method-name>method1</method-name>
<method-params>
  <method-param>java.lang.String<method-param>
  <method-param>int<method-param>
  <method-param>java.lang.Object<method-param>
</method-params>
```

Note that the `<method-params>` element must be placed immediately after the `<method-name>` to which it applies. The type of each method parameter must be identified in a separate `<method-param>` element, which is nested inside the `<method-params>` element. See the preceding example.

You can limit the application of a method permission to methods in a particular interface by identifying the target interface in the optional `<method-intf>` element.

The three styles of assigning method permissions are virtually identical to the three styles for assigning transactional attributes, except for one subtle but important distinction. When assigning transactional attributes, the more specific assignments override the broader assignments. But when assigning method permissions, assignments at all scopes are applied. So you should never include a method in a method permission unless you want it to be callable by the security roles in that method permission.

Listing 15-4 illustrates the definition of method permissions in an EJB deployment descriptor. Remember that you can only define method permissions after you've defined security roles.

Listing 15-4   Defining <method-permission> Elements

```
<ejb-jar>
  ...
  <assembly-descriptor>
    <method-permission>
      <role-name>account-holder</role-name>
      <method>
        <description>A wildcard declaration.</description>
        <ejb-name>AccountBean</ejb-name>
        <method-name>*</method-name>
      </method>
    </method-permission>
    <method-permission>
      <role-name>account-holder</role-name>
      <method>
        <description>A wildcard declaration.</description>
        <ejb-name>DepositBean</ejb-name>
        <method-name>*</method-name>
      </method>
    </method-permission>
    <method-permission>
      <description>
        I am granting the account-holder, bank-teller, and
        customer-service roles permission to invoke any
        method in the AccountBean.
      </description>
      <role-name>account-holder</role-name>
      <role-name>bank-teller</role-name>
      <role-name>customer-service</role-name>
      <method>
        <description>A wildcard declaration.</description>
        <ejb-name>AccountBean</ejb-name>
        <method-name>*</method-name>
      </method>
    </method-permission>
  </assembly-descriptor>
</ejb-jar>
```

In Listing 15-4, I've defined three `<method-permission>` tags, each of which applies to a different EJB component. In the beginning of each tag, I identify the security roles that can be applied to that component, using the `<role-name>` tag. I can include as many security roles as I need. The `<method>` element identifies the name of the entity bean in which the `<role-name>` elements are required. In all three examples, I use the wild card operator * to indicate that I want all of the specified security roles to have permission to invoke all the methods of the specified EJB component.

A method permission grants a security role *permission* to invoke a method. So, as you define method permissions, you can verify that your assignments are correct by constructing a sentence that describes the permission granted in a `<method-permission>` element. For example, referring to the bold `<method-permission>` element in Listing 15-4, I could say, "I am granting the `account-holder`, `bank-teller`, and `customer-service` roles permission to invoke any method in the `AccountBean`." That sentence not only allows you to check your assumptions, but it also clearly communicates your intentions regarding method permission assignments to others. I plugged it into the `<description>` tag.

Blocking Access to Methods

While most application security is designed to constrain access to certain activities within an application, the EJB specification allows you to completely block access to certain methods. You can do that by using the `<exclude-list>` element, which is defined in the `<assembly-descriptor>` section of the deployment descriptor. The `<exclude-list>` element identifies a set of methods that shouldn't be invoked by any user of a system. If a method is identified in the `<exclude-list>`, any other method permission assignments are overridden and the method is made completely inaccessible. The `<exclude-list>` has the following subelements:

- `<description>`: Blah, blah, blah. (Did I write that?) You should probably use this element to inform others about why you're excluding the specified methods, but you're not required to do so.

- `<method>`: This element identifies the methods within a particular EJB component. You can specify multiple method elements in an `<exclude-list>`. I explain the syntax for this method in detail in the previous section. Note that the style rules of the `<method>` element in the `<method-permission>` element also apply to `<method>` elements in the `<exclude-list>`.

You can use the `<exclude-list>` to block access to methods that aren't fully implemented or to methods that are deprecated — and hence no longer supported — in an application. The `<exclude-list>` probably doesn't make sense for other scenarios.

Listing 15-5 illustrates the use of an `<exclude-list>` to prevent access to deposited funds in a bank. This is the kind of draconian effort you might take to prevent a run on the bank. Don't try this at home.

Listing 15-5   An <exclude-list> in Action

```
<ejb-jar>
  <assembly-descriptor>
  <exclude-list>
    <description>Must stop withdraws.</description>
    <method>
      <description>A wildcard declaration.</description>
      <ejb-name>WithdrawBean</ejb-name>
      <method-name>*</method-name>
    </method>
  </exclude-list>
  </assembly-descriptor>
</ejb-jar>
```

In this example, I specify only a single `<method>` element, which uses the * wildcard to block access to all methods in all interfaces of the `WithdrawBean`. You could use an `<exclude-list>` to prevent users from accessing parts of your EJB application that are under construction, or which have become obsolete and haven't yet been replaced.

Auditing User Activity

While not required to do so, EJB containers can define auditing facilities that trace the activities of users while they access the EJB container. These auditing systems are system services and don't need to be considered in the development of your EJB application. Look at the documentation for the EJB container that you choose to determine whether auditing is implemented by the container. If it is, then the system administrator for the EJB container is responsible for managing the auditing service. If auditing isn't supported, you can implement it programmatically inside an EJB component.

Even if auditing is supported, you may want to capture the identity of a user for storage in a database when changes are made to your data. To do so, you must access the security principle for the user. Accessing the security principle of a user is pretty simple. The `javax.ejb.EJBContext` interface defines the method `getCallerPrinciple`, which returns the `Principle` object associated with the caller. This method returns an object called `java.security.Principle`. The `Principle` object contains the method `getName`, which returns the identity of the user. Thus, by using the following snippet of code in your EJB class, you can retrieve the identity of any user that accesses your EJB system:

```
/* context in the following statement refers to the context
        object of
 * the EJB component - either the SessionContext,
        EntityContext, or
 * MessageDrivenContext.
 */
java.security.Principle userId = context.getCallerPrinciple();
String userName = userId.getName();
// Now you have the user's name and can do whatever you want
        with it.
```

Remember that auditing is important because it allows you to track the changes that a specified user made to your application. If you discover that the user's identity has been stolen and that the changes the user made were unauthorized, you can trace those audit logs to identify these illegal changes — and possibly restore the state of your system to where it was before those changes were made.

Chapter 16

Developing EJB Client Applications

*E*JB client applications are the programs that provide users with access to the services you've implemented with EJB applications. Because EJB applications don't have a user interface, you have to create one to put in front of the EJB application you build. The good news about EJB applications is that they provide an excellent mechanism for abstracting the business process out of an application, so you can easily add a variety of different user interfaces without changing the EJB application at all.

In Figure 16-1, you can see two different kinds of client applications connecting to the same EJB application. The first client has a Swing user interface, a Java technology for building applications that resides on a user's local computer. The Swing application connects directly to the EJB container to interact with EJB components.

The other two clients in Figure 16-1 are using a browser, which connects to a Web server, which connects to the same EJB container and uses the same EJB components. Java Web applications — developed using Servlets and JSP (JavaServer Pages) technology — can be used to interact with an EJB container in order to generate Web pages to present to a user across the Internet.

Figure 16-1 also shows that, when invoking message-driven beans, the clients interact either directly (in the case of Swing applications) or indirectly (in the case of Web applications) through a JMS (Java Messaging Service) Server, which handles the delivery of messages to the message-driven beans in the EJB container.

There are entire books devoted to developing Swing applications, Servlet applications, JSP applications, and JMS applications, so there's no way I — in the space of a single chapter — can go into the gory details of developing each kind of user interface. Nevertheless, I illustrate a couple of tricks in this chapter that you can use to maximize the flexibility of your EJB applications. One of the most important tricks is to use standard JavaBean technology to provide a ubiquitous interface for your EJB application. You'll see how that's really useful as you proceed through the chapter.

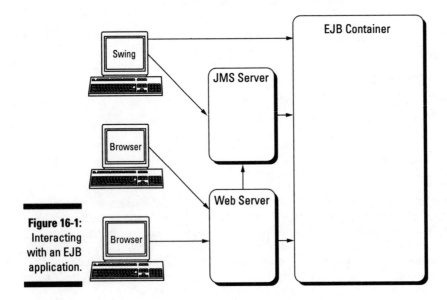

Figure 16-1:
Interacting
with an EJB
application.

Accessing EJB Components through JavaBeans

JavaBeans is a convention for creating compact, simple classes that manipulate data. Most people call these classes *beans* for short. JavaBeans are useful because they provide a portable interface that can be used by client applications to interact with EJB components. You can develop a JavaBean component that both interacts with your EJB application and contains all of the security and JNDI implementation details. The same JavaBean can then be easily added into either a Swing or a JSP application, making a very flexible software component that hides a lot of the complexity of accessing EJB applications from your user interface developers. JavaBeans have some simple rules that must be adhered to when they're created. The basic rules follow:

✔ **JavaBeans must have a public, no arguments constructor.** If you have a class named `MyBean`, you must define a constructor with the signature `MyBean(){...}`. The Java Virtual Machine(JVM) — the container that runs all Java applications — needs to have this constructor so that it can create instances of your JavaBeans without your having to invoke the constructor directly.

✔ **All member variables of a JavaBean should be `private` and must be initialized when an instance of the class is created.** All the primitive member variables must have a default value and any class reference that isn't initialized in the JavaBean's constructor must be explicitly set to `null`. All member variables should begin with a lowercase letter.

✔ **For each member variable that a client application needs access to, the Java bean should define a set of methods called accessor methods.** *Accessor methods* are methods that provide access to member variables of a JavaBean. If a member variable has accessor methods, it's referred to as a *property* of the JavaBean. Accessor methods must be defined according to the following conventions:

- To set a property, a setter method must be defined. Setter methods must be named in the form `set{VariableName}` and must accept a single argument that is of the same type as the variable being set. So if you have a `String` variable called `firstName`, the setter method must be `setFirstName(String firstName){...}`. Setter methods must have a `void` return type.

- To get a property, a getter method must be defined. Getter methods must be named in the form `get{VariableName}` and must have an empty parameter list. Their return type is generally of the same type as the member variable. Thus, for the `String` variable `firstName`, the getter method should be:

```
String getFirstName(){...}
```

The return value of a getter method doesn't have to be the same as the type of the property it retrieves. You just need to be able to convert the type of the member variable to the type of the return value.

- If a property is of type `boolean`, you can define a getter method in the form `is{VariableName}`. This convention is allowed so that the getter can be invoked in a more natural, readable format, as I illustrate in the following:

```
if(person.isBlind()){/*play audio*/}
```

JavaBeans are very useful for EJB client programs because they hide all of the details associated with looking up a home interface or component interface to the EJB component, instead allowing the client program to interact with the EJB application as if it were a direct communication. You can compare Listing 16-1 and Listing 16-2 to discover the power that JavaBeans offer. Listing 16-1 is a simple JavaBean with a property called `message` that contains the value "Hello World!" Listing 16-2 is a JavaBean with a reference to an EJB component called `helloWorldEJB`. When the bean's `getMessage` accessor is invoked, the bean returns the value of the EJB component's `getMessage` method.

Listing 16-1   The HelloWorld JavaBean

```
public class HelloWorld{
   private message = "Hello World!"; // the message

   public HelloWorld(){} // the no-args constructor

   public String getMessage() { return this.message;} // the
           accessor
}
```

Listing 16-2   The HelloWorldEJBAccess JavaBean

```
import javax.ejb.*;
import javax.naming.*;
import javax.rmi.*;
import java.rmi.*;

public class HelloWorldEJBAccess {
   Context context = null;
   HelloWorldRemoteHome home = null;

   public HelloWorld() throws NamingException,
           RemoteException,
   ClassNotFoundException {

     System.out.println("getting initial context");
     context = new InitialContext();

     System.out.println("getting home reference");
     Object obj = context.lookup("ejb/helloWorldEJB");

     System.out.println("casting RemoteHome Interface.");
     home = (HelloWorldRemoteHome)
       PortableRemoteObject.narrow(obj,
       HelloWorldRemoteHome.class);
   }

   public String getMessage() {
     HelloWorldRemote hello = null;
```

```
      String msg = null;
      try {
        System.out.println("Retreiving HelloWorldRemote
            Interface.");
        hello = home.create();
        msg = hello.helloWorld();
      }
      catch (CreateException e) {
        e.printStackTrace(System.out);
      }
      catch (RemoteException e) {
        e.printStackTrace(System.out);
      }
      finally {
        hello = null;
      }
      return msg;
    }
}
```

While the code in Listing 16-1 is very simple, the code in Listing 16-2 carries a lot more complexity. But whether a client uses the HelloWorld JavaBean or the HelloWorldEJBAccess JavaBean, the interaction is the same. There is still only one method called getMessage, and that method returns the same type of object. So the client of either JavaBean doesn't need to worry about the complexity of the internal code of either JavaBean; all the client needs to do is get the message by invoking the getMessage method.

Aside from hiding complexity, JavaBeans provide a couple more great benefits for your source code:

✔ In JSP applications, a Web developer can access the bean properties without writing a single line of Java code. JSP pages provide HTML-style tags called *action tags* that can be used to both create an instance of a JavaBean as well as to invoke the getters and setters of the JavaBean's properties. You'll see an example that uses this feature in the upcoming section "Building JSP Interfaces for EJBs."

✔ In Swing applications, when you implement a Swing user interface component with your JavaBean, you — or a user interface developer working for you — can use a design tool to graphically create screens that include your JavaBean components. That's possible because screen designer tools for developing Swing applications can put your JavaBeans into a tool palette and allow the developer to interact with that palette in a graphical environment. You'll see an example of a Swing JavaBean that applies this technique in the upcoming section "Building Swing Interfaces for EJBs."

Accessing JNDI Resource Names

When you develop an EJB client application, you need to have access to the JNDI names of the EJB components running in the EJB container. There are a couple of strategies to pursue for getting these resource names, and the strategy you use depends on where your client application resides in relation to the EJB application. The information you need to access the JNDI resource names of the EJB container is stored in a special properties file called `jndi.properties`.

No matter what kind of EJB container you use, the resource names for the container will always be accessible via the `jndi.properties` file. The first task in accessing the JNDI names is discovering where the `jndi.properties` file for your EJB container is located. You should find it somewhere below the home directory for your EJB container.

Accessing JNDI through the CLASSPATH

If your client application is located on the same computer as the EJB container, then accessing the JNDI names is very easy. All you have to do is add the `jndi.properties` file into the CLASSPATH for your client application. Accomplish this by using either of two simple techniques:

- You can declare a CLASSPATH variable in your computer and place the path to the `jndi.properties` file in that variable. This approach is the least preferred because when you follow it, all the Java applications you run have access to the same CLASSPATH, whether they need it or not.

- When you run your client application, you can specify a custom CLASS-PATH with the `java` command. You execute the `java` command to run an application. If you want to specify a custom CLASSPATH for the `java` command, you do so by using the `-classpath` parameter, followed by a semicolon-delimited list of paths that you want included in the classpath. The following `java` command illustrates the use of the `-classpath` parameter:

```
java -classpath helloWorldEJB.jar;
   %JBOSS_DIST%jboss-3.0.0alpha\client\jndi.properties
   com.sextanttech.hello.interfaces.Client
```

In the preceding example, the CLASSPATH `helloWorldEJB.jar; %JBOSS_DIST%jboss-3.0.0alpha\client\jndi.properties` is used when the class called `Client` is invoked. The path `%JBOSS_DIST%jboss-3.0.0alpha\client\jndi.properties` points to a directory containing the `jndi.properties` file for the JBoss application server on my computer. When the `java` command is executed, the information in the `jndi.properties` file is automatically added to the environment of the `Client` class, thus allowing the `Client` class access to the JNDI names in the JBoss EJB container.

Loading JNDI Properties Programmatically

When the EJB container you need access to resides on a different computer from your client application, you can pursue a simple technique for loading the JNDI properties programmatically. To access the properties files, follow these steps:

1. **Get the UNC file name for the** `jndi.properties` **file.**

   This file must be accessible to the computer that's hosting the client application. A UNC file name begins with two slashes \\, followed by the computer name, then another slash and a public directory on the computer. Finally, the path to the `jndi.properties` file should follow. Thus, if I made the client directory of my EJB server public, the UNC file name would be as follows:

   ```
   \\myComputerName\client\jndi.properties
   ```

2. **Create a program that opens a file I/O stream to the** `jndi.properties` **file.**

   A file I/O stream allows a client program to either read information in a file or to write information to a file. The following code illustrates a standard implementation of a `FileInputStream`, which you need to use to access the contents of the `jndi.properties` file:

   ```
   java.io.FileInputStream fis = new
           FileInputStream("UNCFileName"):
   java.io.BufferedInputStream buf = new
           BufferedInputStream(fis);
   ```

   In the preceding code snippet, the `FileInputStream` gives your program access to the contents of the `jndi.properties` file. The `BufferedInputStream` does the same, but it increases the efficiency of reading from the `FileInputStream` object.

3. **With the input stream, create a Java object called** `java.util.Properties`.

   This object is a Java representation of the contents of a properties file. The following lines of code illustrate the technique for creating a `Properties` object:

   ```
   java.util.Properties props = new Properties():
   props.load(buf); // loads the InputStream into the prop-
           erties file
   ```

   The `Properties` object now contains the contents of the `jndi.properties` file, and your system can easily read it. The last step in this process is to add the `Properties` object to your `System` environment. Accomplish this with the following line of code:

   ```
   System.setProperties(props);
   ```

After you've accomplished this task, your system has access to the JNDI names of the EJB container. The complete process can be added to your client application using the code in Listing 16-3.

Listing 16-3   Loading JNDI Names Programmatically

```
try{
    FileInputStream fis = new FileInputStream("UNCFileName");
    BufferdInputStream buf = new BufferedInputStream(fis);
    java.util.Properties props = new Properties();
    props.load(buf);
    System.setProperties(props);
    /* Now you can obtain the initial context with the JNDI
             names for the
     * EJB components on your EJB server.
     */
    Context ctx = new InitialContext() // with JNDI names above
    // get your EJB component...
}
catch(Exception e){/* Handle exception*/}
```

While the process in Listing 16-3 works okay, it's not ideal because your reference to the `jndi.properties` file is hard coded into your program. If you want a more flexible solution, consider creating a local properties file that contains references to the UNC file names for the properties files that you need to load in remote systems. Then you can use the technique that I describe in the previous steps to load your properties file containing UNC file names and use those UNC file names to load the remote properties files. This approach is a little more complex, but you can do it without too much additional effort.

If you need to access a properties file from across a wide area network or the Internet, then you'll need to create a URL connection to the properties file first, before obtaining the input stream. Here's an example:

```
java.net.URL fileURL = new URL(
    "http://www.sextanttech.com/client/jndi.properties");
BufferedInputStream buf = new BufferedInputStream(
    fileURL.openStream());
```

Building JSP Interfaces for EJBs

If you want clients to access your EJB application over the Internet, JSP components are ideally suited for the job. JSP application development is divided into two major roles: Web developers who create graphically appealing user interfaces, and Java developers who supply business components for the developers to access. Those business components are provided in the form of JavaBeans, which I discuss in detail in the previous section. While I don't have space in this book to present the complete process for developing a JSP application, my goal is to present a sample application that illustrates the use of the JavaBean component that I describe in the previous section.

When interacting with a JavaBean in a JSP page, the JSP page developer has to perform a couple of simple tasks:

✔ **The page developer must supply an HTML template that organizes the layout of the content to be obtained from the JavaBean.** This task requires nothing more than the understanding of some simple HTML code.

✔ **The class file for the JavaBean has to be imported.** You accomplish this by using a simple tag known as a page directive. The page directive is very similar to HTML. The page directive opening tag is `<%@ page` and the closing tag is `%>`. In between, the developer supplies an import property that identifies the fully qualified name of the class to import, as in the following example:

```
<%@page import="com.sextanttech.hello.interfaces.
         HelloWorldEJBAccess"%>
```

✔ **The JSP page developer creates an instance of the** `HelloWorldEJBAccess` **JavaBean using the** `<jsp:useBean>` **tag.** The tag takes a couple of arguments, the name of the class, the name of the variable to create, and a parameter indicating what the scope bean tag will be. The following example illustrates a `<jsp:useBean>` tag:

```
<jsp:useBean class="HelloWorldEJBAccess" name="hello"
         scope="page"/>
```

✔ **Finally, the page developer places a** `<jsp:getProperty>` **tag at the point in the HTML page where the message of the** `hello` **bean should be displayed.** The `<jsp:getProperty>` tag takes two arguments: `name` tells the tag which JavaBean to get a property from, and `property` identifies the name of the member variable to retrieve. The `property` value is retrieved and automatically converted to a `String` when the page is executed. Here's an example of a `<jsp:getProperty>` tag:

```
<jsp:getProperty name="hello" property="message"%>
```

The code in Listing 16-4 illustrates a complete JSP page that uses the preceding syntax to retrieve a message from your EJB application:

Listing 16-4   The HelloWorld.jsp Page

```
<html>
<head>
<title>Hello World</title>
<meta http-equiv="Content-Type" content="text/html;
        charset=iso-8859-1">
</head>
<%@page import="com.sextanttech.hello.interfaces.
        HelloWorldEJBAccess"%>
<body bgcolor="#FFFFFF" text="#000000">
<jsp:useBean class="HelloWorldEJBAccess" name="hello"
        scope="page"/>
<p>The message of the day is: <jsp:getProperty name="hello"
  property="message"%/>
</body>
</html>
```

The JSP tags that I previously discuss are shown in bold in Listing 16-4. Note that when the page is run, these tags are removed from the page content and the only thing left is the HTML that's generated. In this example, an HTML page that displays the message, "The message of the day is: Hello World!" is displayed.

I've provided a complete Web application solution for the sample code in this book. The example illustrates the use of JSP pages for developing a client application that invokes EJB components. You can download the sample code from www.dummies.com/extras/ejbfd.

The creation of JSP applications is too broad a topic for inclusion in this book. However, you can discover more on the subject by picking up a copy of *JavaServer Pages For Dummies,* written by yours truly and published by Hungry Minds, Inc.

Building Swing Interfaces for EJBs

When you build a Swing interface for an EJB application, you can still use JavaBeans, but you have to put them on steroids. JavaBeans used in Swing applications have to include a couple of different features:

✔ Swing JavaBeans have to include visual presentation code that provides information about how to draw the contents of the JavaBean on a computer screen.

✔ Swing JavaBeans have to include event response information that indicates what they should do when a user interacts with the visual interface of the bean by clicking on the bean, typing in the bean, moving a mouse over the bean, or any number of different user event actions that might be performed.

Swing programming is a broad topic — another one of those subjects that could fill an entire book. But I'd like to illustrate a simple example of our HelloWorldEJBAccess JavaBean so that you can see a Swing example in the flesh. Here are the steps I follow:

1. **Begin with the** HelloWorldEJBAccess **class, which you can see in Listing 16-2.**

   This bean has all the code I need for the non-visual bean components, but I need to enhance it with some graphical components. The content displayed by this bean is text. In addition, this bean can't be changed; it can only be displayed because the bean doesn't provide a setter method.

2. **Pick a graphical user element that's used for displaying text.**

   In Swing, the class for the task is the javax.swing.JOptionPane. To support the functionality of the JOptionPane in my HelloWorldEJBAccess, I have JavaBean extend the JOptionPane class:

   ```
   public class HelloWorldEJBAccess extends JOptionPane {}
   ```

3. **Next, you want the** JOptionPane **to display the message from your EJB component.**

   The JOptionPane has a method called getMessage that returns the message that the JOptionPane is created with as an Object. In my HelloWorldEJBAccess class, I also have a getMessage method that returns the message of an EJB component as a String. To get my HelloWorldEJBAccess bean to work for a swing client, the getMessage return value needs to be changed to Object. That change is required because the getMessage method must have the same return type as the JOptionPane.getMessage method.

If my method name were different from the JOptionPane getMessage
method, I would have to override the getMessage method of the
JOptionPane. For example, if I had to invoke a method called
getAccountBalance, and I wanted to display that in a JOptionPane,
I'd create a new getMessage method and supply the following code:

```java
// This method is hypothetical...not in the examples
public double getAccountBalance(){
    AccountRemote acct = null;
    double balance = 0.0;
    try {
        System.out.println("Retrieving AccountRemoteHome
            Interface.");
        acct = accountHome.findByPrimaryKey(this.accountKey);
        balance = acct.getBalance();
    }
    catch (CreateException e) {
        e.printStackTrace(System.out);
    }
    catch (RemoteException e) {
        e.printStackTrace(System.out);
    }
    finally { acct = null; }
    return balance;
}

// This method overrides the getMessage of JOptionPane,
            displaying the
// result of the getAccountBalance method instead.
public Object getMessage(){
  StringBuffer message = new StringBuffer();
  message.append("Your balance is
            $").append(getAccountBalance());
  return message.toString();
}
```

You can find the complete code for a working example of a Swing application
connected to an EJB application at www.dummies.com/extras/ejbfd, along
with the rest of the source code for this book.

Accessing a JMS Server from Your Client Application

If you create message-driven beans in your EJB application, the client application will have to access those beans via a JMS service. Most EJB containers contain an integrated JMS server. When your EJB application is deployed, it is the deployer's responsibility to set up the topics or queues that your message-driven bean listens to. Your client application will then access those topics or queues to send messages to the EJB server. In Chapter 9, I provide some background on client access to JMS servers. Go there to get some fundamental information that you need to start posting messages to your EJB application.

Part VI
The Part of Tens

The 5th Wave   By Rich Tennant

YOU KIDDING!! TRUE INTERACTIVE CONTENT?! ME CAN'T WAIT, PULL LEVER, OPEN SCREEN!

In this part . . .

It's not a *For Dummies* book without The Part of
Tens. This part introduces you to some excellent
online resources, such as introductory articles on
EJB programming and forums where you can post any
questions you might have. You'll also see some excellent
performance tuning advice that you can use to turn your
EJB application into a racehorse.

Chapter 17

Ten Great Internet Resources for EJB Development

In This Chapter

▶ Discovering the online resources you need to succeed

Sure, Enterprise JavaBean development is challenging, and yet I believe it's still within the realm of the possible for most programmers (including you). I do have to warn you, though, that it's going to take some work to transition from a For Dummies consumer to a confident EJB programmer. I'm proud to say that this book offers a great introduction (and more) to the basic principles of programming EJB applications, but there's still a lot more information available on the topic. In other words, don't expect to grow from beginner to expert by reading these pages alone. The resources in this chapter provide even more valuable advice, show different perspectives, and identify forums that you can go to when the going gets tough.

Download an EJB Container

There are a lot of great resources on the Internet when it comes to choosing an EJB container. Typically, EJB containers are packaged with programs called *application servers,* which host a variety of server-side application components. While this category historically has included a number of vendors, the tightening economy has separated the wheat from the chaff, leaving only a few top contenders on the playing field. Here's a summary of my top three picks for vendors:

✔ **JBoss Application Server:** This product is a solid application service that performs quite respectably and has the most respectable price — it's free. While you won't have any trouble running your EJB applications on this server, this product isn't certified by Sun Microsystems. Take that with a grain of salt. . . . Sun is coming under increasing pressure to certify JBoss Application Server. The product is a hit with the open source community, having over 50,000 downloads per month from Source Forge. Be sure to get Version 3.x, which provides full support for the EJB 2.0 specification. You can download JBoss at `www.jboss-group.com`.

✔ **BEA WebLogic Application Server:** BEA's popular server is one of the top three commercial application server products. WebLogic version 6.1 provides full support for EJB 2.0 applications. You can download a trial version from BEA at `www.bea.com/products/weblogic/server/index.shtml`.

✔ **IBM WebSphere Application Server:** IBM's application server is another top contender for the application server market share. WebSphere caters to the upper-end of the market, but you can still get a trial version for free. Be sure to select version 4.0. To discover more about WebSphere — and to get a free trial version — visit IBM at `www4.ibm.com/software/webservers/appserv/`.

Reading Up on How to Avoid J2EE Project Disasters

My first recommended resource is an article from the March 2001 issue of *JavaWorld Magazine,* titled "J2EE Project Dangers" by Humphrey Sheil. When developing EJB applications, there are more wrong ways to build the application than right ways to build it. This article identifies what Sheil considers to be the top ten risks to avoid if you want to run a successful project that makes use of Enterprise JavaBeans or any other J2EE technologies. I'm a big fan of this article and can recommend it highly because it provides solid advice that I can identify with from previous experience and — wonder of wonders in the world of computing technology — it's well-written.

All developers go through some rough projects at some point in their lives and in the process they discover how to discern good choices from bad. Sheil has been there, done that, and he's earned the Purple Heart. So learn from his experiences, and you'll be ahead of the game. You can find "J2EE Project Dangers" at `www.javaworld.com/javaworld/jw-03-2001/jw-0330-ten.html`.

Download the EJB Specification

The EJB specification is the official resource for all things pertaining to Enterprise JavaBean development. As the primary resource for EJB development, you'll find that it's loaded with information that's relevant to almost any question you might have. The specification is written for an experienced developer audience, so you might find some of it hard to tackle. But once you get used to the style, you'll find that it's pretty easy to locate the information you're searching for. Here are my top tips on how to search the EJB specification for information:

✔ **The specification is available in PDF, with a detailed set of bookmarks that you can use to browse the table of contents and hyperlink to the section that interests you.** Be sure to familiarize yourself with the chapters in the specification so that you'll know about where to start when looking for something.

✔ **The EJB specification is intended for developers of EJB applications as well as for developers of EJB containers.** As an application developer, you don't need to familiarize yourself with the sections devoted to container development. The writers of the specification have provided meaningful chapter and section titles that will help you determine which sections are relevant to you. Look for the following terms in order to keep chapters and sections straight:

   • **Client view:** This term in a section title will address EJB components from the perspective of applications that use them.

   • **Responsibilities of bean provider:** These sections identify — in a concise bulleted list — all the responsibilities that bean providers should be aware of for any particular development topic.

The EJB specification is available from Sun Microsystems at `java.sun.com/products/ejb/index.html`.

Visit the Java Ranch

The Java Ranch is the best destination on the Web for Java greenhorns. With venues that are reminiscent of an Old West cattle ranch, visiting Java programmers can take a load off while they discover the lay of the land. Here's what you'll find:

✔ **The Big Moose Saloon:** When you first arrive at the Java ranch, you can hang your hat at the saloon and visit with fellow Java programmers. There are a number of moderated forums in the Big Moose Saloon that cover a variety of topics, including J2EE and EJB development.

✔ **The Campfire:** If you're a fan of campfire stories and would like a fun way to brush up on some Java fundamentals, the Campfire is the place to go. The campfire stories include "How My Dog Learned Polymorphism" and "Getting in Touch With Your Inner Class."

✔ **The Code Barn:** This is a repository for code samples that you can refer to when the going gets tough.

There are a number of other excellent forums that you'll want to catch, so be sure to put this site in your Browser Favorites. The address is www.javaranch.com/index.html.

Take a Walk on TheServerSide

TheServerSide.com is a forum for J2EE programmers and is suitable for posting intermediate to advanced questions. Here are the resources you'll find:

- **News and articles:** TheServerSide does a good job of staying up on current events pertaining to developers of server-side applications. You'll find news on industry developments, as well as articles on intermediate to advanced software development problems.

- **Discussions:** Here you'll find a number of forums focused on topics for server-based and distributed applications including EJB application design and development.

- **Design patterns:** A lot of TheServerSide readers are very interested in software design patterns. *Design patterns* are software designs that provide proven solutions to a variety of software development problems. Just as you can get a set of plans for building a shed or a pattern for sewing an article of clothing, a design pattern offers a reusable solution for creating a software component. If you're interested in honing your skills in application design, be sure to read up on design patterns and watch the Patterns forum at TheServerSide.com.

You can visit TheServerSide at www.theserverside.com.

Java Users Groups

I'm a big fan of Java Users Groups (or JUGs for short). It would be fair to say I can't get enough of the JUG. That's because JUGs offer developers a chance to network in their local community, to share experiences, and to gather feedback from a group of people that tends to be more courteous and thoughtful than those who frequent the anonymous forums hosted by big industry players. You can find the JUG closest to you by visiting the home page of JavaSoft, the official home of all things Java, at java.sun.com. In the lower-left corner is a list of active and forming JUGs in the U.S. and around the world. You can wait for a location near you to scroll by on this list or you can click the list banner to search for a JUG in a particular city.

When looking at the JUG locations on the scrolling list, click the Stop button on your browser before selecting your desired location. I was frustrated by the fact that, as I attempted to select my desired city, the list scrolled two or three positions before my mouse click registered.

Visit the Java Developer Community

The Java Developer's Community is the official forum — sponsored by Sun Microsystems — for all technology topics pertaining to Java development. This forum is an excellent place to go if you have a question about EJB development, Java development in general, or information about a particular product. I've found the advice people offer in this forum to be generally helpful and good-natured. You can find the Java Developer Community at developer.java.sun.com/developer/community/.

 Occasionally, the organization of Web pages at JavaSoft changes. I was recently caught with a page that had a number of invalid links. If you can't find the Java Developer Community at developer.java.sun.com/developer/community/, navigate to java.sun.com and follow the link to "Community Discussion," located on the left side of the page.

Get Sage Advice from jGuru.com

jGuru is another location I visit occasionally to catch up on industry news and to participate in discussion forums. I've found interesting and useful information at this forum when I was drawing blanks from other locations. One very nice feature of jGuru is their PeerScope section, which lists articles from across the Web that may be of interest to Java developers. PeerScope is maintained by jGuru members, which means that you can add to the list by joining the jGuru community. As a result of active user input, the PeerScope section has developed into a huge anthology of Java-related topics.

In addition to PeerScope, jGuru hosts discussion forums, publishes articles, and provides access to online training resources. You can check out all the services jGuru has to offer by traveling to its home page at www.jguru.com.

Tune Your Programming Skills with Java Developer's Journal

Java Developer's Journal is my favorite industry magazine. While you can subscribe to the print edition, it also offers an online version that contains all the same content. If you want to get the latest issue, you still have to subscribe. But you can get the full text of all back issues for free. Java Developer's Journal magazines tend to be somewhat thematic, which means that you can get a lot of different perspectives on a specific technology with a single issue. Check out the content of Java Developer's Journal at `www.sys-con.com/java/`.

Join the iSavvix Community

Of all the resources I've seen on the Web, the iSavvix site is my favorite. At this site you can do the usual stuff: chat in discussion forums, download free code samples posted by other developers, get technology tips, and stay on top of the latest news and information about Java development. What sets iSavvix apart, however, is the fact that it provides each user with the following free services:

- **Free DevSpace:** This service allows you to create and host your own JSP Web site and also supports JSP, XML and JDBC technologies. On the DevSpace you get 10MB of free storage, which is an excellent deal at any price.

- **BackOnline Code Repository:** Again, this is a free service you can use to make off-site backups of your source code and store them on the Internet. This service compresses your storage, so with your 10MB of space you could store up to 50MB of source code and other content. If you're a contractor, or if you have a large toolkit of code you've developed over the years, this service could prove incredibly useful.

You can access the iSavvix community by pointing your browser to `java.isavvix.com/`.

Chapter 18

Top Performance Tuning Tips

*O*ne of the top concerns EJB component developers should be conscious of is performance. The many features of EJB programs can come at the expense of performance — unless you're careful about the way you implement your EJB components. In the following pages, you'll see some of the best advice available — not only from me but from many people I've talked to on this very issue. These performance tips are being used in many production systems today, and they're proven ideas that work. Be sure to evaluate each idea as you begin to work on EJB applications, and think about how they can be applied in your context.

Don't Make Assumptions about Performance

Analyzing performance is probably one of the most complex tasks in designing any application. It's an imprecise science because there are many factors that come into play. These are augmented in EJB applications, where performance is largely dependent upon the implementation of the EJB container you use. The bottom line is that you can't know if you're making the right performance decisions until you test them. Here are some issues that you should keep in mind when considering performance issues:

✔ **Not all EJB containers are created equal.** While each EJB container must conform to the EJB specification, vendors have wide latitude in implementing the EJB container. Their requirements focus on the outcomes of operations, not on an operation's efficiency. Some vendors will do a better job with different portions of an EJB container. You must determine where efficiencies can be gained in an EJB container and where performance bottlenecks are going to occur. The only way to know that with certainty is to try before you buy. Even after you purchase a solution, major design decisions, such as whether or not to use EJB entity beans, should be tested.

✔ **Performance can depend on the efficiency of your application.** There are rules of thumb that you can use to help determine which application designs are better than others. Many of the performance recommendations in this chapter are rules of thumb. But these rules of thumb can be easily invalidated with a sloppy implementation. The best way to ensure you avoid sloppy implementations is to perform regular *code reviews* — that's when you sit around with all your coding co-workers and have them review your work — during your EJB project. You should focus your code reviews on analyzing the source and ensuring that it's both well designed and efficient. I find that code reviews offer a great opportunity for programmers to learn from each other.

✔ **Develop a prototype to test your performance assumptions.** Here's a sample scenario. As an EJB application developer, you should decide early on whether or not to use entity beans to manage interaction with a database. Your two basic choices are to

- **Create entity beans to manage database interaction.** Entity beans can simplify your database interaction from an application programming perspective. But they can also exact a performance penalty. Some of that penalty can be controlled in the way that you implement entity beans — that is, by using local interfaces versus remote interfaces or by making entity beans coarse-grained objects. (You'll see more on both of these topics later in the chapter.)

- **Code JDBC database calls directly into session beans and avoid the use of entity beans altogether.** JDBC can be more difficult to work with than using entity beans with container-managed persistence. This course may also undermine your ability to take advantage of EJB container-managed transactions.

To determine which of the two courses is more appropriate, you can perform a simple test:

1. **Create an entity bean and a session bean that both perform operations on the same set of data from a database.**

2. **Write a simple program that measures the amount of time required to invoke a set of inserts, updates, queries, and changes to the database.**

   This second program should invoke the session bean for one test and the entity bean for another test — performing the same set of operations on each.

3. **Analyze the results to determine whether performance will be an issue.**

   If you want a more fine-grained performance analysis, you can time individual steps — to identify the most expensive operation — and then try modifying those operations to generate performance gains.

For an entity bean, you may want to measure performance on the following operations:

- ✔ How long does it take to obtain a reference to a remote interface or a local interface?
- ✔ What's the difference in performance between performing an update on a remote interface and a local interface?
- ✔ What's the difference between updating multiple rows in a database in JDBC and performing an update on multiple rows using the home method of an entity bean?

The answers to these questions will be different from EJB container to EJB container and will also be influenced by: a) the JDBC driver you choose; b) whether or not you use database connection pooling; and c) the efficiency of your implementations of the entity bean and the session bean. You will probably be surprised by some of the results you get — tests like these have a way of challenging your assumptions about the performance of entity beans.

When you're tuning an EJB for performance, don't make random changes. Instead, focus your attention on the steps in the application that cost the most in terms of performance. *Note:* Performance measurements usually reveal that a business process has only one or two points where significant improvements can be made. This observation has been made often enough that it led to the creation of the Pareto 80-20 rule. That rule states that 80 percent of the execution time of a program is due to 20% of the code. Your goal should be to identify which 20% of the code is most expensive in terms of system resources and focus on optimizing that portion.

Choose the Right Type of EJB Component for the Job

When you go to buy a pair of shoes, you probably don't ask the clerk for just any kind of shoe. If you want to go snow skiing, you're going to prefer ski boots to stilettos. If you're going to the gym, penny loafers aren't the best choice. If you're getting shoes for a board meeting, don't buy the roller blades.

Choosing EJB components is like choosing shoes. The same principle can be applied to EJB application components. Each type of EJB component is like a different style of shoe; they have different purposes, different performance characteristics, different benefits, and different liabilities. When designing your EJB application, you need to pick the right type of EJB component for the job you perform. When it comes to basic performance, I rank EJB components in the following order:

✔ **Message-driven beans:** These components receive my top performance ranking because the client application doesn't have to wait for a result from the component. That means that message-driven bean performance is virtually of no consequence to the clients that use them. But be sure that the task your client performs is appropriate for message-driven beans. If the client needs to know the result of the EJB component's operation to proceed, then message-driven beans are the wrong choice.

✔ **Stateless session beans:** These components get the second highest ranking because they're pooled and shared by many client applications. They don't get allocated to a single application beyond the scope of a single method invocation, which means that each can rapidly service many client requests. Depending on the vendor implementation, a stateless session bean may continue to serve other client requests before the transaction context of a single client request has been completed. This is possible because stateless session beans don't preserve client state and their state isn't transacted. Thus, they don't have to sit around and wait for the outcome of a transaction.

✔ **Stateful session beans:** These components get the third place award for performance. Stateful session beans rank lower on performance because they're assigned to a particular client application for the duration of a session, which could span multiple method invocations. To top if off, if the client application doesn't terminate its own session, a stateful session bean will hang out and wait for invocations from its client until the EJB container tells it to go away. The timeout duration for a session bean is specified by the EJB application deployer. While it can be controlled, it means that session beans might be sitting around doing nothing — except consuming your application server's resources — for a while after each client is finished working with them.

✔ **Entity beans:** These components come in last place. An entity bean's performance is constrained by a couple of important issues. First, only a single entity bean can be assigned to any given entity. So if you have multiple clients that want to perform operations against the same entity, they all line up in a row and work on the entity one at a time. Second, the state of an entity bean is typically transacted, which means that for the duration of a transaction in which it participates, it can't be invoked by other clients. You should only use entity beans if the multiple client applications must have a consistent view of the same data that's represented inside the EJB component. Even then, you may opt not to use entity beans at all and allow your database to perform the coordination of access to the data instead.

As a rule of thumb, you'll get a big benefit from using entity beans when you have to perform updates and changes to data. But if you just need to read information out of a database, then you're better off creating a session bean that accesses data directly using JDBC. That's because the session bean JDBC combination is more efficient for reading data, particularly if the data isn't changed by the application.

Use Local Interfaces Whenever Possible

In EJB applications, when a method is invoked on a remote interface, it requires the serialization of any data that's passed across the method. Object serialization is a labor-intensive process that should be avoided when possible. You only need a remote interface if you're invoking an EJB component from an application that resides on a different computer from your EJB component. Here are a couple of tips to keep in mind:

✔ When you invoke an EJB component from within the EJB application (that is, bean-to-bean invocations), you should use a local interface.

✔ You'll often need to invoke an EJB application from a Web application that resides on the same computer. Traditionally, each application you start on a computer resides in its own Java Virtual Machine (JVM). Local interfaces can only be used within a single JVM, so if you start a Web server and an EJB container in separate processes, they can't talk to each other locally even though they reside on the same computer.

However, many application servers have the ability to be co-located with a Web server. So, for example, you could launch Tomcat Web Server and JBoss Application Server in the same JVM and use local interfaces to invoke your EJB components from the Web server.

To optimize your application and support local method invocations, you'll need to consult with the vendor documentation for your EJB container and your Web server. Not all EJB containers support co-location of the container and the Web server, while some have built-in Web servers.

A further point to consider when optimizing remote method invocations is to understand the difference between *pass-by-value* and *pass-by-reference*. In Java, every argument you pass across a method is passed by value, which means a copy of the argument is made and passed to the method that's invoked. If you pass a reference to a Java object, a copy of the reference is made, but if you pass a Java primitive data type, the value of the data type is copied and passed. Serialization has a detrimental impact on performance when object references are passed across a method invocation; instead of making a copy of the reference, the application must make a copy of the entire object, including all its attributes, and then pass the entire object to the invoked method. But there's virtually no impact when primitive data types are passed across an interface. A primitive data type is passed by value no matter whether you use a local interface or a remote interface.

Avoid Defining Distributed Transactions

A distributed transaction exists whenever you create a transaction that spans a remote interface. Sometimes you can't avoid the creation of a distributed transaction. EJB applications are designed for building distributed applications, so there are going to be points in the EJB application when you define a transaction that spans a remote interface. But if you keep those remote interface calls down to a minimum, your transactions will be more efficient. When you execute a distributed transaction, each time the transaction crosses a remote interface the EJB container must serialize the transaction context and pass it across the remote interface as well. In essence, you're serializing more than just your method arguments when you invoke a remote interface method. When you invoke a component using a local interface, you don't serialize the transaction context.

The bottom line for this issue is that there's more at stake in making remote method invocations than the arguments you pass. The EJB container also has a number of services (transactions are but one) that must be serialized and transported across the method invocation. You don't see this overhead when you develop your EJB application because the EJB container handles it for you. But you certainly will see it when you actually end up running your EJB application.

Use Bulk Accessor Methods for EJB Components

Accessor methods are methods that provide access to the attributes of an object. The two types of accessor methods are getters and setters. Getters return the value of an attribute while setters are used to set the value of an attribute. The idea behind a *bulk accessor* is to support access to multiple attributes in an object all at once. Listing 18-1 shows an example illustrating the implementation of a bulk accessor.

Listing 18-1   Implementing a Bulk Accessor

```
// This class has a bunch of attributes in a bulk accessor.
public class Person{
   private String firstName; // an attribute
   private String lastName; // an attribute
   private String id; // an attribute

   // This is the bulk getter.
   PersonState getAccountHolderState(){
```

```
      return new PersonState( firstName, lastName, id);
   }

   // This is the bulk setter.
   void setPersonState( PersonState state){
     this.firstName = state.getFirstName();
     this.lastName = state.getLastName();
     this.id = state.getId();
   }

}

// This is a class for a value object in another file.
public class PersonState{
   private String firstName; // an attribute
   private String lastName; // an attribute
   private String id; // an attribute

   // The constructor
   public PersonState(String firstName, String lastName,
     String id){
     this.firstName = firstName;
     this.lastName = lastName;
     this.id = id;
   }

   public String getFirstName(){ return firstName;}
   public String getLastName(){ return lastName;}
   public String getId(){ return id;}
}
```

The benefit of using a bulk accessor is that, using a single method invocation, you can pass all the attributes associated with changing an EJB object. This means that there's only one object to serialize on remote method invocations. The bottom line on this issue is that it's much more efficient to set all the attributes or get all the attributes of an entity through a single method invocation, rather than by invoking individual accessors for each attribute that you need.

Define your value objects so that they only contain the required attributes for specific business purposes. For example, if you have a human resources application that presents two different views of an employee, define a separate value object for each view. Likewise, if you need access only to a single attribute in an entity to perform your business process, don't use a bulk accessor to get the attribute.

Never Expose Remote Interfaces for Entity Beans

Exposing remote interfaces to an entity bean allows a client program on a different computer to interact with the entity bean. Invoking entity beans through a remote interface adds a lot of overhead to their use. Instead of giving client applications direct access to an EJB entity bean, you can hide entity beans behind a facade that controls and coordinates their work. For example, my sample application has a session bean called the `ATMTransaction` bean. This session bean is a facade that external clients can invoke to perform some business process, such as a deposit, withdrawal, balance inquiry, or other process. The facade hides the access to entities from a client application, which means that I can perform most of my entity bean invocations through local interfaces.

Because each `ATMTransaction` requires a set of data that's complete for implementing some business process (that is, all the data for a deposit, withdrawal, or transfer), I can limit each type of transaction to a single remote call and a set of related local calls. The benefit is a small performance boost for each remote interface invocation that I avoid. In a heavily used EJB application, each one of those boosts can make a big difference in overall performance when it's being accessed by multiple clients at once.

Use Entity Bean Home Methods When Possible

Entity bean home methods can be used to perform operations on sets of entities when you don't need a reference to each member of the set. For example, if you need to perform an update on a group of entity beans, but you don't need a reference to each entity after it's updated, you can use a home method to do the job. With home methods, you don't have the overhead of assigning instance data of an entity to an entity object because the EJB container can work directly with the underlying database and doesn't have to return an object reference to you. This confers the following benefits:

- ✔ The home method invocation doesn't remove any entity objects from the object pool held by the EJB container; those entity objects are available for other client requests.

- ✔ The changes to the set of entities impacted by a home method invocation can occur in parallel instead of serially. You can potentially update multiple entities all at the same time, rather than changing one entity, and then the next, and the next, and so on.

Make Your Entity Objects Coarse-Grained

A *coarse-grained entity object* is an object that contains a large set of related data. This is contrasted with a *fine-grained entity object*, which contains a narrowly defined set of related data. In database design, entities tend to be fine-grained objects. The science of designing a database is identifying each entity and its attributes, and then drawing a line between each individual kind of entity. Thus, if you were to consider an invoice from a fine-grained perspective, you would have an invoice-header entity that contains information about the entire invoice, and an invoice-detail entity that contains information about a particular item on the invoice.

Considering the same invoice from a coarse-grained perspective, you would have an invoice and a collection of invoice details all represented in a single entity, as I illustrate in the following example:

```
// An invoice entity bean
public class InvoiceBean implements EJBObject {

    // the entity bean has a collection of items
    private Collection invoiceItems;
}

// An invoice item is not an entity bean.
public class InvoiceItem{...}
```

Coarse-grained entity beans are more efficient to manage because there's less overhead for the EJB container. In a fine-grained entity, the EJB container has to manage the overhead of multiple invoice items for each invoice header it manages. With the coarse-grained model, however, the EJB container has only a single instance to maintain.

Although the invoice items are an attribute of an entity bean, when you design the database you'll probably separate the two. That means that when you design coarse-grained entity objects, you have to supply your own JDBC code to manage the storage and retrieval of the objects in the entity bean that are stored in separate database tables. You can see an example of a JDBC management solution on the Web site for the book at www.dummies.com/extras/ejbfd.

When defining coarse-grained objects, be careful about how you group entities together. An invoice header and invoice line item make a great coarse-grained entity object because line items have no meaning without a header. But if you were to consider a relationship between an adult and a minor, the coarse-grained paradigm doesn't work as well. The minor will become an adult in time and then be able to make decisions without the consent of an adult. Thus, the minor needs to be a separate entity bean.

Use Message-Driven Beans for Procedural Programs

Procedural programs are programs that execute a set of operations but don't return a result. A prototypical procedure is a program that generates a set of monthly statements. The statements are generated, but they aren't returned. The client application that invokes the procedure needs to do some set of operations, but doesn't need to hang around waiting for the result of those operations.

Imagine if you were to generate all the statements for your credit card company using a session bean. That kind of operation could take hours or days to complete. And while it was running, you couldn't do anything else with your client program (unless you developed a multi-threaded program). When using a session bean, your client program is tied to the server application for the duration of a method invocation.

On the other hand, using a message-driven bean in the same situation allows your client program to start the statement generation process without having to hang around for the result. Message-driven beans are great for this type of operation because they decouple the client application from the EJB application, allowing the two to work in parallel and independent of each other.

Glossary

• •

abstract class: A class with one or more abstract methods. An abstract class cannot have a constructor.

abstract method: A method with no body. Abstract methods must be implemented in a subclass (unless the subclass is also abstract).

abstract persistence schema: A schema defining the persistence attributes of entity beans as well as the relationships between entity beans in an EJB application.

accessor method: A method that provides access to a member variable in a class.

API: *See* application programming interface.

application: A collection of classes that work together to provide a collection of services to a business.

application exception: In an EJB application, an exception thrown from an EJB component that isn't a subclass of the `java.lang.RuntimeException` class. Application exceptions are used by application programmers to identify business-specific exceptions, and they don't trigger any system-level behavior in an EJB container.

application programming interface: The set of publicly accessible methods in a class. Usually refers to the classes and methods that can be used in a large collection of related classes, such as in the Enterprise JavaBean API.

asynchronous: A process that happens on a separate timeline from the process that invoked it. The two processes aren't synchronized with each other and can thus occur in parallel to each other.

bean: *See* JavaBean.

bean class: An EJB class that implements the `SessionBean`, `EntityBean`, or `MessageDrivenBean` interface. A bean class is like a template for creating EJB objects.

bean-managed persistence: An entity bean process whereby the fields of the entity bean are preserved in a database — and retrieved from a database — via programmatic instructions supplied by the bean provider.

Binary Large Object: A database type used to store large amounts of binary data. A Binary Large Object usually stores photographs, audio files, or video files.

BLOB: *See* Binary Large Object.

BMP: *See* bean-managed persistence.

bulk accessor: A business method in an Enterprise JavaBean that can retrieve or update multiple fields in the EJB component at once.

Cartesian product: The result of multiplying sets of information together.

cascade delete: A delete command that removes an entity bean as well as all the entity beans that depend upon it.

Character Large Object: A database object that contains a large amount of character data, such as the full text of *War and Peace.*

class: A template for the creation of objects. The class defines the methods and member variables that an object contains.

CLOB: *See* Character Large Object.

CMP: *See* container-managed persistence.

collection: A group of objects that may contain duplicate entries.

collection member variable: A member variable of an entity bean that has the type `Collection` or `Set`. A `Collection` can contain duplicate entries while a `Set` cannot.

commit options: For entity beans, a set of options that influence the behavior of an EJB container when it commits the changes made by a transaction.

component interface: The interface an EJB component provides so that client applications can invoke operations in the EJB component. The two types of component interfaces are local and remote.

compound primary key: A primary key of an entity bean that's composed of more than one of the CMP fields in the entity bean.

constructor: A special method defined in a class that allows the class to create and initialize new instances of itself. A constructor must have the same name as the class and must have a return type of `void`.

container-managed persistence: A process whereby the EJB container manages the storage and retrieval of entity bean fields in a data source such as a database.

create method: A method on the home interface of a session bean or entity bean that's used by a client application to create an instance of the EJB component.

declarative programming: A form of programming where the programmer tells the computer what to do, not how to do it. XML is a declarative programming language.

default package: The root level package in a classpath, the default package has no name and contains all the classes and interfaces of an application that aren't in named packages.

dependent value object: An object or collection of objects inside an entity bean that has no meaning outside the context of the entity bean. For example, a set of line items has no meaning outside the context of the invoice that contains them. Thus, line items can be dependent value objects of an invoice entity bean.

deployment descriptor: An XML file used to describe both the structure of an EJB application as well as the services the application needs from an EJB container.

direct insert: An insert into a database that doesn't get managed by an EJB container.

distributed application: An application that can reside on multiple computers at once. EJB applications are distributed applications.

distributed transaction: A transaction that includes operations on multiple computers. EJB applications support distributed transactions, but distributed transactions are inefficient.

Document Type Descriptor: A document that describes the format that a given XML document must conform to.

DTD: *See* Document Type Descriptor.

EJB QL: *See* EJB Query Language.

EJB Query Language: This is a language defined in the EJB 2.0 Specification; it provides a platform-independent way for entity beans to retrieve data from a database. The EJB Query Language is very similar to SQL.

EJB server provider: Similar to the EJB container provider, the EJB server provider provides a server in which an EJB container resides. The EJB server can also include a number of other application services, such as Java Messaging Service, Java Mail, JNDI, and Web application services. Most EJB container providers provide a complete EJB server.

empty tag: An XML tag with no value. The empty tag is delimited by the < and /> characters.

entity: A thing that exists in the real world, such as a business document or a computer, and so on.

entity bean: An EJB component that contains business data.

entity bean object: An instance of an entity bean, the entity bean object contains the data for a particular entity.

entity class: The class object associated with an entity bean.

exception: A special kind of Java object that contains information related to the failure of a method invocation.

Extensible Markup Language: The full name of XML, a language used to describe data.

finder method: A method on an entity bean that finds an instance of an entity bean that matches the arguments supplied in the finder method.

getter method: A method, usually in a JavaBean, that's used by a client to retrieve the value of a member variable. Entity beans require getter methods to be defined for persistence fields and relationship fields.

helper method: A method in an EJB component that's hidden from a client application and is simply used to help the EJB component perform a task.

home interface: This is the interface a client application uses to create or to find instances of an EJB component. The two types of home interfaces are local home interfaces and remote home interfaces.

home method: A method in the home interface of an entity bean that performs operations on a set of the entity bean's instances.

HTML: *See* Hypertext Markup Language.

Hypertext Markup Language: A language used for creating Web pages.

initial context: The context of an application that provides access to JNDI resources; this refers to the context when it's first obtained.

inner class: A class that's defined inside another class.

interface: A set of public methods and static data that a class of the type of the interface must implement.

JAR: *See* Java Application Archive.

Java Application Archive: A file containing a number of classes that make up an application, along with another file — called a *manifest* — that describes the contents of the JAR file.

Java Database Connectivity: A Java API that provides a mechanism for interacting with database systems.

Java Messaging Service: A Java technology used for implementing messaging applications.

Java Naming and Directory Interface: The API in Java used to register names of application resources as well as the references to those application resources. Java applications can look up application resources in the Java Naming and Directory Interface (JNDI) and retrieve them from the directory.

Java Virtual Machine: A host environment in which all Java programs run.

JavaBean: A special form of Java class containing member variables, called *properties*, which are accessed via getter and setter methods.

JavaServer Pages: A Java technology for creating dynamic Web pages. JSP is a client application technology that integrates well with EJB applications.

JDBC: *See* Java Database Connectivity.

JMS: *See* Java Messaging Service.

JMS queue: This is a type of JMS messaging service in which the creator of the message places the message in a queue, and the consumer of the message reads the messages out of the queue one at a time. After a message is consumed, it's removed from the queue.

JMS server: A system application that hosts JMS topics and queues.

JMS topic: A type of JMS messaging service in which the creator of a message sends it to a topic. There, multiple subscribers to the topic are able to consume the message concurrently, or asynchronously.

JNDI: *See* Java Naming and Directory Interface.

JNDI ENC: *See* JNDI Enterprise Naming Context.

JNDI Enterprise Naming Context (ENC): Each EJB component has its own JNDI ENC, which can be used by EJB components to make abstract references to JNDI resources, without knowing the actual resource names when the component is developed. JNDI ENC can also store real resource names for resources that are private to the EJB component. The application assembler or application deployer must map the resources named in each component's JNDI ENC to actual resources before the application is deployed.

JNDI name: This is the name assigned to a JNDI resource. Any class that wants to use the resource identified by a given name looks up the JNDI name using the context object.

JSP: *See* JavaServer Pages.

JVM: *See* Java Virtual Machine.

local client: An EJB component's client that resides in the same Java Virtual Machine. A local client can invoke EJB component methods through a local interface, which is much more efficient than invoking them through a remote interface.

local home interface: A type of home interface supplied to local clients. The local home interface is used to retrieve local interface references to an EJB component. *See also* home interface.

local interface: A local reference to an EJB component, through which a client can invoke business methods on the EJB component.

MDB: *See* message-driven bean.

message consumer: A class that registers an interest in receiving messages from a particular topic or queue in a JMS server.

message-driven bean: An EJB component that consumes messages from a JMS server.

message producer: The object that creates a message and sends it to the message server.

method-ready state: The state of a message-driven bean when it's ready to consume a message from a topic or queue.

multiple-object finder method: A finder method in an entity bean that returns a collection or a set of component interfaces.

multi-valued attribute: An attribute in EJB Query Language that contains multiple values. A multi-valued attribute must be of the type `Collection` or `Set`.

navigation operator: Also referred to as a *dot operator*, the navigation operator supports navigation from a wider scope to a narrower scope. For example, `className.methodName` uses a navigation operator to navigate from a class to the method in the class.

object: An instance of a class.

object pool: A container that contains a number of objects of the same type. The object pool holds references until they're needed by some application, at which point the application requests — and receives — one of the objects in the object pool.

path expression: A term used in EJB QL to describe the expression resulting from navigating through a set of relationships using the navigation operator.

primary key: An object used to uniquely identify an entity bean of a particular type. No two entity beans of the same type may have the same primary key value.

properties: (1) In the context of JavaBeans, an attribute of the JavaBean that has a getter method and optionally has a setter method. (2) In the context of system properties or properties files, a name/value pair where the name identifies the property and the value is the content of the property.

properties file: A file that contains property names as well as their associated values.

query method: A method in an entity bean component that invokes an EJB QL statement to retrieve data from other entity beans or references to other entity beans.

reentrant: A process whereby a thread of execution invokes methods in the same EJB component twice, effectively reentering the EJB component. Reentrance poses special problems in EJB applications and generally isn't allowed. This term applies to entity beans.

remote client: A client application that accesses an EJB bean component through the EJB component's remote interface.

remote home interface: The home interface of a remote component, which can find or create new instances of the component and return a reference to the remote interface of the component.

remote interface: The interface of an EJB component that provides remote clients with access to business methods of the component.

remote method invocation: A process that allows client applications on remote computers to invoke methods on objects across a network.

RMI: *See* remote method invocation.

rollback: When a transaction is interrupted, changes made to persistent data during the transaction are restored to their previous states.

runtime exception: A system-level exception that causes the EJB container to stop processing a transaction and rollback any changes made to data in the context of the transaction.

serializable: A term describing an object that can be represented in a portable way for storage or transmission, and then reconstituted later either by the same program or by a different program.

setter method: An accessor method, typically for a JavaBean component, that allows a client application to set the value of a member variable associated with the setter.

single-field primary key: A primary key that contains only a single field in the entity bean class.

single-object finder method: In an entity bean, a finder method that returns only a single object reference, such as `findByPrimaryKey`, that returns a single component interface.

single-valued attribute: An attribute of an EJB component that contains only a single value, as opposed to a collection or a set of values.

single-valued path expression: In EJB QL, a path expression that evaluates to a single value.

SQL: *See* Structured Query Language.

state: A term describing the present condition, or values, of an object.

stateful session bean: A session bean that can preserve the state of a client's data across multiple invocations.

stateless session bean: A session bean that cannot preserve the state of a client's data across multiple invocations.

Structured Query Language: A language used to interact with relational database systems. SQL can create relational databases, manipulate data in relational databases, and retrieve data from relational databases.

subclass: A class that inherits the methods and member variables of another class. A purist would say that any class is a subclass of itself, but that's one of those chicken-and-egg issues.

subinterface: An interface that inherits methods from another interface. Any interface is a subinterface of itself — another bone for the chicken and egg enthusiasts.

superclass: A class from which a given class inherits methods and member variables.

superinterface: An interface that a given interface inherits methods from.

Swing application: A Java application that uses the Swing library to provide a graphical user interface (GUI). These applications are typically used by users on desktop computers.

synchronous: A process of communication between two objects in which the first object must wait for a response from the second object before it can continue with its next operation. Synchronous communication requires the caller of a method and the method called to perform operations serially, or in order, as opposed to asynchronous communication, in which the caller of a method and the method called can perform operations in parallel.

system exception: *See* runtime exception.

tag: An XML or HTML structure that has some meaning within the context of the language. `<BODY>` is an HTML tag.

transaction: A set of operations that must all succeed or all fail as a set.

transaction attributes: Attributes used in an EJB application's deployment descriptor to describe the expected transactional behavior of particular methods and EJB component classes.

UML: *See* Unified Modeling Language.

Unified Modeling Language: A graphical language used to specify and design object-oriented applications.

WebLogic: An EJB application server provided by BEA.

WebSphere: An EJB application server provided by IBM.

XML: *See* Extensible Markup Language.

Index

• *F* •

Q

R

Notes

Notes